SALEM COLLEGE
LIBRARY

Purchased Through The

Louise Horton Barber C'11

Memorial Book Fund

THE GREAT WAR
AND THE
LANGUAGE OF MODERNISM

THE GREAT WAR
AND THE
LANGUAGE
OF MODERNISM

Vincent Sherry

OXFORD
UNIVERSITY PRESS

2003

OXFORD
UNIVERSITY PRESS

Oxford   New York
Auckland   Bangkok   Buenos Aires   Cape Town   Chennai
Dar es Salaam   Delhi   Hong Kong   Istanbul   Karachi   Kolkata
Kuala Lumpur   Madrid   Melbourne   Mexico City   Mumbai   Nairobi
São Paulo   Shanghai   Taipei   Tokyo   Toronto

Published by Oxford University Press, Inc.
198 Madison Avenue, New York, New York 10016

www.oup.com

Oxford is a registered trademark of Oxford University Press

Library of Congress Cataloging-in-Publication Data
Sherry, Vincent B.
The Great War and the language of modernism / Vincent Sherry.
p. cm.
Includes bibliographical references (p.) and index.
ISBN 0-19-510176-6
1. American poetry—20th century—History and criticism.
2. World War, 1914–1918—Great Britain—Literature and the war.   3. Eliot, T. S.
(Thomas Stearns), 1888–1965—Views on war.   4. Americans—Great Britain—History
—20th century.   5. Woolf, Virginia, 1882–1941—Views on war.   6. Pound, Ezra,
1885–1972—Views on war.   7. Modernism (Literature)—
Great Britain.   I. Title.
PS310.W679 S47 2003
811'.5209358—dc21   2002070921

1 3 5 7 9 8 6 4 2

Printed in the United States of America
on acid-free paper

TO SOPHIA

The gentler hour of an ultimate day

ACKNOWLEDGMENTS

Like its historical subject, this book has taken a good deal longer than expected to complete. Strangers, developing acquaintances, and long-standing friends have aided it in every way conceivable. For help that has ranged from points of local advice on topical problems to detailed readings of a lengthy manuscript, I want to thank a number of people whose individual spirits exceed their place in a series of names, who, one by one, have been generous and skeptical, curious and demanding: Scott Black, Jessica Burstein, Ronald Bush, James Chandler, Reed Way Dasenbrock, Jed Esty, Paul Fussell, Sharon Cournoyer Howell, Romana Huk, Samuel Hynes, David Kadlec, Cathy Karmilowicz, Seth Koven, Edna Longley, John Matthias, Ella Ophir, Patricia Rae, Lawrence Rainey, John Paul Russo, Tim Redman, Jill Stevens, Connie Titone, John Whittier-Ferguson, and Laura Winkiel. To William Blissett, I express special gratitude for continuing education; to Melita Schaum, for standing by words, and for the courage of standing by; to Marjorie Perloff, for her openness, intelligence, and honesty; and to A. Walton Litz, who has gathered from the air a live tradition, and who knows it was not folly. To my daughter, Sophia, I dedicate this book in the words of a poet, which she and I will specially understand.

To the staff at the Newspaper Library of the British Library, London, I express my sincere gratitude for the special consideration they have extended to me. The extraordinary resources of the Photographic Archive and Documents Library of the Imperial War Museum, London, have been made available to me with the most helpful courtesy. The support that Villanova University has provided for this book has been in every sense exemplary. I want to thank especially the Reverend Kail Ellis, dean of the College of Liberal Arts and Sciences; Charles Cherry and (now, sadly, in memory) Phillip Pulsiano, chairs of the English Department; Susan Burns, for the inexhaustible skill and wit of her office; my graduate assistants Nancy Comerau, Ellen Massey, and Ellen Fiskett; and the staff at Falvey Memorial Library, especially Judith Olsen. I record my gratitude to the Office of Research and Sponsored Projects, Villanova University, for two summer research fellowships, and to the National Endowment for the Humanities for the opportunity of codirecting a summer seminar, "Ezra Pound and His Contemporaries," at Brunenburg, Merano, Italy, where Mary de Rachewiltz remains legendary for her grace and hospitality. I was able to further the work of this book considerably with the Mountjoy Fellowship in Modern Poetry at Durham University, England, and I want to thank Ric Caddel and Diana Collecott for kindnesses little and large. At Oxford University Press, New York, the readers for this project have given anonymity a good name; I have profited much from those suggestions. Jeremy Lewis provided invaluable assistance. And Elissa Morris proved the truest values of the trusted editor: steadfastness as well as humor, the wit of an accomplice.

Grateful acknowledgment is given to the New Directions Publishing Corporation and Faber and Faber Ltd. for permission to quote from the following copyrighted works of Ezra Pound: *Personae* (copyright © 1926 by Ezra Pound); *The Cantos* (copyright © 1934, 1937, 1940, 1948, 1956, 1959, 1962, 1963, 1966, and 1968 by Ezra Pound); *Pound/Lewis* (copyright © 1985 by the Trustees of the Ezra Pound Literary Property Trust); *The Selected Letters of Ezra Pound to John Quinn, 1915–1924* (copyright © 1991 by Duke University Press and the Trustees of the Ezra Pound Literary Property Trust); *Gaudier-Brzeska* (copyright © 1970 by Ezra Pound); *Selected Letters 1907–1941* (copyright © 1950 by Ezra Pound); and *Ezra Pound's Poetry and Prose: Contributions to Periodicals* (copyright © 1991 by the Trustees of the Ezra Pound Literary Property Trust). Grateful acknowledgment is made to Faber and Faber Ltd. and Harcourt Brace Jovanovitch and the Literary Estate of T. S. Eliot for permission to quote from the following copyrighted works by T. S. Eliot: *Collected Poems 1909–1962*; *The Waste Land: A Facsimile and Transcript of the Original Drafts*, ed. Valerie Eliot; *Inventions of the March Hare: Poems 1909–1917* (copyright © 1996 by Valerie Eliot, used by permission of Harcourt, Inc.); *The Letters of T. S. Eliot 1898–1922*, ed. Valerie Eliot (copyright © 1989 by SET Copyrights Limited, reprinted by permission of Harcourt, Inc.); and *The Sacred Wood*. Grateful acknowledgment is made to Harcourt Brace Jovanovitch, to the Random House Group (U.K.), and to the Society of Authors as the Literary Representative of the Estate of Virginia Woolf, for permission to quote from the following works by Virginia Woolf: extracts from *Mrs. Dalloway* by Virginia Woolf (copyright © 1925 by Harcourt, Inc., and renewed 1953, reprinted by permission of the publisher); excerpts from *To the Lighthouse* by Virginia Woolf (copyright © 1927 by Harcourt, Inc., and renewed 1954 by Leonard Woolf, reprinted by permission of the publisher); excerpts from *The Letters of Virginia Woolf*, vol. 2, *1912–1922*, ed. Nigel Nicolson (copyright © 1976 by Quentin Bell and Angelica Garnett, reprinted by permission of Harcourt, Inc.); excerpts from *The Diary of Virginia Woolf*, vol. 1, *1915–1919* (copyright © 1977 by Quentin Bell and Angelica Garnett, reprinted by permission of Harcourt, Inc.); excerpts from *The Diary of Virginia Woolf*, vol. 2, *1920–1924* (copyright © 1978 by Quentin Bell and Angelica Garnett, reprinted by permission of Harcourt, Inc.); excerpts from "Mrs. Dalloway in Bond Street" in *The Complete Shorter Fiction of Virginia Woolf* by Susan Dick (copyright © 1985 by Quentin Bell and Angelica Garnett, reprinted by permission of Harcourt, Inc.); excerpts from "A Society," "The Evening Party," "The Mark on the Wall," "Solid Objects," and "An Unwritten Novel" from *A Haunted House and Other Short Stories* by Virginia Woolf (copyright © 1933 and renewed 1972 by Harcourt, Inc., reprinted by permission of the publisher); excerpts from *A Room of One's Own* by Virginia Woolf (copyright © 1929 by Harcourt, Inc., and renewed 1957 by Leonard Woolf, reprinted by permission of the publisher); excerpts from *Jacob's Room* by Virginia Woolf (copyright © 1922 by Harcourt, Inc., and renewed 1950 by Leonard Woolf, reprinted by permission of the publisher); excerpts from "A Sketch of the Past" in *Moments of Being* by Virginia Woolf (copyright © 1976 by Quentin Bell and Angelica Garnett, reprinted by permission of Harcourt, Inc.); to the Society of Authors as the Literary Representative of the Estate of Virginia Woolf for extracts from *The Voyage Out, Jacob's Room, A Room of One's Own, Mrs. Dalloway*, and *To the Lighthouse*; and to the Random House Group for *The Essays of Virginia Woolf*, vol. 3, *The Letters of Virginia Woolf*, vol. 2, *The Diary of Virginia Woolf*, vols. 1 and 2, and *Moments of Being*, by Virginia Woolf, published by the Hogarth Press, and for extracts from *The Complete Shorter Fiction of Virginia Woolf*, ed. Susan Dick and published by Chatto and Windus, used by permission of the Executors of the Virginia Woolf Estate and the Random House Group Limited.

For permission to reproduce photographs of Ezra Pound and T. S. Eliot by E. O. Hoppé, formerly in the Mansell Collection, London, acknowledgment is made to TimePix. For permission to reproduce the studio portrait of Virginia Woolf, grateful acknowledgment is made to the Estate of Quentin Bell. For permission to reproduce the illustration by Wyndham Lewis, grateful acknowledgment is made to the Tate Gallery, London, and the Estate of Mrs. G. A. Wyndham Lewis. Reproductions of the following photographs appear by courtesy of the Imperial War Museum, London: figures 1 (Q14997), 2 (Q28759), 3 (Q14995), 4 (Q79416), 5 (Q90737), 6 (Q80726), 7 (Q45843), 8 (Q52357), 9 (Q4481), 10 (Q81768), 11 (Q33120), 12 (Q33063), 13 (Q33080), 14 (Q5624), 15 (Q5106), 16 (Q106379), 19 (Q82364), 20 (Q82361), 21 (Q82372), 22 (Q80152), 26 (Q4430), 27 (Q11688), and 29 (Q14966).

CONTENTS

CONTENTS

ILLUSTRATIONS

THE GREAT WAR
AND THE
LANGUAGE OF MODERNISM

"History has many cunning passages, contrived corridors / And issues," T. S. Eliot could write in "Gerontion," in July 1919. The timing of this observation summoned recent history as its reference and rebuke. The "peace" treaty to end the Great War of 1914–18 had been signed at Versailles, in the Hall of Mirrors. In this great room, history repeats in receding series—as in the "cunning passages" and "contrived corridors" that Eliot figures in his judgment of its documents, its "issues." The guilt that the Allied powers officially imposed on Germany and the war reparations plan this maneuver authorized—such cunningly contrived issues already portended their terribly complicated consequences to Eliot (he was working in the Colonial and Foreign Department in Lloyd's Bank, London). His speaker represents these procedures accordingly as an insidious trick of perspective, some shrewd illusion.

Eliot's speaker revisits the scene near the end of the poem, in a comprehensive survey of the contents of his own consciousness. His "small deliberations" expand now to "multiply variety / In a wilderness of mirrors." A roomful of reflections is *be*wildering, no doubt, but "a wilderness of mirrors" shows as its pointed conceit an irony special to the history now inscribed at Versailles. For this royal estate stood once as a monument to Enlightenment civilization. In its finished condition, this demesne mapped the rationalist's universe to the microcosmic plan of its reflecting halls and formal gardens, its schemes of metered and reasoned degree. This ideal of measured control had obviously dissolved in a war fought in excess of all precedent measure and concluded, if it were ever ended, in the rituals of barbaric, retributive justice just conducted at Versailles. This early postwar moment expresses its profounder dread then in the apocalyptic vista Eliot depicts in the poem's finale, where the speaker sees

3

President Wilson and representatives of the Allied powers signing the peace treaty in the Hall of Mirrors, Trianon Palace, Versailles, 28 June 1919.

British troops passing in triumphal march down Constitution Hill for Peace Day celebrations, 19 July 1919.

Dr. Carl Renner, after receiving the peace terms for Austria, makes an impassioned plea to the Allied delegates. Presidents Wilson and Clemenceau are seated at the table in the background.

Demonstrations against the peace terms outside the Hotel Adler, Berlin, early summer 1919.

his miscellaneous accomplices being "whirled / Beyond the circuit of the shuddering Bear / In fractured atoms."[1]

If the cunning passages and contrived corridors in this disquisition on history were meant to be part of the speaker's experience of war, some critics and literary historians might counter, these verbal images must invoke instead the maze of trenches networked across the midsection of the European continent. "I was neither at the hot gates," Gerontion admits near the opening of the poem, "Nor fought in the warm rain, / Nor knee deep in the salt marsh, heaving a cutlass, / Bitten by flies, fought."[2] For reasons of age, the "little old man" of Eliot's title would obviously be exempt from military service. At his civilian distance from the front, however, this personage seems to have been stationed far from the scene of valued action—given the vividness of his combat fantasy. Yet his participation in the conflict shows in other ways. The claims that total war enforced on the general population were sufficiently strong to compel the embarrassment Eliot works into his speaker's apology, into the extraordinary awkwardness with which Gerontion contorts the syntax of his confession. To the precise point of Eliot's most suggestive wording, moreover, in the imaginative prospect of his speaker's personal Versailles, the "small deliberations" of one little old man may reflect the large deliberations, the discourses the men of this Great War will have left as the record of history. The pressure that this event exerts on the speaking sensibility of the poem shows even in the short course of his central meditation, where, by its own cunning passages, the consideration of history arrives at a pair of summary paradoxes. "Unnatural vices / Are fathered by our heroism," Gerontion proposes, leaving us to wonder how an "unnatural" quality can be "fathered," and how a bad thing is begotten from a good. "Virtues / Are forced upon us by our impudent crimes,"[3] he answers, as though in conclusion, repeating the opposing terms of the first statement— but in reverse order, as in a mirror-reflecting mirror. The conceptual image recedes indeed into some infinite series of mysterious contradictions.

How such cunning passages reach through Eliot's developing idiom; how his imaginative language recalls the words of history, questions the status of that abstract category of understanding, and formalizes its own apprehension of those exceptional times; how Eliot's attitudes and practices are matched in the work of his major contemporaries and companion talents, the London modernists Ezra Pound and Virginia Woolf: here are the preoccupations of this book. But these concerns, one might object, seem hardly worth taking up— again. By the rule of well-established associations, the Great War of 1914–18 locates the moment in which the new sensibility of English—and international—modernism comes fully into existence. Phrases like "The Lost Generation" and "The Men of 1914" have long been employed to designate the effect of the war—a centering event, if a destructive legacy—on these writers. What can one possibly add to—or take away from—the nearly sacral character of these critical formulas?

Indeed, these sayings have gained the status of numinous rubrics. They have been used routinely in a sort of ritual invocation, which serves to silence, not to stimulate and certainly not to organize, further inquiry. The actual dearth of commentary on the modernist war—as a *historical* subject, as an event reconstructed from its record in contemporary political and intellectual culture—is remarkable. How easily these formulas are set aside by critics unwilling to grant their major premise, in fact, indicates all too clearly that "the modernist war" owns a coherence that is wholly rhetorical, or plaintive. It has established no solid scholarship, no language of factual basis and rational elaboration, no thickness of intellectual resistance.

Paul Fussell's *The Great War and Modern Memory* and Jay Winter's *Sites of Memory, Sites of Mourning: The Great War in European Cultural History* offer two of the most important formulations of the war, each a representatively best effort in establishing and asserting its frame of reference on the event. The literature of combat experience finds its most eloquent and compelling commentator in Fussell, while Winter retells the story of the war in an impressively extensive narrative of European history, addressing mainly the "watershed event" premise in conventional understandings. Both critics center the memory of the war within traditions that appear—ostensibly, even forcibly, in the arguments of these books—to be immune from the sensibility usually attached to the label and category of modernism, that is, some exceptional, counterconventional, technically inventive temper. If the absence of viable intellectual authority in the idea of the modernist war allows Fussell and Winter to override it thus, these critics also overplay their claims in ways that reveal what they have left out of account—and the problems that follow on this omission.

Fussell argues that the actual conduct of the war contrasted with current (Edwardian and Georgian) expectations in a way that helped to establish irony as the primary, defining mode of modern literary awareness. In its most intense demonstrations, he reserves this modern sensibility for writers who report from the combat zone. The vanguard of history, the brink of those outmoded conventions, lies on the firing line. ("Gerontion" correctly anticipated this critic's censure of the status—the validity—of a noncombatant's imaginative part in the war.) Civilians such as "Joyce, Eliot, Lawrence, Pound, Yeats were not present at the front"—Fussell calls the roll—"to induct them into the new idioms."[4] To *induct*: the verb preserves associations of military conscription and the processing of mass armies, even while it intimates a rite of passage into some exceptional understanding, the awareness shared by a literary clerisy, baptized by fire. A kind of "combat gnosticism"[5] underlies Fussell's consideration of war literature as its intensifying, but limiting, condition.

This critical restriction leaves a problem that Fussell acknowledges. The "roster of major innovative talents who were not involved with the war is long and impressive," he concedes, including "Yeats, Woolf, Pound, Eliot, Lawrence, and Joyce—that is, the masters of the modern movement." By contrast, the writers who were moved "to recall in literary form the war they had *actually experienced*" were "*lesser talents*—always more traditional and technically prudent." Memoirists and poets such as "Sassoon, Graves, and Blunden are clearly *writers of the second rank*" (emphases added). If "their compulsion to render the unprecedented actualities they had experienced brought them to grips with the modern theme which we recognize as the essence of [the] ironic mode,"[6] their actual writing—the "traditional" forms, the "prudent" style— did not alter in answer to that world-changing event. Conversely, in this account, the main event of Fussell's modernity remains unengaged by those "masters of the modern movement," who, presumably, will have developed the literary methods and sensibility requisite to these new conditions, of which the war is the forming incident. The picture that emerges from this version of literary history witnesses an odd allocation of timely and anachronistic temperaments, majority and minority statuses.

One of the reasons for this unequal picture lies in a disproportion between the background and foreground narratives. Fussell is trying to claim major place for writers whose importance is scaled in relation to minor traditions. Even in shock and outrage, the Edwardian and Georgian literature that provides the backdrop for Fussell's focused concerns simply does not sustain the kind of consciousness he wants this war to have forged as the dominant modern sensibility. Yes, the *Modern Memory* of Fussell's *Great War* makes some nominal claim to cultural history as its promissory framework of analysis and understanding. Yet the current Fussell is attempting to follow as the conduit of his characteristically modern awareness is simply too narrow to carry the broad range of implications and consequences he intends. His eloquent attentions are best spent on the psychologized record of this historical event, on the private crises of his individual writers, whose pathos is enhanced by the extremity of the frontline circumstance.

The wider, more comprehensive setting that would be relevant to the kind of claims Fussell makes lies in the public, civilian culture of the English war. It is in this environment that the cause and meaning of the war were first projected, and its language affords thus an original record of the ultimate import this event owns—as the watershed it represents in political, intellectual, and literary history. This cultural space needs still to be reconstructed, however. And the readiness with which Winter's *Sites of Memory, Sites of Mourning* dismisses the claim that such a disruption occurred instances again the problems of a long-standing failure to establish the record of this historical condition.

Winter's account documents the persistence of older, "traditional" modes of cultural representation during and just after the war. Thus he asserts the relative stability and flexibility of the tradition and its readiness to assimilate a not-so-novel shock, a capacity to resist any fundamental reorientation of view. He focuses particularly on the commemoration of the dead and, even, on the configuration of the "apocalyptic" feeling that attended the event—an extrem-

8

ity of the intellectual imagination that reveals its precedents from the mid-nineteenth century. Whether or not this occultism is "public," its eschatology "populist," Winter makes a major claim on the basis of this evidence. "[F]ar from ushering in modernism," he counters triumphally, "the Great War reinforced romantic values" in poetry and encouraged "traditional elements" in a more diverse cultural representation.[7]

Presenting modernism as a rebellion against the traditional or conventional, Winter's assertion turns upon a construction of tradition that takes little stock of what this charged and valorized word actually means. "Tradition" acquires its real significance within specific locales with particular intellectual and political constituencies (Winter's prospect is comprehensively pan-European). If modernism draws its content and depth in some large respect from the set of conventions against which it positions itself, this countervailing material needs a close proximity of focus. The interior, special coherence of the English war must be recovered accordingly. In this setting, the cultural crisis in Britain may be reclaimed as documentary fact, a script from which the endgame drama of a whole civilization may be fairly restaged. For a "modernist" literature that is consistent with the counterconventional valence of this designation will find at the center and capital of that national campaign its furthering circumstance, its profoundest provocation.

Political London presents one of the liveliest sites in the global picture of this world war. A crisis internal to the governing party of Britain defined this moment in local political time. English Liberals had to maintain support for a war which, by precedent and convention, by partisan tradition and intellectual principle, they ought to have opposed. (Resistance to involvement in Continental wars had been a policy constant for the Liberal party, a principle whose compromise in 1914 will be followed as a process through the first chapter.) Committed to the value and practice of public reason, most important, the Liberal party conducted a largely suppositious discussion about the "causes of the war." The "logic" of the policy emerged in a number of popular media, which, ranging from journalistic editorials to newspaper reprints of government documents and parliamentary apologias, presented arguments of increasingly specious kind. The case this majority consciousness was obliged to make for a war it should not have supported reveals more than a series of embarrassing paradoxes. A deep mainstream of established attitudes—call it public reason, call it civic rationality—was convulsing under the effort to legitimize this war. Increasingly, irresistibly, the "reason" through which its causes were spoken ceased to mean anything recognizable, as its conduct reached areas of the previously unthinkable, the unimaginably sordid. The scope of that crisis provides the outline for this book, which follows literary modernism as it evolves in England in response to those particular—and immense—provocations.

This echoing critique found constant stimulus in the Liberal disquisition on the reasonableness of the war. The basic intellectual consistency of this Liberal idiom, moreover, is as striking as its range and variation, which might be sampled in advance for the extraordinary resource it affords.

The partisan gentry could offer no spokesperson more exemplary than J. A. Hobson. Endowed through his family with an income from their provincial journal, the *Derbyshire Record*, Hobson rose to the position of public moralist, writing as cultural commentator as well as an editorial correspondent for the *Manchester Guardian*, long affiliated with political Liberalism. When in 1917 he projects a vision of future prospects in *Democracy after the War*, he expresses the intellectual partisan's expected commitment to rational progress. The emphases added to this passage, however, underscore the strange new accent in which the language of logical optimism is spoken:

> Whether the war ends in complete victory, followed by a dictated peace, or in some less complete decision followed by a negotiated peace, either method is likely to leave seeds of future strife, because the terms it embodies are not in themselves conform*able* to the sense of justice or reason*able* will of the parties concerned, but are a mere register of the preponderance of power when the conflict is brought to a close. Even if the terms of settlement were in substance equit*able*, a supposition in itself unreason*able*, the knowledge that they were a register of force and not of reason*able* assent would leave a dangerous legacy of discontent with each disagree*able* item of the generally equit*able* compromise. Thus, in any case the presupposition remains that war maintains and nourishes militarism. Only the effectual substitution of a mode of settling grievances conform*ably with reason* and justice can break the vicious chain of mutual causality by which war and militarism support one another.[8]

Hobson clearly displays the liberal's resistance to war as an instrument of political will and design. At every turn of the passage, however, he responds more volubly to the pressures being placed upon this typical liberal position and, above all, upon the free reason of liberal intellectuals. Since partisan thinkers have been called upon to rationalize their government's cause, often against the evidence of its necessity, the practices and categories of rationality so required building up, indeed making up, that they were up for grabs. Thus, if the better state of Hobson's humanity is "reason*able*," the rationalist's own *ability* appears as the crucial condition of improvement. That telltale suffix pins, tags, and props the participial adjectives denoting the several protocols and values of ethical and prudential logic. The frequency with which Hobson lapses into this grammatical mannerism is as astonishing in an articulate professional as it is indicative, his reader might suspect, of tendencies in current intellectual discourse. In this situation, the rationalist's task could be taken up either by the dextrous or the maladroit, the scrupulous or the opportunistic, the cleric or the mountebank. The seriocomedy of Hobson's performance, which moves *able* from the deliberative measure he intends to the comic wobble it becomes, represents the spread of tones this moment encloses as its volatile potential.

The need to make sensible a policy previously deemed irrational often plays out as a kind of involuntary comedy of itself. Its script is reasonable absurdity. In this verbal culture, an obscure individual like Charles Hayward attains his strange distinction—a standard oddness. His *War and Rational Politics* (1915) registers the public dialect of the new reason, which is marked by paradox, contradiction, and worse. Thus, while Hayward opens by conceding that "war" and "rational politics" denominate an impossibility, he proceeds immediately to a fierce attempt to reason out the rightness of the English cause. "Before this war is permitted to close," he proposes, "we must get our heaviest foot on the neck of Prussian militarism so firmly and solidly that we can safely lift the other foot high enough to effectively stamp upon any attempt to supplant it with any brand of militarism either in England or any other country. This can be done by sanity and reason."[9] "Before this war is *permitted* to close": the command Hayward extends to this already unstoppable war reaches with failing hand to the conduct of his own logical protocols, which are arranged in the ridiculous postures and gestures of his warlike peacemaking. The rationalist's standard vocabulary of "sanity and reason" has lapsed into a language of physical farce.

These writers provide a background for the evolving response of a modernist literature that owns its shaping occasion in wartime London. Woolf, Eliot, and Pound will develop a register to echo and inflect the prodigal logic of Liberal war policy. To identify and clarify the answer these literary initiatives represent will be to understand anew the meanings that modernism reveals in a consideration of cultural and political history. The difference this crisis of ideological reason actually made in the sensibility of their generation may be suggested even by the readiest survey of the literary record. Let us focus on some major stations in these three writers' developments.

"As the streets that lead from the Strand to the Embankment are very narrow," Woolf proposes in the opening sentence of her first novel, *The Voyage Out*, "it is better not to walk down them arm-in-arm. If you persist, lawyers' clerks will have to make flying leaps in the mud; young lady typists will have to fidget behind you."[10] Completed in 1913 (situated in 1906), this novel of an Edwardian woman's education begins under the guidance of a friendly advisor. The good sense relies on the observance of correct logical process. Grammatically, the usage conforms to the normative standards of reasonable speech: the movement from subordinate to main clauses follows a sequence of cause to effect, condition to consequence. The readers who appreciated this comforting reliance on sound logic might well have been unsettled by the opening words of *Jacob's Room*, her next major novel: "'So of course,' wrote Betty Flanders, pressing her heels rather deeper in the sand, 'There was nothing for it but to leave.'"[11] Woolf starts this tale, undertaken early in 1920, with a gesture of con-

11

clusion, which is narratively unearned. The conjunctive "So" invokes the whole process of thought that leads to this summary phrase: "of course." Yet the course of linear thinking recedes into the anterior time of the novel's plot, an unknown zone.

The well-considered sequences of *The Voyage Out* have complicated themselves thus, in a dozen years. The later gesture represents not just some quirkily personal imaginative prank. The shift in linguistic temperament manifests itself more widely, suggesting the broader import of a historical instigation.

In 1913, as Woolf was finishing *The Voyage Out*, Pound drafted "A Pact," bargaining thus with his poetic forebear:

> I make a pact with you, Walt Whitman—
> I have detested you long enough.
> I come to you as a grown child
> Who has a pig-headed father;
> I am old enough now to make friends.
> It was you who broke the new wood,
> Now is a time for carving.
> We have one sap and one root—
> Let there be commerce between us.[12]

In style as well as in substance, the poem offers an aesthetics of directness. Concise, idiomatic, clear-voiced, the poem shapes its statements to the values of commonsense reasoning that Pound shares with his predecessor.

Seven years later, however, just as Woolf undertakes the new work of *Jacob's Room*, Pound opens a retrospect on the poetic career he has lived out in the interim, in the fictional autobiography *Hugh Selwyn Mauberley*:

> For three years, out of key with his time,
> He strove to resuscitate the dead art
> Of poetry, to maintain "the sublime"
> In the old sense. Wrong from the start—
>
> No, hardly, but seeing he had been born
> In a half-savage country, out of date,
> Bent resolutely on wringing lilies from the acorn,
> Capaneous, trout for factitious bait;
>
> ''Ιδμεν γάρ τοι πάνθ', ὅσ' ἐνὶ Τροίη
> Caught in the unstopped ear;
> Giving the rocks small lee-way
> The chopped seas held him, therefore, that year.[13]

Just as with the later Woolf, the rhetorical curve appears to conform to the prosody of argumentation, replicating the process of expostulation, reply, and conclusive synthesis—"Wrong from the start," "No, hardly, but seeing," "The chopped seas held him, therefore, that year." It is impossible, however, to understand what proposition is at stake, what debate is under way. If the Greek script offers the promise of some secret coherence to these quatrains, its message is reserved to few readers (who will know that it resolves nothing). Pound's trouble in developing his earlier poetics provides the implicit subject of the passage. The clearest register of the difficulty and the difference between 1913 and 1920, however, shows on this verbal surface—in the interrupted functions of imaginative reason and poetic statement.

"And so the conversation slips," remarks the poetic conversant in the dramatic lyric of Eliot's "Portrait of a Lady." As this speaker continues, however, he hardly missteps:

> Among the windings of the violins
> And the ariettes
> Of cracked cornets
> Inside my brain a dull tom-tom begins
> Absurdly hammering a prelude of its own,
> Capricious monotone
> That is at least one definite "false note."[14]

Written in 1910, this sentence poises its statement elegantly on the well-timed pauses of line breaks and (off-)rhyme words. Eliot's syntax is suavely comprehensive, tautly periodic. When the contemporary and counterpart of the lady he addressed in 1910 speaks in 1919 as the generic old man, as Gerontion, the rhythm of linear thinking will disintegrate. The lines may be repeated here in continuous sequence—to catch the pauses on which this speaker is caught, and on which the rationale in his apology is caught out:

> Here I am, an old man in a dry month,
> Being read to by a boy, waiting for rain.
> I was neither at the hot gates
> Nor fought in the warm rain
> Nor knee deep in the salt marsh, heaving a cutlass,
> Bitten by flies, fought.[15]

The "neither . . . Nor . . . Nor" construction projects a balanced antithesis as the promise of a standard rationalistic grammar. The two participial clauses at the end of the sentence interrupt the movement, however, and frustrate the expectation of a well-measured gesture. The sequences of linguistic reason have again failed to hold the line.

How can we account for the development these writers underwent? Between the earlier and later passages, the signal, intervening event was the Great War of 1914–18. It is recalled through the family name of Betty *Flanders*, which summons the site and symbol of the mass deaths of the first mass war, while Gerontion, like other old men of his generation, reveals his uneasiness about not fighting in that conflict. Pound's poetic sequence will center its auto-biographical chronicle in two lyric memories of the Great War and the impact it had on himself and other members of his generation. The internal record of that historical experience is revealed in the consistency of the shift these three writers exhibit. In their varying fashion, they reenact the disestablishment of a rationalistic attitude and practice in language, in the verbal culture of a war for which Liberal apologies and rationales provided the daily material of London journalism. This circumstance exerted an influence whose import and consequences will be followed through this book for the first time.

If this literary sensibility speaks with a coherence previously unreported in critical accounts of English modernism, however, the inattention may have been deserved. Is antic rationality or spoof logic really a compelling topic for critical observation and commentary? Which is to ask, first of all: How much is actually at stake in the tradition at risk? What kind of importance may we attach to the values and practices being travestied in the language of the English war?

In *Political Liberalism*, John Rawls gathers his arguments about his title subject under the heading of "Public Reason," and he historicizes the origins of this political philosophy and practice. Rawls situates its beginnings in the Protestant Reformation, when a need to achieve agreement between equal but opposing views presented the new challenge and opportunity. This diversity of conflicting interests generated appeals to a power that was not only tonic and resolving but, most important, unaligned. Public reason locates an ideal forum and summary attitude, which accommodates oppositions in a spirit of tolerance for propositions whose "reason" may be demonstrated.

How the quality of reason is claimed presents the most complex and interesting dimension of this institutional idea. Rawls proposes that the notion of "reason" relies on no absolute, abstract standard. It involves the compatibility of a proposition with the conventions and precedents of a tradition. This body of comprehensive doctrine has evolved out of past exchanges and stands in the present as a frame of effective reference for the socially sensible.[16] This emphasis underscores in turn the importance of verbal argumentation in securing the reason*able*, a quality to be claimed mainly through a mastery of rationalistic grammar and language. The suffix, so prominent in the Hobson passage, reaches back through a long record of case-making in the tradition of public reason, where rationality is a strategy for the management of facts, and where the terms and standards of what is fair or socially reasonable are more a matter of discussion and construction than simple assertion. Indeed, a whole tradition of liberal intellectual conscience impinges on the case-making efforts of Liberal England at war, where a legacy claiming considerable representative value, ethical as well as intellectual import, is being put on the line.

The "liberalism" of early post-Reformation, pan-European intellectual culture represents, of course, no partisan coalition. The *liberty* that the term recalls as its namesake describes mainly a framework of values and a complementary state of mind, not as yet a chartered or institutionalized grouping of like-minded persons aiming toward similar and specific ends. It is under the aegis of free reason, working to the service and purpose of a liberation that is shared by other rational agents, that the contract of liberal civility is observed, originally, in its unwritten condition. The political organization of these values, most notably the establishment of the Liberal party in nineteenth-century Britain, marks a turning point. This development is marked by a difference in punctuation: we observe a distinction between the capitalized value of the established party (a proper noun and a proprietary adjective) and the lower-case instance of a more general intellectual attitude and orientation (the embodiment of these values in cultural institutions as specific as England's retains, appropriately, the upper-case formation). This development also shifts the location for the debates of public reason, ultimately, to the British Parliament. Yet the consolidation of liberal temperaments in the Liberal party in the mid-nineteenth century can be seen to extend those same impulses that Rawls locates at the inception of intellectual liberalism. Thus, in a citation of Jonathan Parry, one commentator maintained in 1840 that "any party which sought a rapport with public opinion had to respect 'freedom of judgment.' The Liberal Party, he argued, was the political equivalent of the Reformed churches: it was founded on the principles of tolerance and the encouragement of free inquiry, among independent, respectable and religious men." As Parry states, comprehensively, "Liberals . . . presented themselves as the party of Protestantism and pluralism, and their faith in the progress of human reason allowed them to deny any incompatibility between the two"; this "confidence in the power of discussion and reason" was "[i]nherent in Liberalism."[17]

To Rawls's formulations, however, Parry's summary marks a point of major variation. The "rapport with public opinion" that partisan Liberals sought could hardly be construed as the work of public reason. The difference between "public opinion" and public reason goes to a split within political Liberalism that underlies partisan identity and commands the attentions of its membership through the nineteenth century. If English Whigs wished to preserve Parliament as a place for "the party of wisdom, property, and rational debate," that is, as the forum of some ideal public reason, a more populist and potentially radical contingent pressed demands to be "the party of the people," to hear and respond to "public opinion." This pressure eventuates in a contested but inevitable shift in the locale and character of public discussion, which moves from Westminster to newspaper journalism: in the third quarter of the nineteenth century, the number of Liberal dailies increased by a factor of five.[18] If the Whig clerisy perceived these developments increasingly with a feeling of lost dominance, their fears found an image in William Ewart Gladstone. As prime minister, Gladstone flourished in the various media of mass politics, situating the Protestant bases of Liberalism on his High Church ground and extending the appeals of public reason with a moralistic logic that revealed an extraordinary popular power.[19]

These varied constituencies and practices of Liberal politics moved to a defining moment at the outset of the Great War. The conditions of modern warfare called for the cooperation of the total populace in the national effort, and the intellectual patricians of the party had learned how to address the electorate with the lofty and censorious moralism of Gladstonian rationales. Their case was specious, mainly. "Sweet words and dire actions":[20] the aphoristic rebuke Dora Marsden leveled at the machinations of Liberal discourse in 1916 reached back through a record of contradictions and inconsistencies that appears, with the grim conviction of her riposte, as a rueful but routine truth. Indeed, the lie that contemporary revelations were giving to the language of public reason represents no unprecedented event in the history of this majority consciousness. An idealistic philosophy like liberalism collides with history as a matter of usual course. Nonetheless, the war marked a point of critical mass in modern times: the sheer scope of the British enterprise extended the horrors of war from the fringe affair of professional or mercenary armies to a conscripted populace. Dead bodies by the millions weighed out the disproof of the nineteenth-century myth of progress through technology, that grand syllogism of liberal history. Whether or not the dishonest logic of Liberal war policy represented some novel atrocity, it produced consequences by 1918 wholly unforetold in previous experience.

If the year 1500 marks the joint origin of "liberalism" and "modernity" in our contemporary scholarly chronology, as it does for writers as varied as Rawls and Jacques Barzun,[21] that date establishes the longevity of a philosophy that comes to term in 1914. In the political discourses of the Great War, where the language of public reason goes so massively and disastrously wrong, the first words of a truly novel consciousness may begin to spell themselves out in the reverse lettering of this discredited myth, in a modernity against itself, in modernism.

This much-contested term ought to submit first to the clarifications of its own grammar, the cognizance of its verbal as well as cultural etymology. Modern*ism*: as an intensification, "ism" suggests some extreme instance of the primary quality. The suffix adds its force to one of (at least) two available meanings, however. It may augment the sense of liberal rationality that Rawls posits as one original meaning of "the modern." In this sense, "modernism" denominates accurately the activity to which this word first applied. Originally and particularly, "modernism" referred to a religious movement occurring at the turn of the twentieth century within the Catholic churches of England and France primarily, where a pressure identifiably or nominally liberal submitted Scripture and dogma to rational, usually skeptical, analysis.[22] Alternatively, however, and in view of a more radical and elementary meaning of "modern," which, as a word, derives from *hodie*, meaning "these times" or, more accurately, "on this day":[23] here, the "ism" attached to "modern" may represent a particular moment of history, a specified Now, which is defined by a sense of itself as separate. In this account, modernism involves the consciousness of a *special* present, which is made more intense by virtue of some self-conscious *difference* from what went before.

If the literary production we know as modernist holds together at all, it hardly coheres as an extension of the hyperrational attitude of religious liberalism. Whatever memory "modernism" may have preserved of that turn-of-the-century reference, when it entered wider currency in midcentury as a term in cultural history, it evidently served to label an energy once perceived and, long ago, even feared (from one vantage) as insurgent, counterconventional. One of the main values that literary modernism challenged was the liberal rationalism of the previous centuries. If, in our retrospect, that convention and precedent must appear all too vulnerable, given the unreason deepening with the course of twentieth-century history, the term modernism still preserves the orientation—it needs to recover the memory, and the shock—of the first, massive reversal that history turned on liberal rationalism. A historically responsible case can be made for a modernist literature, that is, and it may be undertaken in a consideration of the work emanating from and echoing back to wartime London—in a reading that identifies the timely crisis of this special present. The literature stemming from this moment presents itself as the defining type of an impulse we recognize more generally in a standard bibliography of modernist fiction and poetry; those examples range from Joyce's *Ulysses* (especially its second half), where verbal logic stands as straight man for the author's comic improvisations on it; to the ludic reason Stevens manifests in the verbal fabric of his verse; from the dream-talking sequences of Faulkner to the vaudeville logic of Beckett. While these writers express a characteristically modernist incentive to address and redirect the regimens of linguistic rationality, this impetus may be focused and analyzed most revealingly in relation to the historical moment I am attempting to frame and enclose in this book.

The claim I am making for this event may be strengthened in view of the issues that Robert Pippin addresses in *Modernism as a Philosophical Problem*, a book that retells the long story of modernity's debate with itself. The terms are familiar. A long-standing faith in the Enlightenment ideals of rational inquiry and empirical science has coincided with an equally long-lived tendency to question the premises of those practices. This skepticism, which extends at least as far back as Kant's *Critique of Pure Reason*, ranges in its expressions from the heckling objections of Rousseau to the disciplined, reciprocating exchanges of Hegel. For Pippin, this evidence is consistent with an ongoing, alternative, contrarian line within the majority consciousness of Enlightenment (and post-

Enlightenment) rationalism.[24] What Pippin builds into the official tradition is a critical and self-critical condition that makes its own claim to being a dominant consciousness. He can standardize these exceptions, in effect, because the mainstay standard of logical methodology remains in place even—or especially—among these objectors.

In this gallery of established adversarial rationalists, however, one figure offers Pippin the promise of some purer alternative, some uncompromised possibility. Nietzsche speaks a language Pippin hears as the closest available approximation to an idiom of difference. This vocabulary and manner may enable a real break from that all-encompassing grammar of Enlightenment reason. In Pippin's commentary, Nietzsche pitches his resistance along a fairly standard, predictable series of philosophical issues. More significant to our consideration is the claim Nietzsche makes, crucially vague in Pippin's representation, that "some massive, traumatic event, the 'great event' of modern times, has occurred. Some possibility of going on as we had before has come to some sort of end."[25] The most expressive word in this chronology of crisis is, of course, "some." The inability it witnesses to locate the moment it invokes goes to a failure to realize, to make real as a function of lived experience, the starker truth of that major claim. Without this historical grounding, Pippin cannot help but imply, the language and attitude of that greatly valorized fracture in the rationalist establishment are, well, just that—language and attitude. The much-trumpeted voice of Nietzsche's adversarial prophet might belong all too recognizably to a tradition of sheerly verbalist iterations.

An event of the intensity and dimension requisite to Nietzsche's presentiment may be found early in the century after his death: in the Great War of 1914–18. In it, the discontent that Enlightenment (and post-Enlightenment) Europe had long attempted to express found more than adequate pretext. That the Great War locates a watershed between Enlightenment ideals, like the constant progress technology promised, and their gruesome disillusionment—in the mass grave into which technological war converted the earth of Europe—is hardly news, of course. These events need to be held against the language that attempted to rationalize and support them, however, to reveal anew the really novel shock of that atrocity. The grammar and vocabulary through which the war was constructed in political Britain, in particular, represent an idiom whose coherence reaches deep into the major traditions of intellectual liberalism and, in its disturbance, opens into an equally profound range of resonance and implication.

Why has not the agony of Liberal England's rationalistic language been heard as the target and urge of London's literary modernists? In our own moment, after all, the "cultural studies" perspective usually purports to encompass the determining conditions of artistic production and, in that claim, would seem already to have assimilated the idioms of Woolf's fiction and Pound's and Eliot's poetry to Liberal England's now-failing master language.

Insofar as the modernist echo represents an attempt to challenge or subvert the Word of that dominant consciousness, moreover, this imaginative program bespeaks the insurgent, counterprivilege, underclass initiative that the cultural studies vantage often claims in its mapping of literary activity. What are the presumptive constructions of its modernism, and why hasn't the literary impulse being studied in this book come into its critical narratives?

A developing consensus, theorized to varying degrees of coherence, has tended to present the "newness" of modernism as a general, even mass, condition. Humanity will have moved into this next dimension, or so goes the plot of this cultural history, simply by passing over those (putative) Rubicons, of which the Great War is nominally the greatest. This vision extends an understandable attempt on the part of younger literary historians to reorient the apex-base, top-down model of modernism that dominated scholarly commentary since about 1950. Those assumptions find their culminating expression perhaps in the imperial claims of *The Pound Era*, in which Hugh Kenner references a whole cultural age to the aesthetic premises of one major poet. The rhythm of resistance against the age of Kenner builds thus into the opposite model of the new historicists. Modernism now enjoys a populist provenance, a sort of mass (even anonymous) authorship. Its new readers inspect texts they have drawn from a forcefully expanded and variegated frame of reference, ranging from advertising lingo to lyric poetry, propaganda and obituary diction to poetic elegy. The synergy or complementarity that these documents reveal challenges ultimately the preferred category of "the literary."[26]

When Winter opposes the notion that the war "usher[ed] in modernism" and helped to consolidate its dominance, after all, he is questioning—and identifying—the new claim for the majority status of this novel consciousness. He is devaluing this new modernism as a mass phantom. He is reserving artistic modernism to a coterie or minority interest, not (in my view) wrongly. For the answer these writers project to a master language in collapse represents no anthem for social, specifically underclass, advance; it heralds no movement into a state where conditions will be improved for all humanity. It bespeaks instead an attempt at their own answering mastery, indeed, an equivalent privilege, which will have occluded this project from view in the construction of the new modernism.

What Winter and I make of this diminished thing, however, differs in no small way. In his mapping of cultural history, modernism identifies itself as a ghetto of regrettable idiosyncracies. His modernists sideline themselves from the Main Street of a developing continuum of cultural history. The London modernists appear in my account as representatives of a vanguard awareness. Woolf, Pound, and Eliot will take the change they intimate in the language of established value as the basis for an experimental verbal art, an impetus for imaginative heroisms of variously daring kinds.

The situation I outline positions these London modernists in relation to cultural norms at an angle congruent with the one usually attributed to an international avant-garde. The opposition of art to prudent bourgeois values, which represent the dead center of political and cultural liberalism, designates a temper to which the sensibility of these modernists is routinely assigned. Tellingly, however, one of the best books on the European avant-garde and the 1914 war, Modris Eksteins's *Rites of Spring: The Great War and the Birth of the Modern Age*, makes only glancing reference to an Anglo-American faction.[27] While Eksteins's lack of systematic attention to Pound, Eliot, and Woolf (among others) might have been reasoned out more clearly, their relative absence from his study does not seem wrong. Its correctness turns on a fact now well established in scholarly commentary, though it is still surprising to readers equipped only with long-distance images of a rebellious avant-garde: the alignment of this artistic energy with nationalist aspirations in the capital cities of Europe. From this conscription, the London modernists maintained some distance. The Americans Pound and Eliot were certainly vulnerable to the appeals the Liberal government made on behalf of its War for English Civilization, but their alien status also helped them to preserve a critical edge. Woolf, among other feminist writers, exercised an attitude of well-practiced skepticism on the language of nationalist politics, from which women were still disfranchised in early 1918 (the several stages of enfranchisement began in the last year of the war).

Further: these London modernists were responding to partisan attitudes and manners that show some significant difference to those with which Eksteins's major players were involved. Along the usual axis of Paris-Rome-Berlin-St. Petersburg, the activities of the Continental avant-garde that he maps find a credible center in the political milieu of liberal Germany. This Teutonic strain celebrates an intellectual ethic quite distinctly opposed to the social rationalism of British liberalism: it is an *emancipatory* impulse. Expansionist in imaginative character, this side of liberalism expresses a policy of openly nationalist self-aggrandizement and, in the timely grammar of turn-of-the-century enthusiasms, a poetics of mechanical dynamism.

Aspects of this Continental sensibility may be seen, of course, in London, in proximity to the vorticism with which Pound and Eliot were affiliated to differing degrees. It was expressed vividly if briefly in the name and style (even the exploding typeface) of the journal Wyndham Lewis formed as a record of this outburst: *Blast*. On these pages, in particular in the War Number issue (its last) of July 1915, the insurgent energies of a Continental avant-garde take up the cause and case of an English War for Civilization. Idiosyncratic as that outlook might be, it found its one (lonely) center of coherence on this specifically British flank of Europe's advanced artistic guard in the Englishman Lewis.[28] Pound and Eliot have enough in common with him to make the difference in their implementation of avant-garde aesthetics interesting,[29] but they are not readily assimilable to the nationalist premise that the war defined with heightening import and prominence in Lewis's work. That difference deepens with the years but reveals near its beginning the alternate experience that Woolf, Pound, and Eliot underwent in the war. Their status as resident or relative aliens allowed and indeed compelled them to make something out of the disruption the war represented—in the civic and political mythology of the nation in which they found themselves, sometimes (at this time) oddly.

The opportunity to which these modernists responded lay in the discrepancy between the intellectual principles and practical actualities of British Liberalism. While this partisan faith was committed to the preponderance of public reason in the deliberations of policy, its representatives had also pledged the nation, through a series of secret agreements, which will be documented in the next chapter, to an inarguable involvement in a Continental war. The resulting friction represents a systemic unrest. A seismic wave rolls a whole tradition of liberal intellectual conscience toward the crashing apotheosis of its support for the war. The terrible reversal of those otherwise estimable precedents establishes the conditions in which the major literature of record comes into existence.

That the story is not known in these terms is the result to some considerable extent of George Dangerfield's *The Strange Death of Liberal England* (1935), an account of British political culture between 1910 and 1914. This early, highly readable, hugely influential book leaves nearly completely out of account the intellectual dimension of its political drama. The chief agents of partisan power act through individual whim, clique concern, or some random calculation of the demands of local situations. Their efforts, moreover, have played to most significant consequence before the war. "[B]y the end of 1913," Dangerfield asserts, "Liberal England was reduced to ashes." Comprehensively: "the true prewar Liberalism—supported as it was in 1910 by Free Trade, a majority in Parliament, the ten commandments, and the illusion of Progress—can never return. It was killed, or it killed itself, in 1913."[30] Dangerfield can make these claims in advance of the story he tells, where the unseemly procedures he documents certainly diminish the validity of high partisan ideals. Yet the events discrediting Liberalism were part of an ongoing story, an intellectual as well as political history that rose to its climax and climacteric in the Great War.

Liberalism, that is, went on dying. The agon and pathos of that death may be heard in the contortions of the rationalist's language, which will prove to be of such tremendously consequential account for English literary modernism. Those political procedures presented an incentive for stylistic developments that propelled a revolution against the major, precedent conventions of the previous centuries: a rationalism of language as well as of attitude. In the culture of the English war in particular, we find this linguistic and intellectual tradition of liberal modernity in extremis, and in public. The writers of a specifically English modernism will distinguish themselves by identifying this crisis and realizing—incorporating—its meaning in an imaginative literature. It is the work of this book to recover the echo, to understand the resonance, and so to restore their poetry and fiction to a historical importance that is original, specific.

1

Liberal Measures

Prolegomenon to a Poetics
of English Modernism

I

Harmonic Politics

When the editors of the Home University Library of Modern Knowledge were seeking a writer to provide the most authoritative account for their projected volume *Liberalism* (1910), their choice of Leonard Trelawnly Hobhouse was unsurprising. A descendant of John Cam Hobhouse, first editor of the *Liberal* and friend of Byron, L. T. Hobhouse had seen diverse service within the political and intellectual culture of turn-of-the-century Liberalism. A journalist as well as a university professor, he was alert to debates currently dividing the party; he was aware as well of their backgrounds in intellectual history.[1] He was also formidably equipped to project solutions for these problems. But he would not feature the kind of simple answer or single-minded definition that this one-subject-at-a-time Library was purveying. The main interest of Hobhouse's book lies in the record it offers of a timely sensibility, one that is open not only to the coalitions forming in contemporary Liberalism but to the discontents dividing its membership. The consensus position was maintained within a heavily contested terrain.

The meaning of "liberty" essential to the definition of "Liberalism" had been subject in recent decades to strongly competing claims, most notably those of individualists and corporatists. Herbert Spencer's construction of the social life as a free Darwinian struggle had cast the human character in the individualist role as the self-seeking egoist. Liberalism's progressive and social democratic constituency was urging opportunities for the working class and underclass in the form of collectivist, leveling demands.[2] Yet these two rival types might comprise one ideal, a single model citizen as well as a consistent philosophical value.

23

The new possibility turned upon an older principle. It was the resolution of reason, and Hobhouse achieved it in a fashion at once characteristic of "the liberal mind" at that moment of English cultural history and representative of this sensibility's particularly English traditions and emphases.

The rational faculty that liberals since John Stuart Mill had posited (with self-interest and liberty) as natural to human capacity served Hobhouse's purpose, but not completely. He turned it past its contemporary conventions and specific applications as induction or practical calculation and back to a resource of suggestion and hortative power accumulated from its Latin etymology, *ratio*, meaning "measure" (to *ration* means, if obsoletely, to "reason"). The word recovers thus the full range of its cognate associations and functions: "scale, balance, harmony." The rogue individual in Spencer's scheme might regulate his self-development, then, rationing his appetite to preserve a "common good," which stood, in effect, as a product of similarly rational calculations on the part of other individuals.[3]

The aesthetic premise on which this understanding turns shows more clearly still in the definition Hobhouse offers (in his central chapter, "The Heart of Liberalism") of "the rational impulse." Reason works to strike a balance that is admittedly, in fact professedly, "harmonic." "Just as the endeavour to establish [a] coherent system in the world of thought is the characteristic of the rational impulse which lies at the root of science and philosophy," he proposes, "so the impulse to establish harmony in the world of feeling and action—a harmony which must include all those who think and feel—is of the essence of the rational impulse in the world of practice. To move towards harmony is the persistent impulse of the rational being."[4]

This aesthetic understanding of reason extends its applications from principle to practice, shaping the texture of the language of argument and adapting its strategies to tasks as various as propositional statement and paragraph structure. The sentence adducing his major proposal reads indeed as a nearly perfect demonstration of reason as artistic conceit: "The first condition of universal freedom, that is to say, is a measure of universal restraint."[5] The role of the word "measure" in the sentence is at once crucial and indeterminate. As the medial and mediating term, it intends to present "freedom" and "restraint" in some resolving relation, which remains nonetheless undefined, unrestricted, indeed unmeasured. Those opposed terms balance around a word that affects aesthetically what it means (intentionally, at least) logically. This artistic, harmonizing application of "rationality" then expands characteristically:

> Liberty then becomes not so much a right of the individual as a necessity of society. It rests not on the claim of A to be let alone by B, but on the duty of B to treat A as a rational being. It is not right to let crime alone or to let error alone, but it is imperative to treat the criminal or the

mistaken or the ignorant as being capable of right and truth, and to lead them on instead of merely beating them down. The rule of liberty is just the application of rational method. It is the opening of the door to the appeal of reason.[6]

The stipulative restrictions and antitheses—"not so much . . . as a," "not on . . . but on," "not right to . . . but it is imperative"—seem to develop a dialectical argument, which relies, on closer inspection, on a musical accumulation of effects. The theme words of "reason" and "rationality" repeat sufficiently frequently to ease away any memory of strict intellectual procedure, and so take on the nature of a refrain. By the end of the passage, the incantation has smoothed out the obvious contradiction of the first assertion, neutralizing those real antonyms of "liberty" and "necessity" on one level, "right" and "duty" on another. The "appeal of reason" finds success mainly as a function of affective repetition and syntactic balances, that is, as a demonstration of Hobhouse's aesthetic conception of *ratio*nality.

The emphases detectable in these representative selections reveal the motive of their method more clearly in reference to the larger, pan-European commentary on Hobhouse's topic. Here the nascent formulations of "crowd psychology," with which this holder of the first chair of sociology at London University was certainly conversant, propose notions wholly opposed to his. These were new and disturbing theorems about human behavior as it related to and was revealed by "the collective"—an entity constituted, not civilly, politically, or ideally, but in its rawer, "natural" state. Works like Gustave LeBon's *The Crowd* (1895; trans. 1896) presented human action in groups as random, highly suggestible, scarcely reasonable, and utterly undeliberated.[7] The presence and power of the irrational in human action was establishing itself simultaneously in Freud's writings. These new, seemingly empirical, at least semiscientific accounts present a challenge to which Hobhouse responds most tellingly. His ideally rational calculus formulates an equation and relates the individual to the state (and to other individuals) in terms that ostensibly decline the findings of the new sociological and psychological sciences. A classical rationality operates rhetorically, not analytically, let alone empirically. If Hobhouse's sociological case cannot be won in terms of materialist reasoning, his aesthetic rationality performs its work musically, that is, unarguably.

Hobhouse's strategies also exhibit a consistent proclivity within the political tradition of Liberal reason. There is an inveterate tendency to turn logic away from a rational management of fact and back to the consolations of philosophical principle—a self-hypnotizing rhetoric of reason. This is a slippage that an ex- or antipartisan Liberal like Matthew Arnold seems all too eager to identify. In that catalogue of folly he compiled as the summary chapter of *Culture and Anarchy*, "Our Liberal Practicioners," the most indicative example is surely the "reason and justice" refrain, which the Nonconformist core of the party was intoning in a campaign to disestablish the Irish church. In Arnold's unforgiving analysis, this phrase (which he repeats to the point of mockery) bespeaks no superior, cerebral, or unimpassioned attitude. It expresses instead the compulsive workings of these Dissenters' subrational "fetish."[8]

If most criticism is to some extent self-criticism, this erstwhile Liberal aims his most vehement critique at a weakness that his own text reveals all too clearly. He repeatedly invokes the standards of a classical rationality to lend "sweetness and light," the aesthetic charm of clear-sighted mind, to the urgings, coerced and coercive, of his own "fetish": the anti-Semitism (anti-Hebraism) that compels this book and its campaign for a valid culture.[9] The more profound irony in this performance lies not in the way it disables his own prejudicial claims, which in no case submit to reason. In the example of himself, Arnold has proven the truth of his own critique of Liberalism's prime liability: a readiness to believe in the suasive charms of a purely rhetorical rationality.

The tendency to escalate a rhetoric of reason in nearly inverse ratio to the credibility of the cause is the acutest susceptibility in the liberal mind. A chronic possibility, it is revealed in the seeming reason of Arnold's unseemly decencies. It shows also in the attenuated enmities of Hobhouse's proposition, which attempts to score demotic politics to rationalist harmonics. The pressure that social realities were exerting on the prosodies of an older and resolving logic could be contained, however, at least to a level commensurate with the skill of these rhetorical fictions of reason. This convention would be stressed beyond any precedent tension, it is fair to predict, when it needed to attend to the emergent event of the Great War.

i
___

Armed force appears in Liberal tradition as the chief type of unreason. The problem finds its means of address in an apparatus of specifically moral rationality. Hobhouse attempts to invest this mechanism with the energy of a legacy still living at the end of the first decade of the twentieth century. He reiterates the principles that evolved the foreign policy consciousness of mainstream Victorian Liberalism. He follows the Gladstonian dictum that war, while hateful in itself and requiring resistance up to the end, is finally justifiable—not on strategic grounds, but for ethical reasons. Military intervention is a step to be taken as a decision reached freely and openly from a morally informed act of reason.[10] Yet the strategic and opportunistic alliances that the custodians of the empire felt compelled to maintain certainly went against the prevalent temper of Gladstone's ethic. The reader of history witnesses a division between the dictates of a moralistic discourse of public reason and the strategic interests of the party's imperialist wing. This division coincides with a substantial tension within Liberalism, moreover, one that plays out a real struggle for control of the party.

In this ongoing contest, the signal figure is Sir Henry Campbell-Bannerman, prime minister for a brief period in the Edwardian decade. Hobhouse takes him up in his chapter "The Future of Liberalism" and makes him frame a set of optimal possibilities for the party's near term. Campbell-Bannerman had stood against the Boer War and the support it was receiving from the influential minority of Liberal imperialists, challenging the betrayal of partisan principles that he perceived in this initiative and stigmatizing it in a phrase that remained still for Hobhouse in vivid memory: the famed "methods of barbarism" speech. The key word reverted to its first sense—*bar-bar*, "to babble"—to mark his adversaries. Conversely, in the field of current political and intellectual conflict, Campbell-Bannerman was using the word to claim some deepened coherence for his own speech, the language and policy of moral reasoning. The contest reappears in similar terms in Hobhouse's account, in images that characterize the intellectual orientation of Liberal imperialism as a slide of mind into unreason, in effect, a bad dream. "[I]n the Liberal ranks, many of the most influential men had passed," he rues generously and perhaps even genuinely, "*without consciousness* of the transition, *under the sway* of quite opposite influences. They were *becoming Imperialists in their sleep*."[11] Acknowledging the lapse of the preceding decade as an unintended fall from the expected behavior of rational (liberal) humanity, Hobhouse expresses the confidence of his own political moment in the renewed prepotence of moral logic as the leading standard in foreign policy affairs.

With some reason. The landslide Liberal victory in the elections of 1906 included a repudiation of sheerly imperial interests in favor of a program of social conscience that extended from the domestic to the international. A moderately collectivist agenda at home established a standard of governmental responsibility and accountability. The language of diplomatic policy echoed to the strains of the moralistic, Gladstonian faith when it came to questions of international relations. Yet "the most influential men" of the turn of the century, advocates for involvement in the Boer War, had survived politically, and they would reappear in the premier positions: Prime Minister H. H. Asquith, Foreign Secretary Sir Edward Grey, and Armaments Minister Lord Haldane were all true and proven players on the side of Liberal imperialism.[12] The situation forced their strategic interests, developed mainly through alliances with France, into private. These "secret agreements" would necessitate Britain's eventual—and early—entry into the Great War, when, still, those older codes of Gladstonian probity maintained control of the public statements of official record. The language of those conventions owned an authority and power that would allow these speakers to make a suasive case for what was, otherwise, an unsupportable cause.

ii

The strength of the Gladstonian convention might be measured in advance through one representative demonstration. The Liberal idiom of ethical reason finds a most discerning register in Gilbert Murray, Oxford classicist and public intellectual. Murray combines the high ideals of the Gladstonian with a personal turn of mind that is otherwise skeptical and independent. He offers thus—by the inverse measure of a resistance overcome—the best record of the effect of the great performances of partisan moralism in the Great War.

Murray first earned his credentials as a Liberal intellectual on the dissenting side of the Boer War controversy. He joined with F. W. Hirst and J. L. Hammond to write *Liberalism and the Empire* (1900) and raise a voice of principled dissent to the strategic schemes of the new imperialism. The fealty he swore to moral idealism appears no more wide-eyed, however, than it seems clear-sighted, even hardheaded. There is awareness of the actual machinations of international affairs and demagogic politics. "The present writers believe," their testament begins,

> that for many years past the aggressive and vainglorious instincts of Great Britain have been unduly stimulated; that adventure, conquest, mastery, and race-pride, strangely wedded with speculative finance and culminating in the fatal lust of Empire, have been so long held up to the worship of the populace by men whose position and antecedents would have rendered them capable of higher, or at least saner, ideals, that the reason of the country is in abeyance and its imagination intoxicated.[13]

Murray was able to maintain this fine combination of moral loftiness and practical sagacity into the early days of August 1914. On the day before England's entry into the war, he appeared with an eminent gathering of party intelligentsia as signatory to a document protesting, in effect, the same "abeyance" of reason in the unwisdom of Continental involvement.[14] Then, with most of them, he withdrew the objection.

The most obvious consequence of this reversal (the pressures resulting in it will become evident shortly) is his composition in 1915 of a pamphlet-length apologia, *The Foreign Policy of Sir Edward Grey*. Murray declares the minister cleared of the charge that he had bound England to a policy course as furtive, suspect, unreasoned, and immoral as the secrecy of his dealings with France in the prewar years.[15] The allegations had been substantially proven already in the radical press by E. D. Morel (below). By 1916, nonetheless, Grey's Foreign Ministry stood in Murray's eyes as a paradigm of Gladstonian probity. The war now owned an ethical rectitude as complete as the moral self-righteousness of this statement: "I am most proud of the clean hands with which we came into this contest, proud of the cause for which with clear vision we unsheathed our sword, and which we mean to maintain unshaken to the bitter or the triumphant end."[16] This defensive rationale echoes a number of catchwords and slogans in the propaganda of the current Liberal government. If such a demonstration seems surprising in an intellectual who has styled himself as independently minded, it also testifies to the will, effort, and success of the government's own rhetorical performance.

Murray's vow to maintain the righteous cause "to the bitter or the triumphant *end*" pledges his more specific allegiance to the liberal ideal of progress. The same faith permeates the 1900 jeremiad, where, even in the rhetorical negatives of his rebuke, the "reason" and "high ideals" of rational morality identify the promise those Liberal imperialists have forgone; they were "capable of higher" things. He mourns this loss overtly as a clerisy's squandered privilege and promise, but he grieves really as a believer in the ethical perfectibility of humanity. This idea inscribes a master narrative in history, one that Murray rewrites, in 1916, as his own version of the official ideology. The English cause and case looked for support to a morally reasoned sense of destiny. A providential logic as strong as any Gladstone could concoct extended its sanction to the English side, where the standard of an advancing "civilization" borrowed the aura of religious justification in its ultimate rationales. The righteous conclusion to this argument may seem far off, given the "bitter . . . end" to which events were currently pointing. The moral authority of that destination, however, is not forsaken; the feeling relocates itself. A sense of lost (or deferred) victory mutates into a high and noble pathos. With stoic indignation, Murray settles into the rhetorical position of being in the right. The discourses of right reason supplant the course of actual history as the measure and test of ethical rectitude. This recentering represents no evident defeat. Witness the morally triumphalist stance in which Murray positions himself. His move proves the durable and flexible strength of this prevalent convention of liberal modernity: progress.

iii

The extent to which the myth of a model progress prevailed over the Liberal war and dominated not only its attitudes but its verbal logic is the substantial burden of a little book published in 1931, Herbert Butterfield's *The Whig Interpretation of History*. Allowing for the fact that the "Whig" identification draws a smaller and more tightly defined target than "Liberal," Butterfield nonetheless takes aim at the center of intellectual energy in the cause- and case-making machinery that compelled partisan efforts through the recent conflict. He focuses mainly on the attempt by an intellectual liberalism to write an ideology of history into its account of very specific, highly various incidents and situations. In his analysis, the Whig writer tends to reduce thickly contingent masses of detail to speciously easy focal points. This history invents causal or consequential centers of energy, isolating and radicalizing these as the origins of tendencies to be favored in later developments. Predictably, these consequences will tend to affirm the liberal sense of historical time as the realization of liberty's value by gradual, inevitable degrees.[17]

Butterfield's close reading of representative liberal texts shows the attitudes and practices of a strongly rationalistic conception of language. Causal sequence and reasonable procedure reappear as features equally in the march of time and the regimen of words. In this artifice of language, Butterfield implies most suggestively and crucially, a writer may sustain a mythic vision of history as a wholly linguistic fiction. A pattern of predication in grammar thus substitutes its own rule of cause and effect for a welter of historical forces, converting these rawer and divergent actions into one as unitary and continuous as a conclusion-driven proposition. For Butterfield, writing in the late 1920s, the "right" sort of history will have set aside this liberal fallacy, this verbal facility with reasonable speech. "The process of historical transition will then be recognised to be unlike what the whig [sic] historian seems to assume—*much less like the procedure of a logical argument*" (emphasis added).[18]

This vision of history proceeding reasonably—but only because of the rationalistic language that compels it—may be attributed, Butterfield asserts, to "certain features in the technique of history-writing, and to the exploitation of that dubious phraseology which has become the historian's stock-in-trade."[19] The perfect tense in Butterfield's report suggests the currency of procedures that have been featured recently. His focus sharpens accordingly, drawing the now-typical liberal trick of rationalistic language into this special temporal location. When "the whig historian stands on the summit of the 20th Century and organises his scheme of history from the point of view of his own day," Butterfield specifies, the several liabilities of this backward-glancing perspective may be emphasized to demonstrate the main point of rebuke:

> [H]e is a subtle man to overturn from his mountain-top when he can fortify himself with *plausible argument. He can say* that events take on their due proportion when observed through the lapse of time. *He can say* that events must be judged by their ultimate issues, which, since we can trace them no farther, we must at least follow down to the present. *He can say* that it is only in relation to the 20th Century that one happening or another in the past has relevance or significance for us. He can *use all the arguments* that are so handy to men . . . so that it is no simple matter to demonstrate how the whig historian, from his mountain-top, sees the course of history only inverted and aslant.[20]

The "plausibility" of a Whig historian's statement seems to rely on the mere fact that "he can say" it. The idea of progressive history seems to lie as a kind of residual myth in the language of rationalism, in the syntax of reasonable argument, where the linear, consistent, and end-driven quality in logical proposition extends to a conception of historical time. There is no shortage of examples in the texts of the Whigs' most recent war to support this perception.

The most startling thing about this striking book, however, is the fact that Butterfield never once mentions the intellectual environment of the Great War, let alone cites examples from the Liberal endeavor undertaken there. He draws nearly all of his cases from Victorian and early twentieth-century historians of the Reformation.[21] Perhaps he fails to register the evidence of this most recent incident in his chronicle of folly because he is too young (he was born in 1900) to take in its intellectual import, at least as a function of lived, day-by-day experience. Yet the absence of explicit reference is also expressive. It registers as a matter of received fact the discredit the cause- and case-making of the recent war will have visited upon the myths and principles of liberal history and historiography. Not that the import of his book turns wholly on what it does not overtly say. When Butterfield specifies the Protestant Reformation as the primary and defining site of liberal historiographic principle, he situates the timelier crisis of the recent present in the full context and continuum of its intellectual history. The values of rational gradualism and logical tolerance that were begotten with the constitution of public reason in the early sixteenth century are the same ones that the political discourse of Liberalism at war has manipulated and discredited.

iv

Where Butterfield's analysis recalls the problems that the concept and logic of progress encountered in recent history, the foremost representative of the older order expresses this dilemma as a point of personal pathos. Writing "The Hope of the World" in 1916, L. T. Hobhouse presents this essay as the most substantial chapter in his *Questions of War and Peace*. The main debates of the day take the form of a Ciceronian dialogue. His counterpart is a Liberal who identifies himself explicitly with the rational meliorism of the nineteenth century. With the plangent despair of his intellectual class, Hobhouse's spokesman records the demise of progressive reason as an ideal system, mourning a now-foregone order of history and language. "We lost three or four times as many men at Loos as at Waterloo. If this is progress I grant you the world moves onward, but the word ceases to express anything in which a rational man can take interest."[22]

This speaker yields to Sister Agatha, who restates the case for meliorist reason, but as a matter of faith alone. " 'I don't pretend,' she replied, 'to be able to formulate it in any way that is beyond the reach of cavil, but I should call it a state of confidence and trust in the validity of the best things—reason, justice, and love.' " However, she needs to concede, this "confidence" is based on a simple "conviction that reason is so much better than anything else that you must follow it, even when it leads you into darkness." She expatiates: "The very fact that reason leads you nowhere and yet you consent to be led by it, is a proof of your faith."[23] Sister Agatha's "dark" apocalypse of reason images clearly the negative conclusion to which the old master syllogism of history seems to have led now, by 1916.

Sister Agatha performs a number of adjustments, then, on the ideas of Hobhouse's beleaguered counterpart. Most obviously, she differs from his articulate skepticism about rational progress in her strong affirmation of reason as procedure. Indeed, the *methods* of rationality have acquired for her a value so absolute as to appear unquestionable, infrangible, invariable, even in view of the meanings (or meaninglessness) they induce. This is a shift of major import and consequence, and it measures the extent to which Hobhouse's own former ideals have been transformed over the course of the war. Not only has Hobhouse dissolved his former confidence in the ultimate, material realization of human reason in history. The empirical basis of a positivist logic has disappeared into the spiritual zeal of Sister Agatha, in her faith in some supernal logos. Not that the sociologist Hobhouse can affirm such transcendent entities readily. The one constant value of progressive rationality has shifted for him from its newly disproved destiny to the now-exalted medium and procedure of language itself. The means of verbal reason have turned into an end, in which Sister Agatha attests a faith only as complete for her as it is desperate for a writer who signs himself in this text as "Pentire." Hobhouse autographs his essay then with an indication that the resources of written history, in particular the compositional logic that affords the Whig historian's stock-in-trade, are exhausted. The demise of a living tradition is being told here, one that will help nonetheless to further the development of a new literary sensibility. The story of those last days may be told in pieces, day by day, in the popular, journalistic culture of the Liberal war.

II

The Journalistic Turn

Resistance in the partisan press to involvement in a Continental war was rising with the international crisis in July 1914, and nearly every argument for avoiding a European embroilment turned on an appeal to the "rational." The prospect of conflict was dismissed, initially at least, as an accident that would not happen, that prudent reason would forestall. Peering with a faintly patronizing air into the recesses of the eastern principalities, a writer for the literary weekly the *New Statesman* could still on 25 July hope for the best that might be expected of those "more or less reasonable" peoples. This same writer found "not only improbable but absurd" the notion that a local tribal feud could escalate past its natural borders; "an act of something like insanity" by Austria was required to allow such an eventuality to occur.[24] Evolving with the irony of the situation, reason decamped for British Liberals, who withdrew to their insular position. They renewed the old principle of neutrality and reclaimed their allegiance to it. "Any other policy would be treason to Liberal principle," warned a leader in the *Daily News* on 3 August, since any move to action here would be undeliberated. A "rush into war . . . at all costs and against all reason"[25] needed to be deterred. The partisan chief who compromised the intellectual principles of Liberalism in prosecuting so "causeless" a war, that is, in failing to argue from moral premise to logical consequence, warned the *Nation* on 1 August, "would cease to lead the Liberal Party."[26]

This coalition of political interests and intellectual values sprang up nearly fully formed from mid-July to early August because, in large part, the consensus ran true to long-standing Liberal traditions. The intellectual freedom needed for reason's proper deliberations had usually been identified with resistance, not only to specific alliances in Europe, but to compliance with the entire balance-of-power system. In this scheme, the logistics of alignment preceded and preempted the liberty of moral logic in the individual agents of national policy. John Bright, Gladstone's close political affiliate, thus labeled the doctrine "that foul idol of our foreign policy."[27] Fake deity it may have been, but the actions that Asquith and others had taken under the public cover of another faith led the partisan press to invoke Bright's phrase repetitively and increasingly as the worrisome evidence was emerging that some bond to the Continental powers was making British involvement a real possibility.[28]

To break the spell the government was carefully casting, these journalists were eager to repeat the assurances extended during the preceding three years by Asquith and Grey that they had entered into no "secret agreements." These varied writers were thus able to assert, in their most strenuous and concerted effort, the ongoing life of free ethical rationality as the guiding principle for England's Liberal statesmen. On 3 August, the *Manchester Guardian* went so far as to apply the Gladstonian sanction, not to endorse the response being proposed by the government for the likely German invasion of Belgium, but to respect that ingress itself. The argument was fetched from no further away than the home values of English Liberalism: Germany's move instanced one nation's freedom to decide a case on the evident grounds of its own rightful need. The real "crime against reason," this editorial continued on an equally representative line, was to yield the right and duty of individual review to the preordained mandate of any alliance, secret or not. To enter this system of coerced relations was to lapse back into that old "network of promises and counter-promises"[29] and, in the shifting sands of that ethical morass, to lose the surety of absolute principle; it was to forgo, most important, the freedom to reason and choose.

"It is war to the knife between it and Liberalism," the *Guardian* of a few days earlier had warned, responding to the premonition that debts of alliances long unacknowledged were about to be called in.[30] Already, however, partisan

Sir Edward Grey

The Right Honorable H. H. Asquith

intellectuals were registering the pressure to speak the ethical reasoning behind the government's move into war on the side of France. The ease with which this clerisy would take up the new brief, moreover, represents a facility as strong as the value placed in liberal tradition on the rational capacity of language. That capacity represents a fear conveyed as early as 1 August, in the *Nation*. This writer worried that the true rule of reason in England's rightful role—as neutral mediator between the hostile powers—would dissipate itself in "light-spoken words, the froth of an academic theory,"[31] and would provide the rationale for British entry into the war.

The discrediting that verbal reason will suffer as it serves this purpose occurs within a larger context of shifting allegiances. Nearly unanimously, in fact, the major papers on the Liberal side felt compelled to take the part of Germany (and, usually, Austria) as the issues and sides were being drawn up in July. This alignment flowed from a feeling of transnational, ethnic continuity, which included a special claim by the Anglo-Saxon peoples on the highest priorities of liberalism. This sense of intellectual fellowship was sufficiently strong to prevail, at least as a matter of professed belief, over the real rivalry between the two nations' commercial empires (and naval fleets). Whatever differences existed between the social rationalism of Anglo-French liberalism and the more aggressive libertarianism of their Teutonic relatives, moreover, English partisans in particular tended to view themselves as partners with the Germans. The principles they shared were grouped under the polemical heading of "civilization" and identified explicitly with a commitment to social progress and the matching values of rational gradualism.[32] Under these standards, the linkage of England and Germany was scripted to the ideology of liberal modernity, which marks the beginning of the modern age with the establishment of the values of public reason. If the Reformation had begun in Germany, after all, it had extended itself most readily to England.

The intellectual concord between Liberal Britain and prewar Germany finds a representative expression on 3 August in the *Manchester Guardian* in "England's Duty: Neutrality the One Policy," a manifesto authored by a joint eminence of Anglican deans and bishops and professors (mainly from Cambridge). Now that France had entered the conflict on the side of Russia, the growing sense that England must become involved is met with the case of "Germany, . . . a nation . . . wedged in between hostile States, highly civilised, with a culture that has contributed enormously in the past to Western civilisation, racially allied to ourselves, and with moral ideals largely resembling our own." This sense of kinship is reinforced by an equal feeling of antipathy for the lowly Slavs. These are peoples "only partially civilised, governed by a military autocracy largely hostile to Western ideas of political and religious freedom." Any assistance by British Liberals in victory for such illiberal despotism is as unthinkable as the dominion it would ensure in Europe of "Russia, a half-Asiatic, half-civilised, wholly autocratic and reactionary Power."[33] The contumely and rebuke are redoubled on the same day in the more voluble columns of the *Guardian*'s leader. This piece responds to the notions that "Russia 'will fight upon the side of European moral'" and that "'the cause of civilised relations between peoples' . . . would gain by our backing her." The writer labels the words proposing fellow feeling with Russia as the "crowning effort of cant" and counters: "Of all the smaller powers in Europe, Servia is, quite decidedly, the one whose name is most foully daubed with dishonour. . . . If it were physically possible for Servia to be towed out to sea and sunk there, the air of Europe would at once seem cleaner. . . . And what Servia is among the lesser powers, Russia, so far as regards her Government, is among the great ones."[34]

A week later, once the war had begun, these values changed—with the side England had to take. Relying on the standards of "civilization" and rational morality, finding the opposites of these principles as constant standards now in the Teutonic camp, the *Daily News* of 10 August testifies that Germany "exhibits the human mind in a state of complete disablement from reasonable action." "Apparently one of the least intelligent and moral groups in the world," the Germanic peoples leave "religion, science, art, literature," that is, the whole cause of "civilisation . . . voiceless and powerless." The language of logical progress and moral rationality belongs now to Liberal England and its new conversant—the recently barbaric Russian, the once babbling Slav. "[F]rom a compact among those Powers whose capacity for civilisation is sufficiently developed," that is, from the joint discourses of a London–St. Petersburg axis, this editorial ventures that "a new Europe . . . may accrue."[35] What passes the standards test for membership on the right side of this struggle may include the reconditioned Slav, after all, in just the same way that the case for war is acquiring its new (and unexpected) rationale.

This twofold process of civilizing the Slav and making the war reasonable can be seen as the joint burden and motive in a pair of editorials appearing in the *Westminster Gazette*. They are separated by less than half a week; their positions witness the complete shift in Liberal policy and attitude. The first, reiterating the typical prewar view still ascendant on 28 July, finds "[t]he Serv . . . a man of primitive emotions and tastes, for whom town life seems to have little or no attraction. . . . There are few towns in the country worthy of the name." In a land in which the light of civilization is eclipsed, the commentator continues, "the staple industries" are those benighted activities of "pig-rearing" and elementary "husbandry."[36] Three days later, however, acting on the kind of information this unofficial yet privileged organ of the Liberal party was often able to obtain, the feature article redraws the portrait of the Serbian national character in a piece of ethnographic conversion as stunning as it is unacknowledged. "Posed gracefully before me," this writer opens, "stands a typical Servian: the lines of Apollo flow easily and naturally round his robust figure. It is a good, honest, sun-scorched face." If "the majority are illiterate," as this writer concedes strategically, so too, the immediate appeal goes, "they are quite intelligent." Indeed, this unsavage nobility offers to the more civilized side of the hostilities now begun an advanced science of war, a virtual academy of "artillery officers . . . well grounded in the theoretical branches of their work."[37] The figure of fun that partisan intellectuals have drawn in the Serb is thus transformed in accord with the government's need to align the war with its own case and campaign in "the war for civilization." The heavy pressure of this need goes so far, in reconditioning that national type, as to rearrange its deities and tutelary spirits. Apollo has thrust out Caliban. Where those "lines of Apollo" settle as a mask on the primitive visage, moreover, one sees the face of this new and unexpected ethnic hero recomposed in name to the god, not only of poetry, but of logic. The poetry of the case is already being written, and the spirit of reason prevails over the enterprise as its dubious muse.

The supreme effort in this campaign doubtless belonged to Sir Edward Grey. The foreign secretary was committed in public for most of July to neutrality. However, his private memos of understanding with the French had allowed that nation's fleet to be shifted to the Mediterranean,[38] leaving the northern and western coasts of that country exposed. The secret agreements compelled an English defense of an unprotected France. Grey needed nonetheless to address matters of foreign policy through the still-regnant conventions of Gladstonian probity. He had to reason the move to France's side as a decision taken freely on ethical grounds. This is the predicament toward which the various and conflicting strains of intellectual and political Liberalism had pushed the situation by 3 August. On this day, he addressed Parliament, in a speech whose text would be printed in all of the major dailies of 4 August and reprinted through the course of the war as the founding document of its moral authority.

Grey meets his difficulties with a vocabulary and manner addressed to familiar expectations and standards. Using the likely invasion of Belgium as the nominal provocation for the English response, he uses the moral hortative to implore: "[L]et every man look into his own heart and his own feelings, and construe the extent of the obligation to himself." Claiming this liberty of ethical deliberation for the process, he maintains the openness of the case as the truly liberal condition of its making: "I construe [the obligation] to myself as I feel it, but I do not wish to urge upon anyone else more than their own feelings dictate as to what they should feel about it. The House, individually and collectively, may judge for itself. But now I speak for myself, from the point of view of feeling."[39] This freedom of principled decision, given the real strategic constraints operating on the case, is the rhetorical fiction Grey needs to maintain.

He sustains the effect, moreover, through a masterful collocation of present realities and precedent texts. The appeal to Gladstonian diplomacy and the principle of free ethical decision occurs in letter as well as in spirit. He cites the elder statesman's understanding of an 1839 agreement among other European powers on the neutrality of Belgium as a document enjoining "honour and in-

British propaganda, distributed by balloon, Air Post 49. "Hindenburg: 'Majesty, the People are depressed [oppressed] and are grumbling incessantly.' Majesty: 'Why are they grumbling? We don't feel anything [any weight].'" Images of an oppressive, atavistic *Kaiserreich* appeared frequently in English representations of Germany. Since the election of January 1912, however, the German government had been run by a socialist majority (SPD), which corresponded in its main aims and professed values with British Liberalism. The intimacy of that acquaintance is hinted by the wordplay in the caption, where the literal significance augments the idiomatic sense.

Hindenburg: „Majestät, das Volk ist gedrückt und murrt unaufhörlich."
Majestät: „Weshalb murren sie? Wir spüren keine Last."

Voivode Poutnik, generalissimo of the Serbian army, is transported in his sedan chair across Albania, 1915. The unprogressive conditions of Serbian military and civilian life included many such images, matching ironically with the depictions of an oppressive *Kaiserreich*.

Sir Douglas Haig, commander in chief, British armies in France, joins forces with King Nikita of Montenegro, at Beauquesne, south of Doullens, November 1916.

Unidentified trench front in the Great War for Civilization.

terest" equally on England's response to Germany's violation of that country. If such diplomatic language seems indeterminate, it works perfectly to Grey's purposes, insofar as it leaves all the room required to construe freely and reasonably the moral reckoning of this debt of "honour." Not that he leaves this ethical decision to the chances of individual rationales as various as the dissenting consciences of the Liberal party. Reaching deep into parliamentary archives, he adds:

> I have one further quotation from Mr. Gladstone. . . . It will be found in Hansard, vol. 203, page 1,788. I have not had time to read the whole speech and verify the context, but the thing seems so clear that no context would make any difference to the meaning of it. He said:—
>
>> We have an interest in the independence of Belgium which is wider than that which we may have in the literal operation of the guarantee. It is found in the answer to the question whether under the circumstances of the case this country, endowed as it is with influence and power, would quietly stand by and witness the perpetration of the direst crime that ever stained the pages of history, and thus become participators in the sin.[40]

As the "case" moves through these two sentences, it shifts into a linguistic register that is clearly linked to the vivid, impending situation of 1914. A sense of urgency translates the pressure of realpolitik in Grey's contemporary moment into the mandate of a principled, wholly ethical indignation, which reserves nonetheless every discretionary freedom in the reasoned deliberation of the *moral* claim.

As the suasion escalates, however, the freedom of ethical decision reveals itself as the sheerest verbal artifice. The rhetoric will have developed its own stylistic mannerism by the end of the speech. "Let us suppose . . . let us assume . . . let us assume . . . let us assume":[41] these logical subjunctives speak the mood of free moral reason throughout the public deliberation; prior logistical constraints, however, have suborned the true grammar of ethical rationality at liberty. The strenuous effort of Grey's performance tells by contrary force the real and evident pressure of those otherwise unacknowledged facts.

The emergence of these facts, beginning already in 1914 with the investigations of E. D. Morel and the publications of the Union of Democratic Control of foreign policy (see n. 38), created the conditions under which Grey's speech—and the traditions it brought to so ceremonial a consummation—assumed a strange double life. To the ears of Liberal believers, surely, these remained the words of the Gladstonian hero, entering history as a sphere in which the speech of free ethical reason enjoyed a forceful authority. To nonpartisan readers of Morel's report, however, Grey's words must be edged with a discredit so evident that the whole performance sounded mock-ironic. Already double and shifting, the literary resonance of the speech catches the exact point at which a venerable intellectual legacy, social liberalism with its rich bibliography of concerned humanitarianism, touches awake that equally rich if more cryptic tradition: parodic liberalism, featuring in its most familiar instance the burlesqued voice of the concerned humanitarian in Swift's "A Modest Proposal." While the lines of irony or satire lie silent perforce in Grey's speech, this oratorical construct may shift, at the slightest touch of factual knowledge, from the vatic to the vacuous, from the serious reasonings of a Victorian moralist and statesman to the incendiary measures of a (neo-)Augustan wit. To this quick convertibility, the verbal imagination of London modernism would respond as the moment and opportunity of a new imaginative language. The provocations were as constant as the daily journalistic record.

i

If the press affiliated with the Liberal party initially resists the verbal perfidy of the war government, these writers turn with astonishing swiftness to assist in that campaign. An instance of this early development and an indication of its impact on the language of the partisan cause may be found in the response to Grey's speech, already on 4 August, in the pages of two of the most representative journals of political Liberalism, the *Manchester Guardian* and the *Westminster Gazette*.

The main editorial in the *Guardian* holds true to the standard of reason at liberty, of which it finds Grey's speech in such subtle but violent abuse. The writer protests openly that citizens and Parliament have not been given information sufficient "to form a reasoned judgment on the current of our policy." Interrogating the secretary's address at its points of greatest weakness, where it attempted to cover the strategic needs with a rhetoric of moral choice, this editor identifies the absolute, ineradicable paradox of Grey's claim and case: England, while remaining supposedly free to choose its policy, has extended assurances allowing France to make a naval move that has exposed that country's northern and western coasts. In Grey's conclusion that Britain must go to France's aid, even when Germany has vowed not to move on those undefended areas, this writer accurately intuits that the pressures at work on the secretary exceed those of the moral rationale he has claimed. "His reasons are extraordinary," the editorial demurs. The incredulity goes further, supplying the force of this rhetorical peroration against an obviously compromised logic. "Is it rational? Can it be deduced, we will not say from the terms of the Entente, but from the account of secret conversations which was given yesterday? Can it be reconciled with any reasonable view of British policy? It cannot."[42]

Can*not*? Consider this report of the same speech, in the news leader of the *Westminster Gazette*, which begins with a wholly credulous echoing of the foreign secretary's key words, of Grey's appeal to every man in the House to look into his heart and feeling and solve the question of our obligation himself.

From this Sir Edward Grey passed to the consideration of the present position of the French fleet in the Mediterranean which *evidently* sprang out of the plans for co-operation. The French fleet was in the Mediterranean *because of the feeling of confidence* between the two countries. *Hence it followed* that if a foreign fleet came down the channel we could not stand aside and see it attack the defenceless coast of France. *The House was brought to the conclusion* that we had a definite obligation to defend the coast of France from attack, and, generally speaking, it showed that it was prepared to support the government in taking action. France was *therefore* entitled to know and know at once that she could depend on British support in the event of an attack on her northern coast. There was a loud burst of cheering at this announcement.[43]

Tellingly, this report of "The House and Sir Edward Grey's Statement" bears the subtitle "Logic of Events." Complying entirely in this paraphrase with Grey's own rationalistic stratagems, the reporter reproduces that prosody of adventitious logic, paying special attention to insert those conjunctions that establish cause and reasoned transition in the argument. The effort generates already the official pitch and idiom of the Liberal war. A rhetoric of reason is being imposed on a resistant circumstance. The force of this rationalistic vocabulary increases—witness the density of logical connectives in the emphases added—in nearly inverse ratio to the reason inherent in the case.

The *Gazette* report expresses this loss of confidence in the older moral logic, moreover, as its last word. The writer feels compelled at the end to concede the disquiet Grey's address has stirred among its partisan faithful: "[T]he speech made a painful impression on the Liberal Party, which above all has sought to avoid a war with Germany." The piece reverses every effort of reason and argument it has been at pains to recreate, then, in its final sentence, as the author turns the consideration in another, specially revealing direction: "But its logic seemed the logic of events beyond our control."[44] On one level, this diminuendo could be read as a feeble recognition, a last gasp acknowledgment of the forces operating through the alliances that the secretary would not admit. The possibility it countenances, however, presents to the liberal ideal of reason at liberty a menace so threatening that the pressure it exerts is irrepressible, even in the spotlighted sentence of the finale. It is the same primitive terror that a writer for the *New Statesman* addressed a few days earlier, on 1 August: "The chain of events that we have to fear, the dragging first of one country and then of another into the conflict . . . seems to have all the inevitableness of ancient tragedy, where persons and events are controlled not by reason, but by the spell of an ironic fate."[45] When the presentiment being expressed is realized on 4 August, the most profoundly powerful source of phobic horror for the liberal mind is being opened up, as the *Gazette* report of that day intimates in its closing sentence. This vision sees a sheerly external logic of events. The logistic of affairs appears impervious to individual ethical decisions and the truly inward order of moral logic.

The two articles of 4 August conform to a double rhythm that demonstrates already the tensions generating the language and attitudes of the Liberal war. The more the origins and prosecution of the war suggest a determining force in that horrifically "external logic" of historical necessity, the more strenuous the dependence on the show of ethical rationality and its apparatus of control. Those verbal structures of moral reason will grow at once more pretentious and phantasmal, equally—and increasingly—sweeping and precarious.

This need in the partisan press for "reasonableness" shows in another revealing pattern of journalistic irony special to the *Guardian*. The approval of the Guildhall speech, which Asquith delivered in early September 1914, includes a perfectly reversed echo of the editorial censure the same paper applied to his foreign secretary's August address. Where Grey's "reasons are extraordinary," in the ironic report of the earlier editorial, Asquith's presentation of the same policy in September generates a "speech of extraordinary reasoning power." Augmenting this irony and revealing all the more clearly the need in the liberal mind that compels it is the fact that the September speech contains the more confident, strengthening note of the older, apparently unregenerate Liberal imperialist. Asquith makes the insistent point that verbal rationales do not matter. "The issue," he states, "has passed out of the domain of argument into another field."[46] If he suggests thus that the sound of any systematic reasoning in the report of this speech will be inserted by the journalist, the partisan reporter is undeterred, even—or especially—in face of this evident rebuff. The need to confront the raw fact of naked power with the habit of rationalistic language is too strong to be resisted. The same necessity supplies the otherwise odd title, in the *Guardian* of 9 November, to a review of a collection of Asquith's war speeches: "The Greatest *Need* of All." The reviewer finds the requirement met by a language of political address that is "extraordinarily good—high spirited, vigorously reasoned."[47]

This need for reason is met, however, at the price counted in the *New Statesman* of 24 October 1914, in "Why Did We Go to War?" The writer's own "vigorously reasoned" reply to the question in the title includes an all-too-rigorous reiteration of the vocabulary and syntax of rationality—locutions like "it follows" and "we do not think it can be controverted" establish the sequence of argumentative logic. However, the rationalist's grammar is articulated in the manifest absence of facts. The writer explicitly rejects any attempt to require the government to produce the record of its internal deliberations on the war question, insisting instead that "attempts to investigate the motives which inspired the Foreign Office are, under the circumstances, idle and unnecessary."[48] The willful ignorance of fact points to a willingness in the liberal mind to receive a sheerly verbal reasoning, a need deepening with the fear that things are not so reasonable after all.

ii

A language of rationalistic stratagem has taken over the speech of public reason, and this development may be seen also in the verbal culture of state censorship. The far-ranging effects of the Defence of the Realm Act (DORA), which was passed by Parliament early in August 1914, began in the language of official military reports. The press had to augment the government's versions of developing events to create stories, equally readable as accounts and unrevealing in detail.[49] The verbal artifice of censorship erases the claim of specific and local fact in favor of a language of vacuous generality. "A grain of detail is usually more important than a ton of generality," Arnold Bennett rues perceptively (already) in the *Daily News and Leader* of 22 October 1914. The generic counter, the class category rather than the cited particular, can allow a judgment or implication to be tilted in the wished-for direction. Truth is looser at the abstract remove. Yet these terms of pseudoreference need to create their own comprehensive significance—to generate a grammar that renders them meaningful as verbal statements. This sense-making effort is what Bennett parses as the most suggestive but telling point of his early analysis. "Intensely ridiculous," as Bennett insists in his account of its methods and effects, "it still imposes itself even on the sagacious."[50] Wholly bogus tokens of verbal (non)reference, that is, are working in the stateliest of ways—in the reason-seeming idiom of the Liberal war.

Consider the validity of Bennett's formula as a description of these representative practices, deployed only one week later and on the pages of the same paper, in the account titled "Towards Victory":

> The Allies are doing very well in both the western and the eastern theatres of war. . . . The German assaults all along the line from Nieuport to Arras have been beaten off. They are now losing in violence, and near Ypres and La Bassée the Allies are steadily pressing forward. . . . The tide was turned, apparently, by the arrival of British and French troops to strengthen the Belgian forces heavily tried by continuous fighting. These, with the co-operation of the guns of the Fleet, recovered the lost ground, and repelled the enemy. We may take it that this was the turning point of the battle; and, although the battle is not yet over, there is every reason to assume that the Germans have definitely failed in their march on the coast. . . . [F]ailure in this battle for the coast really means the passing of the offensive in the West from the enemy to the Allies.[51]

Gestures of open and searching speculation witness the constraints applied to hard information by the government. The writer is laboring in a vacuum of actual details but, not to be undone, is substituting in their stead a language of reasonable deliberation, prudent surmise: "we may take it," "every reason to assume," "apparently," "really means." Reverting to this rationalist grammar as a kind of default position, moreover, the reporter manages to convert the chronicle story he cannot write into the sort of propositional logic he can compose, being equipped with the rough-but-ready idiom of liberal reason. The global tide of world war is being turned even now on a single battle, indeed on a reading of one engagement on its already multiple fronts, but the author's own rationalistic language determines this eventuality.

This partisan imprint shows in the *Daily News* piece and in comparable accounts of other majority papers. This dominant inflection appears more distinctly when it is read against the minority voice of the Tory opposition, which appears in the pages of the (London) *Times* (a paper with a relatively small readership in 1914).

In the report of 9 September 1914, the huge battle going on in France around the Marne River is assimilated by the *Times* writer to the struggle of "Armageddon," the face-off between the forces of good and evil at the end of biblical time:

> The battle which may decide the fate of Germany, and must in any case decide for a time the fate of Northern France, is now raging. There has been no combat to equal it in magnitude since war began in the world. Our Military Correspondent estimates that three million men are engaged. The line of conflict extends roughly due east and west for a distance of very nearly two hundred miles. It begins near Meaux, on the Marne, and continues to a point beyond Nancy. Its centre is in the broad, level plain south of Châlons, where ATTILA was overwhelmed and where prophets innumerable have declared that some day Armageddon would be fought. It is being waged upon the very ground where NAPOLEON conducted his campaign of 1814, which still remains a masterpiece of defensive strategy. Fère-Champenoise, where the encounter waxes hottest, and where the Germans are striking their hardest, was the scene of the famous resistance of a French force which refused to surrender to the Allies even when its general had delivered up his sword. The whole region is full of inspiration for the Army of France. Both French and British are plainly fighting to-day with a desperate and intrepid valour which augurs well. They are no longer on the defencive. After a skillful series of withdrawing movements which has taxed their endurance to the utmost, they have turned upon the foe on ground of their own choice. We must not think of this huge conflict as one long and continuous line of battle without an interval. It is

rather a series of battles between a number of opposing armies. Its dominating characteristic appears to be that everywhere the Allied Armies are assuming the offensive, the form of fighting which best befits their temperaments and their proud traditions. The change from the weary marching to the rear, and the disheartening rearguard actions, will renew the ardour and the high hopes of the British and French troops.[52]

Similar predicaments apply to Liberal and Tory journalists, insofar as the manifest lack of information—the broadest geographical coordinates of the battle are all that can be drawn from this shortage of fact—needs to be talked around, by both. Yet the manner of strategizing this difficulty differs as clearly as the partisan affiliations of the two papers.

The Word of biblical revelation in the *Times* projects a design that requires no further rationalization. The alliance implied between the British-French coalition and the right side of Armageddon provides a moral orientation that witnesses, in the ultimate way of that promised and beneficent end, an ever-improving prospect. Unlike the *Daily News*, the *Times* resorts to no apparent grammar of ratiocination, argument, or proof. The account assimilates contemporary events to a framework of traditions and legends, where the precedents of previous history portend favorable developments, most crucially, usually, when the facts seem least encouraging. The *Times* story differs entirely and instructively as such from the *Daily News* account, which, no less all-encompassing, shows its global optimism wholly as a function of reason's strenuous artifice; it is a work of more obviously human exertion and character. The strain that actuality must place on the biblical fiction will meet a resistance as durable as religious belief, which, exempt in this crucial respect from the burden of proof, will intensify for many through the course of the war. The test that history will set to the syllogism of progressive time, however, is harder to pass. These propositions need to be embodied in the sort of solid evidence now unpresentable. That rationalistic apparatus of language will grow increasingly evident as the construction it is.

When a liberal intellectual's need for reasonable speech and logical optimism meets the power of the Liberal government to withhold evidence, then, the result is a product like this report of the *Manchester Guardian* on 1 July 1916, on the day the Battle of the Somme commenced. These sentences gravely reason the wholly positive conclusion that needs to be drawn from an absolute absence of fact: "The news from the British front in France is not as yet of a nature that it is advisable to discuss. So far as there is any doubt as to its meaning, that doubt is in our favour, and nothing should be said that would help to resolve it."[53] The same restriction of essential evidence at the source of information, in a government document that the *New Statesman* reprints on 14 April 1917, leaves statistical ratios and verbal reasoning in a similar condition:

> The machines which we are turning out to-day are equal, if not superior, to any that the Germans have hitherto produced, and they are being produced at a rapidly increasing rate, the details of which it would be unwise to give. The average efficiency of our machines now in use is equal to the average of the German machines. The average of casualties in the machine which has been most severely criticised is less than the general average on all our machines.[54]

This is a specifically algebraic cipher, a system in which quantities exist in *relation* to one another rather than in concrete measure. Yet the evident pressure to make this abstract language serve as warrant and rationale for improved prospects in the British war effort turns the neutral usage of mathematics to the fool's idiom of pseudoreason. The reckonings of liberal meliorism add up to their verbal—if not numerical—worst in the language of official Liberal record. Remembering that to *ration* means originally to "reason," since *rationality* owns first of all the idea of "measure," we may get the outline of the sizable crisis to which the current situation has brought the intellectual tradition of liberal reason: this is ratio, in extremis.

III

The Literary State

The editorial response to that last piece of government sophistry comes in this framing remark:

> On the general subject of our air-supremacy much light was thrown on Wednesday in the speeches made by Sir R. Borden and General Smuts, who had gone into the matter at the Imperial War Cabinet. What they had found was, in Sir Robert Borden's words, "very reassuring." His summary deserves quotation:
> The machines which we are turning out to-day . . . [55]

Those quotation marks surround the "very reassuring" words of official optimism with a skepticism as evident as it is unexpressed. The same incredulousness edges the formulas and statistics that follow. As a "literary" paper, after all, the *New Statesman* seems obliged to notice the verbal absurdity of the government report. The question that the framing gesture raises, nonetheless, involves the extent to which a literary initiative might be taken. How might the minimal resistance of those punctuation marks expand and adapt into a more ample, widely working literary response?

i
—

Tellingly, one might say necessarily, *pseudo*history instances the first literary
turn that writers perform on the current predicament of political Liberalism.
In a sort of mock chronicle, its author assumes the persona of a court historian
or appointed clerk. This recorder views the events of the present from some
imaginary future, in fabulous retrospect. Familiar details of the contemporary
scene thus become strange. The exotic, conversely, seems oddly congruous.
The logical preposterousness that is the concocted tone echoes all too obviously
now to the dominant sound of the Liberal war, where, too, English reason
speaks an apparently alien dialect.

"Looking Backwards: A Fragment," published in the *Nation* of 10 March
1917, situates its view on events of the current war at a hundred years' remove.
While the title echoes Edward Bellamy's fictionalized version of his own historical present and establishes the literary tradition in which this effort belongs,[56] the 1917 piece features scenes and details that represent this writer's
apprehension of the local political moment. Most tellingly, the practices of this
fantastical narrative reenact the outlandish rationalizations of the Liberal war.
Drawing on sources that are obviously fabricated, inventing references as
doubtful in documentary factuality as they are flawless in bibliographic protocol, this writing recalls the logical nonsense those other, serious, official versions submitted as their account of events in the real 1917:

> . . . We are now entering the obscurest period in the social history of the
> Five Years' War. This middle year lacks the dramatic interest alike of
> the heroic opening and the strange close. . . . The close study of the con-
> temporary press, with the aid of the memoirs of public men which are
> now gradually becoming available, enables us, after a hundred years, to
> see these decisive months perhaps more clearly than contemporaries
> saw them. . . . The Liberal leaders, who roused themselves to opposition
> towards the end of 1918, were either silent, or else contented them-
> selves with registering a formal but compromising acquiescence in the
> policy of the Directory. . . . The standard "Life of the Duke of North-
> cliffe" (Vol. III, *loc. cit.*), which is, of course, the indispensable source
> for the politics of the period, suggests that there is some ground for be-
> lieving that the Directory, when it was formed, had originally adopted
> this policy. . . . [T]here is further evidence to be found in a rare book,
> which disappeared (suppressed, perhaps, by the Censor), within a few
> hours of its publication ("Collected Speeches of the Rt. Hon. John
> Hodge," *1918). . . .
> . . . But indeed the England of these years bears little resemblance
> to that of our own more fortunate days.[57]

The (all-too-)logical preposterousness catches the deeper truth of a historical moment it has to back far away from, it seems, to represent at all characteristically and vividly.

The issue of fictional distance figures explicitly in *1920: Dips into the Near Future*, a gathering of pieces serialized in the *Nation* through 1917 and published in 1918. This nearer account loses no acuity in critical perception. This writer notes the same tendencies that inform "Looking Backwards" with equal force and clarity: "No! What really won the day for the Supreme Sacrifice was the sheer logic of the situation. It was best set out in the new Government's reasoned poster: 'To save defeat the nation must eat less; soldiers and workers cannot eat less; therefore, the aged and idlers must not eat!'"[58] The "*sheer logic* of the situation" encloses a wonderfully dense pun, doubling its meaning as "mere" and "transparent." Here then is a penetrating record of official syllogistic discourse, which adduces equally outrageous conclusions in the same way—through the merely apparent (here, exclamatory) clarities of reason's seemly forms. The difference of this piece from "Looking Backwards" appears as a function of the position in which its writer situates its political fiction. The relative proximity of the imaginative consciousness to the events of the current day accounts for an exchange like this, which sounds the author's characteristic note:

> "Well, you know," said Roxborough, "speaking strictly among ourselves, where we first took on Dora and her sisters, all of us were subject to the same delusion—how that Britons stood for personal freedom, every man to be the arbiter of his own fate, and for something called civil liberty, the right to have a voice in making the laws one was called on to obey, the consent of the governed, and all that sort of thing. Do you know that it took us at least four years to discover that all this was nothing but the rhetoric of sentimental self-esteem—that it had nothing behind it."
>
> "And you actually mean to tell me that you find no bottom to the popular servility, just as Paston claims to find no bottom to the popular credulity?"
>
> "Servility! Credulity! You choose harsh terms, my friend, to describe what we have all agreed to call patriotic submission to our country's needs. And, after all, we do the thing quite handsomely, preserving the graces and amenities of the old political order. Just as we still keep up the forms of Parliamentary procedure, even to the ludicrous degree of voting money that has long ago been expended."[59]

The language of report does not achieve the blandly fantastical, weirdly serene feeling that "Looking Backwards" manages to achieve from the empyrean distance of a hundred years. The closeness of contemporary political controversy involves *1920* all too earnestly in the substance of those debates.

The pseudonym that the author of *1920* assumes—Lucian, namesake of the ancient Greek satirist—suggests the need this writer feels to get that better distance and, with it, the edge of fabling difference. The vantage of that backward chasm of time never establishes itself, however. The proximity of the present prevails in a way that reveals a good deal about the liberal sensibility that has fashioned this characteristic document. Not the highly spirited, antic sport of a dialogue sponsored by Lucian, a Socratic interaction comes to dominate the piece, and it dissolves the possibilities of some novel (il)logic into a standard, rationalistic process of argument. The need to engage in reasoned exchange on serious themes preempts the full imaginative freedom of literary response. Given the discredit visited so amply now on case-making argument, that is, it is not surprising to find the main lines of imaginative initiative, and a correspondingly high level of linguistic interest and artifice, in a satire that is rather adamantly stanceless. One's stand needs to be taken in some historical or attitudinal distance, where matters of verbal procedure can dominate the consciousness of literary invention. This freedom from reasoned exchange proves counterintuitive for intellectual partisans, however. On a wide and varied scale, they will decline that immense promise of literary elaboration. Their refusal may also record the extent and depth to which the gnosis of official Liberalism dominates the consciousness of the political and cultural present.

To this rule, one more exception may be found near the end of the war, again in the *Nation* (2 November 1918). "A Press View" positions its fiction within the verbal-journalistic culture of the war. In this extreme version of the typical "press view," the writer adapts the logical preposterousness of the Liberal war (whose insignia will appear here) into the manner of a mock-logical chronicle, where the fantastical occurs as a matter of rational course. The effect is carefully detailed and sustained at considerable length:

> There again were the familiar vans of the fair. This was their first appearance on the green since the beginning of the war. One huge van was specially notable. Its gilded scroll work was richer and more elaborate than anything the villagers had ever seen. . . .
>
> Surmounting the van was a coronetted microphone, moved by clockwork, so that it turned by degrees to all points of the compass, blaring at each momentary pause a new cry of alarm (as though it were sentient and really thought for itself each time) like: "Fire!" "Out Him!" "Mad Dog!" "Spotted Fever!" "Haldane!" "Black Book!" "Peace Trap!" "We Are Lost!" "Bolshevik!" "Infantile Paralysis!"
>
> . . . The noise became a sonorous chaunting, and quite distinctly the listeners heard the uplifted voice declaim: "Our gallant lads, in this French land where plumed English knights were once almost as roman-

tic as I feel now, were approaching that enormous wall of belching smoke and lurid explosions . . ."

It was then that a door opened in the caravan, and a remarkable figure appeared. It looked like Father Time, but his hour-glass was broken and the measuring sand was gone. Instead of a scythe, he carried an empty sack. He took no notice of the multitude, but appeared to contemplate a secret joke. His old beard shook with mirth. . . .

The caravan had a central corridor with cages on either hand. In the first cage an elegant man of the new military age was pacing up and down smoking a cigar. . . . Though the audience regarded him seriously, the face of Time, watching the man in the cage, continued to look as though there were something amusing about it all. "Right," presently decided aloud the man with the cigar, "as the Earl of Jones has bought the paper, that means the war must go on to the last man." He flicked the end off his cigar.

"Didn't want much thinking about," suggested Time. . . .

They passed on to the next cage. "Here," said Time, holding his hand before his smile, "you see something better." The audience instinctively removed their hats. "This is a fine specimen of the Brazen or Bellowing Blufferlo," said Time. "We're not afraid of losing him. We can't. He draws most of the audience, and he knows it. His consumption of hay is enormous. He was only discovered during this war."

In the cage was a figure which looked like a haughty strong man every time a photographer with him said, "Now, sir!" He kept trying on, in turns, a steel helmet, a gas-mask, and the casque of Minerva. When the photographer gave the signal, the Blufferlo made the necessary adjustments to his features, and cried, "I have been with the soldiers in the support trenches, which are more dangerous than the base"; or "You can take it from me that this rain means wet weather; I can't tell who told me so, but you can take it from me"; or "The Cross will prevail against the Hun—I speak with deep humility—but you can take it from me the Cross is always a winner. God will not let evil get first past the tape."[60]

The cracked and drained hourglass, the ungathering sack: these are the empty insignia of a Time who, scytheless and not so grim a reaper after all, laughs the wisdom of his proverbial truths to himself only. Meaning in these times appears as a cryptic riddling of its own possibility, delivered in a verbal symbolism that may be recognizable for its traditional or extrinsic forms, like Father Time's, but, like those vacant shapes, is void of recognizable content or extrinsic significance. A sheerly formal pretense of meaning, this now-familiar riddle of the sensible fraud owns a power that is totemized vividly in the *Blufferlo*, a creature whose broadcast fakery is pointed by the language and accents of a reason-seemingness that represents the special dialect of the times ("You can take it from me that this rain means wet weather"). The use of this creature has been newly and "only discovered during this war." Rather than pulling against this development, the wit of imaginative art in this piece plays along with the timely conceit, at every point working to reinforce the humbug with the tones of reassuring reason.

"A Press View" offers a remarkable consonance to a manner that Ezra Pound develops virtually concurrently, in the essay fables he composes in 1917. These attempts will be read in due course as the first efforts of a modernist response to the war, being echoed nearly simultaneously by the newly developed styles of T. S. Eliot and Virginia Woolf. This modernist production appears equally exceptional in literary history and rare in contemporary practice.

ii

The body of work that the modernists will evolve attains a good deal of its significance in the exception it presents to the mainstream standards of liberal modernity. It bespeaks an extremity of the kind that intellectual historians like Pippin (with Nietzsche) require as the accomplishment of a modernism that really challenges the older dominance. The solid majority of liberal concepts in English history underwrites the control of the imaginative language of literature by the values of a cultural establishment: these are the conditions under which a new literary order will be wrought, but with a struggle that forms a large part of its significance. The counterconventional energy of this enterprise may be assessed in advance, then, through a reconnaissance of the considerable resistance that established attitudes put up to just those possibilities.

In the *Nation* of 30 March 1918, a review of Lucian's *1920* conveys an appreciation within conditions that mark the limits of this commentator's liberal sensibility:

> If the militarist were perfectly conscious, perfectly reasonable, perfectly logical in the pursuit of the conclusions from his premisses, how would he act? That is the method which "Lucian" has followed in "1920." . . . [W]e venture the opinion that Lucian's work is by far the most powerful piece of satire which has appeared during the war. . . . Swift looked at the motives and consequence of war; Lucian works out its logic. . . . He has satirised war by assuming that the men who promote and perpetrate it are rational beings.

If "militarism stands for certain ideas,"[61] according to this reviewer, those "ideas" appear so inherently unreasonable that their development through the standards and practices of proper logic must verge on the preposterous. In this critical syllogism, martial reasoning seems to be a kind of comic hypothesis, impossible in itself or invalid in its consequences but, just so, worth following out for the satiric nonce by Lucian or his intellectual partisans. The ability to discriminate between proper and improper logic, the major value and the minor exception, which the reviewer assumes is Lucian's own special *virtù*, presumes that those rationalistic standards remain more rather than less reliable. We recognize, now, however, that logical atrocity, which the commentator regards as the special exception to reason's seemly forms, represents nothing less than the general tenor of an official Liberal discourse. Rationalist values nonetheless own an authority so formidably established in the language and attitudes of English culture that the reviewer shows every sincerity in assuming this stance about their general credibility and ongoing viability.

Perhaps the best measure of the control that liberal attitudes maintain over any insurgent energy lies in the degree to which this culture already possesses the methods—and so neutralizes the effect—of a literary riposte. This is not a matter of ostensible censorship or evident suppression. As we have seen, the premise of reason in all things sets a tremendous emphasis on the aesthetic presentation of a case—on the values of balance and harmony in argumentation. The dominance of those artistic qualities in the political discourse of Liberal England at war coopted the readiest reflex of literary response. Where the satiric artist might be expected to simulate and stylize the current *folie* of logical nonsense, the language of this parody rationalism has already taken its official place, performed often with an awkwardness that suggests the somewhat roughed-up version of spoof logic. The performance of these compromised values conforms in ready and due course with the pattern and psychology of dramatic hubris: a former strength, exercised to the excess which current extremity calls forth, has become an overpowering weakness, one that will open to the contrarian vantage of modernist authors. Not that the representatives of the former cultural order recognize their own folly (yet): their analogy with the protagonists of dramatic tragedy is confirmed by the extraordinary confidence of their appeals to aesthetic reason, indeed, by their out-of-all-measure appeal to the code of artistic—balanced—rationality.

On 5 December 1914, a reviewer in the *New Statesman* responds to George Bernard Shaw's *Common Sense about the War*. Shaw's pamphlet asserts the absence equally of common and evidential sense in the Liberal case for the war.[62] In doing so, moreover, he sets out the conditions in which partisan rationale will revert to a sheerly aesthetic demonstration. Shaw's reviewer proves this prognostication from the start of the piece, even by the manifest drift of its title. There is no substantive argument here. "On Controversy" takes its high ground on the *principle* of dissent, leaving the sharper stuff of disagreement below and moving into a smooth meditation on the value of reasoned exchange itself. The reviewer conducts this discussion in the same spirit of the polite, nearly ritualized pas de deux that he prescribes for the reasoning of Liberal ideology in the war. Thus English soldiers will march "forward to victory with the music of good arguments,"[63] that is, to a melody whose notes need not be translated into the clearer, starker, more accountable score of a convincing—or con-vinced—justification.

The same drift recalls a writer in the *Nation* of 4 March 1916, when the moral resolve of the war is wearing thin, to the opening moments of the campaign. Here, in the founding documents of Belgian diplomacy, the right reason of a (now-)failing effort might be replenished by "a style which itself carries conviction." Returning to the early controversy of German atrocities in Belgium, the writer quotes an especially revealing piece as the intended justification for Allied intervention. "You want to persuade yourselves that [German atrocity] is not so, because it cannot be so. And, constrained by the evidence," which the writer sees no need to reproduce, "we reply to you that it can be, because it is."[64] The repetitive circularity of the syntax and vocabulary constitutes no logical tautology, at least for the writer, but resolves into the *ricorso*, the return of the musical rondo that closes artistically and so, for the writer, unar-guably. The passage manifests the same capacity for sheerly musical argumentation that called the tune of the Liberal war.

This reliance on the artifice of reason and prosody of logic could reach so extreme an expression as Gilbert Murray's mid-1915 review of Arthur Ponsonby's *Democracy and Diplomacy: A Plan for Popular Control of Foreign Policy*. Ponsonby's book indicts Grey on charges of secret diplomacy and calls force-fully for the direction of policy by a mass electorate. These are opinions to which Murray is, predictably, wholly opposed. Rather than contest these views on their own, however, Murray sets out to convert their proponent. He seeks to repatriate Ponsonby to the Liberal ranks (this M.P. resigned his seat over the war issue). He does so, moreover, by attributing ideological meaning to aesthetic practice, which, it turns out, is all that matters.

No, Ponsonby's professed argument "does not convince my reason," Murray admits, nor does it need to do so. The method of its advocate matters most. "Even if this book were less good than it is," his review opens,

> it would deserve reading for its admirable manners. It . . . leaves me with a profound respect for the tone and method of English politics at their best. No one would ever suspect from these pages of temperate and courteous argument that the author was a man who had just sacrificed his Parliamentary career for his principles, whose meetings were broken up by roughs, his person attacked, his reputation assailed by gross calumny. This temper of mind is not only fine in itself, but particularly valuable in the present instance.[65]

To Murray, the only radical value to which this former Liberal M.P. ascribes is the root valence of *ratio*nalism, which is lived out variously in the syntactic measures and attitudinal balance of his book. An intellectual temper so individual and reasonable in its expression, Murray is saying, could hardly align itself with the interests of those mobbish thugs. Murray is reassuring us that the practices of rational balance and seemly reason define absolute values, and these standards will prove as durable in history as they are vital and credible on these pages. What is finally "at stake in foreign politics is much more an issue between reason and unreason, between prudence and recklessness, between moderation and chauvinism" than between those opposing social creeds of "democratic and oligarchic sentiment." Intellectual and political conflicts have been redefined entirely now in terms of the rival styles of these ideologies, where, on the correct side, reason does not so much argue the case of partisan Liberalism as prove its true colors through demeanor and technique. This is "the tone and method of English politics at their best"—on the Liberal side of that all-defining opposition "between reason and unreason."

The literary skill Murray brings to the performance of his conceit obviates his main problem: the impossible logic of the unreasonable war. While this contradiction may be resolved through the harmonic qualities of grammatical and syntactical ratio, the level of finesse requisite to the task proves to be far from standard fare in the journeyman writing of the partisan press. If *hubris* means (literally, etymologically) "blind spot," Murray's highly accomplished style may succeed in concealing from himself and (up to a point) his reader a mechanism and tendency a good deal more evident in his less distinguished fellow-travelers.

On 29 August 1914, in "Atrocities," an unnamed writer in the *New Statesman* extends the aesthetic conception of rational argument in this attempt to outreason the inherently illogical folly of war:

> It strikes many people as a paradox that looting and other atrocities should be forbidden to soldiers whose object is to terrorise their enemies into submission by death, wounds, and the other sufferings of siege and battlefield. It seems absurd that you should be allowed to drop bombs from the sky on a man's wife and children, but that you should be forbidden to steal the clock from his dining-room mantelpiece. Even in this, however, there is reason. War is a multitudinous foolishness, but its foolishness can be mitigated in some degree by carrying it on according to the rules. And it is a chief rule of honest war that it should be a social affair, and not a mad confusion of private enterprise.[66]

In the prosody of logic to which this script conforms, the argument pivots where the caesura falls: on "however." That conjunction of dialectical deliberation takes the concession that "[e]ven" makes to the paradoxical content of the preceding sentences and turns the whole effort in the direction of a rational control and consistency so ludicrously secure—in view of the recalcitrant inanity of its subject—as to foreground and stage itself. Note how the claims of this conclusion are secured affectively only, that is, aesthetically. Observe the self-reassuring return of "reason" to the site and source of unreason, the empty triumphalism of "multitudinous foolishness," and the superiority this phrase crows over the lower order of war through its polysyllabically Latinate music. Highly performative, wholly precarious, it is on shaky stilts that this hero, Reason, comes on stage, offering to none-too-scrupulous a view the theater of its own hubris, its strong weakness.

The susceptibility that aesthetic reason expresses in extending its methods, and the compensatory measures it takes when so exposed, may be seen with special directness in two *Daily News* pieces of mid-September 1914. These were written in response to the rumors of a huge Russian army landed in France.

The first of these, "Is the Tide Turning?" (eager to see the way clear to war's end already on 9 September), countenances the fabulous news through a no less remarkable artistry of rationalistic language:

> The news to-day is on the whole distinctly hopeful. We do not, in this connection, refer to the statement which came from Rome yesterday and which was passed by the French Bureau, that 250,000 Russians had been landed in France. This may or may not be true. It is not out of the region of possibility. The idea of a Russian expedition from Archangel to the West of Europe, as has been pointed out, is no new thing, and there is nothing in the circumstances that makes it impracticable. There have been widespread rumours in this country of the subject during the past fortnight, and if it turns out that the rumours are well founded there will be no surprise.[67]

A rhetoric of negative affirmation retains some skeptical reserve, but only to establish a strong attitudinal balance for the writer's persona. This measured temperament gives the final credence he extends to these legendary events the appearance of a well-reasoned probability. The impossible is countenanced through a wholly tonal economy, one in which prudence triumphs over incredulity and secures a (likely) truth in what is otherwise an outlandish idea.

What happens when the ruse is exposed, a week later? The *Daily News* follow-up response comes in "The Phantom Army":

> No story could have had a wider circulation and seem to be strengthened by testimony more various or more respectable. Policemen had seen these Russians, mayors had entertained them, bus-drivers had observed them, engine-drivers had driven them, men had traveled with them and photographed them, women had spoken to them, scholars had interpreted for them, shipowners had lent their ships for them. Here was an accumulation of witnesses which would have convinced the normal mind of the truth of any assertion not in itself manifestly absurd. Now we are assured on the sufficient authority of the War Office that the whole story is without foundation in fact. . . . [Yet] the solid residue of serious rectitude will constitute an imposing monument to

humanity's power of self-deception. Here is a warning to which every student of history, and *in particular every student of the history of religions*, will have to give heed. (emphasis added)[68]

A mirage apology, "The Phantom Army" identifies the logical folly that the same paper perpetrated only a week earlier. The list of national gullibilities is as long on details, however, as it is short on any incriminating mention of the *Daily News*'s own part in the foolery. Instead of admitting complicity, the journalist uses that credulity to adduce the superiority of its presently reasonable attitude. What, after all, does the "religion" of suggestively archaic "history" and type have to do with the subject of recent beliefs—more, say, than the same paper of a week earlier? Nothing, in fact, but everything, at least as a matter of deflection and scapegoating. The suggestibility of a week earlier may thus be attributed to the backward irrationalism, the proclivity for superstition that religion can be silently relied on to provide. Above it, this writer implies, the light of true liberal reason may shine more brightly.

The writer forgoes thus the potential for insight and self-awareness that the moment of reversal encloses. "The Phantom Army" demonstrates the tendency within Liberalism to react to such doubts about reason's reach and validity, not by extending the scope of skeptical regard on its own linguistic artifice, but by appearing more supremely reasonable. Is it more solidly logical? Is there some greater clarity of fact in its rational argumentation? Not commonly. Mainstream Liberalism tends to compensate for the increasingly obvious complications and contradictions in its policy by intensifying its appeal to the reason*able*. It may deny the impossible logic of its case, that is, by exaggerating the artistic qualities in the presentation.

A revealing example of this tendency comes in an identifiably literary venue, in the *Nation*, on 13 October 1917. Here, Havelock Ellis actually seeks to align the ideals of prewar pacifists with their support for the current war. His command of rationalistic grammar and syntax allows him to speak his reasonable way straight through the obvious contradiction:

> We may recognize the justification of those Pacifists and Anti-Militarists who not only allowed their propaganda to lapse, but even actively diverted their energies in an apparently opposite direction. It is sometimes said by unthinking people that the war has destroyed Pacifism, and even made it ridiculous. That is the reverse of the truth. The war has been the triumphant affirmation, on a scale they themselves could scarcely have anticipated, of all that the Pacifists have ever asserted.[69]

Is this a parody rationality as masterful as that of "A Modest Proposal"? Or is it just the sort of logical monstrosity all too common now in the partisan discourses of the war? The concerned sincerity that works through the rest of

Ellis's piece puts it decisively on the side of the earnest travesty. The performance marks the extremity to which the aesthetic conception of rationality has been extended. Yet this exposure also shows that the liberal belief in the sheerly reasonable style needs only the intent of the controverter to turn its verbal mechanism into timely art.

The operative word in this formulation of adversarial poetics is, of course, "only." In the cultural scene of English Liberalism, the heavy presence of the convention to be overturned entails no small effort. A record of lost or unseized possibility here constitutes a sort of history of literature manqué. The confounding of this majority consciousness expresses itself more readily and recognizably as an instance of hubris which, unrecognized, and exerted at ever greater extremity, begins to shift the frame of generic reference. It moves from dramatic tragedy to mechanical, involuntary comedy, that is, toward farce.

A representatively extraordinary example occurs in a *New Statesman* editorial of 17 June 1916. The deficiency begins with an obliviousness to the implications of its title, "The Ethics of Lying." The phrase recalls irresistibly Oscar Wilde's "The Decay of Lying." There, Wilde used a voice of moral censoriousness equally as instrument and target for his literary invention. Citing the demise of lying in society as the cause of art's recent decline, Wilde's language and manner comport all too naughtily with the constraints of civic and ethical rectitude. His verbal art works to subvert those standards of overt sincerity and probity and so proves the *un*truth of art in his own exemplary performance. Unwilling to forgo the standards of moral correctness and their logical protocols, however, the *New Statesman* writer attempts to establish a rationale for "the official lie" and impose some scale of valid morality on it:

> [W]e do continue to judge statesmen even during a war by a certain standard of truthfulness. Just as we regard killing for the purposes of war as legitimate and killing for any other end even by soldiers as no better than butchery, so we are constantly seeking to limit the right to lie, and we would look on a statesman who became a habitual liar or lied, so to speak, unnecessarily, as a degraded person. We instinctively respect the statesman who can be trusted to speak the truth beyond statesmen of greater brilliance who use truth and falsehood as mere instruments of policy. We like policy, but we do not like too much policy.[70]

The humor of every Liberal man out of his humor, "The Ethics of Lying" attempts to extend logical and moral control over (what is to him) an inherently irrational and unethical activity. It undoubles the irony of the 1890s dandy and cancels his daring into this blander, well-meaning, flat-footed inanity. The failure is standard, representative. Liberal writers might perform the complications of party logic with an outrageous discretion, like the discrete outrage Wilde perfected as his conceit; thus they might turn the moral rationalism of the established standard to an excess correctness, a self-satirizing art. There is,

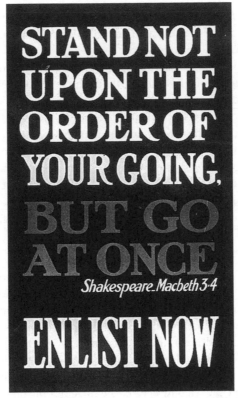

Recruiting poster. The government's purpose finds literature difficult to conscript. The lines quoted (III.iv.118–19) follow immediately on Lady Macbeth's command to Ross and Lennox to leave her husband alone, since he has begun to submit to delusions (the appearance of Banquo's ghost). The inappropriateness of the context goes deeper with a short reach forward in the scene (136–38), where Macbeth utters sentiments all too relevant to the developing conditions of total war: "I am in blood / Stepped in so far that should I wade no more, / Returning were as tedious as go o'er."

however, a general unwillingness or inability to submit the Liberal idiom to literary renditions of this type.

The response that partisan authors make to the provocations the Liberal war affords them may be sampled most representatively by the case of H. G. Wells. Probably the most conspicuous literary personality of his day, Wells also takes his place on the more radical flank of Liberalism, in his frequent affiliation with the Fabianism of Beatrice and Sidney Webb. The independence that affiliation allegedly gave him makes his compliance with the party's official war ideology an all the more telling demonstration of that centrist, established power. (The same recognition might be applied to the prowar writings published in the *New Statesman*, the journal that the Webbs had founded and endowed.)[71] In *Mr Britling Sees It Through* (1916), for most notable instance, the eponymous hero centers a fictional history of Britain at war that is, also, Wells's quintessentially Liberal apology for the policy.

Britling's representative status shows first, within the broadest compass of the plot, in the course of his opinions about the war: opposed beforehand, he lives out the Liberal reversal and promotes the prowar case with a passionate logic. Wells's own residual skepticism about the policy he has shifted to support shows interestingly in the novel. He consigns his negative perception to the youthful enthusiasms of Britling's son, who writes home from the front. In a revealingly unexpected way, the young man characterizes the specifically rational inanity of the *domestic* political war. With the intensity of Wells's own daily (London) apprehension, Britling's son sets out the gravely methodical madness of the military enterprise. "I find myself wondering," he begins with exemplary liberal openness,

> "what we are really up to, why the war began, why we were caught in this amazing routine. It looks, it feels orderly, methodical, purposeful. . . . It goes on for weeks with the effect of being quite sane and intended and the right thing, and then, then suddenly it comes whacking into one's head, 'But this—this is utterly *mad*!' This going to and fro and to and fro and to and fro; this monotony which breaks ever and again into violence—violence that never gets anywhere—is exactly the life that a lunatic leads. . . . I suppose when an individual man goes mad and gets out of the window because he imagines the door is magically impossible, and dances about in the street without his trousers jabbing at passers–by with a toasting-fork, he has just the same somber sense of unavoidable necessity that we have."[72]

The critique of nonsense logic that Wells confines to this boy and situates in the exceptional combat circumstance represents an awareness that the author seeks to beat. He reacts, in a way characteristic of other Liberals, by attempting to outreason it. An attempt to explain and justify the war brings Britling—Wells—to write "An Anatomy of Hate," an exercise in the genre of scientific positivism that is conducted to rigorous standards of linear, propositional logic. The notion this treatise proposes, however, is fetched from possibilities—like the war being argued for—far from the center of an older liberal conscience. " 'Is there not,' [Britling] now asked himself plainly, 'a creative and corrective impulse behind all hate? Is not this malignity indeed only the apelike precursor of the great disciplines of a creative state?' "[73] The answering rhetorical question is, does not the development of this argument represent in substance and method a cartooning parody of the twin liberal standards of creative evolution and progressive reason? Wells's Britling reinscribes the highest principles of liberal tradition in a manner consistent, nonetheless, with their current animadversion. It is an accurate travesty.

Wells's inability to admit or possess the comic downturn of his intellectual tradition can be taken to two opposite but complementary points. On one hand, the obliviousness he demonstrates in view of his own sad caricature of rational gradualism certainly redoubles our impression that the standards and values of liberal modernity have come to term. On the other, the resistance he maintains against this recognition may be taken to measure the embedded strength of the liberal stance, at least on this level of presumptive understandings. Its founding attitudes are sufficiently heavily endowed, that is, to counter or reject the evidence of even this flagrant reversal, which Wells's own aesthetic finesse allows him—in a way representative of a radical *hubris* ("blind spot")—not to notice. The capacity to contain its own parody may testify indeed to the monumental, all-encompassing quality of English cultural and political Liberalism. (This dominance may be attested further by other literary works, which set out to subvert the power of Liberal reason but, in the process, only endorse the core principles of the partisan intellectual tradition.)[74] These are conditions in which the critical and imaginative intelligence of an alternative literature must be equally rare and fine.

iii

The tendency to aestheticize reason was sufficiently evident, however, that it could not go unremarked, unanswered. Irene Cooper Willis offers one of the most sustained, consistently insightful critiques. Her treatise, *How We Went into the War: A Study of Liberal Idealism*, was published in November 1918 by the National Labour Press. This affiliation with the more radical side of Labour activity (the party leadership had entered into political coalition with the Liberal government by early 1916) establishes her angle of view on recent political practices.

The "Idealism" that Willis's title identifies in the authoring position of the "Liberal" war goes in one direction to the aestheticizing tendency in the enterprise and, in the other, to a line of official argument that comports well with this same proclivity. Willis makes her major formulations in discrediting what came to be the placarded, propagandistic cause and meaning of the campaign: the sacred "war for civilization." She shows that the Liberal government fabricated a superior, unifying purpose out of its own demonstrated record of self-contradiction on the advisability of war. She shows how the ground of public discourse was raised from arguable, empirical reasons to supernal, unquestionable faith.[75] Not that these high-minded apologias left the stratagems of case-making below. The major contribution that Willis makes to an understanding of the Liberal war is her alertness to its verbal surfaces. Again and again, she exposes the hollowness of logic behind the holiness of cause. She shows clearly, moreover, how this dearth of evidential sense forced Liberal apologists into making the aestheticized case. A sheerly formalistic iteration of policy logic was all that was possible. If the ideal of reason at (moral and empirical) liberty worked in practice now as reason in chains, its spokespersons could at least pretend some coherent sense in the maintenance of correct, well-measured, rational protocol. "The natural scrupulosity of Liberals could work only up to a certain point," she discerns: "it was denied admittance to the centre of operations. It was reduced to exercising itself outside matters vital to the conduct of the war and within the opening sentences of paragraphs or articles whose conclusions it was forbidden to touch."[76] The logic of the Liberal war devolved its burden of proof thus from the substance of its case to the prosody of its argument.

Willis finds a typical instance of the Liberal case-maker's aesthetic fallacy early in the war, in the reportage circulating from the English front around those early rumors of German atrocities. She notes a willingness to accept the decorous letter, the measured ratio of an account, in place of its factual accuracy or empirical reasonableness. "'The story reads like truth,' remarked the *Nation*, 'but even if it were invented it supplies a sad clue to the mentality of some of the invaders....' '*The story reads like truth*,'" Willis retorts in bold italics, then rues: "Truth is now suggested to depend upon credence, upon a story's reading like truth, a test which many quite untrue stories can easily satisfy."[77] The folly she underlines so fiercely goes to the deeper fallacy underlying the verbal culture of Liberal policy and apologias, where the unreasonable was likewise countenanced through its conformity to an aesthetic conception of rationality, to the measures and gestures of verbal logic.

Dora Marsden witnesses a similar situation in her criticism of contemporary Liberalism. Founding editor of the *Freewoman* (1911), subsequently the *New Freewoman* (1913) and the *Egoist* (1914),[78] where she was chief contributing editor, Marsden took her perspective on English political culture from the vantage of a sometimes radical feminism, which afforded her an extreme–angle vantage on contemporary convention. She comprehended readily the tendency of English Liberalism to aestheticize its apologies for war. She reinforced this understanding with a deep and searching awareness of this partisan tradition's intellectual premises. Chief among these was its linguistic faith, the religion of the era she dubbed "the verbal age."

In reading the progressive idealism of English liberalism after the French Revolution and its establishment ultimately in the Liberal party, Marsden finds a correspondence between the level of optimistic unreality in a social program and the credence given to sheerly nominal categories. In her analytical reading, she suggests that political Liberalism and linguistic nominalism are two versions of a single fallacy: the capacity to wish into existence through names the ideas or values one has envisioned as politically desirable. Liberalism, like democracy for Marsden, takes its social and intellectual charter from a notion of liberty that exists in the minds of its contrivers as a natural fact. It serves thus as a basis for a set of related political "rights" but remains for Marsden a possibility embodied in nothing more than a word. A grammar of the ideological subjunctive, it is parsed efficiently on 1 April 1914 as "the windy wordy business: this latter-day cult of humanity, the Rights of Man and all that is made to go with them." She forces this deficiency to a focus on 1 August 1914, when she aphorizes succinctly and elegantly: "The verbal virtue begins where the living strength ends."[79] She witnesses the same limitation on the efficacy of language that Continental developments are about to visit on the Word of English Liberalism. A field of incipient force and *Machtpolitik* will give the final lie to the rules of verbal logic and sheerly nominal order that Marsden has already discredited. When the old covenant of Liberal verbalism unravels with the onset of war, then, Marsden meets the event with a sense of expectation fulfilled. On 15 August 1914, she rehearses with the bitter concision of her own vindication the reversals of partisan position. In these realignments, she shows a rearrangement of words that reveals Liberal ideology as the softest of verbal confections. "The delicate tact of Mr. Asquith indeed in working a few 'blessed words' into the drab fustian of Mr. Edward Grey's statement of the case for war" consummates this enterprise and consecrates its wholly nominal quality: "The Prime Minister knew well that while to shout for war would strain the pacifists' creeds, to shout against infamy would fit in easily." This simple change in wording proved to be "enough for the promoters of the gospel of peace: they are not the friends of war but the enemies of infamy: the same thing with a delicate allowance made for a verbalist difference."[80]

Marsden extends this critical perspective into a searching exposé of the verbal culture of the Liberal war, as she analyzes the claims being made for the Gladstonian inwardness of its moral campaign. "The rapid growth of political Idealism in the last two generations, the conception of the the 'High' and 'Noble' in politics which we owe largely to the influence of Mr. Gladstone," she writes on 1 June 1916, is a sensibility "which voices and gives direction to 'Liberalism' and the remoter Humanitarianism which comes down to us from the French Revolution." This idealism proves to be none too reliable a guide for foreign policy. She explains its inadequacy as the debilitating indifference of this "remoter Humanitarianism" to the forces and facts of actual history. Its prime liability lies in its reliance on language, on the virtual reality of the verbal: "Its immediate outcome is the establishment of a manner of speech which suggests an excessive amiability of attitude which is incapable of being borne out under the actual conditions of human intercourse, so that it resolves itself into a sequence of 'Sweet Words and Dire Actions.'"[81]

The "verbalist" deceit Marsden overhears in the first days of war resonates through this interpretive frame. The language of high state soon ranges beyond the compass of individual words and their referents—for instance, the speciously manipulated meanings of "infamy"—to touch the propositional function of language, its capacity of reasoned statement. Thus on 1 September 1914, she hears the expression of the official "Reasons for this War" as just so much "cant."[82] She expands on this understanding in the next issue, calculating the extent of the damage done to the language of rationalism by its Gladstonian agents. Rehearsing the now-established moralistic arguments for the war, she repeats the response to the question "Why We English Fight?" by Lord Rosebery: "To maintain," he proposed, "the sanctity of international law in Europe." She then rephrases this Liberal imperialist in a clarifying parody: "'Mumbo-jumbo, Law and Mesopotamia' can always be relied on to work all the tricks, and cloak all the spoof."[83]

"Mumbo-jumbo, Law and Mesopotamia": the literary initiative that stirs in these respondent syllables could be sustained and strengthened. Her imaginative language represents at once an intensified and stylized version of the lingo she mimics. The dissembling sense of the Liberal provocation calls for a sheer meaning-seemingness in the response, one that relies, like Marsden's, on an English speech that appears equally strange and familiar in the sense it purports to make. Whereas the standard language of *1920* flattens all too quickly into the expected measure of rational clarities in partisan exchange, the edge of literary difference is kept from a perspective such as Marsden's and, it turns out, by some of the company she keeps in the *Egoist*. This is the journal of literary modernism, in its nascent day. Writing like hers maintains as its usual and enabling condition some crucial degree of remove from the centers of established political power. An ability to hear and speak the customary tongue as an alien dialect will prove to be the distinguishing feature of the Anglo-American poets Ezra Pound and T. S. Eliot and, although her own feminist sensibility is unrepresented in the *Egoist*, Virginia Woolf.

IV

Critical Poetics

The opposition that English modernism reveals to the discourses of right reason does not estrange that sensibility to sense. The imaginative attitudes and practices that develop under the historical pressures of the war are formulated virtually simultaneously into a poetics at Cambridge. During and after the war, university intellectuals conducted discussions about linguistic philosophy and psychology that responded to the same provocations that English modernist writers found in the crises of British Liberalism. To situate the fiction and poetry of experimental modernism within this institutional frame is not to normalize its verbal art, but rather to reestablish the grounds of its production in a culture of intelligent skepticism and dissent that grew up in wartime England and found a focal and enduring expression at Cambridge. Once we see how the public culture of the Great War helped to form this body of critical writing, we will find a consistency with the literature of English modernism that reveals, here for the first time, the coherence as well as the timeliness of a cohesive historical imagination.

The central figures in the Cambridge literary scene during and just after the war are I. A. Richards and C. K. Ogden. The earliest expression of the sensibility they share lies in the *Cambridge Magazine*. The critical consciousness that forms in these pages during the war evolves through the next decade in a scholarly bibliography organized by its editor, Ogden, and highlighted by contributions from Richards. While Richards enjoys some prominence in standard accounts as an early and astute reader of English poetic modernism, the first ground of this critical affinity has not been claimed in the subsequent constructions of literary history. His commentary will focus and formulate those qualities in the poetry that represent its best depth of engagement with the provocations of the political war.

Ogden's *Cambridge Magazine* frequently announced meetings of the Union of Democratic Control,[84] the organization E. D. Morel had formed. Only days after the outbreak of the war, Morel used the Union as a forum for revealing and discussing the dishonesties of government policy. Around recognitions like these, the literary sensibility of the Cambridge generation was hammered into resistant shape. Able to identify the reasonable lie, they might find in it also a sense of newfound power: language was being freed from those old ratios of measured and decorous sense, the rationalist standards being discredited in an exercise of increasingly evident falsehood. A record of Morel's revelations may serve then to anchor their literary intelligence in its formative moment.

i

As a Liberal M.P., Morel used his access to government archives to prove the untruth of its major public claims for the war. His disclosures appear in a series of articles and speeches he gathered in 1916 into *Truth and the War*, a book brought out by Willis's publisher, the National Labour Press. This was an affiliation Morel could entertain now that he had resigned his parliamentary seat, on the strength of his own revelations. A virtual archaeology of Liberal deceit, the cryptohistory he pieced together out of these materials features a party elite in nearly complete compromise of its professed values and positions. Public reason had been belied in its standards and discredited in its practices, and Morel presents these recognitions with the singular clarity of his own moral passion.

Thus, in "The Betrayal of the Nation, 1912–1914," he sets out to disprove the Gladstonian call for moral war on Belgium's behalf. He shows as a matter of documentary fact that the British took their decision to enter the conflict on France's side several days before the German invasion of Belgium. English resolve stemmed from no ethical imperative; the move had been prearranged through a series of agreements with France that would remain unspoken—the arrangement had been denied outright for years—until Grey's intimation of these "understandings" on 3 August. The extent of those earlier discussions and their manifest intent to bind the interests and obligations of the two nations represent Morel's chief disclosure in "The Betrayal of the Nation, 1906–1911."[85] These years are marked now in Morel's characterization by a shocking disparity of values—the Liberal imperialists Asquith and Grey controlled a covert agenda, unreconstructed by the Gladstonian protocols they were pronouncing as public moralists. The grammar of moral rationalism stands revealed through Morel's documentary account as a sham language. Elliptically but incisively, he attends to this pseudologic, using it in conclusion to typify not only a breach of trust in the official discourse but a crisis in the culture of the public Word, a loss of faith by the British nation in what its language really means. "Thus for the five years 1906–1911 was the nation permitted to live in a fool's paradise," he ends, stipulating sufficiently forcefully to merit the emphases added here, "not as Ministers have since induced the nation to believe, because they, and therefore, the nation, were innocent victims of Machiavellian cunning on the part of Germany; but because Ministers were steering a secret course which *reduced all these fine utterances of theirs and of their colleagues to so much gibberish.*"[86]

In this "gibberish" Morel echoes the "Mumbo-jumbo, Law and Mesopotamia" that Marsden intones as her version of equally "fine utterances"—in Lord Rosebery's appeal to the sanctity of international law as the rationale for British policy. Morel's perception and characterization record the same ironic swerve from the high line of reason's ethical speech, a deflection that turns the substance of moral rationality in its most august institutional professions into a vocal cartoon. The ruins of the Gladstonians' statelier cadences stand in this acoustic residue, which affords also the raw material of an answering literary idiom.

ii

The opportunities that the situation extends to the student wits at *Cambridge Magazine* are obvious. Their Gladstonian grandfathers stand exposed in the moral hypocrisy that Morel's lectures have now made clear. The "garrulous gerontocracy"[87] (in Ogden's memorable phrase) of that oppressive Victorian ideolect already stirs with the obvious possibilities of voluble parody. Yet the critiques that Morel's people were aiming at government policy and practice echo at first in the magazine as a responsive, politically responsible commentary. The reaction to the failing institutional language of Liberalism concentrates a full sense of what is at stake here, morally and historically. If a new usage is going to quicken its literary possibilities in answer to an aging official discourse, its idiom represents more than a back-talking joke. Where the writer of *1920* fails to detach from the manner and attitude of the established arguments, however, the reports in the *Cambridge Magazine* engage in current discourse with a kind of off-angle, playful intensity, all in all, a sort of macabre comedy. These juveniles' shadow discourse owns a world's body of tragic experience and eventuality, which gives a deeper resonance and more somber tone to their sometimes antic revels.

The original density and complexity of this parodic manner are perceptible in the evidence that remains of its earliest expression in the magazine. A mimic sensibility evolves with Ogden's response to the "conscription question," an issue of considerable importance to young men of military age. The government policy of "compulsion" offered a logical contradiction: the consensual reason that Liberal doctrinaires foresaw as the proper means of reaching the decision to serve could hardly be "compelled." Official discourse attempted thus to establish the inherent rationality of this principle of conscription, but the effort became all too evidently strenuous, admittedly partisan, and by the end obviously if grimly ridiculous. Ogden reacts to these convolutions in a fashion that develops gradually and understandably toward a parody of its rationalizing language. He develops this imaginative vocabulary out of very close engagement with the actual question, however, beginning with the instigation of the policy in early 1916.

Writing on 29 January under the pseudonym of Adelyne More (the editor of this fledgling journal had occasionally to "add a line more"), Ogden projects as a prospect for his consideration the "holocaust of young men" the conscription policy will ignite, thus framing the wholly serious occasion within which his verbal comedy will be played. The tonal intent of this piece proves difficult at first to fix, since the proposal—all men up to seventy years of age should be liable for active service—seems modest, at least by the measures of the discourse to which it responds. Ogden makes his pitch in an idiom of egalitarian duty all too familiar in government defenses. Is the burden of his performance a revelation of true if stringent justice or a reveling in the illogic of the government's premise? "In this manner," he postulates,

> the old and middle-aged, whose ignorance and carelessness in all countries have brought this awful thing to pass, could at least have an opportunity to atone for their folly. In this way those whose raucous rant has long resounded through the land would be able, if not as actual combatants, at least in such harmless occupations as mine sweeping, to set free a few young men to go about their work in the world.[88]

The complex and intricate mixture of tones includes mock logic—"such harmless occupations as mine sweeping"—and humorously prudential concern—"set free a few young men to go about their work in the world"—and a full-volume jeremiad on those "whose ignorance and carelessness in all countries have brought this awful thing to pass." Yes, Ogden is mirroring the mani-

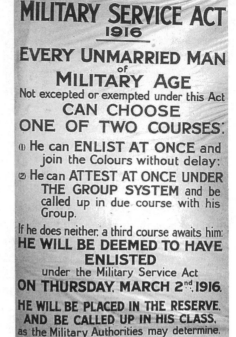

The government's effort to align "compulsion" with the values and practices of the freely reasoned choice reached the extremity of the "third course" offered on this recruiting poster. This set of options was repeated in a wide variety of formats, in much the same wording, through the first several months of 1916.

Freely reasoned choice finds no "EXCUSE for not enlisting NOW!"

fest inanity of government apologias in the stylized and archly rationalistic manner of his own tones. This parodic manner is heavy, nonetheless, with the matter of contingent political fact. His verbal shenanigan proves fully responsive to its historical source and wholly cognizant of the consequences of the syllogisms he reiterates in this riposte.

Awareness of eventualities as grave as those being played out on the fields of France supplies a tragic resonance as well as a range of ethical reference for this manner. The truth of its deep historical feeling and the reality of its moral concern remain as values in its later imaginative elaborations. These founding attitudes become increasingly implicit and inferential, however, and so require this special emphasis. As a critique of verbalism, after all, the parodic style tends to incline increasingly toward the linguistic performance. The answering manner will escalate into ever more intense exercises of verbal absurdity. To later readers, such a linguistic tour de force might seem to have been contrived for its own prankish sake. To contemporaries and those keyed to the master score—modernists and their early auditors—the method echoes back through the usage it cartoons and acquires thereby the aim and substantial point of its rebuke. This is a connection and resonance that a historically informed audition needs to preserve. For the signature style grows into ever-greater preoccupation with its own pseudologos, an apparatus of moralistic argument and proof of increasingly obvious preposterousness.

Already on 18 November 1916, in "The Duty of Suicide—Fiat Justitia Ruat Caelum [Let Justice be Done, Let the Sky Fall]," the conscription issue has fallen out of the range of explicit reference. January's more modest proposal of universal service amplifies now into a call for universal suicide. Matching this shift into the ridiculous is a now-dominating preoccupation with sham argumentation, as in the opening prolegomenon on proper assumptions and procedures: "Specious arguments are put forward by those in whom sentiment rules rather than the reasoning faculty to show . . . that Justice would be dearly purchased at the price of such a universal catastrophe as is implied in the falling of the sky." In the rhetorical fiction of this piece, a Liberal objecting to the government policy establishes the challenge and dare to the war's official Gladstonian rationale, whose personage comes to the rescue from his ethical high ground: "Against such materialist reasoning it ought to be sufficient to call to mind the supremacy of the moral law." The mainstream reasoning that this spokesperson represents is steered then by the parodist into a self-mocking process of proposition and correction. Undertaking to prove "by analytical reasoning" that the sky is about to collapse, he is moved to conclude, "sorrowfully" but wisely, "that there is no immediate prospect that the sky will fall." Ogden now compels his protagonist of the rational passion to further exertions. "[T]o have advanced thus far" in the argumentation "is not enough," this speaker avows, and so, in this mechanical comedy of ratio in extremis, he pursues the course of moral and analytical reasoning to its bloody, bitter end. "We need not despair in attaining Justice. A way is open to us as simple, as speedy, and as effective as the fall of the sky. It depends not upon a world catastrophe, but upon individual initiative. *The same result would be attained if everyone were to commit suicide.* This, then, is our bounden duty."[89]

Out of the current crisis of public language, the growing preoccupation of the magazine goes thus to the verbal performance a writer can turn. Ogden displays this tendency in a piece he drafts only a month after his first attempt at parody. On 26 February 1916, in "What the Public Wants: The Right Words in the Right Order," his Adelyne More proposes a codification of rules to govern the new usage, outlining its poetics and prosody in a suitably mock-ironic format. He offers the services of undergraduate logicians, in this pretend advertisement of university services, to "arrange other people's words." These "CAMBRIDGE SCHOLARS" can stylize the efforts even of "STRONG SILENT MEN" into grace and lucidity. The young masters of the logos will be applying lessons they have learned from their elders in political office. "All that is needed," this promotion assures its would-be clients, "is to impress the general public with a sense of the dignity of words properly arranged." The likely market lies all too clearly indeed in the political capital of London, an appeal this advertisement placards in the upper case. "Special care is at present being given to PATRIOTIC SUBJECTS." There is in fact "NO SUBJECT TOO DIFFICULT." Arguments "TO SUIT ALL CIRCUMSTANCES and ALL OPINIONS" will be cut, thus, to verbal order. The promised ease of the advertised product is not hard to understand: "The trouble does not lie so much with the words themselves—they're all right: it's the *getting them in the right place* that bothers the man."[90] As a logical and heuristic fiction, sense is substanceless; conviction turns on linguistic skill and stylistic nerve, not on propositional content or proper logic. The lesson has been learned from current verbal circumstances, from the versatile Word of Liberal rationales. Its application in a rhetorical and performative art of (serio)comic reason provides its first—its likeliest—turn.

iii

But not its last. The insights that Ogden conveys in the *Cambridge Magazine* inform an equally timely response on the part of his younger contemporary and collaborator. Out of that nexus of shared awareness, I. A. Richards will generate the main critical ideas of this moment.

Of these, the most cogent is the principle of pseudostatement, which Richards first adduces under this heading in *Science and Poetry* (1926; its precessions appear in the work he authored jointly with Ogden, *The Meaning of Meaning*, 1924). In his signal doctrine, he separates the manifold function of poetry into the operations of an "intellectual stream" and an "emotional stream."[91] The intellectual flow, he maintains, serves to offer formulations that match with the standards of conventional discursive sense and appear thus to be reasonable, at least by the measures of normative syntax and grammar. Yet these propositions operate mainly to engage and appease the rational faculty in any reader, thus releasing a current of subtextual energy that comprises a powerfully prelogical sphere of feeling and attitude. "[I]t is *not* the poet's business to make true statements," he avers emphatically:

> Yet poetry has constantly the air of making statements, and important ones; which is one reason why some mathematicians cannot read it. They find the alleged statements to be *false*. It will be agreed that their approach to poetry and their expectations from it are mistaken. . . .
>
> The acceptance which a pseudo-statement receives is governed by its effect on our feelings and attitudes. . . . A pseudo-statement is "true" if it suits and serves some attitude or links together attitudes which on other grounds are desirable.[92]

Richards is not simply reconfiguring the old assertion that "the poet never affirmeth." His awareness reaches into the interplay he perceives between surface and depth, appearance and motive, rational syntax and emotional sense. His inflections on that traditional notion mark a highly timely emphasis.

That the verbal surface of poetry imitates the linear and directed reasoning of logical propositions, but only to confound the expected ends, is a formula that echoes recognizably now to the laws of public discourse in the recent war. Rational speech measures its effect to a degree wholly coincident with its limitation of power. The political and intellectual history of the recent war witnesses the same ratio, if more grimly, that Richards will find as the achievement in the kind of poetry he will so strongly favor. The collapse of a rationalistic apparatus in language serves in verse to recall the most important memory from recent history and to provide thus the specific resonance and ultimate import of a poetry that responds to such timely provocations. We will know it later as the main tradition of English poetic modernism.

The relevance of Richards's critical doctrine to the major issues of recent history is borne out in one way through the difficult process of that concept's gestation and birth. (Richards never historicizes the idea overtly.) Professedly or not, this poetics tunes the voice of literature into intimate complicity with the verbal perfidy of the Liberal war.[93] The residual if suppressed awareness of that fact gathers repeatedly into pointed rebukes of the same principles and values that Ogden and Richards celebrate. A counterrhythm of assertion and retribution marks the articulation of the idea of pseudostatement, nearly from the start.

Ogden and Richards exercise this divided critical mind most notably on the topic of "musical discourse" or "affective resonance." Under their joint hand, in *The Meaning of Meaning*, they formulate this category initially in a wholly negative cast. They use it to represent a mode of verbal sensibility that has reduced language, in effect, to a series of material vibrations. Under this critical heading, the separate counters in a linguistic construction operate like notes in a musical score. The individual words move the auditor/reader into those subcurrents of feeling that are more powerful than an idea or meaning attached consciously, in this account properly, to the logos. Musical discourse works thus to empty propositional logic of all but acoustic content, but under contrary appearances. An apparent grammar of ratiocination and an evident intent of argument operate, but as musical movements only, that is, as a sheerly formal language, which achieves its effects through lower physical channels (in the inner ear) or in a near dreamlike state. This mechanism stimulates associations wholly unearned by those processes of intelligence normally considered necessary for a speech that reaches even the slightest degree of coherence. This analytical construction bears a striking resemblance to the formulations Richards will offer only two years later, under the heading of pseudostatement, where, however, the poet rigs up a rational apparatus of language with an entirely benign irony. By appeasing the reasoning faculty, the poet-master of this stratagem serves the worthy purpose of allowing the auditor to enter the sublogical process of poetry. A nearly point-for-point similarity between the critical concepts of musical discourse and pseudostatement matches up with a disparity, indeed a complete reversal, of attributed merit.

The significance of this difference lies not just in the inconsistency it witnesses. The shift demonstrates the evolving processes by which a historical experience of daunting importance may be gradually appropriated and, arguably, "improved." Musical discourse, after all, enacts a fallacy that Richards and Ogden outline in terms that recall all too clearly the critique of verbalism in the discourses of Liberal war policy. "Turning then to the more emotional aspects of modern thought, we shall not be surprised to find a veritable orgy of verbomania,"[94] their jeremiad opens, fueling the peculiar fervor of the analysis to follow with their lived memory of intellectual and political conscience. Already, however, they also ignite on the lively provocations of their own verbal sounds. "[A] veritable orgy of verbomania" draws its rhetorical vitality from that rustle of respondent syllables. Under the cover of the censure they pronounce on word-as-sound revels like their own, these authors consort with the order they overtly condemn.

As they proceed to detail the debilities of this acoustic condition, then, they also set out the message and pressure of its real appeal. "And Rignano aptly likens this process [of the loss of meaningful reason to sheerly acoustic feeling] to the shedding of the *carapace* by a crustacean." Their account develops:

> But the *carapace*, the verbal husk, is not merely a valedictory *point d'appui*; it also has a certain bombic capacity, an "affective resonance" which

enables the manipulator of symbols such as the Absolute to assure himself that his labours are not altogether in vain. "When language is once grown familiar," says Berkeley, "the hearing of the sounds or sights of the characters is often immediately attended with those passions which at first were wont to be produced by the intervention of ideas that are now quite omitted." From the symbolic use of words we pass thus to the emotive; and with regard to words so used, as in poetry, Ribot has well remarked that "they no longer act as signs but as sounds; they are musical notations at the service of an emotional psychology." So that though at this extreme limit "metaphysical reasoning may be intellectually quite incomprehensible; though, that is to say, it may actually become 'vocem proferre et nihil concipere,' it acquires by way of comprehension," as Rignano says, "an emotive signification which is peculiar to it, i.e., it is transformed into a kind of musical language stimulative of sentiments and emotions." Its success is due entirely to the harmonious series of emotional echoes with which the naive mind responds—*et reboat regio cita barbara bombum.*[95]

"[A] certain *bombic* capacity": how does the restricted meaning of this highly specific word—of or pertaining to the silkworm—become relevant to the argument? If the silkworm's mutations are analogized to the carapace shedding, there is surely a less curvaceously tropological way of saying so. But then, *bombic* is too good a sound, given the subject of "affective resonance," to be lost, even if it means that the loathed noises are creeping into the critics' speech, most audibly in the echo that bombic finds in the gorgeous, stuck-in-the-gorge coda of *cita barbara bombum.* Similarly, across the broader scale of the passage, the interlingual weave of Latin and French phrases comprises its designed effect of rhetorical decoration yet clearly exceeds it, too, converting the logic of the case against music into its own language of en*chant*ment.

Since this passage reveals the appeal of the principle it openly rejects, it will be no surprise when, in 1926, Richards praises "the most characteristic feature of Mr. Eliot's technique" under the heading of a "music of ideas":

> The ideas are of all kinds, abstract and concrete, general and particular, and, like the musician's phrases, they are arranged, not that they may tell us something, but that their effects on us may combine into a coherent whole of feeling and attitude and produce a peculiar liberation of the will. They are there to be responded to, not pondered or worked out.[96]

This "coherent whole of feeling and attitude" and the "liberation of the will" it expresses are entirely sublogical, associative, "musical" in the now-positive sense of the term. This improved attitude reaches through a detailed reading of the verse toward a language mechanics that matches the activities Richards depicts concurrently, and now equally favorably, in the emerging formulas of pseudostatement. Thus the logical freedom he esteems in Eliot's verse results from a strategy of setting verbal reason against itself. The "logical scheme" and "scaffolding" the poet constructs in his verse are not some articulated structure of deliberated significance; they serve instead as reasonable or heuristic fictions, whereby the poet engages and appeases the reader's habituated "need" for intellectual coherence.[97] Thus the better poet allows this apparatus of rationalistic language to collapse gradually over the course of the poem. This technique resolves the reader back into the deeper life of the psyche, that region of "impulses" and "feelings" that the poet has aimed to access. Now unrepressed, the musical note resonates in this virtuoso reading with a confidence and volubility equal to that of the poet who has mastered this wholly valuable attitude and practice.

Richards finds these orientations and stratagems mainly in Eliot's "later work"[98]—in the verse composed (although the exact dating was unavailable to Richards) since 1914. If this critical discrimination ties the now-preferred manner in some suggestive sense to the difference the war made, this setting remains unspecified by Richards. Silence on this score amplifies the reticence he has already shown to confess any change of valence in the evolution of musical discourse as a critical idea. It is not so much dishonesty or even inconsistency, I suggest, as a true record of the historical residue this mutating notion preserves. If poetry converses with the worst history has had to offer, the logical foolery that the verbal culture of the Liberal war institutionalized also shows far more than a set of simple tricks a poet might mimic, vindictively or not. Richards's critical concept puts poetry in touch with the disintegrating conditions of liberal rationalism. It taps equally momentously into areas of sublogical feeling that bespeak the wordless and brutal thing history is, or has been revealed to be, now that its logical accommodation has dissolved. In his model, poetry reenacts nothing less than the demise of the main myth of liberal modernity, as enacted in the public discourses of the Great War. The power of this affective construct is recognized only partially or unclearly by Richards for its full historicity—a testament, all in all, to the daunting force of its origins. A clarification in this respect would entail serious labor.

iv

Such serious labor motivates one of the primary lines of inquiry in the enterprise Ogden undertook in the early 1920s: the International Library of Psychology, Philosophy, and the Scientific Method.[99] An academic literature that featured already prominent philosophers such as G. E. Moore and the emergent work of the philosopher Ludwig Wittgenstein and the psychologist W. H. R. Rivers, this scholarly bibliography reveals a special point of coherence in a different configuration of names. Richards and Ogden combine with

Hans Vaihinger and Eugene Rignano to center attention on concerns emerging from the general editor's historical experience, the verbal culture of the Liberal war, and the more urgent and particular problems it evinced for him. The powers and liabilities of verbal logic, the performance element in reason's customary speech, and the pressure the sublogical exerts upon normative discourse: these interests express the always invigorating and sometimes resisted challenge of sounding through words those areas of emotional experience that appear, as it were, through the cracks or incapacities in its rationalist apparatus. The issues reach toward formulations as various and opposed indeed as Rignano's critique of musical discourse and Richards's later celebration of it. On those paramount questions the entries in the Library comprise a dialogue and dialectic as lively as the exchange Richards and Ogden joined to evolve the concept of the pseudostatement.

Witness Hans Vaihinger's *The Philosophy of "As If": A System of the Theoretical, Practical and Religious Fictions of Mankind*. Written as a doctoral dissertation in Germany in the late 1870s, when it sank quickly from view, it reappeared in German in 1911, but was mainly ignored in England until 1923, when the currents already cresting in the productions of English literary modernism led to its recovery and translation—by Ogden himself. The informing notion is "that 'as if,' i.e., the *consciously false*, plays an enormous part in science, in world philosophies, and in life."[100] Statements admittedly and manifestly untrue are thus maintained for uses and motives that Vaihinger explores in detail. This capacity for the sensible and acceptable lie responds to an equivalent facility in language itself, and Vaihinger opens an investigation that will identify the primary interest for his English editor and translator.

Vaihinger understands linguistic action not as referential, primarily, but as essentially propositional. Processes of argumentation and proof are intrinsic to human consciousness but in fact worthless by any measure of "objective" validity. Any sequential, cumulative, conclusion-driven effort in logical demonstration amounts only to the exercise it performs. Strategies of expository and argumentative logic thus serve to ratify nothing but the habits of language itself, or of a human consciousness that is formed accordingly. Rhetorical and conventionalist rather than essentialist in its understanding of articulate thought, Vaihinger's scheme realizes its more surprising implications when he uses it to parse the grammar and syntax of the typical ratiocination. The main work of propositional logic is presumed thus to be done not by the obvious parts—verbal substantives, argumentative predicates, individual words with specific, credible significance—but rather by the apparent incidentals of language: particles, prepositions, conjunctions, and so on. "[T]he connections of sentences through particles are the real logical joints of the argument," he avers, since the "whole chain of thought is often compressed into a particle, and a logical analysis of a given chain must therefore direct particular attention to the connecting particles." In the feeling these connectives transmit, the reasoning achieved in the whole performance is demonstrated and made credible—or not. The case being made resolves into an idiom of conviction that is mainly aesthetic and affective. If logic is read or, rather, scanned, as a prosody, Vaihinger intends no undue mischief in appreciating its expressions as "artifices of thought."[101]

Categorically: logic affords an artistic language to Vaihinger in the way that its logos resists any reduction to the postulates of common sense, which presumes in real experience a lived wisdom, some substance or residue independent of its linguistic construction. This insistence marks a revealing point of difference from the insights that William James records in *Pragmatism* (1907). James's frame of reference admits to some evident parallels, insofar as he sets out to identify a language of reason-seemingness but, ultimately, he critiques and submits its verbalist artifice to the test of lived experience.[102] Not Vaihinger. Resisting any vulgarizations as "common speech," his verbal artifact indulges the uncommon tongue of its own secret coherence. Assured through its hieratic language of the better than usual sense it makes, it sounds already in the academic Germany of 1878 as the poetic vocabulary of a nascent *symbolisme*. The "operations" of this linguistic discipline, which in every way "run counter to ordinary procedure," are more than Parnassian; they are nearly Masonic. These "methods . . . give an onlooker the impression of magic if he be not himself initiated or equally skilled in the mechanism. . . . And as in certain arts and handicrafts such artifices are kept secret, so we notice that this is also the case in logic."[103]

It is all here. The crisis Ogden heard in the speech of public reason through the war is staged ahead of his time and in full view already of the opportunity it will find in Richards's own responsive formulation. The evident strictures of logic are heard as a rhetoric, even a mummery, but one that exceeds any foolery and that leads its speaker or reader to those interior, covert reaches of human experience. Here, the quick of mystery—the irreducible impulse, the inexpressible emotion—abides. Vaihinger's scheme stands as a mirror plan for pseudostatement. The resemblance serves at once to extend Richards's linguistic mind back in philosophical (and literary) time and to find for Vaihinger the timelier application of England's first postwar moment. If Vaihinger has lived in subsequent literary history as a somewhat recherché figure, supplying a coherence to the poetics of play with verbal statement in other poets (Wallace Stevens, for chief instance), he may reclaim a central, essential place in the circumstances outlined here. Ogden and Richards have endured logical sophistry as a dialect of the most encompassing kind, Ogden has in fact chronicled the travesty of that motley logos, and so the two English writers turn to Vaihinger on the oblique angle of their one extreme need. On this primary site, where false verbal consciousness speaks the deeper truth of its use and need, they find a map to rewrite the manifold confusions of those tumultuous years into a diagram of lively literary energy and controlled poetic power. Indeed, Richards will begin systematically to pull his formulations together in the year (1924) of the publication of Ogden's translation of the German philosopher.

The contribution that Vaihinger makes to the evolution of this critical idea includes for the poetic sensibility it depicts the figure of Nietzsche as its first, surely its most richly problematic, embodiment. In a chapter Vaihinger added to the first German edition of 1911, the now-famed and already scandalized persona of the Superman speaks his part in a drama scripted to the issues and emphases of Vaihinger's own analysis. Thus the "cult of error" and the "joy in illusion" that Nietzsche values in his superior being incorporate these liberating falsehoods as "fictions of logic."[104] To admit that a proposition is substantially untrue but to glory in it just so, as a logical fiction; to develop the grammar and syntax of rationalistic artifice as nothing less than the human will's finest, most strenuous expression: here is that expansive skepticism, the pessimism of strength, the same capacity for tragic gaiety that Nietzsche finds in Greek theater and recycles as the prevailing *virtù* of his mature work.

If Nietzsche stands in Pippin's formulation as the closest approximation to a valid challenge to the dominant consciousness of modern Enlightenment rationalism, the difference the Great War makes for Nietzsche's philosophical attitude is absolute. Where Pippin's Nietzsche lacks the material realization of his skepticism in an actual historical event of adequate dimension, the recent war provided the previously missing basis. It disproved the truth of logical progress to a degree that made Nietzsche's own extremity credible, even necessary. The appropriation of the Nietzsche-Vaihinger episteme in postwar Britain occurs in an occasion, then, that has given Nietzsche's world view the stuff of the earned and inevitable—at least for those who choose to use it.

If the speech of Vaihinger's language philosophy shifts easily into (Nietzschean) song, in the heroic tenor, recent circumstances also complicated the appeal this persona might exert to an English audience at the moment of Vaihinger's revival, in the early years of the postwar period. The grandiloquent tones that Nietzsche pronounces in his expression of Vaihinger's ideas are amplified all too easily to those qualities of vainglory or bluff that the propaganda campaigns of the English war will have fixed on his Superman, there a cartoon of Teutonic atavism. Not that the capacity for rationalistic sham that Nietzsche and Vaihinger—and Ogden and Richards—elaborated in language was originally or characteristically German. To back-talk the logic of Liberalism, nonetheless, is to speak against the force and centering authority of modern English culture. This is the contrarian nerve and dare—and value—of the whole enterprise. The creative inversion of this dominant consciousness requires a kind of adversarial involvement. A strenuous condition in wartime, it may be the special—difficult—privilege of the relative alien.

Lessons for the Relative Alien

On 26 April 1916—the Wednesday after the Easter Monday Rising in Dublin—the London *Times* featured two pieces of commentary on its leader page. A dismissive analysis of the motives and strategies of the insurrectionists in "The Irish Disturbances" counterbalances "The Message of Anzac Day," a commemoration of the landing at Gallipoli on its first anniversary and a formulary of praise for the bravery that Australian and New Zealand troops displayed there. The second writer concedes the misguided nature of the Gallipoli enterprise, but for the sake of a further political point, which binds this section of the page silently but unmistakably to the diatribe on Ireland. The resolve that the Anzac forces demonstrated in that trial of spirit asserts the inwardness of their affinity with the English res. Their performance testifies to their status now as equal members of the Commonwealth, a distinction the Irish have obviously forgone. The double panel coheres clearly around the single theme of proper behavior among the far-flung peoples in the United Kingdom and Commonwealth.

The lesson includes as well some sharply marked assumptions about the proclivities and susceptibilities of people situated in the "colonial" condition—understanding this term less as an official designation than as a description of existence at some significant distance from a cultural capital, some center of meaningful coherence. This concern grows in urgency in April 1916 in view of the still-unresolved position of those other (former) colonials, the Americans. "The Germans have always counted upon armed insurrection in Ireland," the piece on the Dublin situation opens:

> They have striven to provoke it from the outbreak of the war, and at last they have succeeded in getting their dupes to indulge in an insane rising. . . . It is evidently the result of a carefully-arranged plot, concocted between the Irish traitors and their German confederates.

... [T]he Germans may have calculated that a rising in Ireland would influence certain kinds of American opinion in their favour at a moment when their relations with the United States are critical. The German societies and the "extremist" Irish societies in the Republic have been working hand in glove under German direction for a long time past to prejudice Americans against this country and make mischief between the two Governments. They will doubtless exert themselves to the uttermost to win sympathy for "Ireland's struggle for freedom." ... The Casement invasion itself appears to have been the merest *opera bouffe*, and its character will be thoroughly appreciated across the Irish channel.[1]

Alternatively:

There had been nothing more impressive in the capital of the Empire since the war began than the behaviour of these crowds—their reverent silence while the service was held, their fervent acclamation of the troops, the enthusiasm of their loyal welcome to the King and Queen....

Never, to all appearance, was valiant blood spilt for less gain; never "the shield of the mighty" more "vilely cast away." Yet we know that it was not so. The Australians and New Zealanders, when they landed in Gallipoli, set the seal upon the manhood of their peoples, as Mr. Hughes showed in the speech that he made to them yesterday. They did much more than that. They flung wide the door that the Canadians had already opened to a new life for the British peoples of the Empire. The brotherhood thus established no mishaps or disagreements can break in the days to come.[2]

While the Canadians seem to be leading the Australians and New Zealanders with their exemplary behavior, they, too, follow an orientation already formed in England. The map of imperial power this writer transcribes cannot help but suggest that colonial populations will model their action and demeanor on precedents established at the "capital of the Empire." The same mimic strain reaches a negative if risibly sinister extreme among the Irish. These people also copy deportment, but from the wrong source. Their actions consequently invert the values attributed to their preferred colonial brethren. "[D]upes of their German master," the Irish also conform compliantly, but to the wrong tune. They pattern their performance thus on the conventions of musical farce, a mechanical comedy where the protagonists may imitate the pathos of their higher operatic types, but inadequately, automatically, laughably.

Given the mimic condition these rebels and loyalists severally comprise, the writer's eye shifts understandably, but with uneasy hope, to the Americans. These people appear still in terms of the single propensity the two pieces jointly inscribe for the colonial caste. Subject to the suasion of "prejudice" and so unprepared for the reasoning of individual judgment and opinion, the Americans seem liable accordingly to the kind of "influence" that will result in the imitator's undeliberated reflex. Will the copying streak that is natural to the populace of this one-time colony lead to antics as rudely if stupidly defiant as the Fenians'? Or will the performance prove to be as correct and edifying as those New Zealanders' and Australians'? The editorial leaves the Americans poised on the page between two models of policy, which differ substantially, but not, finally, in the mode of response expected and prescribed for them—at least by a writer positioned at this "capital of the Empire" and privileged with the vantage of this symbolic site.

Might conformity provide a means to pursue purposes trickier, however, than its evident or professed obeisance? Could not rebellion be enacted in a fashion apparently flattering to the image a once-master nation maintains of its own rites and polities? One response to these questions comes in Homi Bhabha's "Of Mimicry and Man: The Ambivalence of Colonial Discourse." For the inveterate simulator, the provincial poet or novelist if not the colonial soldier, Bhabha proposes a double function of subversion through appropriation. Here a desire on the part of the colonized person to resemble the apparently superior imperial type takes up a mimic role that plays out a more deeply seditious motive and design. The manners of an imposed and oppressive system may be "put on," assumed, but only in order to be spoofed, thus discredited, and in the end disabled. "The effect of mimicry on the authority of colonial discourse is profound and disturbing," Bhabha expatiates. "For in 'normalizing' the colonial state or subject, the dream of post-Enlightenment civility alienates its own language of liberty and produces another knowledge of its norms."[3]

Where the Word of modern Western rationalism is duplicated with alien bearing, more specifically, one may detect the most particular menace that an Anglo-American poet might represent in Liberal England of the early twentieth century. The threat rests furtively but potently in the susceptibilities that this political tradition exhibits in having its logos copied. The partisan intellectual tradition assumes, after all, that individuals reason their views freely and, so, originally. If the grammar and syntax of verbal logic are standardized, the movements of linguistic logic may be copied—and by speakers so manifestly unfamiliar with its inward spirit as to defy or defile its authorizing ground in the private, self-authenticating mind. The extent to which the political institutions of Liberalism invest their authority in the individualist claims of rationalist language, then, will measure by inverse ratio the force and import of the mimic's "disturbance." And no heavier investment will have been made—and risked—than in August 1914.

Conspicuous and precarious, at once wholly exposed and apparently unwary, this discourse of English rationalism extends itself—openly, availably, vulnerably—to the verbal attentions of (ex-)colonial poets in the London of 1914. Balanced on the medial stroke of a hyphenated identity, the Anglo-Americans are positioned sufficiently off-angle to the central political and cultural institutions of British Liberalism to hear the increasing weakness in the once easy authority of its language. They may take imaginative advantage in a grammar and vocabulary that responds, as a magnificent failure, to the failing magnificence of that erstwhile power.

While Bhabha's writers enact a sometimes involuntary parody of the master language, the subversion such usage entails—inadvertently or not—appears in his calculation to be their primary motive, indeed their final, determining effect. His insistence in this respect turns on the point of a scheme he plays in refrain through the piece: "not quite/not white." Racial distinctions tend to absolutize the difference between capital and colony; under the essentializing constructions of apartheid systems, imitation by the "other" people presents a transgression, right (wrong) from the start. An inappropriateness in the appropriation makes for an unseemliness in the seeming. Bhabha's "not quite white" mime thus raises his voice ever in "an insurgent counter-appeal." Despite the ambivalence Bhabha signals for colonial discourse, then, this simulating tongue utters a fairly single- (and bloody-)minded message: ultimately, a wholly disruptive function.[4]

Pound and Eliot are "not quite" British, however, within a fully "white" compass of possibility. Americans with virtually complete English genealogies, these provincials have returned to the capital and closed a gap of space and generations, not of "nature." Racial colonization authors horrors so obvious, of course, that any consideration of the private psychodramas of these poets—descended from an already "privileged" class of white settlers—must seem impertinent. The colonial condition is not limited to its present ostensible victims, however. To the underclass identity so readily attributed to the colonial subject, it turns out, Pound and Eliot will exhibit an excess sensitivity, which compels statements of superior attitude over their own alleged inferiors—the Jews and the Irish of inveterate, Anglo-American stereotype. In this colonial condition, the roles of agent and victim may be reenacted variously—under the reverse logic of the compensatory correction. The colonial state is a category in which to understand the fully complex initiative of this pair of American poets. These (former) colonials have returned to a London engulfed in a war for the "civilization" to which they relate as the most charged term in their contested poetic identities.

The intrinsic sameness of these relative aliens to the English res serves at once to accentuate their sense of difference and to compensate for it. The exception they represent constitutes a feeling of special authority and (self-conferred) legitimacy. In practice: becoming critics of contemporary linguistic fashion, they exchange their outsider status in the imperial metropolis for an externality of perspective that locates (for them) a superior vantage. In war-

Not Quite/Not White. Colonized populations serve in the Great War for civilization in the subsidiary positions to which Eliot and Pound will reveal such aggravated sensitivity.

King George V inspecting NCOs of the South African Native Labour Corps at Abbeville, France, 10 July 1917, with Colonel S. A. M. Pritchard of the South African Native Labour Corps.

General Smuts inspecting a division of the South African Native Labour Corps at Dannes, France, April 1917. At this level of service, the supervising cane displayed by Colonel Pritchard in the previous figure has become the brandished stick.

Quite White. The appeal of the imperial capital is answered on this Australian recruiting poster with an outlandish humor, which presents no subversive intent to the main message.

time: as skeptical auditors of the language that official Liberalism offers to endorse and rationalize its war, they assume an intimacy and inwardness with the older, deeper thing—the more "genuine" British tradition, which this current practice of logical cant only shams and shames. And proleptically: out of their "better perspective" on contemporary linguistic practice, they write a parody language, more potent by far than its disqualified model. These two provincial poets thus prove themselves adequate—at this early moment of reverse colonialism—not only to spoof the current voice of the capital and ridicule its timely claims but to "send up"—improve as well as mock—the act of mimicry itself. Pound and Eliot indulge in a simulation with such ostentatious artifice as to appear immune or superior to the mere "dupery" that the inveterate colonial might exhibit in the same milieu, under similar "influences." They convert the prompt into a provocation, in the profounder etymological sense: something that calls forth their own creative power and, to them, reveals their hitherto concealed equality with the traditions of origin.

This preview may seem to rehearse a fairly standard narrative of English literary modernism, at least in its major emphases. The plot follows a young America returning to rescue an aging European culture from the ruin it will meet anyway in its Great War. The dominant conflict encloses an individual talent, or pair of talents, within a tradition that is both in danger and at stake. According to the legends these poets left for their own activity, in expressions ranging from Eliot's essay on the formative importance of classical myth in Joyce's *Ulysses* to Pound's counsel to translators of ancient texts to "make it new,"[5] they will have worked diversely but jointly to repossess a literary legacy and reinscribe it to the letter of their existence as contemporary individuals, in the idiom of their own modernity. And modern*ism*, given the full emphasis of the suffix, entails surely this sense of being modern, not just as a chronological fact but as a self-conscious attitude, which involves and requires a sense of division from the past. Under this defining and enabling awareness, these two poets will live out a signature instance of English literary modernism. They use their belatedness, which is their given condition, to stimulate an elaborate artistry of making it new, that is, of making it "mine."

This story has tended to be told recently with a postcolonial turn. The penultimate chapter of Robert Crawford's *Devolving English Literature*, for instance, "Modernism as Provincialism," extends the tendency prevalent in this critical tradition to a revealing extreme. In Crawford's construction, Eliot and Pound become the foremost examples of provincials who bring their native and primitivist strength to the metropolis, which is the primary, driving site of modernism. In this locale, in Crawford's construction, the provincial's intrinsic vigor rises to the opportunity and task of generating a new literary and imaginative sensibility. Its linguistic record displays a novel dominance of the demotic, an accent varying from the Americanisms of Pound and Eliot to the regional dialect of Lawrence to the Scots tongue of Crawford's favored poets.

While Crawford acknowledges the double status of Eliot as "resident alien" in England, the depiction tends to shift the poet's Americanness into a position of unchecked hegemony. Crawford reiterates this picture through the instance of Pound, who, from one (limited) view, can lend himself to such simplification. The American background of these modernist poets thus affords a resource on which they draw, in this account, not so much to reciprocate with things English, but mainly to perform themselves. Thus they fashion the character of the poet as at once more savage and more urbane than the denizens of their chosen place, animating a project whose aim or motive, in Crawford's perception, seems to be chiefly to prove that they can do it.[6]

What Crawford's account fails to credit sufficiently is the internal reality of this London locale and, in that, the force of the appeal to the Americans of English cultural tradition. (The literary initiative he sets forth in his outlandish men makes a strong sound of reverse- or postcolonial triumphalism.) This exchange between the province and the capital provides the generative energy of the productions we will come to recognize as characteristically "modernist," which, as a nominal category, no less as a term of customary reference, presumes some ramifying complication of relation between past and present, and, here, between a metropolis and a colony. This manifold interaction comes to maximum intensity in the war circumstance.

Roughly: the "outside-withinness" that images the relation of the modernist sensibility to tradition is a riddle lived to every complexity of implication and consequence in the local culture of the political war, of the campaign for civilization. The pressures an alien meets to belong to the right side of an established practice become more forceful and more evident than before, more readily coercive and so more urgently answerable. These forces meet a sort of resisting reciprocity in the poets. Eliot and Pound can see the right campaign (for civilization) being waged by its wrong (Liberal) representatives, who, as the current stewards of the cultural legacy and as the target of mimic subversion, offer these modernists at once a soft spot and an entry point into that better tradition. This program does not decrease in coherence or meaning by virtue of the fact that Eliot or Pound might have hardly intended it to work out this way in advance. The historicity of the process of *evolving* modernism—the intersection of prior aesthetic ideals with contingent circumstances, an enriching of original principles with unforeseen eventualities—is one of the stories the subsequent account will tell.

Putting on the manners of London, at once bedecking themselves and spoofing their host, the complexity of motive and behavior in the modernist project identifies all too clearly its agents' out-of-placeness in the literary capital of the empire. Eliot, in ways apparently natural to his character, manages to keep his part in this attitude far from the spotlit center of the stage. One of the incidental values in Pound's more spontaneous honesty is to chronicle the process of an alien's appropriation. The evidence this process leaves, moreover, presents at points the wreckage of earlier, "purer," simpler notions. Thus, the developmental complexity of English poetic modernism comes first through Pound's story, prefaced in prose.

2

Pound's Savage Ratios

I do not wish to be mayor of Cincinnati nor of Dayton, Ohio.
I do very well where I am.
London may not be the Paradiso Terrestre,
but it is at least some centuries nearer it than is Saint Louis.
—E Z R A   P O U N D, *to his mother, January* 1914

In January 1914, Pound has not yet heard of the poet from St. Louis. He speaks beforehand, nonetheless, out of the identity he shares with Eliot, more specifically of the necessities attending that American fellowship: chiefly, of the provincial writer's need to locate himself in—and in relation to—the old imperial capital. Since most commentary on Pound has emerged through an age that has grown more or less satisfied with the victory of reverse colonial—now post-colonial—impulses in literary and political history, one needs to remember the aim of the literary education he undertook with his travels, beginning in 1908. After a brief period in Venice, where his cultivated interests had first taken him, he repaired to the symbol and source of the literary tradition in which he was native: to London, where he would remain for twelve years.[1]

By October 1914, Pound can agree with the current assertion that "London is the capital of the world" and aver that "no course of study is complete without one or more years in London. Scholarly research is often but wasted time if it has not been first arranged and oriented in the British museum."[2] The present centralization of energies in the war effort certainly serves to reinforce the value he appears so eager to ratify for the capital. The orientations of his own art precede and provide for the same development. In the imaginative topography of vorticism, the figure of the whirlpool inscribes an energy, a current of circumambient force, which gathers and clarifies at its point of intensest concentration: its "head." The English painter Wyndham Lewis drew this scheme into vivid and individual form, but the American Pound signs onto it forcibly because it provides an ideogram for his progress as a provincial poet.[3] A *gradus ad Parnassum* has drawn this American from the periphery to the center, from one-time colony to enduring capital.

A career that has already mythologized itself thus responds predictably to the culture of war, to the centripetal pull that the national campaign exerts. He

Ezra Pound, 1916, by E. O. Hoppé

Wyndham Lewis, *Composition*, 1913, Tate Gallery, London. The vortex design, swirling an array of shapes around a keystone figure (the double wedge shape in center right), was troped by Pound as a "fury of intelligence baffled and shut in by circumjacent stupidity."

elaborates these geometries imaginatively, intensifying his sense of membership in the capital enterprise. "It is an appreciation of the great Roman Vortex," he enthuses in March 1915, converting the heady intoxication of his own moment in wartime London into the thralldom of an ancient imperial center. "[T]he value of a capital," he continues, is "the value of centralization, in matters of knowledge and art, and of the interaction and stimulus of genius foregathered. *Ubicunque Romana lingua dominatur!*"[4] The language already breathes his share of the authority he has sought in constructing this fanciful urbs, where he convenes the members of his generation, those selectively equal types of "genius." The words of vatic antiquity bespeak the esteem and power—the legitimacy—for which he is pleading.

The force of this appeal goes to the poet's case for his (and his cohorts') place in—and assimilation to—a specifically English civilization. This process is complicated, but also considerably enriched, by the circumstances of the current war. In the political ideolect of this conflict, *civilization* assumes a use and value as aggressively edged toward German *Kultur* as it is threatening to the uncultivated American.[5] Within the system of oppositional and right-wrong thinking that the war so obviously fosters, belonging to the correct tradition is the one thing needful for a poet uneasy about belonging to any tradition at all. The compensatory zeal with which Pound will advocate the cause and standard of Britain's war will operate by a logic more powerful and personal, then, than the suasion of national policy and propaganda. The loyalty he swears to this campaign also seeks to claim the high, authorizing ground of his own poetic identity.

It is essential to understand the sense of disadvantage that compels this project of imaginative affiliation with the English capital. From prewar days, Pound articulates this insecurity. In 1912, for example, in "Patria Mia," a passage that echoes in English the title of this series concedes that "America, my country, . . . almost a continent and hardly yet a nation, . . . has not yet achieved an 'Urbs,' . . . some city 'whereto all roads did lead.'"[6] The effects of this absence ramify even—especially—when his migration to London might seem to have redressed what is missing. "How can the bloomin provincial poet be expected to keep a pace unless we set it,"[7] he writes in March 1914 from London as transatlantic editor for Harriet Monroe's *Poetry* (Chicago). He is talking back to his former condition in that "half-savage country" in which, in the fictional autobiography of *Hugh Selwyn Mauberley* (1920), he will represent himself as having been born. In the British usage he assumes, however, he speaks still from within his marginal and inferior circumstance: in the underclass idiom of the demotic, cockney pronunciation. Even on Parnassus, it seems, he is a permanent member of a colonial undercaste.

As the letter to Monroe suggests, capital authority speaks through Pound in a voice at once assumed and elusive. Secured rather than secure, quicksilvery, gamey and adventitious rather than confident about its monuments and legacies and material endowments, with its ear ever to the main chance. And its best chance lies in the enterprise to which this poet's colonial character and habit suit him best—an activity to which he will gravitate with all the complexity that attends his provincial estate, that is, to mimicry.

I

Mimicry, with Differences

As an American poet in London, Pound expresses a need for legitimate, imitable models. Equally predictably, insofar as this imaginative desire for primary types bespeaks a yearning for firstness, a bid for originality, he also needs to critique the copying quality in his conationals. These rival values of originality and replication slide back and forth between the two sites of his experience: sometimes the capital of the former empire identifies the place of estimable origins (so that America can merely duplicate the manners and attitudes of the English metropolis); sometimes the aboriginal colony is the source of genuine invention (while London simply imitates itself). This discourse of contested primacies moves into its ultimate intensities in the years of the English war, in Pound's London experience, when, in the global arena, the Allied and Central powers are fighting over ownership of the word that Pound associates with the imperial capital: civilization. If this American progenitor wishes to affiliate himself—and his transatlantic tribe—to this term and category of value, current circumstances turn the difference between imitation and genuine versions into an opposition between right and wrong, true and false, good and evil representatives of the high standard: English civilization versus Prussian *Kultur*. The mimic condition of Pound's American origins also plays out all too readily now to the primitive associations that the British side wishes to affix to the uncivilized Enemy. In this heightened environment, the issues driving the development of Pound's poetic identity arrive at the one climax and long climacteric of his early career.

i

"Nine out of every ten Americans have sold their souls for a quotation," Pound observes of the echoing tendency among his countrymen in 1912 in "Patria Mia": "They have wrapped themselves about a formula of words instead of about their own centres. . . . [P]in an American down on any fundamental issue you like, and you get—at his last gasp—a quotation." "This in no wise hinders them," he protests in answer, "from being the most inventive people in the world. They know what they want."[8] Inventive mimicry? A self-reliant assumption of other's—another country's and capital's—manners and customs? The peculiar *virtù* Pound attributes to his countrymen reinscribes the typical colonial disability, but with this critical difference. In the "naturalness" of Americans he finds no tabula rasa of merely impressionable matter. Rather, he prizes some discriminating quick, a discerning instinct, all in all a readiness to receive and renew what is old and—for the most part—venerable. To this faculty, a dead or failing tradition may look, indeed, for its regeneration and longevity.

The American mimic's indispensability takes as the condition of its importance the continued prominence of the capital of that foregone empire. In the provincial's intimation of his most potent capacity, however, contemporary London becomes a locus of old, or wrongly antiquated, fashion. The colonial poet returns thus to a capital which, in its debilitated condition, submits its manners and habits to a simulator, who not only proves their decadence but improves upon it. This poet's mimic gift will extend to and revivify the better traditions obscured by current usage. Pound enters this exchange consistently and especially over the course of the war, but he has already revealed its importance for him in an earlier engagement.

"Through Alien Eyes," a series Pound writes in 1913 for the *New Age*, sees in "London . . . [a] Rome of the decadence, so far, at least, as letters are concerned. She is as a main and vortex drawing strength from the peripheries."[9] To this capital and its museum of established attitudes, the polar flow of creative force draws the vital provincial character, who, in the daring of the cartoon to which he reduces the customs and postures of this once-dominant power, exhibits most evidently the energy of which he may credibly boast. He addresses the denizens of this formerly privileged place:

> Yet from the personal side your sense of property is a never-failing source of astonishment to me. . . .
>
> This curious atavism! Is it a matter of climate? Did you descend from the walrus, while the rest of mankind was busy descending from the ape? Is there an original difference?
>
> This curious fetish! . . . And where we seek liberty, or what I suppose you would call "irresponsibility" because you cannot see that is a feeling of being responsible for something else than the things for which you find it natural to feel responsible; where we seek liberty, you clamour for a sense of "safety," another *ignis fatuus*.[10]

Knowing (he has claimed elsewhere) what he wants, being one of the most inventive people in the world, this outlandish character seeks to establish his primacy on the supposed site of origins, where, after all, not just civility but sophistication marks the one belonging to the venerable tribe of tradition. Thus he outdoes the locals in urbane irony, gaining the upper hand in this transaction as he tropes himself into the role of the visitor, superior to and amused by the oddities of native usage. The reversal extends to the tone he assumes. Note the properly metropolitan dialect in the third paragraph: he "puts on" the capital in no apparently savage fashion, there are no barbaric yawps. Indeed, he speaks his declaration of personal American independence through a syntax of elaborate, suspended, and then perfected subordination. In this appropriation of the grammar of dominance, he shows his familiarity with the colonizing power, even the superiority that the upper hand of irony supplies. This is mimicry, then, with a signifying difference. If the kinship this American owns with the ape concedes some comic capacity for simian mimicry, the provincial owns up to this potential on the proud warrant of his own linguistic performance.

Mimicry comes into Pound's critical view in the immediately subsequent years in increasingly complex and intense representations. Writing in the autumn of 1915, in "American Chaos," he locates at once a primary liability and original genius in an American poet's inveterate tendency to imitate the literary mannerisms of the former power. Granted, this simulator fears an influence from the worst elements in the character of English culture. "[W]hen I curse my country I find myself cursing her for distinctly English habits, for habits imported from England," he complains in the first number in the series, then specifies, "There is a prudery doth hedge the printed word." That regrettable reticence expresses itself in "evasions and circumlocutions"[11] and exports itself to a colonial poet all too likely to take it on. This poet works in the economy of influence which, in the second installment of this series, he not only outlines but exemplifies. "Whenever I meet an interesting man in either England or America he invariably tells me things which he 'is not allowed to print,'"[12] the American complains. Ingeniously, teasingly, Pound uses the hedge of those quotation marks to signal the self-protective gesture in the remark. In one stroke, he imitates capital obliquity and attitudinizes it.

A conception of satire is special to his evolving poetics of critical mimicry, and it appears as a point of focused concern in the same essay:

> And "satire"? Ah, until American [sic] can understand that a satire consisting merely in a statement of fact (undistorted fact, known perfectly well to the reader) is not intended to be "comic," we must still sigh with Leopardi—
>
>> . . . vedo le mura e gli archi
>> E la colonne e i simulacri . . .
>> Ma la gloria non vedo. (EPPP, II:109)

In these final lines, the Italian words work slyly but effectively to dispel the associations of any provincialism on Pound's part. Thus he joins Leopardi in mourning the simulating function among his countrymen. Suggestively, however, the apparently rival qualities of natural straightforwardness and cultural impressionability in the provincial establish the propensity for a special kind of satire, one that combines the direct observation and the mimetic function. Pound's is, ideally, a vocal mirror that reveals equally the benightedness of the types it is echoing and the native verve of the recorder; all in all, it reflects the decadence of the original and the better *virtù* of its aboriginal mime (under whose designated power, "satire" may be reverting to the associations of its bogus etymology: *satyr*).

Defining the provincial mimic's special genius, Pound responds to a particular aspect of the capital character-in-voice. This is, in a phrase, the mannered untruth. The practice appears in its capital and colonial versions in "American Chaos (II)." "The Englishman," Pound observes,

> lies unconsciously, because he wants to be considered as holding "sound opinions." The growth of "sound opinion" in England is a curious and recondite affair.
>
> The American falsifies, either because, as men of other and older races, he wishes to sell you a horse (or a pup), or because he wishes to seem genteel, or because of a curious sense of humour. (*EPPP*, II:109)

The intentional character of American mendacity defines the difference and contributes the figure of the rogue impersonator to the colonial's mimic role. This trickster character picks up on a set of creative possibilities—opportunities, targets—that Pound draws into view. Whatever may be "curious" about the colonial's "sense of humour," the adjective gestures through the echo it represents to its chief point of attention: those British manners that Pound frames as equally, answerably, "curious." The point of his duplicating humor lies in the strange matter of the recondite, English lie.

Its cognate practice is obviously most timely, now, in 1915. Reason-seeming nonsense describes accurately the linguistic style of the Liberal war. To that primary English model, Pound's American riposte is the promised, literary answer.

The echo that this literature affords may include more than the rebuke it needs to feature. Consider the complexity of a gesture Pound makes in the same essay, "American Chaos (II)," where he identifies and critiques the American's tendency to imitate English indirectness. Here, in the visible language that punctuation provides, he lowers a timely and controversial remark, like a dramatic aside, into the discrete silence of parentheses: "(This is not a matter of war censorship; I am aiming no shaft at that very necessary board.)" (*EPPP*, II: 109). While this silencing effect ironically simulates the "evasions and circumlocutions" that characterize English usage, the parentheses include as expressed content an evident endorsement of the national war. This effort appears so estimable indeed as to allow Pound to sanction in its service those practices of censorship that exhibit the same suppression or reticence that, elsewhere, provide the basis of his complaint against the English. The critical simulation of those benighted British practices allows Pound to accede indeed to the interior mystery, the secret coherence that this "Great War for Civilization" actually signifies. (The parentheses enclose and signal his inward affinity with the English res.) The American anticipates thus the double measure of his mimic purpose and strategy.

The first condition of this enterprise, however, lies in a sense of belonging, already and beforehand, to (his) origins. Firstness—originality—locates the vexed point in his poetic identity. A self-invented legitimacy shows its problems most notably then in the unstable, ever-reversing valence of primary terms, of the words for primacy itself. Originality reverts readily to aboriginality, which may represent the energy and canny wit behind the whole program of reappropriating—and reinvigorating—the materials of a (mostly decayed) civilization. This characterization encloses its own double measure, however: a native *virtù* coincides with *un*civilized, atavistic practices. The erstwhile provincial needs to find the *more* primitive and less noble savage, his own anti- and antetype. Pound can appeal this need, it turns out, through the ideological discourses of the current war, through the diatribes on Ireland and Germany especially.

ii

In this largely defensive and compensatory engagement, Ireland comes into view as the prodigal colony (hardly the site of a difference esteemed in post-colonial models like Crawford's). No actual place with a specific political history, Pound's Eire forms rather as a rhetorical topos, a repository of the traits he fears that he may reveal as a provincial and so discloses in a series of distancing negatives. The same enemy appears in the German he reconstructs out of the stuff of popular ideology. This "foe of civilization" appears as an adversary with which any outlandish provincial fears affiliation and so disowns—through the virulent cartoons of the barbaric Hun that Pound reproduces.[13] A strenuous effort to exorcise these identities coincides then with an attempt to write himself into the larger enterprise, a war for civilization that will establish the grounds of his own legitimacy as a poet.

"Gentle reader," Pound gestures in "The Non-existence of Ireland," in February 1915. Through the quiet irony of an antiquated manner of address, he does not silence the feeling of intimacy he needs with the readership of an imperial capital. "[C]an it possibly matter," he questions his affiliates rhetorically, "what becomes of a place that writes like that?" *That* is the provincial ignorance shown in Dublin by the public objection to Synge's *Playboy of the Western World*, and *that* is a manner Pound exiles to the hinterlands of an empire in which he has moved to the central, capital position. "Can a dignified empire care two straws whether or no it keeps or casts off a province where this passes for public opinion?"[14] Pound has perceived similar inadequacies in his own country before the war, in "Patria Mia," but the pressure of current circumstance brings him now to withdraw those objections—with the advantage that the Irish comparison affords him. "There is no city even in America so small or so provincial that it would not have welcomed these pictures," which Dublin turned down in the instance Yeats publicized in his poem on the Municipal Gallery controversy. "There is no State, no recently promoted territory in the Union, which has not more claim to being a nation in itself than this 'John Bull's Other Island,' this stronghold of ignorance and obstruction" (*EPPP*, II:21).

The American constantly improves himself by virtue of the contrast he draws with the Irish, most specifically in the claim he makes to kinship with the standards of civilization. In 1917, the comparison he develops between a secessionist scheme in nineteenth-century New York and the current initiative to separate Ulster thus induces the assertion that "some trace of civilisation has been permitted to remain" in the United States because of the continued union "and, despite many of their faults, to continue, if not to progress." "[T]he present sub-sectional criers within your Islands," however, show "no voice raised on behalf of civilisation." "Neither from South Ireland nor from Ulster," he continues in refrain, "has anyone spoken on behalf of civilisation."[15]

The same strategy of the self-advantaging contrast appears in Pound's response in January 1920 to the emergent fact of the Irish Republic. "I am about as much interested in the Irish Republic," he attitudinizes, "as I would be in a proposition to set up the Nation of the Cherokees with text-books of the original language, in the bad lands of Oklahoma."[16] The linkage he intimates between Irish and American natives allows him to assume a vantage toward the "backward" peoples of his own continent that matches exactly the advantage that the imperial Englishman should (still) enjoy over those rude Celts, whose efforts at cultural nationalism, exerted originally in the recovery of the Gaelic language in the Revival, provide the more pointed target of this belittling comparison with America's Cherokees.

The defensiveness in this aggressive disdain goes to an excess of sensitivity on Pound's own part about the liability of the colonial, of mimicry in particular. He frames this concern with the dupery of cultural duplication through the revealing example—again, at the expense—of the Irish, who are moved back into view in a letter to John Quinn of 15 November 1918. He warms rhetorically on the now well-worn site of Irish intransigence in the recently concluded war, aligning that people with the several liabilities attributed to them by the (London) *Times* of 26 April 1916. Whereas "Ireland tried to stab the Allies in the back" at Teutonic provocation and "was ready for another try during the spring offensive," which Germany launched as its final effort in March 1918, the depiction he proceeds to detail through Maud Gonne's example features the more particular debility of provincial (Celtic, primitive) mimicry:

> So far as I can make out M. G's only constructive political idea is that Ireland and the rest of the world should be free to be one large Donegal fair.

She now favours a "republic," but she was Boulangerist in France,
and I think they were once royalistic.

Have *all* the Irish a monomania? M. G. is "reasonable" to a point,
just as Yeats is on psychism, but then there comes the. . . . . . . I suppose
"glamour."

I believe the Zulus or Oceanic tribes make war by marching out in
companies and hurling invectives at each other by the hour.[17]

Chameleonlike, Maud Gonne assumes a coloring corresponding to the political
ground on which she finds herself. Thus Pound likens the political culture of
Ireland to the performative rites of the "Zulus or Oceanic tribes" and draws the
parallel to the familiar point of the aboriginal mime. In the anatomy of folly this
picture of the backward copyist portrays, Pound appears in the reverse mirror
of his own anxieties about colonial simulation.

If he attempts strenuously to defend himself against the worst susceptibilities that he limns for the provincial, however, Pound also lays claim to the sort
of creative strength this Donegal mimic must forfeit—in his eyes, by the rule of
her inferior Irish nature. While Gonne quotes unthinkingly the partisan slogan
of any social locale on which she finds herself, Pound places quotation marks
around "reasonable," the motto of his own moment in the political time of English Liberalism. In the slight, dubietive movement this piece of rhetorical
punctuation performs, he makes a gesture that expresses his independent orientation to a word whose value this Celtic duplicator can ken only "up to a
point" and so will reproduce in the parody version of her own partial, inadequate apprehension of it. Not that the "reasonable" speaks, for Pound, some
primary language or authentic voice of the civilization of which these Celts
know not. Through his punctuation, he exerts a respondent force, a pressure
that signals that pressure is already being brought through this word. "[R]ea-
sonable" bespeaks the standard that the colonial is *supposed* to want to try to
meet. A writer capable of labeling it thus gains an independence and superiority to the whole mechanism of expectation and obeisance. The same bettering
of expectation will generate a poetics of mimicry in deliberate excess, all in all,
an elaborately ostentatious duplication. This motivational energy drives the
poetic enterprise he will have undertaken by 1917.

The poetics Pound forms out of current circumstance also reveals a paradoxical truth. His lampoon of English Liberal reason at war is also working—
by his own intention and design—in service to the cause for which this same
value is otherwise fighting: civilization. Thus, in the Quinn letter, he observes
that "these [Irish] are people who have no sense of the value of 'civilization' or
public order" and have demonstrated this deficiency most tellingly "during
war time."[18] While it is obvious that Pound debars the Irish from membership
in the cause for which the Great War has been nominally fought, his placing of
the theme word within quotation marks signals a double function similar to the

To an American eager to be part of that campaign, the Irish rebellion against Great Britain clearly represents the wrong side in this world war.

Irish Rebellion, May, 1916.

Sackville Street in Flames. A photograph taken by a "Daily Sketch" Photographer under fire.

Night fighting in the Battle of Dublin, an image reminiscent of evening scenes on the Western Front, which were also lit by flares, artillery, and automatic fire, May 1916.

Irish Rebellion ~ May 1916.

Soldiers holding a Dublin Street.

British soldiers "standing to" in a trenchlike defense in a Dublin street.

The arrest at Bayle of men who raided Rockingham House, the residence of T. Stafford Bart, on 14 March 1918. The parading of prisoners matches the practice on the Western Front, notwithstanding the children and partisans surrounding the march.

THE BIRTH OF THE IRISH REPUBLIC -1916.

Irish Republican poster, April 1918. The Irish rebels also appropriated the imagery of the Great War. Embattled Republican soldiers hold the line. As in imagery depicting Britannia, the spirit of a free Ireland—holding the tricolor in one hand, a palm branch in the other—is garbed in classical attire.

one his punctuation exerts through "reasonable." There is a meaning or value preconceived for each term, of which this poet is aware and to which he orients himself in the self-conscious manner the punctuation signals. His status as a relative alien provides the basis of this attitude.

Creative parodist, Pound is engaged in a poetics of appropriation, an act of imaginative seizure on the part of a colonial poet. If he leaves the fingerprints of that activity in the punctuation he puts around "reasonable," as the supposed possession of his much-sought civilization, evidence of the same angle of relation to things English shows in "glamour," a counter that seems otherwise unremarkable. Why should this word call attention to itself? "[G]lamour" includes a piece of etymological history exactly apposite to the character of Celticity that Pound's imaginative project is constructing. For glamour represents a Scottish corruption of gramarye,[19] or grammar, that is, the study of those relational structures in language that are tantamount to the rationalistic organization of speech. A mispronunciation of the word that bespeaks a classically rationalistic conception of language thus stigmatizes the tongue of Pound's Celt. His Irish speak still within a modern Gaeltecht, in the Celtic babble of Gonne's Donegal fair. To the supreme "reasonable[ness]" of the capital *Verbum*—to a logical word central equally to Liberal England and the Roman Imperium—Pound's Celts relate in a fashion that characterizes the provincial primitive's perennial, outlandishly simple way of knowing and controlling the world: through glamour, that is, more idiomatically, by the merest set of charms (the fabled "Irish charm" may supply the provocation for Pound's tapping the resources of this loaded term). The advantage this characterization assumes for the poet who drafts it tells elsewhere in a verse art fully conscious of the imitation it enacts of an imperial capital's rationalistic language.

The peculiar combination of obliqueness and vehemence in this critique suggests for the grievance it releases an excess of personal sensitivity. The off-angle attack points back at Pound himself. Uncritical mimicry is perhaps the most obvious quality in the topical writing he produces on the official causes of the war. In the four-part series he drafts for the *New Age* in the spring and summer of 1917, "Provincialism the Enemy," for instance, he concedes the weakness America will reveal in being led by the imperial power: "America was so provincial that it took her several years to understand that militarism must be put down. Even now, she does not much understand; she is stampeded, thank God, in the right direction, towards the annihilation of Kaisers."[20] Does he permit his own prose to be stampeded, "in the right direction" perhaps but under a linguistic will not his own? A copyist practice like this would maintain the crusade for civilization only as a manifest travesty of its current and normative standards, which presume the freedom of individual decisions and the legitimacy of personal views.

Consider his performance in the first installment of the series, where he draws his perspective on the current scene through the eyes of Henry James.

"The master" is the colonial writer who represents an idealized version of the persona Pound will be assuming through the series: an American who (in Pound's view) has most successfully naturalized himself to those English values and traditions this poet also seeks to possess as the substance of his true inheritance. He would secure this legacy by signing on to the right side of the current war. Opening with a figure James drew (for Pound, prophetically) in 1883, he uses this image of the Prussian character to adumbrate the current enemy of civilization. Thus James's

> Dr. Rudolph Staub writes from Paris:
> "You will, I think, hold me warranted in believing that between precipitate decay and internecine enmities the English-speaking family is destined to consume itself, and that with its decline the prospect of general pervasiveness, to which I alluded above, will brighten for the deep-lunged children of the fatherland."
> "Universal pervasiveness." We have heard a lot of this sort of thing during the last three years. My edition of the "Bundle of Letters" was, however, printed in '83, thirty-one years before Armageddon. . . . Provincialism is more than an ignorance, it is ignorance plus a lust after uniformity. . . .
> England and France are civilisation. They are civilisation because they have not given way to the yelp of "nationality." That, of course, is a debatable statement. All the same, they have not, at bottom, given way to the yelp of "nationality," for all their "Little England," "La France," "Imperialism," etc.
> More profoundly they have not given way to the yelp of "race." France is so many races that she has had to settle things by appeal to reason. England is so many races, even "Little England," that she has kept some respect for personality, for the outline of the individual.
> This is modern civilisation. Neither nation has been coercible into a Kultur; into a damnable holy Roman Empire, holy Roman Church orthodoxy, obedience, Deutschland über Alles, infallibility, mouse-trap.[21]

The concession Pound makes in his defense of this war for civilization—his "statement" on its behalf is "debatable"—serves mainly to reinforce his claim to membership in its cause. The dialectic he invites thereby and the self-qualification he offers enact values of rational circumspection that match up with the declared standards of the Allies' campaign. The reference to the multi-racial basis of modern France and its consequent need to "settle things by appeal to reason" establishes the ideology of post-Reformation, liberal modernity as the charter document of the civilization to which he seeks to belong. This rhetorical identity has run through the life cycle of its merely local opportunity, however, by the end of the passage. With an apparently unconscious irony, the tribal rant he proclaims against Deutschland as the enemy of

Britain expresses the same attitudes he otherwise exempts from the civility of France and England, which, he has just been at pains to point out, have refused to speak like this (of course, they have not).

This passage reveals a disaffinity between Pound's intellectual imagination and the rationalist standards of the English war that points to a different, truer, or less compromised line of relation to the language of the Liberal rationale. (The values of liberal, post-Reformation Europe remain nonetheless the most cogent framework within which to assess the import of the English war and the literary impact of its crisis.) The position from which he orients himself to the verbal culture of that partisan war may be sampled fairly in the tenth install-ment of a twenty-part, round-up account of current journalism that he under-took for the *New Age* in 1917.

He offers a report on the conservative *Chambers' Journal*, which his title labels "The Backbone of the Empire." "Madame," he gestures to this Tory journal's imagined readership, "one copy of this paper is sufficient to form your boy's character—and irrevocably. It is the Nelson Column, the Bull-dog breed, the backbone of the Empire, the Trafalgar Square among papers. I do not make mock of it."[22] The tonal complexity of this last statement involves the complication of Pound's endorsing the same war of which the Chambersites approve, but with their emblems of artless aggression: the Nelson Column, the Bull-dog breed. Such regalia stand manifestly at odds to the insignia of poetic aestheticism and imaginative originality that this poet identifies with the civi-lization for which the Chambersites are also fighting. He hints at these differ-ences more tellingly as the article continues, conceding a disparity on this mat-ter of verbal aesthetics more remarkable in the end for the effort he expends not to widen, but to reconcile it. "Style," he admits,

> is not for them; they are wholly impervious; to rally them on their rhet-
> oric would be as useless as trying to persuade a bronze lion with argu-
> ment. No true Chambersite would regard a problem with style as any-
> thing but immoral, a sort of absinthe, an aestheticism in the worst sense
> of the term. We must meet them on their own ground, on the high
> moral tone of their subject matter. (EPPP, II:288)

"We must meet them": whether or not Pound plays the double sense of con-frontation and collusion, he manifests a powerful attraction to the absolute conviction of right these Chambersites maintain for the English side in the war. The certainty that the American shares presents an equal zeal of belief in the imperial cause and a joint skepticism toward any niceties of verbal argument. His disbelief reaches silently but unmistakably to the Liberal Word at war, the aestheticized language of reason. This target appears in the livid image of lin-guistic anesthesia—the verbal absinthe—which, to Pound's taste, these Cham-bersites are right, at least demonstrably not wrong, in reviling. To rely on *ra-tio*nalization, to allow balance or harmony in argument to carry what is for the

Chambersite—now for Pound—a truth that should be indisputable: this Liberal practice betrays a weakness of spiritual allegiance with the English thing, an infirmity of political purpose from which the American must distance himself with all the force his otherwise unlikely alliance with the Chambersites requires. The apparently radical disparity of their manners and his programs reveals a need on Pound's part to cultivate, in the affinity he insinuates, the root truth of his own poetic identity and perspective. From the "backbone of the empire" he orients himself toward the verbal culture of the war, which will provide the sounding board for his poetry's adversarial response. This is the material he lays out, in his critical and documentary prose of the moment, in all of its demonstrable folly.

II

The Student of Contemporary Mentality

In July 1918, Pound looks back to the moment immediately preceding the war and views the journalistic culture of the dominant liberal consciousness. "[T]he *Nation*, chief envoy of the Dublin lower-class to the English suburban back-parlour," brought the advanced guard of social egalitarianism politely to bear on a middle-class readership. As genteel emissary, the *Nation* served as a strategic complement, in Pound's prescient gaze, to the journal with which it would eventually merge, "to the *New Statesman*, last refuge of doctrinaire committees." Here was harder matter, more intellectual stuff. Dominated still by those Fabian ideologues of material progress, Beatrice and Sidney Webb, the *New Statesman* featured an empirical tilt to its schemes of meliorist reason. It bore the lasting marks of those "statistic Webbs, the haven of Shaw's worn out theories" about progressive evolution, which, worn-out or not, proved as durable, or at least (in Pound's view) as dogged, as their author. While the closeness of affiliation with the Liberal party may have varied in these two journals, the degree of coherence that this culture of liberalism achieved is marked by the fact, in Pound's recollection, that "in every one of these papers a set point of view was demanded. To every possible question," he continues, "for every possible situation in life, art or politics, there was a carefully prepared, 'correct,' opinion. The writers for these papers knew to a jot just what was the *proper* view in every possible case." The emphasis Pound supplies goes silently but unmistakably to the one comprehensive logic, the "reasonableness" liberalism maintains as the dominant propriety in art and life.

"Suddenly," this cultural history continues, "hell broke loose," in August 1914, when

> the normal and comfortable conditions of occidental life were suddenly
> cast into confusion. There were cases for which no ready made answer

was available. On none of these antique staffs, or of these staffs suffering from premature senility (as the *New Statesman*'s), was there anyone
accustomed to form conclusions from external facts. Neither were their
editors acquainted with people of "that sort," i.e., people accustomed to
think from facts. They were "flummoxed."[23]

In Pound's calculation, the catastrophe revealed an intellectual mechanism for
what it was. Its "answers" had responded to problems unconstituted by "facts."
A set of *verbal* procedures merely, the linguistic machinery of these liberal
journals maintained the values of the Liberal party's stable constituency, a
middle-class well balanced in the attitudes of political and economic rationalism: those "normal and comfortable conditions of occidental life." In the instance of war, however, this conventional set of mind confronts the exceptional
"case," that is, an instance *fallen* (*casus*, "fall") from some defining ideal—here
the immense exception this war represented. The members of the generation
that Ogden labeled the "garrulous gerontocracy" had to manufacture more and
more language to discount the increasingly obvious disparity between word
and world. They were, indeed, "flummoxed."

Why set this otherwise idiomatic term resonating within those quotation
marks? So marked, "flummoxed" reaches back through its dialect sources to
call up the original onomatopoeic sense of clumsy fluster and the attendant
image of the country bumpkin—as unlikely a counterpart for England's intellectual gentry as it is risible. This personage merges the figure of the rural
clown, caught out by surprise in a rustic farce, and an academic clerisy, maintaining its theories and procedures despite all contemporary evidence to the
contrary. The state of perplexed persistence that Pound's verbal image fixes for
the condition of Liberal England at war adds a full and searching view to the
rueful humor it affords and to the profounder seriocomedy it represents. The
grand syllogism of history (and the English cause), that is, may be maintained
with an equal combination of earnestness and absurdity.

That paradox catches the tone of things. Pound clarifies its further literary
possibilities, moreover, as he examines its manifold record in the journalism of
the war. The twenty-part series that includes "The Backbone of the Empire"
presents in its overview of English periodical publications a portrait of the national character at war. In these "Studies in Contemporary Mentality," published throughout 1917, Pound draws an intellectual profile of an enislanded
and, now, embattled cultus. The dominant quality proves to be an indominat-
able reasonableness, a trait that appears most clearly for the duration in duress.

Thus Pound interrupts the wisdom of the *Quiver*: "Does the popular
'common sense' consist in the huddling together of proverbial phrases, with incoherent deductions, contradictions, etc., leading to yet other proverbial
phrases; giving the whole fabric a *glamour* of soundness?" (emphasis added).
The "glamour" Pound marks in the Quinn letter recovers its judgmental force

here, too, to underline a mispronounced ideal. A pseudogrammar, a quasi logic only shows in the "proverbial phrases" of this "popular 'common sense.'" The Word of public reason, which bespeaks the greater tradition of liberal modernity, speaks its corrupted utterances thus, in these "incoherent deductions, contradictions, etc." The same verdict emerges in the simpler instance of this sample passage, where he marks the centers of verbal attention:

> "Just as the coming of war linked up our far-flung" (not battle-line, but) "dominions, so it gathered together the members of my family, glad to have the common centre of a beloved home." The action of the adjective "beloved" is a little hard to determine. However, we must accept the metamorphosis from centrifugal to centripedal [*sic*]. The family mobilised. Pharmacy was, "of course," useful in hospital.[24]

Of the several phrases Pound's punctuation puts on display, "of course" stands out conspicuously, insofar as the words would seem, under usual circumstances, not to call attention to themselves. Yet the conclusiveness that the wording assumes has run no valid "course" of reasoning. "[O]f course" offers thus a defining, answering example of the "common sense" he has targeted by the same quotation marks as the unit and value of his analysis, aimed at a passage that samples the language fostered particularly by "the coming of war." In the commercial setting of a popular journal, this public "glamour of soundness" appears, in lieu of a solid grammar of logic, as a framed, stylized product, a sort of verbalist confection. The public taste that expects this candied language of rationality might be all too easily beguiled by the sheerest speech of sweet reason. And Pound proceeds to outline the cultural economy in which these needs are appealed to, and in which the meaning of one of the major figures of English public culture is revealed and deepened.

Pound assesses the immense success of the Sherlock Holmes stories in his piece on "The Strand." In this character, the store that Britain sets by the logical mind finds its primary icon, indeed its gigantistic type: "Sherlock with his superhuman strength, his marvelous acumen, his deductive reasoning . . . has all the charms of the giant." "He is also," Pound points out, "a moral Titan: right is never too right. The logical end of these likes is, or was, God."[25] Holmes's practice of moral rationality intimates a divinity as the conclusion of its methods and so recalls the larger sanction that the British liberalism of the nineteenth century conferred on it. There, a meliorist reason conceived the grand program of progressive and providential history and thought its way forward to its own destined end in the ultimate logos, the supernal Word and truth of God.

Pound's far-reaching analysis takes those liberal attitudes to their one climax and only climacteric, their ongoing apocalypse and sustained revelation in contemporary history. "Sherlock's peroration (supposedly, August 2, 1914) is a mixture of moving—prognostication of the 'cold and bitter' wind which will blow over England and wither many in its blast, and a hurry to cash a £500 cheque before the arrested spy (then actually in their Ford motor-car, and about to be taken to Scotland Yard) has time to stop payment. Watson is urged to 'start her up'" (*EPPP*, II:271). From the historical crisis England has reached in the first half of this passage, the deflection Pound registers in the second reads equally as a farcical sequel and an indictment, severe if oblique, of the sensibility Holmes's author has typified in this character. English reasonableness manifests an absolute inability to recognize, let alone deal with or correct, the accident it has just encountered.

A literary response to this moment in cultural time finds a likely model, in this last passage, in the signature incident of mechanical comedy. "Start her up": the engine of materialist and meliorist reason whirs on, impervious to the collision into which it has just entered with the main event of late modernity. The ethical, prudential reasoning Holmes exemplifies as his hallmark trait thus demonstrates, not only a failure to forestall the gruesome eventuality of war, but also and especially, in the face of its own irrelevance, the obliviousness of the automaton. Holmes's is the representative rationality, now laughably out of all measure. His reason-machine appears as fully risible as it is wholly undeterrable. The protagonists of the high drama of the former century, playing its logistical schemes and logical word to the best consequences, meet their contretemps in recent history thus, in Pound's irreverent casting, as a troupe of rude mechanicals.

Not the least of these is Holmes's author, who plays a signal role in this intellectual farce. "Sir Arthur," Pound gestures, "is as illogical as any other sort of fanatic. He is loud in praise of Sherlock's faculty for reason, but his own flesh or mind, or whatever it is, falls a little short of divinity" (*EPPP*, II:271). An out-of-ratio rationality provides the pattern for a grimly mechanical comedy, its institutional status echoing through the knighthood conferred on Conan Doyle, in the honorific title slyly observed by Pound. The agitated bathos of Sir Arthur's embattled rationality manifests at once the fallen condition of official usage and the insurgent, now-regnant convention of reason in burlesque.

Pound demonstrates this sensibility at its most comprehensive extent in the fourth installment in the series. He gathers the gradually expanding set of examples he finds for this language of ratio in extremis into an instance so representative that it exceeds the now-insignificant category of partisan ownership. "The 'Spectator' is by hearsay 'conservative,'" Pound opens, inserting between those marks of punctuational skepticism a distinction he proceeds to query: "It has 'dictated the conservative policy,' whatever that phrase may mean."[26] The irrelevance of partisan identity shows Pound a unity with the mainstream style of these times. The *Spectator* thus speaks a language most recognizable to him from the pages of the *New Statesman*, the liberal journal that he goes on to cite. Among the writers appearing here, he offers the primary type in the author we recognize now as the defining icon of English liberal rationalism, whom he invokes through this signature phrase. "And there, my dear Watson," he proclaims in mock-ironic discovery, aligning with those Holmes fictions the whole literary-intellectual-political culture he proceeds to sum up,

> we have it. I knew that if I searched long enough I should come upon some clue to this mystery. *The magnetism of this stupendous vacuity! The sweet reasonableness, the measured tone, the really utter undeniability of so much that one might read in this paper!* Prestigious, astounding! . . .
> . . . The "New Statesman" is what might be called a shining (if not rugged) example, in action, incipient, under weigh [*sic*]. Aimed at the generation which read Bennett, Wells, Shaw, Galsworthy, rather than Lord Macaulay, this weekly has done, is doing, the "same stunt," if we by so gutter-snipish and saltimbanquic a phrase may describe anything so deliberate as the on-glide of the successful and lasting "Spectator."
> (*EPPP*, II:270)

These formulations bear well the emphases I have added. A reasonableness that consists of "*measured* tone" only and so coalesces into the merest feeling of *ratio*nality, a logic as hollow as it is polished in presentation, well managed indeed in all its impressive "vacuity," its "stupendous" emptiness: these are the sounds of contemporary Liberalism at war, exposed at the extremity of Pound's ridicule in its vapid sagacity and absurd sententiousness.

Even in caricature, moreover, the sentences Pound selects as representative may be parsed to further, confirming revelation:

> Observe in the last quoted passage the gradual development of the idea of multitude. How tenderly the writer circles about it, from "large" to "legion," with its scriptural and familiar allusiveness; from "considerable" to "enormous," and then this stately climax, this old but never outworn or outcast comparison with the number of the sands of the seashore—measuredly refraining from exaggeration. . . .
> That is really all there is to it. One might really learn to do it oneself. . . . The "New Statesman" is a prime exemplar of the species, leading the sheltered life behind a phalanx of immobile ideas; leading the sheltered thought behind a phalanx of immobile phrases. This sort of thing cannot fail. Such a mass of printed statements in every issue to which no "normal, right-minded" man could possibly take exception!
> (*EPPP*, II:270)

The metaphors of mobilization and images of military formation suggest the connection between the hollow if polished logic of *New Statesman* prose and the logistics of this now-hallowed war. Given this insidious linkage, might—or should—one really learn to do it oneself?

The taunt also addresses, in the image of the Roman "phalanx" specifically, the record of Pound's current work. This figure echoes explicitly to the Latinate, mock-heroic vocabulary of his *Homage to Sextus Propertius*, which Pound is now composing,[27] and which, as we will hear in due course, represents an echo of the contemporary political ideolect. The simulation he enacts there (and reenacts here) represents an incentive worthy of the boast he whispers inside this challenge. Yet the aesthetic and ethical dare it represents has already taken him in a direction that registers, in its new and unusual character within his oeuvre, the novel and exceptional development this enterprise entails. The earliest record of this intent lies in the prose fables he composes from late 1916 to early 1917.

III

The Arranger of Inanities

"Jodindranath Mawhwor's Occupation," "An Anachronism at Chinon," "Aux Étuves de Weisbaden [*sic*]," and "Our Tetrarchal Précieuse": the titles Pound assigns these vignettes are not only striking. In their interlingual vocabulary and cross-cultural markers they strike a keynote. The English words that he surrounds with a foreign or nonce vocabulary sound all the stranger in this exotic company. These titles prefigure an art of linguistic defamiliarization. Domains previously unknown, fetched from afar or from thin air, reveal their strangest, most outlandish aspect in the schemes and patterns of the established language that Pound uses to access these imaginary areas. The protagonist in this adventure is the personage Pound assumes as his new persona, the prosaic character-in-voice he freshly adapts. He fits his traveler with the sturdy, serviceable, sensible shoes of an English prose, reasonable in the ways of an insular British character, but increasingly risible the farther he strays past his native limits, his own enislanded domain. Pound stages this verbal performance at no dark backward of space, however, no abysm of time. He plays at the present extremity of his 1917 England. His rationalist inanity matches up with the same tendencies he perceives nearby—virtually concurrently—in his "Studies in Contemporary Mentality." Here, the standard-issue reason of English Liberalism has ventured toward the equally foreign possibility of a Continental war and revealed the balance it is attempting to keep in terra incognita as a wobbly logic indeed. To this moment in political time, Pound's response coalesces into an imaginative literature that represents one of its first sustained registers. The dare the whole program entails, moreover, shows in the relative distance—of genre, of imaginary locales—at which it needs to be realized, at least initially. Pound has situated this literature sufficiently far away, in fact, to allow most of his commentators to overlook the record it presents of an essential moment in his poetic development[28] (and to

miss the precedent texts for the political imagination of *Propertius*, no less ostensibly remote from present provocations).

By the time Pound writes the fourth tale, "Our Tetrarchal Précieuse," his
practice proceeds to a culmination that acknowledges in its subtitle its more
particular, if now surpassed, literary source. The "Divagation from Jules
Laforgue" identifies the prototype he has also modified. The difference
catches the contemporary stress, the local accent of Pound's individualized
adaptations.

Pound has represented the main value of Laforgue's verbal imagination in
the term *logopoeia*. A making (poesis) out of language, the Greek heading refers
most indicatively to the manipulation of a given, restricted, or specialized
idiom. Pound outlines the qualities and possibilities of this method in his 1917
essay, "Irony, Laforgue, and Some Satire," where he casts the French poet primarily as a scold of established manners in language, always their skeptical di-
agnostician if sometimes their mischievous accomplice. His Laforgue "is, nine-
tenths of him, critic—dealing for the most part with literary poses and *clichés*,
taking them as his subject matter; and—and this is the important thing when
we think of him as a poet—he makes them a vehicle for the expression of his
own very personal emotions, of his own unperturbed sincerity."[29]

If the tuning fork of Laforgue's poetic music is, in effect, a set of quotation
marks, which places the representative phrase on display, so Pound's use of this
device strikes the timely note of his own appreciation. His Laforgue is "'verbalist'" (*EPPP*, II: 297). The prongs he puts around this word suggest its special contemporary resonance. Dora Marsden has offered its summary rebuke
on the linguistic debilities of contemporary Liberalism.

The term is sufficiently charged to invite and sustain an extended discrimination by Pound. "Bad verbalism is rhetoric," he motions to one side. This
negative valence carries the specific gravity of inertia, of inadvertence. "[T]he
use of *cliché* unconsciously" (*EPPP*, II:297) may thus pertain in his critique
equally to those characters of unthinking habit that Laforgue was taking off
and those automatons of logic that Pound has cast as the rude mechanicals of
the official Liberal Word. "But there is good verbalism," he rejoins, establishing the principle of the echo that talks back. Where this voice utters an idiom
specifically "distinct from lyricism or imagism" (*EPPP*, II:297), moreover, the
stipulation that Pound enters shifts from the ostensible reference in Laforgue
to the implicit instance of his own practice. "Lyricism" and "imagism" name
the primary models of his own poetic activity in the preceding years. To these
well-accomplished methods, the language he confabulates out of the current
political parole represents a difference so great that he needs to go to prose to
embody the novelty it constitutes.

The text Pound takes as the starting point for his "divagation" lies in "Salome," where Laforgue manipulates an idiom specific to Flaubert's historical
fictions. Detail-laden, exact and exacting in the probities of obscure reference,

those performances already sounded almost mock-scholarly: Flaubert could elaborate his own *penchant pour les mots et les choses recherchés* to an unwitting extreme. Thus Laforgue's parodic retelling of that manner finds its local habitation and name in the "Esoteric White Isles." To that antique repository, the antic riposte he offers moves into a signature image of authorial character: "Ordainer-of-the-Thousand-Odds-and-Ends."[30] This hierophant presides over a hodgepodge only, as the master manqué of particulars equally diverse and unassimilable. How Pound reorients this pseudochronicle and recomposes its persona shows in his creative translation of this French phrase, "l'Ordonnateur-des-milles-riens," in the title he confers on his own muse and likeness: "the Arranger of Inanities."[31] Orderly nonsense, a sort of sensible absurdity, this double measure presents the verbal performance he choreographs less as a remembrance of Laforgue's text—an antiquarian miscellany all in *dis*array— than as a record of those systematic absurdities, those protocols of seemly but merely reason-seeming logic, which Pound hears in British rationality at war.

The English accent in Pound's piece sounds clearly, once it is listened for, in the final sentence. While Laforgue's speaker reproves his Salome's "desire to live in a world of artifice and not in a simple, wholesome one like the rest of us,"[32] Pound takes the irony—as straightforward as the simplicity Laforgue so obviously mocks—and ties it up in a verbalist knot: his Salome has died "less from uncultured misventure than from trying to fabricate some distinction between herself and everyone else; like the rest of us" (*EPPP*, III:131). Beneath these apparent clarities of syntax and vocabulary, a sheerly nominal logic hardens into a paradox as impenetrable as it is laughably transparent. Pound's conceit nonetheless bespeaks the unreason deepening day by day, in the practice of an analogous nonsense, in the verbal rationales of current war discourse.

Pound has built this contemporary resonance into the last word of his series, moreover, through a number of topical references in the preceding three texts. In "An Anachronism at Chinon," for example, the Socratic dialogue Pound establishes between Rabelais and his student finds the timely context and point of its beforehand prank in the local moment of the Great War. He features a concern with the effects the public culture of conflict has exerted on language, in particular through censorship, whose exertions are replicated thus in dialogue:

> . . . some Rabelais
> To. . . . . and. . . . . and to define today
> In fitting fashion, and her monument
> Heap up to her in fadeless ex. . . . .[33]

If Rabelaisian scatology provides the obvious provocation for censorship like this, the literary case being invoked expands under the pressure of current circumstance with a sense of present general usage. "At present there is a new tone," Pound's counterpart observes from his own study of the contemporary mentality, "a new *timbre* of lying, a sort of habit, almost a faculty for refraining from connecting words with a fact." "Let us keep out of politics" (*EPPP*, II:213–14), Rabelais responds, aiming through the avoidance he counsels straight at the Liberal war that provides the underlying, ramifying occasion of their exchange.

In the ideal form of its Socratic paradigm, this exchange enacts a discourse that aspires to the highest kind of rational argumentation. The dialectic it exercises constantly modifies and refines the proposition under discussion to the point of a circumspect, well-reasoned conclusion. Where the spirit this format serves has been turned currently to political purpose, its intellectual travesty may identify the literary opportunity a writer finds in it. The *Nation*'s "Lucian" thus appropriates the formal possibility of the comic dialogue, which the Greek pseudonym offers him, but this scribe defaults quickly to the familiar liberal ground and argues his points of personal political grievance to conclusions in which he far too sincerely believes. The defining mark of difference in Pound's achievement shows him taking on the rationality of linguistic proposition itself as his target and urge, his animus and provocation.

"The Church has always been dead set against washing," Maunsier proposes in the colloquy of "Aux Étuves de Weisbaden." The conversation proceeds along the lines of a tightly formal inquiry, but that opening note augurs fairly the preposterous logic of the exchange. "St. Clement of Alexandria forbade all bathing by women," Maunsier continues. Whether or not the statement is true as fact, the method of its sensible development and reasonable exposition represents Pound's own sort of reductio—or elevatio—ad absurdum. His Clement

> made no exception. Baptism and the last oiling were enough, to his thinking. St. Augustine, more genial and human, took a bath to console himself for the death of his mother. I suspect that it was a hot one. Being clean is a pagan virtue, and no part of the light from Judaea.
>
> Poggio: Say rather a Roman, the Greek philosophers died, for the most part, of lice.[34]

To the "No Bathing Allowed" injunction of the early Church, absurder for the several recondite citations Pound's speaker furnishes in refining it, Poggio adds the further turn, taking the "rather" of oppositional refinement to the ridiculous instance he cites.

"*Civilized* man grows more frog-like" (*EPPP*, II:225), Poggio ventures later. A whole verbal culture resonates through the added emphasis: the word presents the value most heavily stressed and contested in the theaters of intellectual conflict. The partisan campaign of Liberalism associated civilization with the standards of procedural reason, the same protocols that Pound's speakers follow to his own seriocomic measure. As the froglike man of Poggio's civilization grows, and, as the consequence to this proposition, "his members become departmental," the conclusion that this protagonist of civilized reason has developed out of that emblematically ludicrous premise moves into the intenser inanity of Maunsier's two-word rejoinder: "But fixed" (*EPPP,* II:225). This fragment sounds as sententious in its apparent sagacity as it is absurd—as the *terminus ad quem* it affords to the argument. Hardly the better half of a Socratic dialogue, the gag line of a two-man vaudeville act puts on the last word of dialectical propriety. Pound represents in the exquisite buffoonery he performs the high farce that English Liberalism has already forced onto the conventions of rational dialogue.

"Sententious," Pound pronounces the Chinon piece soon after its appearance, "a bit dull."[35] He seems to blame his "Anachronism" for succeeding: the reason-seeming grandiloquence that he builds into these dialogues (at Chinon and Wiesbaden) catches its contemporary resonance, after all, from the hollowly pompous logic of the Liberal war; the emptier the sentence, the better the echo. Yet the dissatisfaction is accurate. Pound's impatience goes to the deficiencies of a simple mimicry. He is replicating the mechanism of dialectical logic in the to-and-fro exchange of the two conversants, but this imitation betrays a failure to forge a new form and language of imaginative critique, rather in the same manner that is manifest in Lucian's *1920.* The consequence shows a similar disability. Like Lucian, he cannot detach himself from the questions of the political day sufficiently to convert their vocabulary into the stuff of a new literary language. With an irony as immediate as it is unwitting, Pound's speaker proceeds to "speak in no passion," to

> say that the whole aim, or at least the drive, of modern philology is to make a man stupid; to turn his mind from the fire of genius and smother him with things unessential. Germany has so stultified her savants that they have had no present perception, the men who should have perceived were all imbedded in "scholarship." (*EPPP*, II:211–12)

While Pound may well find philology to be the signature idiocy of German academic comprehensiveness (the opinion goes back to his experience of the system in his study, to the master's level, in romance language),[36] this point of personal rebuke grows more virulent as a nationalist animus appropriates, animates, and expands it. The degree to which this propagandistic language takes over the passage may measure at once the dominant power of that political ideolect and the requisite strength of literary invention, which, in the manner of Dora Marsden's example, might turn this lingo of *Kulturkritik* into a poet's own "Mumbo-jumbo, Law and Mesopotamia." The fabling difference that some distance in linguistic or imaginative time might provide in the formation of an alternative literary idiom comes to Pound from Roman antiquity.

IV

Homage to Sextus Propertius

"I hope to God I have in my 'Propertius' escaped from all matters of politics, public instruction, uplift of America, etc. etc. etc.,"[37] Pound protests to John Quinn in late December 1918. Thirteen years later, however, memory reorganizes the same verse as a turn *toward* the determining pressure of contemporary history. *Homage to Sextus Propertius* thus "presents certain emotions as vital to me in 1917, faced with the infinite and ineffable imbecility of the British Empire," he recalls, "as they were to Propertius some centuries earlier, when faced with the infinite and ineffable imbecility of the Roman Empire."[38]

The two remarks together comprise the complex phenomenon of the poem's instigation and performance. In 1918, the noisy hortatives still echoing around Pound sustain his understandable need to distance poetic speech from the false consciousness of this popular ideolect. The involvements that the public language of mass war enjoin on this poet with the force of a demagogic politics (to which he is not inured) might well prompt the response he seems in 1918 to be reiterating—writerly flight into subjects of distant antiquity, which the first words of the sequence might promise:

Shades of Callimachus, Coan ghosts of Philetas
It is in your grove I would walk,
I who come first from the clear font
Bringing the Graecian orgies into Italy,
                    And the dance into Italy.[39]

In 1931, however, he claims the point of political contact too explicitly and politically to have invented the connection at this later date. Not that the later statement renders the earlier protest meaningless. His poem assimilated the political pressures he admits in 1931, but in a fashion that stands at manifest odds with the public language and attitudes from which he seeks to distance himself in 1918. The two remarks offer together some indication that *Propertius* may have found a novel imaginative language for the words of its own political day.

The polysyllabic, Latinate vocabulary in which Pound pitches his invectives in 1931 also recaptures the sound of political rebuke in Propertius's text. Pound's Propertius is not the poet who has excused himself, in the more endearing constructions of some modern commentators, from the false obligations of an imperial verse. He is rather a writer keyed directly into the sound of his times, which he reproduces on the off-note. Propertius already performs a sort of Laforguian tour de force on the established manners of social advancement in the court of Augustan poetry. The mock-heroic diction of his *Elegiae*, his parodic Virgilisms, the hollow triumphalisms and empty finishes of those all too heavily labored martial cadences; the august inanities, the "ineffable imbecility" Pound appreciates in 1931: all these features speak clearly in the Latin lines. The accurate representation Pound makes in 1931 also preserves a memory of the conceits operative in 1917–18: the psychopompery of the Liberal logos stirs again—and still—in the critical figure of "infinite and ineffable imbecility" that he inscribes thirteen years later. Here is the "stupendous vacuity" Pound registered in 1917 in the "sweet reasonableness" and "measured tone" of English usage in the Liberal war. The impression it made leaves a memory as irrepressible as Pound's own echoing ingenuity with it. One measure of Pound's inventiveness with this political idiom shows in his critics' steadfast inability to hear the reverse echo he plays in this verse.[40] How Pound sets a contemporary sensibility resonating in his text and elaborates its possibility in an imaginative language of comprehensive extent represents the timely—and enduring—achievement of his *Propertius*.

i

Of the various voices impinging on Pound's poem the partisan majority is Liberal, which represents the spoken consciousness of the dominant policy logic. The war this sensibility authored, however, also occasioned a less-specialized language of rationale. This generalized idiom of compensation and consolation echoes through *Propertius*, too, as further record of Pound's immersion in the vocal culture of this public moment. Consider as an initial instance these two verses from the Roman Propertius, where, under the glass shield of an excessive earnestness, the poet pledges to write a martial-minded verse:

> Quod si deficiant vires, audacia certe
> Laus erit: in magnis et voluisse sat est.

> But should strength fail me, yet my daring shall win me fame: in mighty enterprises enough even to have willed success. (Loeb translation)[41]

And then the curve on Pound's version:

> If I have not the faculty, "the bare attempt would be praiseworthy."
> "In things of similar magnitude
>   the mere will to act is sufficient." (*P*, 212)

"*[E]t* voluisse," "*even* to have willed": the nobility of sheer effort that Propertius pronounces in the mocking earnestness of one adverbial conjunction provides the dominant tone of Pound's whole performance. The note of strenuous hope that he redoubles in these phrases—"the *bare* attempt," "the *mere* will"— amplifies and exceeds the sense of the original to catch a truer rhyme, the more voluble sound of his own time. This heroism-in-despair-of-itself echoes reports from the Western Front. Sayings like these have rallied a populace day by day to the daily impasse and offered the solace of victory in spirit, in the nobility (alone) of mighty efforts (only). The quotation marks that Pound places around these phrases show him echoing his own time.

Of these contemporary mentalities, the writing style of English Liberalism takes the major place. Pound registers its preponderant pressure already in the opening verse paragraph of the poem, in an (ironic) invocation:

> A valeat, Phoebum quicumque moratur in armis!
>   Exactus tenui pumice versus eat.

> Away with the man who keeps Phoebus tarrying among the weapons of war! Let verse run smoothly, polished with fine pumice. (*GD*, 87, 89)

> Out-weariers of Apollo will, as we know, continue their Martian generalities,
>   We have kept our erasers in order. (*P*, 205)

Apollo reigns as deity over the partisan case for war, as we remember from the policy document the government issued in the privileged place of the *Westminster Gazette* in the editorial of 31 July 1914. There, the Serbian peasant, redressed from his appearance only several days earlier (in the same paper) in the lowlier mien of pig farmer and husbandman, assumes the likeness of the Greek god of logic (and poetry and music)—a discrepancy that measures the amount of help a case for war on his behalf really needed from the seemly reason of Liberal partisans. Pound works these contortions into a figure of his poem's verbal instigations, reworking the wording of Propertius's text to the extremity of this current situation, which provides his ironically inspired purpose. Apollo, that Liberal divinity, has been wearied and worn out, not by generals but by the *generalities* of war—by political abstraction. Arnold Bennett heard the same "generalities" as the parlance of censorship. Here, the abstraction of euphemism has emptied words, as it were, of specific and credible reference; "erasers" have thus become the ready instruments of Pound's expression. The reorientation he performs on Propertius's Latin text gives away the timely complaint: war has indeed suborned the work of current verse.

Pound rewords the Roman poet's protest, moreover, to redirect attention to further consequences, to a more exacting impact on the language of poetry. "Out-weariers" implies for the verbal exertions it depicts an extended temporal frame. This god of poetic logic presides over a continuous discourse, so that he performs his obverse work, not just on those tokens of specific reference, which come up blank one by one, but on the propositional, deliberative, statement-making function of language. Pound's Liberal Apollo tells his tone-setting role to this greater extent, where meaning supposedly coheres at its greatest reach. This muse—with his timely provocations—accounts for a style new to Pound's developing poetic range. It is "as if" there is serious meaning, but we cannot be sure if it is really there. The outlandish propriety of these verses, which combine the presumption of scholarly exactitude in antiquarian translation with slangy throwaways, catches the same conceit. There is a mock sententiousness, a capriciousness edged and offset by an urgency whose significance remains indeterminate—a poetics and prosody of pseudostatement.

English idiom plays a crucial role in this rhetorical fiction. The colloquial phrase references the reader to a zone of shared knowledge or common sense. This token of the known represents the main point of Pound's creative mutation. He takes his poetic cue from the odd logic of the Liberal war, which also attempted to make familiar the unthinkable, indeed, the unheard of. Pound replicates this negotiation in the transaction he undertakes between the assurances of his Anglo-American vernacular and a more exotic lexicon—an often imponderable set of references to classical mythology:

> Orphea delenisse feras et concita dicunt
> > Flumina Threicia sustinuisse lyra:
> Saxa Cithaeronis Thebas agitata per artem
> > Sponte sua in muri membra coisse ferunt:
> Quin etiam, Polypheme, fera Galatea sub Aetna
> > Ad tua rorantes carmina flexit equos.

> They say that Orpheus with his Thracian lyre tamed wild beasts and stayed rushing rivers, and that Cithaeron's rocks were driven to Thebes by the minstrel's art and of their own will gathered to frame a wall. Nay, Galatea too beneath wild Etna turned her steeds that dripped with brine to the sound of thy songs, Polyphemus. (*GD*, 88, 89)

> For Orpheus tamed the wild beasts—
> > > and held up the Threician river;
> And Cithaeron shook up the rocks by Thebes
> > and danced them into a bulwark at his pleasure,
> And you, O Polyphemus? Did harsh Galatea almost
> Turn to your dripping horses, because of a tune, under Aetna?
> We must look into the matter. (*P*, 206)

"Make it new": the aim that Pound famously extended to other translators hardly applies its advisory motto to this effort. The colloquialisms he imports may presume a conversational acquaintance with the classical *res*, but this familiarity appears superficial. Its cozy but wholly local knowingness enhances the otherness of these poetic materials, searched out it seems from the deeps of Mediterranean antiquity and served up in allusions more obscure for the sense he pretends they make to a contemporary readership. Who, most of us must ask, was Galatea? And how close did she get when she "almost" turned to the horses of Polyphemus? The precision this last interpolation claims resonates in the blank space that it reveals in the original Latin text.

Pound sets this rhetorical fiction of reason-seemingness going from his first interpolated word, "For." The conjunction he adds at the head of this catalogue adds a cause-and-effect sequence, a feeling of logical progression. It builds some presentiment of commonsense meanings, one that Pound complements with the reassuring words of common speech. He steadily undercuts this prescription, however, by enforcing the awareness that we do not know these mythological personages very well, if at all. "We must," yes, "look into the matter," but when we do, we see through the easy loquacity, the familiarizing fiction of interpolated phrases like these, and find the splendid emptiness of incomprehensible words. The sheer seemingness of meaning echoes most significantly to the background sound of these times.

This influence works with a pressure sufficient to ramify through a range of poetic applications. The verse line, the unit of value and attention for which Pound's place in the development of modernist prosodies is probably most secure, presents a particularly plastic, adaptable measure. He frames his response to current provocations in his rejoinder to this Latin passage, in a translation that gives his own lineation due importance:

> Multi, Roma, tuas laudes annalibus addent,
>   Qui finem imperii Bactra futura canent.
> Sed, quod pace legas, opus hoc de monte sororum
>   Detulit intacta pagina nostra via.

> Many, O Rome, shall add fresh glories to thine annals, singing that Bactra shall be thine empire's bound; but this work of mine my pages have brought down from the Muses' mount by an untrodden way, that thou mayest read it in the midst of peace. (*GD*, 88, 89)

> Annalists will continue to record Roman reputations,
> Celebrities from the Trans-Caucasus will belaud Roman celebrities
> And expound the distentions of Empire,
> But for something to read in normal circumstances? (*P*, 205)

The dubious value that "celebrities" brings to its first appearance redoubles in the terminal position of the same line, where the repetition replicates the self-mirroring, self-congratulatory character of the fame it claims. Into this echoing ring of English words, in effect, Pound shrinks the original domain of Roman imperial compass. Where empire "belauds" itself through verbal measures as hollow as the ceremony that Pound's antiphon encloses, moreover, he records the same provocations he will identify later as the source of this poem. The "infinite and ineffable imbecility" of the British (or Roman) Empire at war for the world echoes here. The dominion that its Word may have once claimed now dissipates in the dying fall, the diminuendo in repetition. This is indeed the end of the poetic—and historical—line.

115

Pound's alertness to current circumstance and its monumental folly shows in a poetic lexicon of critical figures. In keeping with this last example, the scheme of verbal—and global—enclosure inscribes the circle as one of the chief pieces of imaginative plastic. The hollow round of sounds he features in this scheme reappears in a series of tropes he has turned out of figures hardly so mischievously shapen in the Latin texts:

Surge, anima, ex humili iam carmine, sumite vires,
Pierides: magni nunc erit oris opus.

Awake, my soul! Ye Pierid maids, leave these humble strains and take a stronger tone; the work that waits you needs a mighty voice. (*GD*, 103, 104)

Oh august Pierides! Now for a large-mouthed product. (*P*, 212)

Nec mea conveniunt duro praecordia versu
Caesaris in Phrygios condere nomen avos.

[N]or has my heart power in verse severe to trace the line of Caesar to his Phrygian grandsires. (*GD*, 103, 105)

And my ventricles do not palpitate to Caesarial *ore rotundos*. (*P*, 213)

Nec mea tunc longa spatietur imagine pompa,
Nec tuba sit fati vana querela mei.

For me let no procession walk with long array of masks, let no trumpet make vain wailing for my end. (*GD*, 107, 108)

Nor at my funeral either will there be any long trail,
        bearing ancestral lares and images;
No trumpets filled with my emptiness. (*P*, 214)

Nec minor his animis aut, si minor, ore canorus
Anseris indocto carmine cessit olor.

[A]nd the melodious "swan," less lofty of accent, yet no less inspired when he sings the songs of love, sinks not to tuneless cackle like the "goose." (*GD*, 121, 122)

For the nobleness of the populace brooks nothing below its own altitude. One must have resonance, resonance and sonority . . . like a goose. (*P*, 224)

The cavernous vacancy these sound-producing circles inscribe in the first three excerpts redraws itself in the fourth as a mouth speaking *to* the people, as vox populo. The strenuously demagogic effort that the contemporary Word has undertaken to justify mass war stands behind these several images of resonant emptiness.

The hole Pound has shown in the logos of empire, moreover, he fills in with a timely and personal testament. Under his own name, he signs the art of erasure he has wrought out of this political moment. Among those "celebrities" who "ex*pound* the distentions of Empire," this poet is the celebrated figure, autographing this line in the single instance the epic poet has been permitted by tradition to appear in his work. His name also resonates as an emptiness: an "*ex*-pound" echoes the draining away of reference and meaning in the words of this time.

A prodigious vacancy, a "stupendous vacuity" of "sweet reasonableness," Pound's critical genius generates a poetic improvisation that comprises but exceeds the local, sometimes minutely textual applications on which we have focused. The inventiveness reaches to a degree commensurate with the scale of the provocation.

ii

The circle, which Pound turns into an image of hollow logic, represents his response to modes of argumentation most readily schematized as linear. Sequential and progressive, the grand plan of history has shaped the making of the Liberal case for war in a deliberated series of premise-(evidence-)conclusion. Pound measures the merit of those appeals as he reworks the trope into his figures of the voluble zero. As an instrument of critique, this image draws its force from perceptions that energize to literary application as well. From the ruined order of linear time, a new model for poetic temporality emerges in the *ricorso*, the circular return and refrain. Granted, the concentric circles configured in Pound's vortex have already imaged an alternative possibility to the straight line of time. In his prewar writing, nonetheless, the whirlpool presents a pattern more decorative than essential. Described in particular and local tropes, the vortex inscribes no organizational force in a poem like "The Game of Chess," which bears the subtitle "Dogmatic Statement concerning the Game of Chess: Theme for a Series of Pictures." Pound simply redraws the painterly figure to the shapes on the game board but leaves the argument his subtitle asserts undeterred from its own linear course.[42] Methods of progressive logic have met with their ghastly animadversion in the rationales of the current war, however, and its violence serves to undermine finally the structures of progressive and conclusive time in ideal history. Pound may now reorient his verse more searchingly and earnestly to the sort of temporal orientation the circular scheme represents.

In the first section of the poem, Pound exhibits a pattern reiterated over its sequence: a repetition of words or syllables that curves the narrative back on itself and knots its evolving process into points of specifically linguistic consolidation and interest. The invocations that Pound has entered into this overture,

> *Out-wear*iers of Apollo will, as we know, continue their Martian *general-*
> ities,

repeat in the last lines of the first part:

> Stands *gen*ius a deathless adornment,
>   A name not to be *worn out* with the years. (*P*, 205, 207)

The circle this opening section comprises anticipates a consistent effort on
Pound's part to avoid any semblance of linear narrative in the love story
Propertius tells and, so, to reorient the process of poetic time to a verbalist
scheme. Thus he repeats the key phonemes of this initial suite, returning in a
pattern that features an accruing variation of sense in the sounds it keeps
echoing:

> And *weary* with historical data, [the Muses] will turn to my dance tune.
> (*P*, 206)

> No keel will sink with your *gen*ius
>   Let another oar churn the water. (*P*, 208)

> Neither Calliope nor Apollo sung these things into my ear,
>   My *gen*ius is no more than a girl. (*P*, 213)

> We, in our narrow bed, turning aside from battles:
>   Each man where he can, *wearing out* the day in his manner. (*P*, 214)

> There comes, it seems, and at any rate
>   through perils, (so many) and of a vexed life,
> The *gen*tler hour of an ultimate day. (*P*, 217)

> And behold me, small fortune left in my house.
> Me, who had no *gen*eral for a grandfather! (*P*, 224)

This outline also presents the evidence of the incentive Pound will extend and
refine in the nascent project of the *Cantos*. He echoes ahead of time his version
of musical technique, where a refrain of words or verbal images sustains and inflects any one of the ongoing concerns of the longer poem. A framework at
once comprehensive and intensive, "musical technique" or "subject rhyme"
provides a way equally of concentrating attention on the particular and local
moment and establishing the recurrence of larger, architectonic themes. In the
Cantos, the figure of the Odyssean voyager, or the edifice of art's religion in
Malatesta's Tempio, reappears in the constantly if slightly altering form of its
recognizable words.

In the response this initiative represents to the specifically linguistic crisis of the Liberal war, which the documentary imagination of *Propertius* otherwise records, Pound reveals an essential dimension of his developing poetic intelligence. A skepticism about what language is and can do begets this technical complexity. He voices this suspicion already in the way that the thematic propositions in *Propertius* remain wholly musical, eluding any composite logic in their formation. Loose and cumulative as the comprehensive significance appears to be, meaning emerges mainly as an inference of the pattern the repetition comprises. While its cohesive sense remains elusive, the form creates nonetheless powerfully the *impression* of substantial and organized statement, that is, pseudostatement.

Destabilizing the meaning of verbal propositions in this way, Pound puts the same impulse to work on the reliability and authenticity of individual words. He displays this energy best perhaps in the labor of creative translation. In the series above, for instance, he performs extensive reorientations of the wording of the original text. These variations include an echoing of the Latin *ingenii*, "wit," in the cognate *genius*; a substitution—"gentler" for *mollior*, "easier"; and an extensive adaptation: "no general for a grandfather" wholly recasts *nullus et antiquo Marte triumphus avi* (no triumph from ancient Mars do I hail). The strain Pound places on the original sense of those Latin counters shows its effects most notably in the pattern of his English derivatives. The root syllable *gen* mutates, in repetition, to a radical disparity of meanings: *gen*eralities, *gen*tler, *gen*erals, *gen*ius. The significance of these differences goes back to the association that this core formation owns with notions of originality, of firstness. It is the attendant idea of the *gen*uine that the changing significance develops now to challenge, in effect wearing out the possibility of true, essential, or absolute meaning in this unit of speech. Adamantine assurance in words, some original Edenic equivalence between the linguistic integer and the whole referent:[43] these mythic aspirations certainly flourish under the archaeological conceit that Pound's antiquarian project assumes as his muse and mission in classical excavation. Yet the rhetorical adventure the poem conducts from beginning to end leads the reader down the long roots of this primary phoneme, the lengthening syllable of primacy, to nothing clearly primary at all. The art of erasure that Pound features takes aim at the principle of original, integral meaning.

Writing against the foundational myth of stable linguistic significance, Pound inscribes a charter of freedom from the rule of meaning that he also celebrates, as in the passages above, with a relatively high level of verbal spirits. He partakes of these energies as he realizes anew some of the older motives and hopes in his poetic agenda. His persistent attempts to analogize the poet's craft with the musician's or painter's turn on the ambitions he realizes so clearly here: to convert a vocabulary of regulated significance into the material of verbal plastic.[44]

Under the pressure of contemporary circumstances, then, Pound finds a powerful coadjutor in his work to further those items of long-standing importance, first in his own poetic program, ultimately in the agendas of modernist and postmodernist poetics. Yet an incident as convulsive as the war can hardly be expected to confine its effects to a short list of preconceived aims and desires. Its results comprise but exceed any programmatic specifications this poet might submit to the muse of history (well versed though he may be in the manner of the manifesto). Clio insists on bringing Pound to negotiation. The record of his interaction with his own times tells a story of adaptations, compromises, developmental *reorientations*—deflections at certain points, quantum leaps at others. The literary legacy of this momentous event in political and intellectual history entails first of all a change in the idea of poetic personality itself.

V

Propoundius: His Aftermath

"No trumpets filled with my emptiness": the disembodiments that *Propertius* executes so volubly range from the ghosting of its logos—in the empty references in which its myth diction specializes—to the erasing of its speaking subject. The "Propoundius" figure that this poet weaves out of the interactions between his primary texts and his modern improvisations appears as no discernible personage at all. Individual identity is at once doubled and canceled, variable in its manifestations and adaptive in its functions yet indeterminate completely as an expression of Pound's specific, historically grounded character. The lyric "I" that provides the readiest, most expressive stylization of his poetic personality in his early career has already survived a number of transformations. "I" emerges in *Propertius*, however, as a presence newly and wholly instrumental, not unexpressive but certainly nonessentialist. This development draws its force from sources deeper by far than the self-seconding work of translation. The violence being done to the language of reference and the logic of proposition in contemporary culture supplies the depth of a destructive drive on the basis of writerly identity, at least as conventionally constructed. Verbally derived, constituted as an entity through words correspondingly integral and reliable in significance, Pound's "I" has opened into the force field of current usage as the zone of its unmaking. Potentially, its remaking.

i

The reconceiving of authorial voice and identity that Pound undertakes in *Propertius* represents at once a response to the provocations of the political culture of the war and, from the results of that interaction, a method of addressing problems and needs increasingly clear from his developing work on the *Cantos*. The burgeoning scope and increasingly idiosyncratic nature of this project placed ever-greater strain on the character-in-voice, ready-made as it was, that Pound had called upon from the start to sustain it. Between the drafts of the first three (ur-)Cantos (1915–17) and their revision (extending from 1917 to 1919), the composition of *Propertius* intervenes. This development includes as its crucial breakthrough not simply the advantage most commentators credit to his labor in creative translation, that is, a more relaxed stance and a more expansive manner in the poet's imaginative relation to the materials of the past.[45] The change in *Propertius* and the echoing Cantos involves a revised understanding of the poet's own sensibility as a textual presence.

The novel development of *Propertius*—a style of signifying meaning that is jocoserious, urgent but indeterminate—emerges as a function and effect of matching qualities in its author's character-in-voice. This personage appears equally forceful and unfocused, all in all, a strong dominator of poetic consciousness but identifiable neither as a generic, historical, nor biographical individual. The "make-believe" dimension of his vocal character goes along with the "as if" factor in the poetic statements. This composite manner travels into the new Cantos as the freshest and most enduring method in the poet's resumed work. A wholly *potentialist* character shows now in its verbal citations, not only in thematic statements but in authorial presence as well. Unbinding the poet from the singular "I," unfixing the significance of individual words, loosening the logic of propositional sense: the difference the war makes in *Propertius* continues in the (resumed) Cantos. The revisions Pound performs on the ur-Cantos show this reorienting force most strongly.

Those earlier versions exhibit an increasingly strenuous exertion in responding to the problem Pound assigns himself in ur-Canto I. How can he use and, potentially, extend the model of poetic speech and individual consciousness that Browning has left the modern long poem, in his *Sordello*?

> So you worked out new form, the meditative,
> Semi-dramatic, semi-epic story,
> And we will say: What's left for me to do?
> Whom shall I conjure up; who's my Sordello,
> My pre-Daun Chaucer, pre-Boccacio,
>   As you have done pre-Dante?
> Whom shall I hang my shimmering garment on;
> Who wear my feathery mantle, *hagoromo*;
> Whom set to dazzle the serious future ages?[46]

The quest Pound sets himself aims at the creation of a single speaking presence. He underscores the legitimacy of this individual personage with the emphasis that the prefix *pre-* repeats: an earliness, a firstness, an originality, a primacy and indivisibility. A similar rendition on the same theme appears later, in

1917, in the *gen* topos he inscribes through *Propertius*. His earlier appeals seem undiminished by the ironically redoubling functions he sets going in the later text, however. The artifice he strains to claim in ur–Canto I, moreover, shows its limitations. The requirements that Pound assigns to his individualist sensibility there clearly outsize this functional construction. The widening frame of historical reference, the multiplying context of varied time deposits, all in all, the expanding frame of awareness in a modern epos: these conditions overwhelm any attempt to unify the materials under the rhetorical fiction of a single speaker. The result of this mismatch between task and capacity also appears clearly:

> The moat is ten yards wide, the inner courtyard
> Half a-swim with mire.
> Trunk hose?
>   There are not. The rough men swarm out
> In robes that are half Roman, half like the Knave of Hearts;
> And I discern your story:
>   Peire Cardinal
> Was half forerunner of Dante. Arnaut's that trick
> Of the unfinished address,
> And half your dates are out, you mix your eras;
> For that great font Sordello sat beside—
> 'Tis an immortal passage, but the font?—
> Is some two centuries outside the picture.
> Does it matter?
>   Not in the least. Ghosts move about me
> Patched with histories. (*P*, 229)

Self-sustaining, self-absorbed, Pound's self-presentation serves to crowd other stories out of the vocal spotlight, which he insists, instead, on training upon himself, on his own process of self-questioning self-response. For reasons as complex as those underlying the priority that Browning assigned his speaker, the modern epic needs to feature a subjective center in the construction of its material field. These determining conditions constitute a problem, however, which Pound cannot as yet solve. As he tries to energize the diverse materia poetica from the limited individual viewpoint, he turns back inevitably upon himself. He animates his own character-in-voice as the substitute subject of the poem.

Issues of linguistic psychology and ontology enrich the difficulty of Pound's task, as his overture indicates:

> Hang it all, there can be but one *Sordello*!
> But say I want to, say I take your whole bag of tricks,
> Let in your quirks and tweeks, and say the thing's an art-form,

Your *Sordello*, and that the modern world
Needs such a rag-bag to stuff all its thought in;
Say that I dump my catch, shiny and silvery
As fresh sardines flapping and slipping on the marginal cobbles?
(I stand before the booth, the speech; but the truth
Is inside this discourse—this booth is full of the marrow of wisdom.)
Give up th'intaglio method. (*P*, 229)

The "one *Sordello*" Pound discounts as a model consciousness for *his* poem does not exclude the principle of an individualized character-in-voice. The poet does not identify this construction with himself, however, insofar as Browning and Sordello do not comprise one entity. This poetic construction thus divulges the contents of individual consciousness, the "catch" Pound has drawn in, on areas peripheral or "marginal" to the author's existence. Yet the expressiveness of the writer's own feelings and thoughts remains the point of contested attention. Pound's ideal speaker does not converse with the general language or the common reader. Supraverbal or paralinguistic, this sensibility abides apparently, tellingly, and irretrievably inside the parentheses. The wholly inner validity of individual speech, the truth parenthesized and secreted "*inside* this discourse," need not reconfigure its "wisdom" otherwise, that is, to terms or requirements the reader outside this magic enclosure might be expected to recognize. The inherent resistance that this conception presents to a conventionally sensible linguistic expression accounts at once for the shouting match Pound has to enter in order to impose its flawed claims on public speech and the silence into which he finally resigns it—in the brackets of this signal statement.

A pattern of further inconsistency witnesses more interesting linguistic difficulties. "There can be but one," "But say," "and say the thing's," "say that I," "but the truth"—statement and alternative proposition, conjecture and rebuttal and synthesis: the gestures and methods of verbal reasoning appear, at the key coordinates of the passage, as the evidence of some overriding point in its strategic plan. Pound follows a process of self-qualifying, self-refining dialectic in order to adduce a single "truth" as its stated product, his conclusion. This residual faith in the efficacy of speech, of rationalistic and argumentative language in particular, belies the skepticism the passage otherwise expresses toward true and useful speech, most intimately and tellingly in the secret keep of that parenthetical silence. These oppositions are not staged or manipulated; they are displayed as an inadvertent but primary irony.

The main turn this verse will take comes then in the mock-logical ratios of *Propertius*. A new conception of linguistic (in)significance appears, ranging in its demonstrations from the referential to the propositional functions of language, from those catalogues of mythic unknowables to the pseudostatements of sheerly musical refrain. Freedom to regard authoritative reason as a provisional fiction coincides with new liberties in the presentation of its once-dominant author: the writer's superior ego may be handled, too, as just another piece of imaginative—verbal—plastic. An identikit, "I" offers uses that range from the instrumental presence it affords this poet (dodging and feinting between modernity and antiquity) to the high chicanery of a writer named Ezra Pound, signing himself off now as the "*ex*pound." Where liberal civilization voids its Word of the power to constitute its own supreme value, the rational individual, Pound finds a liberating energy, one that helps to embody in words a range of potential or virtual selves.

Of these personae, the most notable occurs in the reorienting of ur-Canto I (Canto II, in subsequent numberings). Pound extends the travel venture in the earlier version into the voyaging motif that will provide a unifying trope in the sequence. The sensibility of the open-ended series appears already in the personage of the journeyer. In this character-in-voice, he compounds the primary type of an Odyssean adventurer and a delineation more historically specific, the first among many—here, a demotic speaker and sailor from the merchant navy of a less mythic Greece. "The ship landed in Scios," the narrative opens,

> men wanting spring-water,
> And by the rock-pool a young boy loggy with vine-must,
> "To Naxos? yes, we'll take you to Naxos,
> Cum' along lad." "Not that way!"
> "Aye, that way is Naxos."
> And I said: "It's a straight ship."
> And an ex-convict out of Italy
> knocked me into the fore-stays,
> (He was wanted for manslaughter in Tuscany)
> And the whole twenty against me,
> Mad for a little slave money.
> And they took her out of Scios
> And off her course. . . .
> And the boy came to, again, with the racket,
> And looked out over the bows,
> and to eastward, and to the Naxos passage.
> God-sleight then, god-sleight:
> Ship stock fast in sea-swirl,
> Ivy upon the oars, King Pentheus,
> grapes with no seed but sea-foam,
> Ivy in scupper-hole.
> Aye, I, Acoetes, stood there,
> and the god stood by me,
> Water cutting under the keel.[47]

The comprehensive personality of the speaking consciousness includes Dionysus (the grapevine) and Odysseus as well as this ship boy. The god standing next
to him may configure the expansive possibility that the whole manifold represents. The same motive of multiplicity and inclusiveness appears as the aim and
implication of the wordplay Pound engages in his spelling. The shipmate's customary salutation—"Aye"—echoes through "I" and submits this nominal construction and the integral conception of self that attends it to all the numinous
indeterminacy that the voyage promises. This metamorphic potential maintains
as its condition the unfixity of phonetic and linguistic signals, like these. The instability of verbal reference that Pound witnesses in this local instance he complements in the larger dimension by the dissolving of logical proposition itself.
Note the absence of any attempt to unify the passage under a language of rationalistic stratagem. He shows the reprieve he has won from the constraints of a
comprehensive or expository logic already in the looser, more easily cumulative
progressions this series of paratactic clauses reveals. This newfound freedom
anticipates the prosodic energies he will remodel throughout the *Cantos*.

Hypotaxis collapses under forces that register more than a technical-
experimental incentive, however. The process draws on all of the resources of
Pound's historical experience, already so amply chronicled and analyzed in his
critical and documentary prose. This full development offers one account of
the discrediting that a rationalistic syntax and grammar have met in the prosecution of the Liberal war. The significance this event contributes to his poetic
project may be assessed, then, through the asking of a single critical question:
What is the difference between the paratactic cadences of the revised Cantos,
which *Propertius* precedes and for which it provides, and the measures resembling these in the prewar poetry?

ii

Pound's imagist verse generates a rhythm and an idiom that appear to be working in the service of aims allied with his later practice: an indeterminacy in verbal meaning, and an analogously expansive character in the speaking subject.
Yet these qualities appear clearly only to a critical sensibility reading backward—from the vantage of *Propertius* and the post-1917 Cantos. A close reading of the earlier work reveals the difference.

The poems of Pound's imagist phase move routinely to a climactic moment. He has nearly conventionalized this rite of closure already by 1912. His
finale typically synthesizes the line-by-line sequence of sensory details into a
comprehensive impression, a kind of minimal epiphany, a final image:

> April
> *Nympharum membra disjecta*
> Three spirits came to me

And drew me apart
To where the olive boughs
Lay stripped upon the ground:

Pale carnage beneath light mist.

Gentildonna

She passed and left no quiver in the veins, who now
Moving among the trees, and clinging
    in the air she severed,
Fanning the grass she walked on then, endures:

Grey olive leaves beneath a rain-cold sky.

The Encounter

All the while they were talking the new morality
Her eyes explored me.
And when I arose to go
Her fingers were like the tissue
Of a Japanese paper napkin.

Liu Ch'e

The rustling of the silk is discontinued,
Dust drifts over the court-yard,
There is no sound of foot-fall, and the leaves
Scurry into heaps and lie still,
And she the rejoicer of the heart is beneath them:

A wet leaf that clings to the threshold.

In a Station of the Metro

The apparition of these faces in the crowd;
Petals on a wet, black bough.[48]

The transaction Pound records in each of the final lines represents a possession
of the poem's perceptual events in linguistic metaphor or metonymy. "Her fingers were *like* the tissue," while "these faces in the crowd" appear—as "The
apparition"—*like* "Petals on a wet, black bough," and so on. Impressionistic as
these figures may be, the verbal net catching the associations appears equally
flexible and tensile. The more elusive the material of consciousness appears, indeed, the greater the strength of the word laying claim to it. Pound gives away
no faith in language to catch the significance of the represented experience.
While the last two poems accumulate their details in a paratactic syntax and lineation, the comprehensive gesture of their finales works to the same purpose as
the more conventional, linear, propositional syntax of the first three (the third

is periodic, hypotactic). The consciousness in which these poems culminate, moreover, offers no bundle of anonymous functions. An individual subject speaks these pieces. Pound invokes this presence when he describes the process that the poems record as the trajectory inscribed "when a thing outward and objective transforms itself, or darts into a thing inward and subjective."[49] Toward this destination, the rhythms build typically if quietly: to an epiphany, which signals the ordinal presence of the romantic ego, a sensibility from which Pound speaks, usually if not always under the form of the lyric "I." This self-presentation finds its chief instrument in a language fully endowed with the capacity to name. Ontological confidence is running as high as Pound's belief in the representational capacity of language is deep, latent but residual, resilient, and sufficiently strong to underwrite these experiments in self-representation at the delicacy of awareness they depict.

The strain the war places on his poetics may be gauged in the first poem that Pound publishes in response to the provocation its title identifies, "The Coming of War: Actaeon" (March 1915). The initial image runs through a new range of mutations:

> An image of Lethe,
>   and the fields
> Full of faint light
>   but golden,
> Gray cliffs,
>   and beneath them
> A sea
> Harsher than granite,
>   unstill, never ceasing;
> High forms
>   with the movement of gods,
> Perilous aspect;
>   And one said:
> "This is Actaeon."
>   Actaeon of golden greaves!
> Over fair meadows,
> Over the cool face of that field,
> Unstill, ever moving
> Hosts of an ancient people,
> The silent cortège.[50]

Whereas the practice of the prewar image tended to allow the individual line to coincide with a unit of grammatical and referential sense, the 1915 lineation tends to isolate and fragment the details and qualities of sensory perception, unhinging them equally from each other and a continuous, cohesive syntax. These verbal particulars are suspended against the white space of the page.

There is no statement in the poem, no sentence that comprehensively formulates its details, feelings, or perceptions. The more expansive ratios of verbal logic have contracted thus as an operative prosody, collapsed in fact as an entelechy or shape-making force. The impact of this development shows in the epic bleakness that Pound achieves in the final prospect. The scene is recognizable in its general visual lineaments as a type of the sublime, a condition that Pound's poem instances as a more particular, radical manifestation of language.

As one of its primary locations in the Enlightenment, the sublime occupies a verbal site. Presentiments of terror and beauty commingle in the absence, more powerfully the abyss, of linguistic reason.[51] An expanse unmapped by the designs of rationalistic language enthralls. The atmospheric prospect of the finale, as it were the picturesque sublime, thus complements and concludes the linguistic action of the poem, which coalesces to "silen[ce]"—to the statement it cannot make. This indifference of words to the needs of reasonable meaning records an experience of the illogical, unspeakable profound.

These distinguishing effects concentrate in the questionable presence of the poem's speaker. Perhaps the exclamation responding to what "one said"— "Actaeon of golden greaves!"—provides some memory or forward echo for the accent grave Pound edges over the French word into the silence of that final prospect. Do two marks of punctuation consolidate a living speaker? Pound gathers no vocal sensibility as specific (and continuous) as the one underlying and unifying the progressions in the poems of the prewar image. The once-identifiable, sensible representative Pound extended to his imagist verse as his counterpart-in-voice does not appear. The speaking ego has lost its self-endowing, self-constituting Word. The individualist premise behind the earlier poetic is being let go through this "image of Lethe," released as it were through the waters of forgetfulness to lose any confident recollection of the self that "I" once consolidated through reliable verbal references and logic.

This development seems instinct already with a sense of its poetic potency. "The Coming of War" serves certainly to erase the dominance of the writerly "I" that so complicates the developing project of the Cantos; already in March 1915 Pound intimates those possibilities of multiple identity that he will begin to evolve into the manifold consciousness of the Cantos. Yet these eventualities are far from swift in their realization. In early 1915, Pound is still drafting the ur-Cantos. He will not submit these efforts to revision for at least two years. The delay suggests that he finds these awarenesses difficult to reconcile with the direction of his earlier development.

This story of personal reorientations ramifies into a tale of modernism in dispute with itself, in dialogue with history. Surely, the talents Pound gathered around himself in prewar London could be grouped (from his viewpoint) under the standard of articulate individualism, a banner flown in the title and subtitle of the *The Egoist: An Individualist Review*. This programmatic value interacts with the challenges set for it by the conditions Pound has accurately graphed—and taken advantage of—in the state of Liberal England at war. This context provides the setting for a new account of English literary modernism. On this critical score of expressive individualism a plot evolves, one that needs to be spelled out from a historically informed understanding of this unit of salient value. Its status changes, utterly, between its pre- and postwar calculations. Pound exhibits this difference in the record of critical opinion he has left on a writer whose importance for him seems, otherwise, unlikely in the extreme.

iii

Jules Romains is the poet of Unanisme, a loose grouping of heterogeneous talents that concurred nonetheless in espousing ideals of generalized consciousness. Public by profession (if far from populist in its stylizations), this impulse to express nonindividual sensibility comes under no obvious notice of contradiction in the round-up review Pound performed on it, featuring the example of Romains, in February 1918. He accepts the French poetic *à la lettre*, conceding the claim it makes to voicing "the poetic consciousness of our time." "The best poetry has always a content," he proposes in endorsing Romains,

> it may not be an intellectual content; in Romains the intellectual statement is necessary to keep the new emotional content coherent. . . .
>
> > Je suis l'esclave heureux des hommes dont l'haleine
> > Flotte ici. Leur vouloir s'écoule dans mes nerfs;
> > Ce qui est moi commence à fondre.
>
> This statement has the perfectly simple order of words. It is the simple statement of a man saying things for the first time, whose chief concern is that he shall speak clearly. His work is perhaps the fullest statement of the poetic consciousness of our time, or the scope of that consciousness. I am not saying that he is the most poignant poet; simply that in him we have the fullest poetic exposition.[52]

In this analysis, the "intellectual statement" of poetry appears at once extrinsic and necessary to the core of the poetic experience. The inner "emotional content" of the poem relies upon a "statement" to which, by all evident measures, it bears no internal or essential relation. ("I am the happy slave of men whose breath / Hovers there. Their wish hides in my nerves; / That which is me begins to fall apart.") A surface order of words, a sheerly verbal logic, operates opportunistically or provisionally and, in its dissolution, obviously augments the "emotional" associations to which it orients the reader. Pound's characterization reveals a nearly exact congruence to the scheme of pseudostatement, where Richards outlines the work that poetry performs in terms of just such an equipoise of opposite forces. Where this formula has pointed to sources in the verbal culture of the political war, Pound's approval goes to a recognition of the possibilities that his own English situation extends for a new poetry. He reclaims and validates its historicity, using it to understand and appreciate a poet who has indeed produced "the fullest statement of the poetic consciousness of *our time*."

The timeliness of this appreciation shows through the evolution of Pound's view on this poetic subject. In 1913, he patronized Romains's poetry as "very fine and intoxicating rhetoric, no doubt." He dismissed it in fact as specifically anachronistic: this verse "harks back to the pre-Victorian era, when Shelley set out to propagandize the world. It is of the time of Leopardi. If Romains had lived earlier he would have written *Night thoughts on Death and Immortality* or on *The Grave*."[53] In 1913, Pound could not respond to a poetic voice and manner whose import and resonance belonged, for him, to a history that had not yet happened.

While the recondite passion of Pound's later analysis manifests his inwardness with Romains's sensibility, the identification remains incomplete. An ambivalence lies inside the antithesis he proceeds to imply, in noting that "[t]he opposite of Lewis's giant" (*EPPP*, III:51) abides in these lines. Something of contour and grandeur has been lost, or inverted. Not the collective gnosis Pound uses Romains to typify, certainly not some colossal embodiment of the public res, "Lewis's giant" presents—in an enlargement proportionate to its value—the principle of radical individuality. The giant typifies the superior ego, which Lewis asserted as the center of artistic awareness. Where Lewis drew this value into various visual designs, Pound perceived—and named—it in the figure and blazon of the vortex. Its apex locates a point at which the energies of a surrounding field, which is equivalent to a social collective, discover a formal signature as distinctive as its focusing agent's.[54] This subject suffers erasure under the conditions of recent war, not only in its mass character but through the subtler underminings of the individual's capacity for self-definition through integral words, intact rationalizations. Pound meets these developments with reservations more extensive than the objection this single antithesis whispers into his critical text. The demise of this gigantistic ego represents a point of ramifying complication for his developing poetics. The tension shows in the dialogue he tries to establish between these two rival colossi, Romains and Lewis.

"Among all the younger writers and groups in Paris, the group centering in Romains is the only one which seems to me any where nearly so energized as the *Blast* group in London," Pound continues in the February 1918 piece. The commensurate energies he observes in the two movements, he claims, define a force of attraction between them. Unanisme thus comprises "the only group in whom the writers for *Blast* can be expected to take very much interest" (*EPPP*, III:53). He relegates their differences to the more superficial dimen-

sions of their main representatives: "Romains in the flesh does not seem so en-
ergetic as Lewis in the flesh," he concedes, "but then I have seen Romains only
once and I am well acquainted with Lewis." Pound has to admit that "Romains
is, in his writing, more placid, the thought seems more passive, less impetu-
ous." Yet he reconfigures the difference upon which the evidence otherwise
insists. "As for those who will not have Lewis 'at any price,'" this piece of literary brokerage goes, "there remains to them no other course than the acceptance of Romains, for these two men hold the two tenable positions: the
Mountain and the Multitude" (53). These distinctions do not appear superficial, but Pound wants them to be immaterial. In these two tropes the dual figures hold commensurate import.

More pleadingly, Pound seeks to appease a difference that remains as tense
as the antitheses he is attempting to undo. Thus, "It might be fairer to Romains
to say simply he has chosen, or specialized in, the collected multitude as a subject matter, and that he is quite well on a mountain of his own" (*EPPP*, III:54).
The generalized sensibility Romains has grounded in (his idealization of) the
corporate mass is being lifted to the lofty solitude of Lewis's individual.
Pound's effort, however, presents the only undeniable element in the proposition. The syntax of discrimination and alternative evaluation witnesses a strain
that tells most about Pound's own compulsive urge. He needs to attach to his
new enthusiasm for Romains's group a value formerly professed in his affiliation with Lewis's. He must recover for his own poetic practice a condition he
once asserted as primary and essential. He reaffirms this quality through his
erstwhile alliance with Lewis. He protests too much in this review, however, because he has resisted too little in practice. In his commerce with the tendencies
Romains represents, he fears, he has lost that ordaining strength, which, in the
disintegration of the writerly "I," locates the real growing point in his development since 1917. He registers thus a developmental difficulty in the history of
English literary modernism that he is living, recording, and (arguably) forming.

This story begins at least as early as May 1917, when Pound corresponds
with his American friend Edgar Jepson. He sets out his editorial vision for the
Little Review, the magazine in which the prose fables he has written will soon
appear—alongside Eliot's 1917 verse, which answers to the same conceit.[55]
"My corner of the paper is BLAST," he avers, establishing a continuity he proceeds immediately to qualify, "but BLAST covered with ice, with a literary and
reserved camouflage. (I mean, that's what I want: a classic and impeccable exterior: ——— enunciated with an exquisite politeness. BLAST in which the exuberance has given place to external decorum of phrase.)"[56] The conventions
governing the first publication of this letter in 1950 point up the true ambivalence of Pound's original formulation. The objectionable word the censor
deleted threatens to disappear equally beneath the order of formal decorum
that Pound promises for his new usage. He wishes certainly to preserve and

even nourish the impulse this profanity represents. The "politeness" he desires, moreover, edges this motive with a potentially "exquisite" irony in its expression. Silence, however, leaves open a real question about the pressure and effectiveness of this alien presence.

The problem may be detailed further. The "camouflage" and the "classic and impeccable exterior" in which he images a surface order of words bespeak an origin and reference point in the culture of the war. "[C]amouflage" still owns associations with the conflict, indeed with an artistic involvement in the military campaign, insofar as Picasso and other cubists designed those disguises.[57] Pound pushes this connection to his own "literary" focus, moreover, and forms the issue in terms specifically English. Thus he reformulates the conceit of the Liberal war, whose guising ruse of pseudostatement included all the proprieties of conventional sense, which featured, in its reason-seemingness, a sheerly "*external* decorum of phrase." Under this camouflage, the artist may smuggle his "shit," but in order to . . . what? To prove he can do so (like some juvenile bathroom prank)? Simply to undermine its own propriety in execution? Or to intimate some area of awareness alien to that formal order, rather in the same manner that, in Richards's formula of pseudostatement, a logical form on the verbal surface of poetry comports and contrasts with the otherwise unexpressible emotion? This conceit will drive a considerable literary output, both in Pound's recent and ongoing work and in the emergent verse of Eliot. A nervousness of assertion, however, emerges as the most interesting and telling point of this promotional preview. A little memory here serves to reveal his deeper unease about the cover he wants to assume.

Compare the presentation of "shit," in the well-mannered exchange Pound prescribes in 1917, with the headier, wholly unapologetic proclamation of his early (16 February) 1914 promotional essay, "The New Sculpture." To the "smooth answers" of conventional attitudes and their apposite practices in literature, Pound avers for his radical group, "we have nothing to say but '*merde*'; and this new wild sculpture says it" (*EPPP*, I:222). Unpulled, the punch of *merde* puts a Frenchified spin on the avant-gardist's Continental pose. To this sensibility, the lines of opposition are uncomplicated: a wild and vitalist defiance, supplied by the individualism Pound identifies as the high line of value in this avant-garde temper, moves against the entrenched and habituated mechanism of social polity and conformity. At the later date, however, in May 1917, he compels this same rebellious spirit to speak in the language it used to revile.

Protesting in 1917, Pound fears that he has given away the autonomy and power of a consciousness that is uninvolved in the inherited sensibility of linguistic convention. The speech of pseudoreason in Pound's prose fables appears utterly unassignable to an individual. The personage delivering those mock-logical catalogues in *Propertius* appears equally indeterminate. "I" disintegrates also in the revisions Pound will perform on the ur-Cantos. In an effort at intrinsic consistency, he attempts in 1917 to assign to a linguistic medium the resistance he earlier accorded to an individual intelligence. Does he not fear, however, that he has signed away this adversarial strength? The question marks the evolving complications of a modernist literary art.

VI

The Decay of This Generation

This account of literary history comes thus to the critical narrative of the consequences the Great War wrought on Pound's earlier model of modernism. To follow the evolving complications his own register marks is to gain some solid cognizance of the real density and increasing complexity of the energies identifiable with this movement. We may acquire thereby some profounder sense of the historical content of literary modernism in England.

Pound has left this record in prose as well as in verse. In his literary reviews and promotional writings, a pair of terms recurs with the insistence a modernist art must show in claiming the timeliness that is its primary, defining condition. The words "decade" and "generation" repeat with his need to speak from and for an acutely time-mindful state in himself and his contemporaries. While the first term refers most evidently to the present decade of the 1910s, the force of insurgent, counterconventional energy that Pound locates in his representatives of this moment calls up all of the associations of sheerly physical, procreative vitality in the second word. Pound's "decade" also enters into a back-and-forth, cross-talked exchange with the precedent decade of the 1890s, which is (arguably) the first interval in literary and cultural history to be conscious of itself as such, and with whose signal figures and (supposedly) defiant stances he converses revealingly through this period.

Pound is attempting to consolidate for himself the quality of novelty that must constitute a modernist art. What the war does to the language and character of this claim is the story these prose writings tell. And the complex fate he relates in the process of its long realization over the course of the war is told in the intensified present of its end and destination, in 1920, in *Hugh Selwyn Mauberley*. This is a work whose timely memory and contemporary resonance may be recovered through the background narrative that Pound's prose writings recite. In its autobiographical fiction, he implements a figure of self-division—he splits his own poetic character into the double personage of E. P. and Mauberley—that records more than the story of a modernist at odds with himself. Properly situated, as an echoing extension of the engagements he relates in the prose of the preceding years, this poetic sequence may be read anew as the record of a modern*ism* in collision—and dialogue—with history.

i

In mid-July 1914, Pound writes a review of the recently published *Dubliners*. He esteems in particular Joyce's Flaubertian concision of language, a verbal surface highly polished, equally accurate. Specificity invigorates a linguistic texture of shaped and stylized references. These values coincide entirely with the attitudes of Pound's imagist verse. He merges the achievement he appreciates into a story of joint enterprise. His record of the program he shares with Joyce combines, moreover, with the testament he offers to its primary, necessary condition: its timeliness. "The spirit of a decade strikes properly upon all of the arts," he avers. "There are 'parallel movements.'" Thus, in practice, "Mr. Joyce's more rigorous selection of the presented detail marks him, I think, as belonging to my own generation, that is, to the 'nineteen-tens,' not to the decade between 'the 'nineties' and to-day."[58] He defines the moment of literary and cultural history that he occupies with Joyce by insisting on the *difference* it exhibits to what has gone before. He intensifies this distinction by drawing not just one line through a wide compass of time but several lines through recent times. These minute calibrations certainly further the sense of specificity in the current instant. If modern*ism* adds to the merely chronological situation of being modern an acute and defining sense of difference from what has gone before, of belonging to one temporal locale and not another, this last passage reads as one of the initial, initializing configurations of its myth—and a promise of the problem it cannot help but encounter.

The difficulty of accommodating change when earlier novelties have already been enshrined appears only two weeks later, on 1 August 1914, the last Friday before war. The international crisis rising from mid-July has certainly heightened one's perception of time. It is an interval marked indeed with the insertion of a new temporal order or, rather, the experience of a shift from an older to a newer rhythm and pace: the novelty of electronic communication among the diplomatic capitals throws into confusion the process and logic of former diplomatic protocols and augments greatly the feeling of crisis.[59] The impression of some accelerating change, of time picking up its pace, is inescapable at this time. In apparent synergy, in "The Glamour of G. S. Street," Pound qualifies the distinctions he drew earlier in July. The representative work of the 1890s that Street provides now posits a model for Pound's own decade. The difficulty he experiences in making this shift, however, provides this piece its interest and significant texture.

"The generation of men who have preceded me is in the main so loathsome," Pound's positioning begins. In its evident extremity this statement includes an opportunity and indeed the necessity of an adjusted view, opening the space of the negotiation into which he proceeds to enter immediately after repeating its virulent rebuke. "The very mention of their names fills me with such a nausea," he continues, "that I am glad of a change. It is a demand of the system not a mere craving for the bizarre that leads me thus to risk the scorn of my contemporaries and speak well of a book written in the "nineties' or even in 1900. 'The older men are such lice.'"[60] Within those rebarbative marks of quotation, Pound places the same attitude he expressed at the opening of the review, now framing the attitude of *his* contemporaries as the target of address. Thus he obscures firm oppositions; he destabilizes any absolute valences. The relative freedom of intellectual movement that ensues shows him reaching out to an aspect of the earlier age that attracts him in a measure equal, it seems, to its prohibitiveness, to its apparent unlikelihood for "the young men of my decade," who

> with our coarser touch are too prone to abridgement, we do not make ourselves so amusing. Mr. Street is never in haste. . . .
>
> All these and a world of minor matters are explained to us. I feel we should revive Mr. Street. I feel that we of this generation should turn toward him. . . . He spreads before us such a world. . . .
>
> . . . One envies Mr. Street his great patience. One feels that his decade may have something said in its favour. Or perhaps not his decade.
>
> One feels rather that he may have something which we sorely lack in our own decade. We are perhaps too prone to name the detestable, to BLAST it outrightly. (*EPPP*, I:272)

Street's largesse bespeaks the grace and ease of an established cultural class, its facility deriving from its familiarity with convention and tradition. These values appear so antipathetic to the emergent temper of the *Blast* generation that Pound must leave the possibility Street defines entirely in the mood of the personal subjunctive. The Street sensibility marks a kind of minor or private case desire, which Pound would like nonetheless to parlay into the developing identity of the movement. Where this lively environment of late July reveals an implicit but irresistible connection to the imminent war, the sense of change attending it fairly augurs the upheaval of that next event and anticipates its profoundly altering force and effect on the modernism of Pound's generation and decade. This development will bring their art, Street-wise, into closer complicity with the conventions reigning in its day.

Pound chronicles this process and his fear of accommodation as he evolves his "decade-generation" topos over the course of the immediately subsequent years. The key words repeat but alter their meanings categorically. *Generation* leaves behind the sense of productive strength from early in 1915 and picks up the latent but ready association of life cycles, mortality: "There is perhaps no more authentic sign of the senility of a certain generation of publicists (now, thank heaven, gradually fading from the world) than their abject terror in the face of motive ideas."[61] And *decade* undergoes a shift in value so extreme that this new meaning has to mutate from a different root. *Decus*, "ten," yields to *decadere*, "to fall away," thus to "decadence."

One of the values in the recent revival of critical interest in the phenomenon of literary decadence has been to fix the definition—or, rather, the slippage—in this term. While the sense of a fall from an established standard is the ready association, as David Weir point outs, the norm from which this lapse occurs may range from the codes of bourgeois propriety to those of romantic individualism.[62] Accordingly, the style assumed by decadents may be that of an avant-garde fringe or a retrograde center. When rebellion is conventionalized, after all, convention becomes rebellion (Wilde presides over this paradox). The term is relational, that is, rather than referential, and in this function it operates already and first of all for Pound as a register of differences, in his case, a measure of change. And it serves in this respect to reflect the reversing—ultimately, the decaying—of the energy of the generation that Pound saw in its most representative form in himself.

"An age may be said to be decadent, or a generation may be said to be in a state of prone senility," he resumes in the same essay in 1915, "when its creative minds are dead and when its survivors maintain a mental dignity—to wit, the dignity or stationariness of a corpse in its cerements. Excess or even absinthe is not the sure sign of decadence" (*EPPP*, II:4). Where "absinthe" appears as the emblem of an artistic decadence, Pound's last sentence seeks to preserve this positive and valorized image from the wrong sort of decay, the mortmain the members of that elder generation display as the rule of their place in time. To attach this brand to the attitudes of that older decade, even in rhetorical reverse, however, suggests that the categories of polar opposition are no longer intact. Are the counterconventional "creative minds" of Pound's own "generation" also going "dead"? The intimation goes urgently to his premonition of the end that the war under way already foretells for his generation of genius, foregathered in prewar London. Pound's premonitions sound the effect of the pressures being exerted currently on the personae and poetics of his younger group, at least—or especially—on himself. Could the heroic renegades of Pound's aesthetic decadence become the retrograde guardians of the social and cultural status quo ante? The fear bespeaks one's understandable sense of being coopted in a centralization of energies in a national war effort. A subtler suborning will occur in the very compulsion of a time-minded art, which will find in the language of the establishment it used to revile a vocabulary and grammar full of the extraordinary significance that this moment in history really locates, all in all, the materia poetica of a most timely art.

He repeats and clarifies this fear of accommodation in the same piece as he recasts the customary characters of the 1890s, those emblems of defiant and decadent vitality, in his own contemporary setting. "[T]he wickedest and most dashing publisher of 'the nineties,'" indeed, "of the 'vicious, disreputable nineties,'" appears as an icon of entirely rival values now. The rakish dandy has become the one who "demands that our antiseptic works be submitted to lady-like censorship" (*EPPP*, II:4). Pound takes the assimilation and mutation he records further than the sex change this editor undergoes through the turns of those tropes. Pound aims at the point of liveliest defiance in the period manner of that earlier decade: the "effeminate" stylization of homosexuality. As Cassandra Laity has pointed out, the provocative and rebellious character in fin-de-siècle sexuality constituted a fearsome attraction to male modernists,[63] who could only resist their interest with recriminations of this kind. The anxiety Pound reflects in this instance, however, goes well beyond the homophobia he registers as a reaction to those experiments in the stylization of gender. A historicized consideration of the developing identities of literary modernism may locate the focal point of his profounder dread. He sees the future of himself and his own decade and generation in the decayed youth—the compliant age—of the group now in power.

The 1915 critique of dandies from the flagrant 1890s aging into the dainties of contemporary convention registers a development against which he needs still to defend himself—with the heavy hand of caricature. The censorship he identifies with these figures locates after all the growing point of his own practice. This is a poetics of *not* saying it, or of *pseudo*stating it, whose energies he realizes first—virtually concurrently—in the lines of "The Coming of War: Actaeon." The possibility this work represents remains sufficiently contrary to his earlier standards, however, that he must deflect in prose the enemy his verse assimilates so readily.

This reorientation aligns him all too clearly on another score with 1890s writers. "Has any one yet answered the query," he asks in "Renaissance," "why is it that in other times artists went on getting more and more powerful as they grew older, whereas now," that is, in May 1915, "they decline after the first outburst, or at least after the first successes?"[64] The double reference goes to the twin decades of the 1890s and 1910s. The point of similarity lies in the short course of fame, or success, or creative strength: Aubrey Beardsley's brief career of spectacular renown, doubled by the catastrophic fall of Oscar Wilde from the height of his early power, inscribes the pattern and fate (in Pound's presentiment) of his own decade and generation, lived out in the dying fall of the now-fading "outburst" of *Blast*. This fate appears all the more striking in view of the fact that *Blast* will have survived its announced demise, at least for the moment: its second issue was now at press.

He reiterates this loss of promise in December 1916, in "Mr. Yeats' New Book." The history Yeats shares with the English 1890s, which he has relived recently in talks with Pound at Stone Cottage (Yeats was drafting "The Tragic Generation," the chapter on the 1890s in his *Autobiographies*), calls up the paradigmatic narrative of that decade: the brief candle. Yeats may have spared himself that fate, at least in the estimation of Pound, who finds him "the only poet of his decade who has not gradually faded into mediocrity, who has not resigned himself to gradually weaker echoes of an earlier outburst."[65] Such continued vigor, however, provides the contrary model for the work of Pound's own *Blast* decade and generation, which has now outlived its own "outburst," and not even "gradually."

These pieces comprise as it were the later chapters in a story of paleomodernism, of the last days of a first flourish. This contemporary history reflects an initial split between Pound's primary identifications of modernist energy—with the countercultural claims of *Blast*—and a sense of incipient decrepitude, of creeping accommodation.

Pound moves this evolving complication into a comprehensive expression in June 1917, in "Drunken Helots and Mr. Eliot," which he writes in response to the negative notice Arthur Waugh has provided Eliot's first book in the *Quarterly Review*. A landmark document in any conventional history of Anglo-American literary modernism, this review needs to resist the simpler reading—as some unabashed assertion of the new American presence in London letters. In its complexity and ambivalence, "Drunken Helots and Mr. Eliot" registers the new and difficult initiatives that modernism includes as a function of its own historicity.

Consider the situation in May 1917. The first of the ur-Cantos is about to appear in print and reveal vividly to Pound the inadequacies of radical lyricism and imagism to the scope and ambitions of his new project. At least partially in response to this failure, he has undertaken the work of creative translation that will eventuate in *Propertius*. Its verse forms in the same months as his "Studies in Contemporary Mentality." As a poet, then, he animates to the same conventions he otherwise reviles through this critical series—to the pseudologic of the Liberal discourse on the war, which he has already echoed as the chief conceit in his prose fables. He needs to place this sensibility in a position of undivided contumely, however, not only from the counterconventional vantage of the *New Age* chronicle of this "contemporary mentality," but from his earlier standards of direct expression. Add to this convergence of disparate orientations the fact, witnessed by Vivien Eliot, that Pound has just seen five of his fellow American's new poems, which were written by late April and which strike a tone wholly new to *his* developing oeuvre.[66] These quatrain poems constitute Eliot's response to current provocations and will reveal a profound consonance with the experiments undertaken in *Propertius*.

The case Pound makes in the review thus comprises but exceeds any need to redeem *Prufrock and Other Observations* (1917). After all, Eliot composed most of the poems in this book before the war, some even eight years earlier. Pound's strenuous assertion of the value of the current and the timely goes to his apprehension of this most local moment in the growth of the endeavor he and Eliot jointly define. But Pound wishes to configure this sensibility still in terms his reading public will recognize as his, familiar now for several years, all in all, as an expression of one energy, the same project. Thus Joyce's practice, in *Dubliners* in particular, samples the manner and attitude that promise to reinvigorate the production of literature in the hands of this "younger generation."

Yet the "exactitude" Pound esteems has strayed far from the pages of his—and Eliot's—recent work. This reversal curves back into the prose of this review with an extraordinary rhetorical force, turning the defensiveness he feels about these contemporary developments into the aggression he displays. He insists on differences between older and younger *gen*erations and pursues an absolute value of the root syllable of this word, which repeats with a frequency verging on obsession.

"*Gen*ius," he opens,

> has I know not what peculiar property, its manifestations are various. . . .
> [I]f in any land, or upon any floating deck over the ocean, or upon some newly contrapted craft in the aether, *gen*ius manifests itself, at once some elderly *gen*tleman has a flux of bile from his liver . . . there bursts a torrent of elderly words, splenetic, irrelevant, they form themselves instinctively into large phrases. . . .
>
> All I can find out, by asking questions concerning Mr. Waugh, is that he is "a very old chap," "a reviewer." From internal evidence we deduce that he is, like the rest of his *gen*eration of English *gens-de-lettres*, ignorant of Laforgue; of De Regnier's *Odelettes*; of his French contemporaries *gen*erally, of De Gourmont's *Litanies*. . . .
>
> THE EGOIST has published the best prose writer of my *gen*eration. It follows its publication of Joyce by the publication of a "new" poet who is at least unsurpassed by any of his contemporaries, either of his own age or his elders.
>
> . . . Mr. Waugh dates back to that *gen*eration, the virus is in his blood, he can't help it. The exactitude of the younger *gen*eration gets on his nerves, and so on and so on. . . . I have had nothing alcoholic to-day, nor yet yesterday. I said the same sort of thing about James Joyce's prose over two years ago. I am now basking in the echoes. (emphases added)[67]

The contentment Pound expresses in the last two sentences enjoys in the vindication he boasts a sense of consistency over these years in the movement he represents. The temperance pledge this chronicler takes in the sentence before these last two, however, swears him off the absinthe he held up earlier as the instrument and blazon of an inspired youth. Where he blames Waugh for not reading Laforgue, moreover, he leaves unmentioned the fact that Laforgue has helped him to write *against* his own earlier grain, so to respond to the provocations of the Waugh generation, indeed to sound (all too) like the older men. If "[t]he exactitude of the younger generation gets on [Waugh's] nerves, *and so on and so on*," the timely vigor and precision he champions among his fellow travelers hardly appear in the fatigued sweep of this locution. The phrase provides one more sign of a language adapting to those habits it is supposed to abjure ("elderly words . . . large phrases"). Written as *et cetera et cetera*, after all, the usage rhymes with the Latinate diction in which Pound achieves the same effect of resonant emptiness in *Propertius,* or Eliot the comic pomp9osities and pseudosagacities of his quatrain poems. Pound resists these developments by the force of a former principle, however, in the idiom of the critical prose whose vocabulary was formed before this Word-altering world war.

He reveals these divisions more clearly when he recycles the words of the decade-generation topos through his private correspondence, unconstrained by the manifest needs of public consistency or the interests of literary polemic. Writing to Wyndham Lewis in early May 1916, he cites "a book by me called 'This Generation' dealing with contemporary events in the woild–uv–letters, with passing reference of about 3500 words on vorticism. including my original essays on you and Edward [Wadsworth]." A title and cast of characters that recall the volatile force of the *Blast* generation, "This Generation" will never find interest in "an old stodgy firm like MacMillan [*sic*]," he writes a month later to John Quinn. He has sent the pages instead into the hands of a break-off, upstart figure in New York, one John Marshall, whom Pound praises in the same letter as "the only man ready to print it." Marshall's unfixed address or unconventional temper allowed him to misplace and lose the manuscript. The fate this insurgent impulse meets appears consistent, nonetheless, with the several major reversals the whole story records. Already at the start of the negotiation, in a letter to Quinn at the end of February 1916, Pound scores his sense of the imminent downturn of his subject—(t)his generation—in his rewording of the book's subtitle. "The Spirit of the Half-Decade" plays out in this ruefully humorous mispronunciation: "Am. humorists please copy 'half-decayed.'"[68]

The grim joke goes to a point beyond the personal distress it so evidently marks—Pound's companions Lewis and Hulme now gone to the war, which has already killed his great friend Gaudier. The poet is assimilating the fate of his youthful generation to the model of another decade, the one that owns this temporal marker first, and whose legend or plot features premature demise as its primary pathos: the 1890s.[69] His generation owes its decay to no machination of the natural cycles of waxing and waning energies, however. In his calculation, the Great War must be held to account for the demise of this primary *virtù.* The enriching complication this event has injected into the development of literary modernism in England may be read as one of the stories Pound tells in the verse narratives of his own imagined obituary.

ii

"E. P. ODE POUR L'ELECTION DE SON SEPULCHRE": the title that Pound supplies the opening poem in the first half of *Hugh Selwyn Mauberley* seeds the theme of early death that underlies the double structure of the sequence and unites its two poetic characters. First personage in this twofold scheme, E. P. demonstrates a virtue of exuberant experiment, which his author initializes as his own erstwhile identity. This youthful energy, however, is already faded—under the shadow of the commemoration his author monumentalizes, mockingly or not, at the start: "He passed from men's memory in *l'an trentiesme/De son eage*."[70] The French words intoned over the bones of the thirty-year-old Ezra Pound originated as no youth's funeral wreath, however, rather as a clarion assertion of self, in François Villon's *Testament*.[71] The reference to Villon's testament meets the feeling of "pass[ing] early from men's memory," then, to generate the special conceit of Pound's poem: a sort of heroic boast manqué, self-declaration as epitaph, a record, all in all, of a self-definition proclaimed—now lost—in an instant of brief excellence. The poet of a zestily French moyen-âge contributes to the story of Pound's own (early) middle age.

In what terms does Pound reckon his sudden turnaround? In the evidence offered by the two imaginary characters of E. P. and Mauberley, the difference consists of commitments to poetic tenets and practices only as sharply opposite as they are obviously (now) representative of Pound's own altered voice. The heroic singularity Pound features in E. P. focuses mainly on his role as protagonist and champion of a poetics he fables in a single line with a double allusion: "His true Penelope was Flaubert" (*P*, 185). The Odyssean epic of this literary career has guided him to the home and harbor of one constant value, the standards Pound pronounced in his January 1914 review of *Dubliners*—a poet's homage to an art of Flaubertian concision in Joyce's prose, where reliable reference justifies a stylized word. If this poetic protagonist went in fear of abstractions, however, his successor in the sequence, Mauberley, is identified with a style of Latinate abstruseness:

> Invitation, mere invitation to perceptivity
> Gradually led him to the isolation
> Which these presents place
> Under a more tolerant, perhaps, examination. (*P*, 199)

At the extreme verge of this passage, in the gravid classicism that characterizes Mauberley's poetic language, Pound depicts one end of the direction he has taken up, he fears, in the idiom it reiterates: the heavy Latinisms of his own *Propertius*.

While it is difficult to hold the numerals in an imaginative narrative like this to the standards of biographical accuracy, the thirtieth (strictly reckoned, thirty-first[72]) year of Pound's life does not coincide with the development of a poetic style identifiable with the one that appears in *Propertius*. The year 1915 may be held nonetheless to heavy, consequential account. It is the year of Gaudier's death. It marks also the moment in the course of the story Pound has lived in advance that he has recorded as a turning point—where the "generation" of (t)his "decade" shows that it is in fact "half-decayed." It is around this mid-decade year, then, that Pound organizes the fable of his own poetic development and decline, and it is a spot of time that is occupied by a most identifiable event.

In the biographical–historical narrative that the first half of the sequence comprises, the Great War locates this medial point most clearly. Sections IV and V—Pound's extraordinary war lyrics—occupy the moment to which the various developments in the sequence converge, as to a point of critical mass. It locates a crucial nexus in the time line of its poetic character's development. (That the narrative of the fictional autobiography is actually *about* something, an issue long contested in the critical literature on the sequence,[73] is being asserted here.) These pieces read as the determined expression of the poetic temperament being formed in the preceding sections of the autobiography. Their intense directness of feeling and statement presents the fruit of their poet's preparation in the school of imagism, a poetics that legitimizes and intensifies his objection to the obfuscations, eloquent or not, of the elderly gentlemen authoring this war:

> Died some, pro patria,
>   non "dulce" non "et decor" . . .
> walked eye-deep in hell
> believing in old men's lies, then unbelieving
> came home, home to a lie,
> home to many deceits,
> home to old lies and new infamy;
> usury age-old and age-thick
> and liars in public places. (*P*, 188)

Lyric immediacy clearly overrides a language of Latinate abstraction, which is compatible with the mendacities of that authorized war. If Pound rose to an apotheosis of imagist perfection, say, in the 1915 gathering *Cathay*,[74] his involvement with the (otherwise) unavoidable complication of history has resulted in developments he sees now, in retrospect, as a downward turn (*catastrophe*). For the Latinate language he presents in the heckling objection of his lyric speaker represents an echoing—and growing—point in the poetics of his own career, which eventuates as the voice of Mauberley in the poem's second part.

At this point, accordingly, Pound reverses the literary history interior to the sequence. He returns the story after the moment and poems of war to a point in prior cultural time as unlikely at first as it is, now, predictable and revelatory. The sixth poem begins to tell the story of English decadence. The narrative begins, historically, as early as 1870. The connection Pound intimates elsewhere between *decadence* and *decade* may go to a chance echo, not a solid etymology, but his picture of English decadence in the sequence deepens the mirror image this nominal value provides for his sense of the present decade, half-decayed at its top (in 1915, in himself). References to Swinburne and Rossetti crest thus in this account into episodic narratives featuring representative figures of the English 1890s (Dowson, Johnson, Plarr, and Beerbohm, among others), the decade of decadence. The cast of characters in this pageant of literary history is too numerous to sustain the attribution of any single fault, any one unifying value. The main force or underlying intent of the extensive representation, however, goes to the relevance of decadence for his own career. Does the label apply as verdict, or apologia?

The answer to this question goes to the radical sense of the meaning that decadence preserves at the Latin root of the word: *cadere*, "to fall." *Lapse*, or *fall*, provides the theme word in the story of the two-part sequence, where it is obviously dishonest to make an argument for the superiority of Mauberley to E. P. as the embodiment of an aesthetic program. The retreatism of Mauberley, the attempt to refine a bodily character out of physical and historical existence: the fatigued aspirations of this poetic character's late *symbolisme* compare poorly indeed with the heroic *virtù* of E. P.'s engagements with circumjacent actualities, stupidities or not.

What is critically interesting in the consideration of this question entails instead an exploration of Pound's own imaginative understanding of the cause of the "fall." Single sources are, of course, only partial answers to a phenomenon as complex as this reversal of fortune. Yet the main weight of felt judgment clusters around the echoing iterations of a single word, one that presents a verbal category and juridical class for Pound's story of this lapse. It is the participial nominative of *cadere*, that is, *casus*, "case," which presents in English the sense of a fall from some definitional paradigm, an ideal instance. The repetition of the word over the course of the sequence builds an understanding of what was ideal in the poetic program and career of E. P., of why and where this fineness was lost, of what its remaindered substance may be. It is a narrative of sizable dimension and immense consequences. The history underlying and compelling the personal story may be recovered, nonetheless, through the fourfold repetition of this signal word. A full resource of understanding may be restored thus for the developments we have been following.

"[T]he *case* presents / No adjunct to the Muses' diadem": the last two lines in the opening poem in the sequence already present the poetic career of E. P. as a special exception—to itself as well as to the standards of conventional poetic expression. A genius chiefly lyric—"out of *key* with his time" (E. P.'s art is mainly musical)—finds its main problem, in fact, when it loses the tune. The sensually songlike intensity of E. P.'s best imagist verse is forsaken for sure in the poetic textures of this opening piece, which forms, according to the professed need to present E. P.'s "case," as an argumentative site. The method of verse forensic, that is to say, serves at once to address and display the problem of E. P.'s "case":

Wrong from the start—

No, hardly, but seeing he had been born
In a half-savage country, out of date.

The movement between these first two quatrains simulates a case-making logic—positing a wrong, then correcting the gesture, then developing the first assertion through further qualification. The rhetoric of reason deepens its conceit in the narrative of this career: if "[t]he chopped seas held him, *therefore*, that year" (*P*, 185; emphases added), the sense of conclusion Pound inserts with this conjunction summarizes as a logical plot a sequence of events that may feature consecutiveness, but surely no argumentative consequence. The verbal surface presents the mannerism of rationality as a transparent artifice. No worthy sequel to the integral music of the early career, it seems, this manner presents a demonstrable falling off and, arguably, the substance and problem of Pound's case.

This pseudologic shows the tendency that his work has featured as its chief conceit since 1917, which has been fostered by the language of the Liberal war. The poems centered ostensibly in that event might be expected, then, to extend the most searching interrogation of this signal word. The pattern these repetitions comprise cannot be dismissed critically as offering just some simple, connect-the-dots approximation of the complex picture of literary modernism in England. For the "case" word resonates to the history and memory of a culture that features a case-making ratiocination as its main value and practice, a culture that found its moment of awful truth in the woeful effort of making reasonable and acceptable its Great War. Thus Pound recalls the whole story through this theme word, a formation whose resources he explores with an ingenuity edged with his own bitterly intelligent witness.

"These fought in any case," poem IV opens. The ambivalence is subtle, but exact: in one sense, "in any case" catches a feeling of resignation, while, in another, it designates a "no matter what" attitude, a heroic vainglory running high in that first moment of war. The uncertainty already bespeaks an instability in the case-making efforts Pound is recalling from the political history of the war. He formalizes the problem in the next instance, in the next lines, as the cadencing and punctuation serve to place other emphases on this theme word:

> and some believing,
> pro domo, in any case . . . (*P*, 187)

If, in one of its meanings, the first line of poem IV has invoked a situation in which no arguments for war were required, these next two recall the situation in which rationales were called up. The one Pound rehearses, "pro domo," catches in his rhythms and pointings the complex economy of the Liberal logic at war. He dubs in a pause with the comma, then amplifies the sense of reticence in a line left unfinished, lingering on the ellipses. An artifice of ratiocination, too elaborate for so short a space, wherein it shows its contortion, moves at last to inconsequence—a familiar Liberal debility.

The echo Pound has generated out of the sound of these times rises then to form a single question: What can a poet do with the language this moment in history has offered him? Certainly, the pressure of feeling in these two pieces unseams the devious weave of legalistic casuistry. The language reactivates the clear and urgent memory of men and friends who "walked eye-deep in hell / believing in old men's lies" (*P*, 188). Pound's recent verse, however, has believed in these old men's lies, at least in a provisional and opportunistic way. Their rationalistic mendacity provided the credible measure for his timeliest work, in *Propertius*, which will be echoed in the Mauberley section of this sequence. This achievement moves against the grain of human feeling, however, not to mention the standards of an earlier, straighter-talking poetics.

This discrepancy, which generates the major "case" of the sequence, centers the difference in the literary idioms of E. P. and Mauberley. It also locates the point of breakage unarguably, now obviously, in the lived experience of the war. The consequences of that event are registered in the turning, reversed, now-lapsed fortunes of the generation that Pound makes himself represent.

Predictably, then, "case" appears next (last) in the sixth poem, whose quatrains begin to record the literary history of de*cad*ence. Pound retells that fall through Jenny, the prostitute whom Dante Rossetti poeticized—to prompt the more infamous attack on decadence by the "Foetid Buchanan" (*P*, 189), Pound's characterization of the enemy of decadence (platitudinous author of *The Fleshly School of Poetry*) in that portion of the literary history.[75] Pound situates the Jenny figure in imagery and wording that work within his own mirror-and-echo pattern:

> The thin, clear gaze, the same
> Still darts out faun-like from the half-ruin'd face,
> Questing and passive. . . .
> "Ah, poor Jenny's case" . . . (*P*, 189)

Rossetti attaches the epigraph from Shakespeare's Mrs. Quickly, "Vengeance on Jenny's case! Fie on her! Never name her child!" to his Jenny,[76] but the "poor Jenny" formula that recurs through Rossetti's poem (ll. 144, 172, 299) features no use of the "case" word. Pound's wording, "Ah, poor Jenny's case," obviously derives from the Shakespearean epigraph, where *case* includes the learned double entendre of a sexual *fall*. The fusion of these two sources suggests the synthetic effort of his work and an appropriation of this charged counter to the system of verbal reference in his own poem. Pound's Jenny provides a slant rhyme to the "case" of E. P.'s career, especially where her visage merges with the "thin, clear gaze" of the "Burne-Jones cartons" (*P*, 189) that he featured in the preceding quatrain. The clarity he configures as the value of that sensually intense art recalls the standards of his own imagist verse, a high line of aesthetic purism from which Pound has certainly "lapsed."

The reversed fortune Pound records through Jenny goes beyond himself to the mischance of his modernist accomplices. By the chronology he followed in the Lewis letter, he marked "this generation" as "half-decayed" in 1915. He fulfills the premonition of that jauntier wordplay, now, in more rueful retrospect. He depicts "poor Jenny's case," or fall, in the image of the "half-ruin'd face." The memory and echo, private as they may be, give this enigma its embittered precision. The figure is intimate with the saddest story of his generation. The tale that Pound retells in *Mauberley* and centers in the fall of E. P. recalls a history that has turned individual promise to general loss, a single career into a representative case.

The impress the war leaves on E. P.'s career appears ultimately in the poet's early ending testament. Pound erects "Envoi" as a monumental failure, preempting the claims its poetic protagonist (and subsequent critics) may make for it.[77] This poem fails, moreover, at just that point where E. P.'s lyric genius meets the prose of recent history.

"*Go, dumb-born book*," goes the apologia of its opening line. Pound appeals through the silence of print to the finer audition of its promissory song. His overture reads like that of the conventional elegist, who alleges the impossibility of the task, but who assesses thus the better, more estimable worth of the thing that will be done. E. P.'s disclaimer lays claim to its own truth only, however, in the unsingable, unspeakable, obscurely argued thing "Envoi" is:

> *Tell her that sang me once that song of Lawes:*
> *Hadst thou but song*
> *As thou hast subjects known,*
> *Then were there cause in thee that should condone*
> *Even my faults that heavy upon me lie,*
> *And build her glories their longevity.* (*P*, 195)

Where these hypotactic formulations depart from the paratactic accumulations congenial to musical speech, Pound traces the shape of some propositional case that remains vague in the extreme. The lapse reenacts Pound's own regression, from the musical idiom of the prewar years, into the pseudodiscursive measures of 1917. The material residue of the tradition of poetic song lies in a wholly archaic manner, utterly unquickened by contemporary idiom. One major project of literary modernism has failed to come alive. The matter of literary and cultural tradition remains archival, silent, inert. His failure proves exemplary, however. His case, or fall, represents the lapsed ambition of the generation he typifies.

Imaginatively enhanced, Pound's narrative reads as one full story of the energy and intelligence that we know as English poetic modernism—the motive forces as well as the first consequences of that movement and plot. Its poetics will have formed jointly from the hand of his fellow American and (sometime) fellow traveler, the figure whose critical prescriptions (benedictions and maledictions) served for many decades as the charter documents of high modernism. These initiatives may return for an enriched understanding, too, to the forcing ground of contemporary circumstance. Where Pound tended to collide with history, this other poet colludes with crises, opportunities most local and usable. And while Eliot's intervention may serve personal purposes quite distinctly different from Pound's, his background establishes a shared orientation toward their English situation. This common condition may be clarified in advance through a brief consideration of a figure who, except for her own earlier Americanness, seems an unlikely companion indeed for the English adventures of Eliot and Pound.

Stein

The pattern that Gertrude Stein triangulates with Eliot and Pound offers a frame of critical consideration for the import the war owns in their developments equally as individuals, as (ex-)American writers, and as modernists. To Pound's and Eliot's, certainly, Stein's was a materially different war, mainly Continental in its references and French in its local intensities. Limited in her exposure to the English scene, she will prove informative nonetheless about the possibilities it extends to a writer prepared to avail herself of these, in view especially of the preparation her previous development has provided her.

The experiment with language that Stein began in the first decade of the twentieth century already went to the securing roots of an intellectual tradition. Her work represents an early extension and refinement of the critique of European and English rationalism that American Pragmatism found as its original stimulus. This was a tradition known to Pound, well known to Eliot at Harvard, and intimately familiar to Stein. William James, with whom Stein collaborated as an undergraduate at Radcliffe, moved these attitudes into their most condensed expression in his 1907 essay *Pragmatism*, where he focused on the constructions of post-Enlightenment reason and science as verbal or heuristic fictions only.[1] Not that these structures were wholly useless. It was the task of the pragmatist to submit the language of absolute reason, as it were, the statement of a metaphysical rationalism, to the qualifying and refining test of actual experience. This is a motive that finds a not-so-distant echo in Stein's own novel prosody. The incremental variation to which she submits a repeated phrase shows just the sort of adjustment that is the constant discovery of the pragmatist, who adapts the categorical formula to the variant, sometimes recalcitrant conditions of reality. This commitment alerts the American pragmatist to a comparable project in English Liberalism, which, after all, will extend the procedures of a supreme verbal reason to the Great War as its ultimate challenge. If English Liberals do not readily flex their Word to the exceptional circumstance of this war, but insist instead on the absolute truth of their own rationalistic language, the somber folly of that mechanical comedy opens also as the forcing, enriching circumstance of an art especially primed to respond to that provocation. What Stein provides in a consideration of this art, besides a confirmation of the response that is common to those most cognizant Americans, is an instance of extraordinary prescience about these possibilities.

In early July 1914, Stein traveled to England. The explicit purpose was to intersect with John Lane (publisher of *Blast*), who had professed some interest in printing an English edition of *Three Lives*. After their meeting, she decided with Alice Toklas to visit Hope Mirlees in Cambridge, where they remained through much of the rest of the month. Through acquaintances, she gained an introduction to the philosopher Alfred North Whitehead, who invited Stein and Toklas to Lockeridge, in Sussex, for a weekend retreat that would come to include, among other guests, Bertrand Russell, George Moore, and Lytton Strachey. It was the first weekend in August.[2]

Stein recalls the moment in *The Autobiography of Alice B. Toklas*:

> I can still hear Doctor Whitehead's gentle voice reading the papers out loud and then all of them talking about the destruction of Louvain and how they must help the brave little belgians. Gertrude Stein desperately unhappy said to me, where is Louvain. Don't you know, I said. No, she said, nor do I care, but where is it.[3]

The memory Stein rehearses in Toklas's voice recalls an assertion of the moral cause of the Liberal war. Whitehead might well stand as the dean of the party's intellectual and academic membership, soon to be conscripted to the national effort. Certainly, to dissenting pacifists such as Russell and Strachey, the novel logic of that war policy would be as obvious as the contradictions it presented to their special apprehensions of what Liberalism was, or ought to be. Right reason gone wrong would constitute the main objection in Russell's adamantly rationalistic critique of the government's case. The standards of intellectual and behavioral freedom that gave the party its name as well as its ideal would define for Strachey the source of a deeper, more far-reaching grievance—its refusal to admit or legitimize his homosexuality.[4] The condition of freely reasoned choice, which the Gladstonian apologists for involvement invoked at this moment in the name of Belgium, could hardly meet more severe reviewers than these. By unrivaled luck, then, Stein's early if brief experience of the English war coincided with a perspective that identified the political substance and intellectual issues that would dominate public, partisan consciousness for the subsequent four years. In the company that chance and circumstance gathered, moreover, she entered a frame of critical reference through which the sound of these times could be heard and characterized for the somber folly it already was, and would more volubly become.

Not that Stein required an analytical sensibility so exactly adapted as Russell's and Strachey's to clarify or amplify this understanding. Her own predispositions equipped her especially well to listen critically to the machinations of a sheerly verbal logic. Accordingly, the writing she did at this moment, and in subsequent returns in memory to the scene of the British war, will attune its linguistic inventions to the special conceit of Liberalism in duress, to a manifest fracture in the language of ratio. While her earlier writing was already adapting the sequences of an ideal verbal reason to the pragmatist's motives, this practice did not feature nearly so dense a concentration of logical particles, not nearly so strong a self-consciousness of the rhetoric and gestures of the rationalist. The linguistic conventions of English Liberal reason set up the conditions and stimulus for her creative interest—for an exchange and riposte that will speak one of the most searching and revealing records of the collapse of that rationalistic language. That she continues to register the significance of the war in England in subsequent years in this way is a testament to the intensity of the message being sent and to the acuity of her initial reception—all in all, to the select but representative power of its demonstration in other major modernist texts.

As late as 1938, in *Picasso*, where she sees the strategic plan of the Great War in the canvases of cubism, she returns to its first circumstances in her English experience. Her citation of Sir Edward Grey includes an observation that, in her own verbal observance, she underscores:

> Lord Grey said when the war broke out that the generals thought of a war of the nineteenth century even when the instruments of war were of the twentieth century and only when the war was at its height did the generals understand that it was a war of the twentieth century, and not a war of the nineteenth century. That is what the academic spirit is, it is not contemporary, of course not, and so it can not be creative because the only thing that is creative in a creator is the contemporary thing. Of course.[5]

The two complete sentences set out developments in the history of logistics through sequences that are clearly reasoned, consistently achieved. These sentences appear to be unsurprised by the dividing line they identify, let alone by the violence coinciding with it. The irony is formal but not entirely silent. The changes she records in the external dimension she extends into the dodges of her own language, which maintains its logical decorum, so it seems by the end, mainly to enunciate it overmuch, so to accentuate the points of its disruption: "of course not" and "of course." In a rational proposition, these phrases would serve to intensify the possession of reasonable sequence, thus of logical and demonstrable consequence. Stein makes these claims, however, in the two phrases that break an otherwise exemplary cadence and continuum of reasonable, linear thinking. She follows an extended course of grammatical logic, that is, not to record the smooth or continuous progression of strategic science per se, rather to magnify the impact of these fractures. The conclusion of the logical process—in this text, in the history being recalled—is a disruption, detectable just where the claim of the exemplary sequence of verbal reason appears strongest. It is an inconsistency all too familiar from the Liberal discourse of the Great War.

If the 1938 characterization of the 1914 event appears to be more than mildly stylized, a bit too coy perhaps in being so adroit, Stein also accounts for the distancing effect an interval like this makes, at least in principle, in the statement on poetics she is making. She locates the place of greatest creative urgency closest to the historical moment being composed. This assertion works as the first rule of a poetics she proves in the doing, in a persuasively timely way, in the record that appears nearest to her experience of the British war. Much of the writing she did in England between early August and mid-October, when she returned to France, went unpublished in her lifetime, but it suffered this result mainly because of the uncertainty and precariousness of her circumstances. The same conditions account for its interest. Her exposure to the distress of English Liberal reason opens in this literature as a record of extraordinary immediacy.

"In One" combines stylistic concision and local evocation:

> I suggest that that is not what I ordered. I relieve more feathers that way than any other. I hesitate to establish necessary we know of no better and I do mean to oblige. I do mean to offer paper and I do thoroughly reasonably chuck out what has hitherto hindered office of origin. Office of origin has become to me so presently agreeable that between needing it and not needing it, between needing it and not needing it between needing, it, between needing it, shall it be a village. Offices of origin.[6]

"Its words are reasoning words," Virgil Thomson notes in a commentary, which dates it convincingly close to early August 1914, "though the shape is musical."[7] The musicalization of reason's speech: a sequence of argumentative phrases leads to no demonstrable proposition, let alone to a sensible or even identifiable conclusion. While the gestures being made certainly posit a developmental, consequential logic, this rationalist language resonates in a rhythmical rather than linear configuration. There is also in the performance an audibly satiric quality, where, say, the logic goes demotic and heckles the gesture of stipulative discrimination and refinement that it is supposed to be making: "and I do thoroughly reasonably chuck out." This antic element varies and expands to the scale of the mock peroration, the sham parallelism in that triple repetition near the end, where the antitheses she builds up "between needing it and not needing it" proceed to no precision of synthesis, rather to a stammer, and collapse thus into a question having nothing to do with the substance of the preceding exchange: "shall it be a village."

The insistent appearance of these reason-seeming non sequiturs represents the main point of development from Stein's already well-developed range of practices. This novelty leads an otherwise well-informed commentator such as Thomson to attach to its peculiarity the ready but facile tag of "hermeticism."[8] Stein's new usage expresses no private obscurantism, however. It registers an art of logical obfuscation all too public, urgent, and contemporary. She is echoing—dramatizing, amplifying, imaginatively clarifying—the incipient discourse of the Liberal war.

"Offices of origin"? The words suggest official beginnings, the origins of a war whose authorized "causes" are currently (and urgently) being formed, or invented, or coerced. Into her refrain phrase, Stein packs thus a manifold sense, which she plays out in the answering passage as the whole notion of formal causation: its principles, its verbal formulas and rituals, its procedural rules. Prior, higher ideas constitute a rationalist metaphysics of which any American pragmatist is profoundly skeptical. Strategically, then, Stein stalls the words of reasonable cause- and case-making in the exercise of their own procedures. In these preliminaries, the logical prolegomenon of the Liberal war spells itself out as the merest series of reason-seeming premises.

"Against this ever rising tide of national enthusiasm," goes the first of the prefatory gestures that keep opening "Painted Lace" (early August 1914), "while immersed in this prodigious task, with some surprise with some surprise, with thousands of skilled stirrups with no dismay, with what is important with surprisingly great surprises, with some surprise and with no dismay, against this ever rising tide of national enthusiasm, the greatest enthusiasm no doubt, it echoed in the preliminary recitations. No I don't."[9] In the inaugural phases of the war, when "preliminary recitations" recall the preparatory speeches of apologists such as Grey and Asquith, the attitude of their performance is "echoed" in the phrases of Stein's text. Her conventionally sensible speaker assumes the usual postures. Conceding current difficulty but appealing to the deeper human spirit, this character-in-voice sounds like a liberal individual of classically balanced rationality. Beyond the ongoing repetitions of an opening maneuver, however, these overtures go nowhere. A timely inconsequence. Stein's exceptional prescience allows her not only to pick up this deflection in the contemporary *parole* but to echo its attitudes and practices beforetime. Further, more searchingly, she shifts this sensibility back into its fixed, typifying position: as an endless first of all, as a rationalistic metaphysic full of the high sentence it cannot deliver. Stalled on its own primary condition of reason in all things, it commits itself to rehearsing the ceremony of its own initiatives in gesticulations as ineffectual—and, were it not for the history intermingled with them, as ridiculous—as these.

Or these, again in "Painted Lace," where, in the rhetorical fiction, in response it seems to the monitory advice of the popular press, the speaker avers:

> I did not neglect little pieces of garden. It is so easy not to be built with a view to an orchard now the news is correct. It is not without reason that the man is to be reminded to call. Five days earlier it was not without reason. Up there to the left. . . . It's harder work up at that end. Never letting the war run out does making recognition easier.[10]

"It is not without reason . . . it was not without reason": the negation of the contrary strikes again to the point of circumspect balance on which the individual of liberal rationality poises, classically. The repetition of the sentence, however, moves the gesture suggestively in the direction of obsession. Here is ratio, in extremis. It is the usual confusion of Liberal England at war.

The deftness with which Stein extends those "preliminary recitations" of the Liberal war to so great a range of linguistic response and literary consequence certainly allows one to wonder what a four-year exposure to those conditions might have produced as a result. As it stands, however, the English war represents in her oeuvre, not the encompassing circumstance of her own *durée*, but one of its particular spots of time.

She will revisit that insular sensibility later, nonetheless, in the construction of her French experience. "Accents in Alsace" (1919), for example, carries the subtitle "A Reasonable Tragedy." The phrase preserves a memory of the intellectual temper and spiritual crises of British Liberalism at war. Her memories of August 1914 recur, too, when she shifts her attentions to the precincts of her English experience:

> Clouds do not fatten with teaching.
> They do not fatten at all.
> We wonder if it is influence
> By the way I guess.
> She said. I like it better than Eggland.
> What do you mean.
> We never asked how many children over eleven.
> You cannot imagine what I think about the country.
> Any civilians killed.[11]

Packing an assertion into virtually every line, Stein's speaker seems constantly to be summing up some ongoing and developing argument, which, otherwise, remains obscure in the extreme. This disparity goes to the conceit of a parody rationality, whose pretense may be as comic potentially as the renaming of the island—England, "Eggland"—that modeled its usage. This folly dominates the consciousness of her retrospect, nonetheless, with some measured sense of the actual dimensions of the event, of the true sum and consequence of its logical inconsequence: "Any civilians killed."

Certainly, before the war, Stein could enter the space she opens here between reasonable statement and accomplished sense. In *Tender Buttons*, for instance, she establishes the speaking sequences of normative reason so as to intervene in these, but not as a malediction, rather to place and raise in some instantaneous frame the vivid, impending detail of her painterly sensibility: "A temptation any temptation is an exclamation if there are misdeeds and little bones."[12] The irrelevance of linguistic reason makes these sensible particulars more vivid. In 1919, however, as in the late summer of 1914, the quality of thought appears clearly to be *pseudo*propositional, *mock*-logical.

Low tragedy, or high farce, the performance of reasonableness in the work of the English war will live on in Stein's memory as a creative strength that is, mainly, latent. Her fellow (ex-)Americans, however, will generate a good deal more work out of this nexus of critical perception and historical feeling. The difference goes mostly to the durations of their respective exposures. While Stein identifies the tremendous potential that the (long) moment of the English war locates for a writer prepared, in the academy of American pragmatism, to respond to this provocation, Eliot will prove the truth of the promise. The crisis of English Liberalism, which the background he shares with Stein and Pound equipped them especially well to perceive and critique, lives in his career as the main opportunity of his major work. This is a body of poetry and criticism that has long assumed the status of an institutional charter, establishing the values and practices of an identifiably (at least, nominally) high modernism. In this literary history, the formative importance of the English war is a story that needs to be followed, now, through the record Eliot has left of his interaction with its extraordinarily advantageous circumstances.

3

Mr. Eliot's Wartime Services

The Sacred Wood: high-toned and even (already) High Church as this phrase has sounded to some commentators, the allusion Eliot provides in the title for his first collection of prose (1920) moves to a site of more savage ceremony. It is the place that Sir James Frazer has retrieved for (what will prove to be) a distinguished literary use, an extensive imaginative representation: the Nemi grove of ancient Rome.[1] Here, a conflict for succession—between priest-kings in the fertility religions of antiquity—sets the youthful *virtù* of a contender against the decaying strength of an elder. Eliot's reference cycles back as well through the final quatrain of his recently published poem, "Sweeney among the Nightingales" (1919), where "the bloody wood" restages a manifold site of ancient sacrifice.[2] Thus the book title takes the reputation this verse has already earned in a forward direction. *The Sacred Wood* attaches the distinction of the poetry to the prose and fits the emergent whole of the work to the plot and motive of the ritual and myth of succession. The title shows indeed the sly device of an interloping contender in this domain. But what, after all, is Eliot contesting? And who, to begin with, is his main opponent?

I

Oppositions, Repossessions, Performances

"When a distinguished critic observed recently, in a newspaper article, that 'poetry is the most highly organized form of intellectual activity,' we were conscious that we were reading neither Coleridge nor Arnold," Eliot demurs in July 1920, opening the essay he will present as the first offering in *The Sacred Wood*. Speaking through a pronoun that assumes his new capacity to speak for

English literary culture, this American presumes an inwardness with a tradition that, as a relative alien, is still at issue for him. Through this initial gambit, he advances to his grander challenge: possession of this legacy. He may earn this inheritance at the expense of the figure this essay draws into the spotlight of its own title. "The Perfect Critic" edges its subject as victim already, with the menace of evident irony. He continues, striking the target words in that opening quotation:

> Not only have the words "organized" and "activity," occurring together in this phrase, that familiar vague suggestion of the scientific vocabulary which is characteristic of modern writing, but one asked questions which Coleridge and Arnold would not have permitted one to ask. How is it, for instance, that poetry is more "highly organized" than astronomy, physics, or pure mathematics, which we imagine to be, in relation to the scientist who practises them, "intellectual activity" of a pretty highly organized type? . . . The phrases by which Arnold is best known may be inadequate, they may assemble more doubts than they dispel, but they usually have some meaning. And if a phrase like "the most highly organized form of intellectual activity" is the highest organization of thought of which contemporary criticism, in a distinguished representative, is capable, then, we conclude, modern criticism is degenerate.
>
> The verbal disease above noticed may be reserved for diagnosis by and by.[3]

"[B]y and by" understates the extent to which Eliot will engage and address the sensibility he has presented. The true scope of his inquiry lies in the dimensionality of these final metaphors, which shift the "diagnosis" already under way from the specific instance this single citation provides. The "degenerate" condition this writer's "verbal disease" has reached clearly suggests that the problem occurs on a systemic scale.

The sensibility that Eliot frames in this depiction fits with the main tradition of Enlightenment discourse, instanced here in a critical condition. The empirical reasoning that distinguishes this discipline appears to Eliot's gaze as the merest pretense. Its representative phrase raises only "that familiar vague suggestion of the scientific vocabulary which is characteristic of modern writing." A *quasi*-scientific language and syntax, its referents are unbased in fact and its proposition is accordingly unearned. The statement appears to reason its way through a medium of material referents, but it moves instead to its own resonant ends and offers nothing but a form of words, the sheerest rhetoric of rationality. The contemporary sensibility exhibits to Eliot the "degenerate" condition of a specifically "verbal disease"—call it verbal*ism*.

The drift Eliot witnesses shows clearly an orientation specific to English Liberalism. This tradition places so great a faith in the working of verbal

logic—and its capacity to manage a world of fact through the words of reasoned speech—that the will or appearance, the rhetoric or grammar, may be
taken for the deed. Thus Eliot's investigation returns that problematic statement to the depths of this modern philosophical tradition. He reconfigures its
problems as the time-worn difference between the "abstract" and "concrete"
but subdues this dualism to the insidious influence of a "verbalism" identical in
every respect, in spirit as well as in name, with the "liberal" tradition he cites in
his final indictment. "The confused distinction which exists in most heads between 'abstract' and 'concrete,'" he begins by pointing out,

> is due not so much to a manifest fact of the existence of two types of
> mind, an abstract and a concrete, as to the existence of another type of
> mind, the verbal, or philosophic. . . . If verbalism were confined to pro-
> fessional philosophers, no harm would be done. But their corruption
> has extended very far. Compare a mediaeval theologian or mystic, com-
> pare a seventeenth-century preacher, with any "liberal" sermon since
> Schleiermacher, and you will observe that words have changed their
> meanings. What they have lost is definite, and what they have gained is
> indefinite.[4]

The cited "corruption" recalls the "degenerate" condition that the "distinguished critic" exhibited earlier and so identifies his "verbal disease" as one
current form of the "verbalism" Eliot labels here. On the hygienic instrument
of those punctuational tweezers, Eliot holds up the source or ultimate instance
of this pollution as the "'liberal'" condition of post-Enlightenment Europe.
Transhistoric and international as this tradition may be, Eliot fixes it in the initial and signal position of his essay's (and book's) opening sentences in its representatively English instance.

With the aims of the classic antagonist, then, Eliot identifies the liabilities
of a once-dominant power. He targets the weak points in a national culture that
may have once excluded him as an American but now offers him, through the
stress points and soft spots he reveals as he exposes such representative usage,
an ingress into its contested, newly possessed domain. The verse and prose that
provide the basis for his insurgent counterclaim have responded to the infirmi-
ties of that system and religion. The sacred wood of England's Nemi grove
holds up for advantage the ruined clerisy of British Liberalism. Its fate in the
recent experiences of insular political history provides, we shall see, the timely
opportunity for his literary riposte. The encouragement he takes from its demise may be followed, moreover, through the letters and literary journalism he
has left from these years. The orientation he takes to these developments
should be understood initially, however, in terms of the vantage he shares with
that other, equally astute, also transatlantic observer of the English situation,
Pound. The author of "Studies in Contemporary Mentality," "Our Tetrarchal
Précieuse," and *Homage to Sextus Propertius* has set his literary intelligence to

work under the same conditions. He has also modeled a form of imaginative response that is special to their joint place of origin.

i

The mimicry that the American Pound performs on English Liberal reason in distress locates an equally rich complex of possibilities for his compatriot Eliot. Imitation of a rational manner conatural with the values of a higher civilization is, to begin with, the response a (formerly) colonial writer is still *supposed* to produce. Like Pound, however, Eliot witnesses a familiarity with this expectation that signals his—their—ability to deviate from it. He, too, will create himself over and against such expectations.

Thus, in "Imperfect Critics," the piece answering in *The Sacred Wood* to "The Perfect Critic," Eliot recycles the disposition of that most "distinguished critic" into its colonial animadversion. The reasonable demeanor of the original reappears in the American type Eliot features but, at the other end of the world, in another mien. In an instance at once mimic and primitive, the American rationalist remains a savage, a characteristic Eliot elaborates interestingly in his finishing triplet:

> [The American critic] takes the reputations of the world too solemnly. This is probably due in part to remoteness in space from the European centre. But it must be observed that English solemnity and American solemnity are very different. I do not propose to analyse the difference (it would be a valuable chapter in social history); the American solemnity, it is enough to say, is more primitive, more academic, more like that of the German professor.[5]

The figure of the German carries the image of timely rebuke and, in it, a reminder of Pound's use of the same type. In "Provincialism the Enemy," the other American poet deploys the Teutonic caricature to the evident purpose of protecting himself against any identification with this figure—England's war for "civilization" against Germany will not miss *this* American as an ally. The erstwhile provincial, Eliot subscribes silently but unmistakably to the same ideal—still the right side—of that recent campaign, by identifying the fool of true civilization in the barbaric, German academic; in this unwitting imitation of its proper behavior.

Eliot's apprehension of poetic colonialism goes, like Pound's, to a fully double motive. On one hand, both writers appear to be drawn powerfully to the values and attitudes of the English capital; on this symbolic locale, they may regain the authenticity they fear they have lost at their transatlantic remove. On the other hand, they own an acute awareness of the mimicry their condition as aliens enjoins on them. Their self-awareness about this mimic reflex establishes the point of difference, however, between their imaginative strategies and those

Homi Bhabha imputes to his colonial man, who, as rehearsed earlier, engages ever in an insurgent, but erasing, mimesis. For Pound and Eliot, while *not quite* English, are hardly *not white*. The intimation of some secret if foregone affinity with the British res allows them to (wish to) resume or reconstitute its authority. In the furtherance of this motive, however, Eliot begins to differentiate himself from Pound. The rustic mime with whom Eliot is wont to be identified reappears as his chosen subject, a new materia poetica. The primitive mimic appears in this provincial's poetics equally as content and as expedient, target as well as method. Eliot exaggerates the echo he is expected to reproduce, moreover, in a behavior that indicates his own knowing acquaintance with the response he is *supposed* to make. This elaborate ostentation of artifice also betters the expectation of his given condition as provincial mimic. Thus he takes control of his writerly identity in a way that bespeaks the authority he associates with the literary capital.

In September 1918, Eliot provides Lewis's *Tarr* a review, which, for his own purposes, implies this English novelist's identity as Anglo-Canadian. He finds in Lewis's writing a set of traits that, containing opposite qualities so strikingly, seems to delineate a compound special to the perception of the Anglo-American. "The artist," he concludes,

> is more *primitive*, as well as more civilized, than his contemporaries, his experience is deeper than civilization, and he only uses the phenomena of civilization in expressing it. Primitive instincts and the acquired habits of ages are compounded in the ordinary man. In the work of Mr. Lewis we recognize the thought of the modern and the energy of the cave-man.[6]

Thinking primitive: Eliot witnesses a synthesis unique to Lewis—rationalism and atavism in his own peculiar balance. He compounds this perception several months earlier, in a preview of the same novel. He reads *Tarr* as "a commentary upon a part of modern civilization: now it is like our civilization criticized, our acrobatics animadverted upon adversely, by an orang-outang of genius, Tarzan of the Apes."[7] If, in Eliot's later perception, Lewis has allowed his tribesman to put on the manners of modern English civility, the poet reassigns him now to his primary, indeed primate, type. This simian mimic, however, presents the genius loci of the novelist's—this poet's—provincial origin. His is the "genius" of the outlandish mime, a verbal and conceptual repetition of a word Pound has established inside the same discourse. Like Pound, moreover, Eliot privileges this imaginative personality with a heady gift. His perception of Lewis's aboriginal hero goes to possibilities that a sound-alike in Lewis's title sets going for him: *Tar*zan encloses this vocable within *Tarr*, at least for Eliot; we may recall as well that the hero of Burroughs's novel was the orphaned Lord Greystoke.[8]

That "nobler" side of Tarzan locates some of the possibilities Eliot is most intent on addressing—and repossessing—through these several notions of critical mimicry. In fact, the critical faculty Eliot establishes for this imitation locates its crucial quality. Yet Eliot does not specify the point of the criticism. The critique proceeds by the sheer fact that the model can be copied at all. The thinking man's civility, which is presumed to include a uniqueness as well as an inwardness as its needed predisposition, appears thus as a set of external, imitable gestures and manners only—done up (and down) in a kind of gymnastic animation that at once exaggerates and reduces, replicates and ridicules their pretense. This formula encloses the conceit of a most timely poetics. (The fact that *Tarr* was begun in 1909 and completed in large part before the war measures the pressure current circumstances exert on Eliot's reading.)[9] The rationalistic language of the Liberal war for civilization affords the opportunity of a self-improving echo on the part of the poet. And he might prove himself better in the sense that his simulation forgoes belief in the discredited methods of that campaign. Indeed, Eliot's verse of this moment outperforms Lewis's pseudo-human, ratiocinating chimp, as he turns his own somersaults on the speech and episteme of English Liberal reason. In doing so, then, he proves a *virtù* that may be consistent with the older and deeper—and better—things of Britain.

Thus, the civilization being maligned for its contemporary idiom and emphases is, nonetheless, claimed (twice)—reclaimed—as "our[s]." The identification Eliot implies between "our civilization" and "our acrobatics" serves to shift the meaning and value of the word in the first phrase—currently being contested by nations—to the merest sort of extrinsic mannerism, in the second, where it shows itself as a performative quality only. This discriminating perception—affirming the limits and pretenses of that much-charged, valorized term—proves to be of decisive importance. It locates for Eliot the soul of Lewis's own animadversion, the animating wit of that caricature. The gift of critical mimicry with which Eliot privileges his provincial type seems to be instinct with some capacity of finer appreciation, some superior means of possession, or prepossession, of whatever "civilization" may really mean. Negotiable in the end, the significance of this potent counter includes with the contemporary mannerisms Eliot is uniquely vantaged to lampoon—to ape—some permanent, ineluctable sense of its correct but irreducible aura. Thus the same years that will witness Eliot's intensest cultivation of the voice of Liberal reason in distress, in the speaking character of his own verse, feature an equally—increasingly—insistent claim on the inward essence of British civilization. His not-so-gradual advance to respectability as a poet and critic moves to this double measure.

"But remember that I am a *metic*—a foreigner," Eliot writes to the Englishwoman Mary Hutchinson on 11 July 1919, glossing a term that works at once to denote his otherness as an American and set it resonating in that strange word, which, once explained, also serves to countermand any impression of outlandish ignorance. "I *want* to understand you," he continues in the same

T. S. Eliot, 1919, by E. O. Hoppé

sentence, "and all the background and tradition of you."[10] The interest he expresses in apparently awkward earnestness replicates for the attention he promises a complex of attitudes as rich as the one his use of *metic* includes. If he sounds a little gauche in the overloaded last half of the sentence, so like a tongue-tied visitant to the site and source of the real language, he also craftily reverses the current of primary and secondary locales. For the England this American is visiting seems a site as rich with the traditions he wishes to (re)possess as it is, subtly but not at all slightly, odd. A sort of curio, England has acquired the status of an anthropological subject to be studied, as quaint at least as the phrases the visitant needs to use to describe it. If this turnaround of assigned roles recalls the behavior that Pound's upstart colonial displays in "American Chaos," the manipulation hardly diminishes the interest or validity of things British for Eliot. It signals instead a level of witting artifice in his mode of approach to this valued trove. Only two days earlier, he had completed a poem we will read, at the end of this chapter, as the end point of his progress—really, his ingress—into this prized domain: "Gerontion."

ii
___

The progress Eliot will have made as the man of English letters, and the method or ethic of his advance, may be followed in the record he leaves of his passage through several sites. One report emerges in a letter he writes near the time of the Hutchinson correspondence, to Ottoline Morrell, in late June 1919. He apologizes for a visit recently missed to Lady Ottoline's "Garsington Manor," where, in her version of twentieth-century salon culture, she convenes the political and intellectual gentry of English Liberalism. From Bertrand Russell to John Maynard Keynes and Lytton Strachey, and from her husband's diverse acquaintances (a Liberal M.P., Philip Morrell was also an avowed pacifist), the cast of characters at Garsington spoke the partisan idiom in its most gifted and diverse inflection.[11] Surprisingly, however, Eliot seems to want to be part of the conversation—or, at least, to speak closely with the hostess. Citing a surprise visit paid him by an old Boston acquaintance as reason for his failure to appear the preceding weekend, the young American takes up the expected tone of casual respect, friendly deference, nearly intimate formality, as he presses for a renewed invitation:

> I feel completely exhausted and especially depressed by my awareness of having lost contact with Americans and their ways, and by the hopelessness of ever making them understand so many things. I could go on indefinitely with this, but it is probably tiresome, and it was only to explain how much I should have preferred sitting on the lawn with you at Garsington, and to justify my proposing myself again after failing in this way. Will you please ask me *soon* after the next weekend.[12]

The scene Eliot projects of Lady Ottoline speaking with him on the expanse of this ancestral demesne—overrun otherwise by the representatives and attendants of the English Liberalism he loathes—presents the staging area of this colonial poet's imaginative project. The site locates at once a primary desire and a contingent complexity. Garsington represents a nexus equally of poetic ambition and opportunistic but difficult struggle. It focuses the crowning image of one—the first—stage in this poet's career.

What was spoken on the lawns of Garsington may have been the tongue of another intellectual country for Eliot, but he had also and already acquired proficiency, even fluency, in it. From the time of his arrival in England in August 1914, he understood that literary advancement lay along the liberal way. He plotted his route accordingly, moving soon into a position as regular review writer at the *New Statesman*, the *Nation*, and the *Westminster Gazette*. He would also be considered for a staff position at the *Manchester Guardian*.[13] The essayist who would put "liberalism" inside those marks of polite abuse could with equal ease and polity hit the marked, liberal tone. So to speak—or double-speak—the idiom of English Liberalism in the poetry would prove at once the pretense of that manner and his own genuineness with the older, deeper things of Britain.

This countermotive and practice return to a suggestive but central and resonant demonstration at Garsington. The high society to which Lady Ottoline has invited Eliot represents a place of tradition and so the sense of legitimacy he seeks but, in its current habitués, the language and attitude of a pseudostewardship. A miniature of the England of Eliot's mind, its proprietor is addressed with a complexity of due deference—and disdain.

He appeals initially to Lady Ottoline as his most astute reviewer, his most informed auditor (with a canniness now characteristic of him, already evident in that self-improving disapproval of those other Americans and "*their* ways"). "You said, by the way, about my poems, some of the things I should like people to say, and which none of the reviewers have said. So I naturally choose to believe that you were 'on the right track!'"[14] The gestures in this final sentence are subtly but more than slightly patronizing. He is reviewing her review; her insight is the grant of his largesse; between quotation marks he frames the very words of acclaim as the cliché they represent, thus offering a tribute to whose dubiousness he remains superior but to which she appears (in this one-sided report) unsuspecting. The uncalled-for, overstated, exclamatory mark speaks aloud the doubtfulness of her attributed gifts. On the lawns of her own estate, indeed, she has become the unsure one. Thus he shifts positions in this culture of patronage. The repossession this colonial poet has staked as his campaign appears to have been won already. The claim his *Sacred Wood* will entitle him to make on succession in the Nemi grove of English literary culture finds on the lawns of Garsington the likeliest site of its realization.

Perhaps, to be fair, Lady Ottoline does present Eliot with an intellectual personality adequately nuanced to the texture of his verse. At least she combines an established name with a novel extravagance of character—if sometimes brutally cartooned, as by D. H. Lawrence, in the figure of Hermione Roddice in *Women in Love*. She manifests nonetheless a capacity for self-invention within the inherited securities of her class, resembling, all in all, the same temperament and demeanor to which Eliot responds so readily in Leonard and Virginia Woolf (whose fledgling Hogarth Press has just brought out *Poems*, the volume whose reviews Eliot mentions in the letter).[15] With her, the Woolfs could stand at once as insiders and rebels, as it were, way out in the center. His own project animates to a similar counterrhythm of observance and defiance. And whether or not Lady Ottoline as reader has reached to its secret coherence, his verse works a sedition from within the conventions represented so extensively at her demesne. The poetry moves through the liberal behavior it feigns in a risible extreme to reclaim a world—and Eliot's own place in it—that has stood, in relation to this present, in every sense of the term, in *precedence*.

Eliot situates this precedent tradition in a figure indicative of his own growing propinquity to the values of its mythical England, in the person of "The Romantic Aristocrat," among his "Imperfect Critics": George Wyndham. This Tory statesman and man of letters lightens measurably any censure that "imperfection" carries in its heavier charge upon others in this category. Indeed, Wyndham shows a "romantic" element to Eliot that adds up, in the imaginative calculus of this piece, to an altogether positive attribution, to the irregularities of genius. These are the eccentricities of a particularly English genius loci. "[T]his man stands for a type, an English type," Eliot proposes, then proceeds to specify this cultural tradition in the configuration of an emblematic life:

> Wyndham left Eton for the army. . . . After this Coldstream culture there was a campaign in Egypt; later, service in South Africa accompanied by a copy of Virgil. There was a career in the Commons, a conspicuous career as Irish Secretary. Finally, there was a career as a landowner—2400 acres. . . . [T]he key to its topography is the fact that his literature and his politics and his country life are one and the same thing.
> . . . George Wyndham was Gentry.[16]

While Wyndham's ethic may prove to be coterminous with world empire, it stands originally—organically—as conatural to Britain as its basis in the land. It describes, all in all, a political faith that Eliot conveys with too eager a zeal; it shows the hand of the interloper, (too) fervently pointed. To recapitalize the social class to which Wyndham belonged, after all, is to reendow this Gentry—but with all the solvent power it maintains in the political and cultural imagination of Eliot himself. This formation resonates to the same complex of needs and ambitions that Pound sets echoing in the same initial syllable, in similar iterations. Eliot's projection draws from this verbal radical the several relevant senses of his own desire, in the manifold extremity of a provincial returning to and reclaiming that first place. To be of this Gentry is to be rooted, to own the genius of the indigenous, to be genuine.

One measure of the personal pressure that this term exerts appears in the use to which Eliot put it in a letter he wrote a year and a half earlier, in October 1917, to his American cousin Eleanor Hinkley. His description of an English country setting features the appellation as its tonic and resolving note:

> [The] farm is very high up, the lane is steep, between tall pines, all the way from the station, the farm in a little hollow of the highest hill, with a ring of pinetrees all about it, and a little rivulet trickling down into the valley. . . . Two miles away is Leith Hill, which looks for miles over the

downs of Surrey and Sussex. It is the sort of country where old farmers touch their hats and call you "gentry."[17]

Eliot's prose mounts the acclivity in this description with the momentum of expectation, paced to the slightly breathless cadence of its parataxis. He has reimagined and repossessed this social topos with the accumulated thrall of the one-time provincial returning now to his truly indigenous condition and recovering a dominance that, if once lost, was ever promissory. The one word spoken—quoted—from this home terrain seals Eliot's favored place in the re-created economy of English social nature. "Gentry" reverberates within those quotation marks with all of the power he recovers for the same class, in Wyndham's instance, as the recapitalized Gentry.

For the outlandish man, however, recovery of the genuine turns on an art of the disingenuous, an instrumentality equally ingenious and mischievous. "[F]or an American," he writes to his mother on 3 July 1920, "getting recognised in English letters is like breaking open a safe."[18] The moment is indeed rich for him: *The Sacred Wood*, about to appear, gathers and consecrates the fame already attained for *Poems* (1919, enlarged 1920). The treasury he frames in his image of English literary repute offers a prime type of the genuine, as it were, the gold standard of literary worth, but such a validation comes to him, Eliot's tropes insist to his American forebear (on the day before their separation from England is formally recalled), through an act—an art—of felonious intent. Opening this safe involves, not the detonations of Eliot's brief career at *Blast*,[19] rather the handiwork of the cryptographer. Cracking the combination, breaking the code: Eliot keys his figure to those manipulations of English political and cultural idiom that will have unlocked this trove for him. The admission he gains to the inward keep of the English resource will have been won then by the turns and counterturns with which this outsider pulls off the inside job. A language of access that is also a cipher, it spells itself out as the reason-seeming speech of British Liberalism at war. This linguistic sensibility compels Eliot, but only as the target it presents. He follows the code but only to break it, so to break in.

iii

This American opportunism locates motive and energy in a deeply considered engagement with the poetic uses and imaginative possibilities of the pseudo-logic of English Liberalism. Even when Eliot appears to censure this idiom, revealing the limitations of a (quasi) rationality in language, he delineates its considerable potential for him. In these complexities, it appears in its most suggestive and representative instance in a single piece in *The Sacred Wood*.

The essay on Ben Jonson opens by framing the values under which his verse drama seems to be esteemed. Jonson adheres in this initial estimate to a language that manifests an adequacy to "the surface of life," an aptitude that Eliot develops under the manifold aspects of linguistic rationalism. In this application, *ratio* covers all the apposite values and possibilities of an aesthetic rationalism: measure, deliberated fit or sufficiency, fittingness and decorum. Thus Jonson's verbal formulations appear at once to be complete and believable in themselves and coextensive with the world they represent; they enclose a satisfactory proposition of the actual. He presents a sensibility ostensibly preferable then to the opposite prosody of Shakespeare, who, in this reckoning, uses a vocabulary of the *ir*rational and incongruous, which works in the gap between word and referent or meaning to stimulate an intense but, it appears, spurious effect of the mysterious, to simulate an impression of depth. "Poetry of the surface cannot be understood without study," Eliot counters, strengthening the evident appeal of this practice, "for to deal with the surface of life, as Jonson dealt with it, is to deal so deliberately that we too must be deliberate, in order to understand. Shakespeare, and smaller men also, are in the end more difficult, but they offer something at the start to encourage the student . . . ; they are suggestive, evocative, a phrase, a voice."[20] Between the associations that Shakespeare's words invoke and the meanings they claim, there opens an area of the unknown, the dimension of the imaginative profound. This abyss, where verbal logic collapses, will locate the space of the modern sublime, but it is Jonson's distinction, in Eliot's initial calculation, not to fall into it. Here "unconscious does not respond to unconscious; no swarms of inarticulate feelings are aroused." He expatiates: "The immediate appeal of Jonson is to the mind; his emotional tone is not in the single verse, but in the design of the whole."[21]

This critical image centers the attention of Eliot's essay and focuses, ultimately, his complex objection. Initially, and positively, a language of rationalistic adequacy may comprise the design of an entire passage, no less a whole poetic drama, and coincide thus with the significance of a complete work. Eliot proceeds to feature such a capacity in what appears to be its exemplary demonstration, the speech of Sylla's ghost in Jonson's *Catiline*, which he analyzes conclusively in an appreciation of its formal proportions, its well-wrought ratios, its fitting of the dramatic language to the "outline" of its referent, its meaning. He asserts: "At no point does it overflow the outline; it is far more careful and precise in its obedience to this outline than any of the speeches in *Tamburlaine*." The argument continues, making concessions which, however, may be more than strategic:

> The words may not be suitable to a historical Sulla, or to anybody in history, but they are a perfect expression for "Sylla's ghost." You cannot say they are rhetorical "because people do not talk like that," you cannot call them "verbiage"; they do not exhibit prolixity or redundancy or the

other vices in the rhetoric books; there is a definite artistic emotion which demands expression at that length. The words themselves are mostly simple words, the syntax is natural, the language austere rather than adorned.[22]

Eliot seems to be esteeming this literary sensibility for its exemplary work within the standards of rationalistic adequacy. Here a "definite artistic emotion" receives the "expression" it "demands"—just "at that length" and at no greater (Shakespearian, incongruous) length. This is a poetics in which meaning is realized as it is embodied perfectly in words. But there is more than silent irony in this profession of the ideal of verbal incorporation. For Eliot finds its quintessential expression in the language of a ghost. This character-in-voice, Eliot puts it unlightly, speaks unlike "any*body* in history." Is Jonson's not a poetics of disembodiment, a sacrifice of the world's dense and irregular body to the merely apparent clarities of a well-ordered verbal surface? No window on a world already there, this polished veneer seems to mirror more clearly the linguistic form and order of the contriver's mind. The polities and rituals of Jonson's spare but elegant syntax bespeak thus a specifically "*artistic* emotion"; they reflect the purer protocols of language itself. While the level of intention underlying the wordplay in this passage seems impossible to determine (the "deliberated" meaning here proves as difficult to secure as that of Jonson's best dramatic language, in Eliot's subsequent discussion), its adversarial theme will be borne out in the course of the essay.

"[T]he worlds created by artists like Jonson are like systems of non-Euclidean geometry," Eliot continues, bringing his subject into a frame of reference more identifiably—intentionally—modern. "They are not fancy, because they have a logic of their own; and this logic illuminates the actual world," not, it turns out, because it reflects some meaning or order inherent in this "actual world," but "because it gives us a new point of view from which to inspect it."[23] Jonsonian language reveals the interest and value of its coherence to Eliot as the expression of one specific vantage, not as an essential or absolute truth. The former orientation of that salutary "logic" has been altered, and not slightly. This ethic of perspectivism or relativism certainly reverses any absolutist claims for the language of a naturalistic rationalism.

This countermeasure emerges most clearly near the end of the essay. In one passage, Eliot manages to retract nearly all of the major formulations he advanced earlier to explain Jonson's power over him. He has claimed that the value of Jonson's drama lies in the complete speakability of its characters, actions, and themes, all in all, in the adequacy of its rational language to the reality it presents in so "deliberate" and apparently comprehensive a fashion. This testament stands at sharp and revealing odds with the admission now that the real source of interest and energy in this literary imagination lies in the pararational, the sublogical, the nonverbal—in the unspeakable. "[I]f we dig beneath the theory," that is, beneath the theory of the humors and the grammar of understandable motives it prescribes for characters; if we read "beneath the observation" and so beneath the belief in the demonstrability of these characters through a language of rationalistic adequacy; if we search under that trust in the "surface" of words and its concomitant faith in verbal logic as a satisfactory, congruous proposition of the actual; if we see thus

> beneath the deliberate drawing and the theatrical and dramatic elaboration, there is discovered a kind of power, animating Volpone, Busy, Fitzdottrel, the literary ladies of *Epicoene*, even Bobadil, which comes from below the intellect, and for which no theory of humours will account. . . . The fictive life of this kind is not to be circumscribed by a reference to "comedy" or to "farce." . . . It is not merely Humours; for neither Volpone nor Mosca is a humour. No theory of humours could account for Jonson's best plays or the best characters in them.[24]

What magnifies the "kind of power" Eliot particularizes to the *sub* "intellectual" life of Jonson's "best characters" is the collapse of an intricate superstructure, that "elaborate" apparatus of rationalistic language that he took such pains to erect at the start of the essay. The demise of this scheme, it is fair to say, identifies the main point of Eliot's interest in it.

This understanding of antithetical poetic power, moreover, reveals a striking resemblance to the signature idea of I. A. Richards: pseudostatement. For Richards, poetry draws its peculiar force from the same special, inverse economy: the feelings become sensible just where they defy or outsize the surface order of words, the superficial ratios of a rational language. The insufficiency of reasonable speech proves to be the indispensable element in the poetic experience. Hardly a barren paradox, no merely exquisite critical conceit, this concept is consistent in all of its contrariness with the ironies that recent intellectual and political history has inscribed as the truer, more enduring shape of these times. Sweet reason has appealed the matter of bloody fact in the recent war to the standards of a rationalistic language whose inadequacy has grown increasingly apparent. Since the force of history has been assimilated as a failure of reason, so poetry repossesses this experience as sublogical emotion, but requires the demise of rational authority—at least in its rhetorical fictions—to recreate the feeling of an original intensity. In its pace and process, Eliot's essay on Jonson enacts this same dynamic.

The poetry that emerges from these timely conditions is as strongly counterconventional, however, as the tradition of imaginative reason is deep in English literary history. One measure of the force of difference in this new usage lies in the initial move that Eliot, like Pound, is compelled to make as he attempts to write out of his profounder apprehension of this moment. His first efforts at verse must take him outside his native language. His poetry needs to speak English in—as—a foreign dialect. He will have come to this remote pa-role by staying right at home, in Liberal England at war.

II

English, in French

On 23 August 1914, from London, Eliot writes to his mother of the Germany he has recently been forced to flee for reasons of war. (The period of study he had planned took him there in advance for a summer vacation.) "The people in general are persuaded of the rightness of the German cause," he remembers, "and so was I," at least "to a certain extent"—to the same extent, it seems, that a young man's suggestibility allowed. He maintained this alliance only "till I found that the English papers were making exact contradictions of the Ger-man." Then he expresses the division this British journalism has introduced to his previous attitudes. "Germany is animated by an intense spirit," he recol-lects, "but I don't see how she can possibly win. They will do no harm to En-gland; the waters as we approached were black with English warships. And Germany is putting forth every ounce of strength. 'Deutschland kaempft um das Existenz!' they say and they are right. *But I think it is better that Germany should go.*"[25] "[T]he whole experience has been something which has left a very deep impression on me," he writes then on 8 September to Eleanor Hinkley, "having seen, I mean, how the people in the two countries have taken the affair, and the great moral earnestness on both sides." If this transnational vantage "has made it impossible for me to adopt a wholly partizan [*sic*] attitude, or even to rejoice or despair wholeheartedly" at the success or defeat of either side, "I should certainly want to fight against the Germans if at all."[26] A compulsion in doubt of its ultimate "rightness": how like the predicament in which English Liberalism found itself at the same moment.

To hear in Eliot a literary sensibility echoing representatively to the ten-sions of this heightened time is encouraged further, again in early September, as he writes to his brother Henry. "[H]ere in all the noise and rumour," he as-serts, "I can work," citing the provocations of the journalistic day (and night): "Ten o'clock in the evening, quiet for a few minutes, then a couple of men with late editions burst into the street, roaring: GREAT GERMAN DISASTER!" where-upon "the papers are all sold in five minutes; then we settle down for another hour till the next extra appears: LIST OF ENGLISH DEAD AND WOUNDED."[27] The headlines recover their original sensationalism, as Eliot describes a go-and-stop rhythm that makes waiting as restive and excitable as the silence is edgy. He as-similates the idiom and sensibility of the journalistic war, moreover, rehearsing its already premature enthusiasms. "I have a great deal of confidence in the ul-timate event," he pledges, then reiterates his wish for an English victory: "I am anxious that Germany should be beaten." Yet the conviction he proceeds to elaborate wobbles oddly—on these conjunctions of antithesis, which, in being stressed, reveal the real stutter-step in his statement of faith:

> *[B]ut* I think it is silly to hold up one's hands at German "atrocities" and "violation of neutrality." The Germans are perfectly justified in violating Belgium—they are fighting for their existence—*but* the English are more than justified in turning to defend a treaty. *But* the Germans are bad diplomats. It is not against German "crimes," *but* against German "civilisation"—all the system of officers and professors—that I protest. *But* very useful to the world if kept in its place.[28]

Eliot's personal experience has equipped him with an open-mindedness about two-sided truths in this war. Thus he can take the sayings of the side he favors—the lingo of journalistic London—and put these words and phrases within quotation marks. The dubiousness of these counters coincides nonetheless with their service, in his estimation, in the right campaign. Words are at war, then, at every level of the linguistic temperament he inscribes. The antithetical conjunction he keeps reiterating registers a more particular inflection, however. The gesture of a self-refining progression of dialectical argument appears with this intensity of repetition to be little different from intellectual farce. So, too, Liberal *raisonneurs* are currently forcing the case of England's reasonable war; theirs, too, is a ratiocination as intense in its rhetoric and artifice as it is, by force of intellectual principle and predisposition, incredulous; theirs, too, a sputtering confidence in the verbal logic of it. The uncertainty that Eliot's "but" scores into the otherwise voluble report reproduces the sound of the times in this revealing extreme, in this lucid cartoon.

Eliot's readiness to register these contemporary pressures demonstrates no certain or evident purpose as yet. (Nor is the "work" he refers to identifiable specifically.) His correspondence in the early years of the war sometimes displays this uncritical synergy with the popular consciousness. Recalling his stay in Germany in a letter of 4 April 1915 to Mrs. Jack Gardner, for instance, he rehearses the argument of the war for civilization virtually *à la lettre*. He takes the French side against a national character that shows "that hospitality and cordiality which characterises the less civilised peoples," then continues, "And not that I wish the Germans to be crushed—but France is so important, and defeat would do the French so much harm! This alone outweighs any consideration of right and wrong in my mind."[29] The circumspect civility Eliot evinces—the generous (if patronizing) concession he makes to the well-meaning Teuton, the moderation he counsels in the end to which the war should be prosecuted—bespeaks an affinity with the creed being professed. He would fight, it seems, for beliefs he maintains with such fineness of civilized spirit. Or is it just finesse? Where his cause subdues "any consideration of right and wrong" to the sheer "importance" of France, one may read what these *more* "civilised peoples," these French (and their allies), really mean to him. Privileging aesthetics over ethics, he allows the absence of moral cause to be filled with the exemplary attitude of his own civility; this value appears performative rather than prudential. All too English, after all, and specifically Liberal, he reiterates the main conceit of the insular political war. Here, too, a "civilized" correctness performs ratios of well-formed thought to afford an appearance of rightness for a rationale otherwise lacking moral authority and conviction.

The ready echo Eliot provides for the Liberal sensibility of wartime London finds a revealing counterpoint in the invective he centers on the liberal mind in other English milieux. Comparing the academic environments of Oxford and Cambridge in a letter of 21 March 1915 to Eleanor Hinkley, for example, he opposes the two universities on the grounds of their associations with social philosophies and cultural values. He features the scene at Cambridge as the symbol and center of intellectual liberalism. He finds the primary site—and icon—of institutional value "where I read a paper" at "the Moral Science Club." The title (and charter) of this organization presents an echo of the twin principles of ethical and empirical reasoning in the liberal tradition, and it extends in Eliot's report to a membership that presents an academic demography of suggestively partisan stripe. Its social egalitarianism, in particular the opportunity for education and improvement that it would extend to hardworking members of the working class, manifests in an audience that is "serious, industrious, narrow and plebeian." By contrast, "the temper . . . of Oxford is *historical*," he emphasizes and, insofar as "history is a more aristocratic pursuit than natural science,"[30] he responds with obvious favor to the Tory confidence of its claims. This security coincides for him with a sense of inherited assurance, which is uncompelled to argue or prove its authority. The contrast he fashions certainly advantages Oxford.

His distaste for the reasoning faculty he associates with Cambridge liberalism shows in a report that summarizes his own academic experience. If "almost every philosophy seems to begin as a revolt of common sense against some other theory," this better, inarguable, intuitively grounded "sense" may be connected with the entitlements that the "more aristocratic pursuit" of history takes, as granted, at Oxford. The moral-scientific episteme prevailing at Cambridge, however, takes nothing for granted. In his characterizing representation, this liberal sensibility works and worries the details of a reasonable coherence until it "ends—as it becomes itself more developed and approaches completeness—by itself becoming equally preposterous." This logical quality reaches its consummation at a risible extreme that "involves," in Eliot's astonishing trope, "cramming both feet into one shoe."[31]

This figure of the ridiculous seems capable of considerable literary development. It represents a responsiveness and imaginative openness to similar provocations—to those strenuous rationalizations that Liberals were concocting in support of an insupportable war. The somber, involuntary comedy those partisan apologists for the cause were performing in the drearily donnish medium of liberal prose may yield—the promise appears as irresistible as the wit of this figure—to more ebullient, intentionally excessive measures; to a cramming into poetic feet. The verse may take this further turn and inflate the ratios of a rationality already excessively stressed. The forcing of political logic will slide easily, or so it seems, into a farcing of the artistic logos.

This is hardly the motive to be scanned, however, in the rendition of Eliot's political opinions in the letters of August and September 1914 and April 1915. The language of English ideology encompasses the issues of the war so extensively, after all, that his own expression seems for now, at the outset, to be wholly dominated by it. The experience of total war was hardly apprehensible at the start, in fact, in the outline of a philosophical comedy. It stages nothing less than an end to liberal modernity, and the literary modernism we have cued to this provocation hardly writes itself out in some ready-made fashion. The event *is* unprecedented. Were he able to turn the particular perversions of that intellectual campaign into verse from the first moment, the product would be preconceived merely and, drawn from his own rather narrowly academic exposures at this moment, performed perhaps as just a bit of antic academic gaudy. Arguably, it would miss the content and depth of the lived historical and political experience that the delay accumulates and, in what he ultimately produces, preserves. In the resistance that history extends to his special ability, his facility gains for his expression its representative weight.

Resistance is indeed the generative condition of this art. The period between mid-1914 and early 1917 coincides with the driest time of poetic productivity for Eliot. He finds himself in the country of an enemy language, a linguistic, literary, and political culture dominated by English Liberalism. An inimical sensibility might well be turned to its adversary's advantage in a poetry of cartoon and ridicule, but the campaigns of mass war are at the start too massive; poetry cannot as yet outsize this target. While Eliot might like to turn the weakness of the partisan temperament into the nascent strength of his own poetic, he still cannot access the primary language of this performance, which his opponent owns. He must move out of the oppressive ideolect into which Liberal ideology has shifted his English idiom. He needs to take up the language, if not the cause, of his—and Britain's—willing ally. He has to write in French.

i

When Eliot cites the completion of several French efforts, in a letter of 11 April 1917, he intimates clearly the liberating effect of this exercise.[32] Why could it work this way? The elaboration of syntax and grammar for their own sake, which these pieces reveal, conforms to the order of a lesson in language paradigms. Reliance on rules like these combines with the license provided him by an indifference to the finer points of meaning in an acquired language. Thus the block that a poet chiefly lyrical (until now) has encountered in his task of nuanced self-expression is lifted. Yet the drama private to this poetic career plays out on a broader public stage. He shares this scene with Pound, who, also in spring 1917, turns to composition in—and from—foreign languages, not only in the Latin of Sextus Propertius but, preceding this effort, in the French of Laforgue. While Pound implements these attempts to break no stoppage in poetic flow, they serve a further purpose, one that Eliot's attempts also further and help to clarify.

Ultimately in *Propertius*, initially and equally strongly in his rendition of Laforgue (in echo to the tone the other prose fables have struck, also, through their travelers' response to distant locales), Pound uses the alien semantic of the foreign tongue to distance or estrange verbal meaning in his own. An apparently sensible syntax features words of frequently indeterminate significance. The confection reads as a rhetorical fiction of logical non-sense. A resonant echo of the sounds of these English times, Eliot's efforts in French will demonstrate a consonance with Pound's current work and include his own riposte to this shared provocation.

One measure of the coherence this joint project reveals shows in the fact that it was Pound who set Eliot on his French course. In a letter of 21 August 1916 to Conrad Aiken, Eliot reveals that Pound "has just translated (with untiring energy) Laforgue's 'Salome,' and wants me to do the 'Hamlet' to go to make up a volume between us of the *Moralités Légendaires*." "I have done a few pages of it," Eliot goes on to indicate, and whether or not he stopped, as Valerie Eliot speculates later, on account of the copyright problem with the Laforgue estate, the passage he offers at the end of the letter leaves an impression of the amazing instigation this effort represented for him. His sample of the new writing appears as a sequel and conclusion to a piece of intellectual self-portraiture, drawn for his friend Aiken in terms idiosyncratic but also sincere and exact. "I am still a relativist," he proposes, setting up the old standard of well-reasoned meanings, as normative as this standardized word,

> a cracker of small theories like nuts, essentially an egoist perhaps, but I have not the leisure to be cynical, a good thing perhaps, life is always positively something or the opposite, it has a *sens*, if only that

>> the torch-bearers, advancing from behind the throne which King Artaphernes had just vacated, progressed two by two into the centre of the hall. To the shrill piping of the quowhombom and the muffled rattle of the bass trpaxli mingled with the plaintive wail of the thirty captive kings, they circled thrice forwards and thrice backwards, clockwise and counterclockwise, according to the sacred ritual of the rpat, and finally when the signal was given by the pswhadi or high

priest, they turned a flip flop somersault and disappeared down their own throats, leaving the assembly in darkness.

But if you still believe in my sanity, and receive this letter, write to me.[33]

The French original of this performance fosters a special capacity to turn English into an alien language, where the substantive counters retain their alterity even—or especially—within the sense-making gestures of syntax and grammar. The sheer *appearance* of normative meaning emerges as the main conceit. This creative concept will compel his inventions in French. Already in this letter he elaborates it in a fashion adequate to more than the sophistical ruse of a foreign language student. For he tends a sensibility on this continental ground that presents the linguistic consciousness of his own English moment. The insular idiom has nonetheless overpowered and silenced him with the force and scale of its own rational inanities. How to free this sublogical quality—ultimately, in English verse—is the aim and effect of Eliot's French lessons.

ii

"Petit Epître" is the first of Eliot's spring 1917 efforts (the "mi–careme" or mid-Lent date in its imaginative fiction places it in mid–late March of that year).

> Ce n'est pas pour quo'on se dégoute
> Ou gout d'égout de mon Ego
> Qu'ai fait des vers de faits divers
> Qui sentent un peu trop la choucroute.
> Mais qu'est ce que j'ai fait, nom d'un nom,
> Pour faire ressortir les chacals?[34]

> [It's not to disgust anyone
> Nor is it the taste of the sewer of my own Ego
> That I've made verses out of different things
> That smell a little bit too much of sauerkraut.
> But what is it that I've done, the name of a name,
> So as to make the jackals come out again?]

"Petit Epître" already shows in its title—in the close repetition of the *it* syllable—the element that Eliot features in his new French register: sound effects. He intensifies this element to an acoustic density in the opening lines. Here he encloses echoes of whole words within others—"gout" in "dégoute" and "d'égout"—and reiterates similar phonetic formations across differing phrases—"fait des vers" in "faits divers"—to achieve a virtual continuum of sheer sound. He arranges the musical body of these words, however, inside a highly elaborate apparatus of syntactical ratiocination—that very French array of rhetorical negatives, antithetical conjunctions, subordinate and relative clauses. The discriminating thinking that this rationalistic syntax fosters in standard French, however, has turned into a sheer mouthful of Gallic bread and cheese. Foreign sound chokes the locutions of Eliot's (neo)classical reason.

The local and timely provocations of this work emerge with some specificity in "Petit Epître." The worried reference in the fourth line to "choucroute"—sauerkraut—testifies to anxieties about items proscribed under Duration, like this archetypally German food (American delicatessens would put it under embargo). In a French tongue, then, *le farçeur* echoes the logistical forcing of English, which has imposed its rationalistic grammar on the stuff of history but left it, in effect, as dense and impenetrable as these foreign sounds. Further evidence of this local historical pressure shows as Eliot's rhetorical fiction adapts the format of a questionnaire, which *rédacteurs*, newspaper editors, direct at the unit of mass war, the citizen-speaker:

Messieurs les rédacteurs
Et tous let autres maîtres-chanteurs
Et tous les gens étiquetés
M'ont dressé tous, leur questionnaires.
"Il se moque dc l'égalité?"
—"Mais c'est un vrai réactionnaire."
"Il dit du mal de nos ministres?"
—"Mais c'est un saboteur, le cuistre."
"Ici il cite un allemand?"
—"Mais c'est un suppôt de Satan!" (*IN*, 86–87)

[The gentlemen editors
And all the other master-singers
And all the ceremonial people
Have addressed me with their questions:
"Does he mock equality?"
—"But he's a real reactionary."
"Does he speak ill of our officials?"
—"But he's a saboteur, the pedant."
"Does he quote a German here?"
—"But he's a tool of Satan!"]

The answers to these questions present themselves as antitheses that represent no difference to the reply expected. A reactionary, after all, will probably find equality a concept for mockery; a saboteur will speak ill (if in secret) of ministers and betray them; and, in the xenophobic demonology of total war, anyone quoting the enemy's German is identifiable as an instrument of Satan. A word of meaningless difference, "mais" frames the logic of opposition—the rationale of total war—as a rationalistic inanity. This is a riddle all too familiar to the Liberal war of Eliot's English experience.

The British frame of reference for these French improvisations emerges more evidently still in "Le Directeur." The poem takes as its subject the editor of the publication it names, the English *Spectator*:

Malheur à la malheureuse Tamise
Qui coule si prés du Spectateur.
Le directeur
Conservateur
Du Spectateur
Empeste la brise.
Les actionnaires
Réactionnaires
Du Spectateur
Conservateur
Bras dessus bras dessous
Font des tours
A pas de loup.
Dans un égout
Une petite fille
En guenilles
Camarde
Regarde
Le directeur
Du Spectateur
Conservateur
Et crève d'amour.[35]

[Evil to the evil Thames
Which flows so close to Spectator.
The conservative
Director
Of Spectator
Stinks the breeze.
The reactionary
Actionaries
Of conservative
Spectator
Arm in arm
Make their tours
With a wolf's step.

In an alley
A little girl
In rags
Flat-nosed
Regards
The conservative
Director
Of Spectator
And bursts with love.]

With hurdy-gurdy rhymes and rigmarole rhythms, this doggerel prosody extends Eliot's more obviously sophisticated efforts in French, which attempt to present language mainly as a medium of sound. The heightened materiality of these words achieves the same feeling of meaninglessness as he positions each of the signal words virtually by itself in an individual line. This unit of (expected) sense leaves the word echoing in a framework of its sound alone. While the piece lacks the more elaborate apparatus of rationalistic grammar and syntax, the acoustic residue it leaves presents the remains of the same—English— journalistic day. The insular newspaper culture has worn out the verbal logic it has used to support an insupportable war and left the noise, alone. The Conservative-Tory identification of the *Spectator* shows up perhaps in the absence of the Liberal accent, that is, in the very low gradient of rationalistic activity in the syntax. In its own way, however, the poem shows Eliot's agreement with the perception in Pound's "Studies in Contemporary Mentality," which found the linguistic sensibility of the *Spectator* fully consonant with that of the magazine most obviously aligned with Liberalism, the *New Statesman*. To this national logos, in total control of no thinking at all, the most telling response lies in an ideolect virtually bereft of intellectual content. This is the tongue that echoes, in Pound's own memorable phrase on the representative instance of the *Spectator*, to a "vacuity" of meaning as "stupendous" as the one Eliot sets resonating in lines sounding out sounds (alone).

iii

In wartime, moreover, the writing of any foreign language uncovers a further dimension of interest. Is it a code? one worries with curiosity. Its secretiveness goes to the poet's interest in the secret dimensions of speech, in what goes covert or unrevealed in English, in particular in the national language of England at war. This area opens indeed as a major resource in Eliot's developing poetic response to the language of the national experience.

As a foreign national writing home, Eliot could expect a censorship that suppressed any specificity of reference. Verbal substantives could disappear completely beneath the censor's bar, that blanking black.[36] Between these

177

PASSED THE TEST.
A Fragment.

✗ ✗✗✗
The Fragment.

That blanking black. Representation of their work by members of
the Department of the Postal Censor, 1919.

voids, nonetheless, the sense-making gestures of language—conjunctions, particles, the prepositions of relation and reference—are preserved and suspended. This syntactical apparatus would have given propositional—and, presumably, logical—meaning to the words now erased. The censored page reads
thus as the visible idiom of journalistic and governmental Liberalism in defense of its war, a rationalistic language voiding itself of content. Beyond this
somber comedy, however, lies another area of awareness, one to which the
American poets, who must envision their letters being sent under this appearance, could well ignite. Whether it is the letter censor's bar, or the generality
Bennett has found as the new vocabulary of vacuous abstraction, or the euphemized rationales for the war, the counter for unallowed knowledge exerts a
powerful energy, a sort of black–hole–in–space draw. Into those blanks might be
poured all that could not be said. Papered over or blacked out, the empty space
presents the resonant domain of the modern unspeakable—a language adequate potentially to the hitherto unimaginable atrocity of this war.

"It *is*, of course, a check to one in writing, always finding oneself running
up against subjects which it is wiser not to mention," Eliot confides to his
mother on 24 March 1918, "and everything seems to lead to such subjects
now."[37] A self-interfering speech moves against the disclosures of which it
feels the urgency—all the more strongly—in resistance. He expresses this in-

terest most suggestively at a time coinciding with the resumption of his poetic activity, that is, as he turns to France and finds a novel language of composition: 21 March 1917. "As you say," he writes back to Charlotte Eliot, "political topics are barred in letters: it is a great annoyance to me, as I am violently interested in the subject at present. However, one can 'lay down' bottles to be opened when the vintage has ripened."[38] The "lay[ing] down" of "bottles" may suggest as its easiest implication a deferral of free exchange until the embargo has lifted. Yet all of the associations of this trope conspire to align the practice it designates with bolder motives. The wine cellar presents the site and primary symbol of an art of writing in crypt, undertaken currently and most notably in Eliot's composition in the foreign tongue. Lowering into code does not indicate a cancellation or postponement of open political discussion; a whole range of meaning or feeling ripens and grows in potency, even—or especially—as it goes unspoken in English. The unspeakability of Eliot's British experience—the erosion of the logos of reason, even of reference, in the political ideolect of English Liberalism at war—establishes and magnifies the attraction of this cryptographic idiom, in this relatively alien language of France.

iv
―――――

So powerful are the local determinants on Eliot's exertions in French that not even the scenes of a continental holiday in "Lune de Miel"—Honeymoon—can leave the island behind. Whether or not the itinerary Eliot narrates under this title makes reference to events in the early days of his already troubled marriage to Vivien, the two verse paragraphs lead most tellingly to a single constant, the twice-visited site of the church of St. Apollinaire in Ravenna. He images this structure as a projection of his British experience no less vividly than suggestively:

> Pas même une lieue d'ici est St Apollinaire
> In Classe, basilique connue des amateurs
> De chapitaux d'acanthe que tourbillonne le vent. . . .

> Et St Apollinaire, raide et ascétique,
> Vieille usine désaffectée de Dieu, tient encore
> Dans ses pierres écroulantes la forme précise de Byzance.[39]

> [Not even a league from here is Saint Apollinaire
> En Classe, a church known by the lovers
> Of Acanthine capitals that the wind turns. . . .

> And Saint Apollinaire, stiff and ascetic,
> An old manufactory disaffected with God, still holds
> In its collapsed stones the exact outline of Byzantium.]

The patron saint of this Roman church recalls the Hellenic god of logic and light. More immediately, St. Apollinaire echoes in name—and imaginative elaboration—to the figure Pound calls up at the same moment, in the opening verse of his *Propertius*. This is an Apollo "wearied" and worn "out" by the "generalities" of war—the Word of godly reason has been erased by the vacuous discourses of the Liberal campaign. The vacant shape of the namesake basilica in Eliot's poem traces the same provocation.

The issue of poetic influence may be impossible to resolve. What seems certain, and ultimately more interesting and important, is the twinness of the two configurations, and their virtual simultaneity: they present one reply to the same stimulus. While the ghost of a supernal logos haunts the edifice in Eliot's poem, the timelier provocation of war discourse not only prompts this image but invests this figure with its complexity of poetic potential and implication. The Word of ultimate sense has emptied itself of credible reference, absconded from its promise of embodied meaning. Where the old ratios of language show an architecture of syntax only, a structure exposed now and denuded, those ghostlier demarcations locate a starker, more severe and astonishing beauty. In this tradition of the sublime, a thrill of feeling attends the disintegration or disembodiment of verbal logic. The same imaginative space opens as the main resource of linguistic energy for Eliot as for Pound. Poetry draws its force in proportion to what, by the former standards of an established rationalism, cannot be said. The inspiration explains Eliot's initial need to go to the relative unknown, a language in which meaning seems to be recessed at least from the verbal surface. As he turns back to English expression, he brings the aim and method of the French *leçon* into a form that, again at the direction of Pound, he assimilates with the special benefits of his French interlude. This is the signature measure of Théophile Gautier: the quatrain.[40]

III

Powers of Four

The revival of Eliot's ability to compose poetry in English coincides almost entirely with his discovery of the potentials of the quatrain form. Within its tightly closed structures of sound, his metrical progressions could shape themselves to an impression of regimented thought. By the same token, and by virtue of a cadence verging on the mechanical and a rhyme scheme tending toward the hypnotic and at times idiotic, the deliberation runs on its well-paced feet straight into the intense inane. Again and again, the quatrain poems concoct this rhetorical fiction of sagacious shenanigans, using normative patterns of rhythm and propositional syntax to create a feel of reasoned meditation that dissolves constantly into the preposterous. Into a similar register the rationalistic grammar of Eliot's French demonstrations has led the way. The consonance that this earlier *leçon* reveals now with the quatrain poems goes to the controlling and tone-setting presence of the English political circumstance, in particular, the Liberal episteme of reason at war with itself. It is no accident, then, that one of the first of the quatrain poems, which he left unpublished (for reasons that will become clear), takes the culture of partisan war journalism as its target and point of mimicry.

"Airs of Palestine, No. 2" centers on the figure of John Spender, editor of the *Westminster Gazette*:

> God from a Cloud to Spender spoke
> And breathed command: "Take thou this Rod,
> And smite therewith the living Rock";
> And Spender hearkened unto God. . . .

> Swift at the stroke of Spender's pen
> The viscid torrents crawl and writhe. . . .

> And such as have the skill to swim
> Attain at length the farther shore
> Cleansed and rejoiced in every limb,
> And hate the Germans more and more.

> They are redeemed from heresies
> And all their frowardness forget;
> And scales are fallen from their eyes
> Thanks to the Westminster Gazette.[41]

The mechanical inanity to which this cadence takes its scriptural references defines the tonal conceit of the piece. The apparent sagacity of the vatic allusions collapses into the low bawdry of the barrack-room ballad; the high biblical propriety dissolves into a demotic residuum. Eliot repeats a conceit he has learned from his subject and occasion. In Liberal war journalism, too, the ceremonies of moral rationale run down into the ground rhythm of unseemly realities, under the pressure of history's profounder unreason. The organ-grinder meters and lickety-split rhymes speak a sort of doggerel logic, a tone that offers a rough-but-ready replica of the mock sententiousness and pseudoreasonableness that the later, more polished quatrains will smooth out (and so, unlike this poem, will present in print). A radical version, this poem roots the later quatrain style in its forcing ground, its originating context.

These quatrains recover a resonance from their local and immediate context that may be lost too easily, for later auditors, to the nonsense air the poems confabulate. "A Cooking Egg," similarly. On the surface, its miscellany of ostensibly trivial subjects, presented in the know-nothing know-it-all tone of journalistic reportage, seems to add up to a representatively ephemeral noise. A number of references, however, orient these quatrains and their now-characteristic manner to the contemporary political circumstance, which may echo better to a historically informed reading.

"I shall not want Capital in heaven," the speaker motions to start one of its stanzas, then explains,

> For I shall meet Sir Alfred Mond;
> We two shall lie together, lapt
> In a Five Per Cent Exchequer Bond.[42]

Sir Alfred Mond, an Anglo-German Liberal and a prominent M.P., served in Lloyd George's cabinet in the Office of Works and on various trade and tariff commissions, but he emerges out of his well-known success in commerce and banking as the signal figure of war economics, the broader context of which becomes relevant to a reading here. The costs of total conflict were sufficiently enormous to have pushed the government into the role of the borrower—or conscriptor—of private capital, for which it issued bonds promising attractively high rates of interest. That the national effort was running on money borrowed prodigally was a fact the full consequences of which would be told only later, yet already in 1917, especially for Eliot, whose clerical work at Lloyd's Bank had now begun, the impact was immediately—daily—apparent. The great casualty of the war economy was the gold standard,[43] which, fiscal myth and legal fiction or not, had served at least to maintain an appearance of universal value, a degree of reassurance about stable worth. It had offered the promise of some absolute standard, in the image of hard matter being stored in vaults to back up the paper currency on the table. This conventional understanding has been stressed and indeed discredited in the monetary arrangements of the war, which have generated the resources the government needs by promising money it does not have.

Eliot depicts this situation in the visible mimicry of this quatrain's last line. The capitalization he provides this "Five Per Cent Exchequer Bond" signs these notes from the economy of borrowed "Capital"—the keyword in the first line of this quatrain establishes the symbolic value of the punctuation—with the conspicuous insignia of inflation, of willed or invented worth. A dubious system of fiduciary credit ramifies into the linguistic dimension. This pressure appears as inexorable as the parallel underlying the economic and verbal practices of the current Liberal government, whose Bond was indeed its Word. Premised on the notion of an absolute logos, all in all, a gold standard of trustworthy sense, Liberal language was borrowing on resources only as substantial as its official seal. This linkage between the linguistic and fiscal policies of the majority party at war establishes the contemporary political reality as the full ground of Eliot's imagination. In this context, his poem speaks the meaning of these days, recovering a character-in-voice at once surprisingly and fully representative.

"When Pipit's slipper once fell off," goes the provocation in the opening line of the third stanza,

> It interfered with my repose;
> My self-esteem was somewhat strained
> Because her stockings had white toes.

> I wanted Peace here on earth,
> While I was still strong and young;
> And Peace was to have been extended
> From the tip of Pipit's tongue.

> I shall not want Honour in heaven
> For I shall meet Sir Philip Sidney,
> And have talk with Coriolanus
> And other heroes of my kidney. (*IN*, 358)[44]

In 1917, the British lexicon of the Great War owned the two abstractions of "Peace" and "Honour" ("Peace with Honour," went one mantra). Eliot also capitalizes these abstractions, bringing them into line with the activities of Sir Alfred Mond, who, in his manufacturing of financial "Capital" for the war, has magnified and inflated those corresponding units of monetary value. Eliot's verse of the moment has become a poetry of money, all the truer to its time in striking the note of counterfeit. An apparent but insubstantial value in the fiduciary realm is negotiated as the fully logical preposterousness these verses show on their verbal surface.

If this conceit of reason-seeming nonsense appears so extensive as to need little demonstration, this manner shows a capacity for diversified expression that testifies to its imaginative potency. The concept compels the main entertainment of the poem, its psychological fiction, where the speaker's attraction to Pipit, the ingenue flickering through several of the quatrain poems, conforms to the crazed logic of erotic obsession ("*Because* her stockings had white toes"). It works further, moving the substance of literature in the same direction that the language of Liberal political discourse is going—in this poet's own imaginative apprehension, to meaningless sound. Nothing but an acoustic valence, after all, can survive an idiot rhyme like *Sidney* and *kidney*, which forces any discourse of "heroes" into a representatively farcical measure.

Heroic or not, the substantiality of human tragedy in this war asks to be spoken for. Where gravity is ludicrous, as truisms balloon through a verbal atmosphere lightened of all but sententious nonsense, Eliot adapts a thematics of feeling hardly adequate, it seems, to the reality of that demand. How may measures like these speak of heavy suffering? The rhythms demonstrate an indifference to the implications or consequences of Eliot's timely references, but this silence becomes expressive in another sense. The same sort of logical folly that he embodies in these meters has produced conclusions so grimly borne out in the English war. It is a representative sound, stirring with all the disquiet (to an informed auditor) of the war with which it is identified. This point about the historical association and the resource of feeling it holds cannot be proven through direct reference to the quatrain form, whose meaning, after all, lies in its impassivity, all in all, in its extraordinarily business-as-usual attitude. The war affords these poems a resource of background sound, however. The accumulated distress that the event edges into their (tellingly) inexpressive measures may be discerned through the single instance where Eliot breaks the pattern, in the five-line verse he inscribes as the conclusion to "A Cooking Egg."

The closing cadence amplifies its difference against the normative measure of the quatrain stanza immediately preceding it:

> But where is the penny world I bought
> To eat with Pipit behind the screen?
> The red-eyed scavengers are feeding
> In Kentish Town and Golder's Green.
>
> Where are the eagles and the trumpets?
> Buried beneath some snow-deep Alps;
> Over buttered scones and crumpets
> Weeping, weeping multitudes
> Droop in a hundred A. B. C.'s.[45]

Whereas the four-line pace moves in its usual way to a mechanical iteration of names, recited mainly for the sake of their place in a metrical scheme, the widened frame of the finale opens another order of imaginative possibility. As the observing eye dilates through a prospect of visionary figures and immediate details, Eliot loosens the rhythm and frees the feeling into an expressiveness, even a pathos, which encompasses a range of reference recognizably historical and intensely affective. The image of "weeping, weeping multitudes" sets in epic perspective a sight of mass grief all too current in the mass war, where the diminuendo he hits in the last two lines catches the collapse of aspirations voiced in the opening of this cinquaine. The speaker's appeal for "the eagles and the trumpets" sounds, in that *ubi sunt* lament, a triumphalist note in despair of itself, a presentiment of loss fitted to the dimensions of a plebeian tragedy. Thus, in the earlier quatrain, the preferred heroism of Coriolanus, a figure inextricably associated with the crowd, reveals its timelier rationale. Whether or not Eliot himself believes that the plight of the people at war may be idealized in line with the higher typology, that feeling abides as one of the half-voiced possibilities here. This frame of imaginative reference also surfaces in a fashion apparently natural—elliptically but progressively, echoing back through these drooping multitudes to the Coriolanus allusion. The emotion is sufficiently living to be released incrementally and, by the end, revealed movingly in this irregular and expressive meter. The process leaves behind an understanding of the dense and intricate relationship that obtains between the contemporary reality and Eliot's quatrain cadence.

Again, in "Whispers of Immortality." Here the sometimes portentous affect suggests deep philosophical meaning, while the verbal surface remains metrically genial, easy. This piece works that disparity into an exemplary demonstration of the poetics of reason-seeming inanity.

The titles Pound assigned this poem in draft—"Night Thoughts on immortality," "Night thoughts on Gautier"[46]—rightly identify the intellectual exercises these verses undertake. Yet Eliot's quatrain cadence takes the effort at disciplined meditation in the direction he signals through one of his own provisional headings, "Try This on Your Piano."[47] The poem moves into the musical register of ludic reason, now usual to the four-line form:

> Webster was much possessed by death;
> He saw the skull beneath the skin;
> And breastless creatures underground
> Leaned backward with a lipless grin.
>
> Daffodil bulbs instead of balls
> Stared from the sockets of the eyes!
> He knew that thought clings round dead limbs
> Tightening its lusts and luxuries. . . .
>
> Grishkin is nice; her Russian eye
> Is underlined for emphasis;
> Uncorseted, her friendly bust
> Gives promise of pneumatic bliss.
>
> And some abstracter entities
> Have not disused a certain charm.
> But I must crawl between dry ribs
> To keep my metaphysics warm. (*IN*, 365)

The grammar is definitional, the syntax declarative, but what assertion is being refined? In the last two lines of the final quatrain, the antithetical clause seems to draw a process of dialectical argument to conclusion. What have been the stages of its development, however, and what exactly has been at stake?

The "night thoughts" this poem "whispers" might hardly be held to strenuous propositional account. If these stanzas add up to any decipherable meaning, they suggest that the "friendly bust" of Grishkin might offer "*pneuma*tic bliss," but only in the dubious sense of that recondite wordplay on Greek roots and modern technology—what *spiritual* happiness might be experienced from breasts inflated artificially? This is probably not an issue worth deliberating much. Yet the logical coherence that this dream talking features on its verbal surface, as its rhetorical curve and cover, surely teases the appetite for the greater statement. This disparity emerges as the most striking feature. The means of verbal reason appear as the sheerest *extra*vagance, a kind of gratuitous and ostentatious foolery, all in all, a technical conceit of no (new) philosophical concept at all. Perhaps "abstrac*ter*,"[48] as the comparative term of that adjective, presents the signal most clearly indicative of Eliot's intents and methods. The graded form of the adjective extends some sense of a discrimination in process, which reaches at the end of a disquisition like this to some better assessment, some more accurately qualified final measure. "Abstracter," however, owns the (sheerly) formal rightness of the adjective's comparative term. In this particular formation, Eliot turns the gesture with a correctness that is wrong (like a child's conformity to grammatical paradigms even in the exceptions), or wronger than an idiomatic sense would rightly insist on. Likewise, his meditation follows the protocols (only) of logical disquisition. The "night thoughts" that Pound proposed as the framing category of the poem's action are played indeed to the mechanical-piano inanities of Eliot's hurdy-gurdy reasoning, the main conceit of this quatrain art.

IV

Sunday Morning Decadence

The sensibility that Eliot shares with Pound goes to a most vivid and indicative register in a more particular literary idiom: the vocabulary and imaginative attitudes of decadence. As Pound's sustained engagements with the name and representative figures of this tradition have already shown, literary and artistic decadence subsists as a living if contested memory and identification for modernism. The resource it affords Eliot as well as Pound may be developed thus with some greater specificity of focus.

The ceremonial antiquity of the diction of decadence—the heavy Latinisms of Pater, in the most exemplary instance, or the ritualized arcania of Swinburne[49]—offers the most obvious prompt to poetic and critical attention. It needs to be recognized first of all that this set of linguistic mannerisms presents no simple escape into verbal obsolescence. Where words seem to have endless roots, where clear verbal sense comes to an end, we find a lively literary intelligence and a sophisticated political wit. Thus, as Linda Dowling has observed, the tendency that the authors of decadence exhibit to write—inter—their English as a dead language, as a kind of classical subdialect, lives out the truth of discoveries in contemporary philology. When the center of scholarly attention shifts from the written to the spoken word, and so relocates the developmental energy of language in living speech, so the writers of English decadence remainder their own *written* language in this crypt of unspeakable archaicisms.[50] Authors like Pater and Swinburne observe the rites of linguistic demise, but with a good deal of stylistic panache, and in that counterrhythm provide the indication of a critical wit that quickens with implications beyond the strictly verbal. The specifically written tradition of English literature, for instance, had sustained the elaboration of cultural apologists and propagandists as the substance of national distinction and, in that eminence, provided the authorizing writ for Britain's civilizing mission in the world.[51] In a cultural environment still charged with such assumptions, the decadents responded with an English running back onto its Latinate formations. This orientation points to the deeper affinity between the two empires, bound in like manner to organic cycles of ripening and decline.

The wayward antiquarianism of decadence, its particularly mischievous skepticism about cultural nationalisms, reappears clearly as an incentive—and challenge—in 1914. This moment in English linguistic history is dominated by the already long-standing project of the *Oxford English Dictionary*. Struggle in the world war edged with greater urgency a motive implicit in this initiative from the beginning: to recover the interior coherence of a specifically English speech. The untimely irony of this nationalist campaign usually went unspoken: the tools of a philology still identifiably Germanic were being used to reveal roots often Anglo-Saxon and, so, Teutonic.[52] The inconsistency indicates nonetheless the sort of opportunity the situation afforded a poet disposed to take advantage of it. *Homage to Sextus Propertius* defies the expectation that a writer commemorate this event in the history of the British Empire in a language natural to its high enterprise, that is, in a recognizably English idiom. Pound's riposte comes not only through the poem's historical and rhetorical fiction, which spells out the demise of the empire's claim on poetry, but most of all through a working vocabulary that features such heavy Latinity. The depth of verbalist irony in the poem shows a diction of antiquity weighing those verses down with a sense of the fate that its Roman foretime presages for its English descendant.

Pound's conceit reveals its historical provocation, as the ground of its enhanced significance, in the echoing response these circumstances prompt in the concurrent work of Eliot. His prose commentary on the major writers of decadence and the apparent status of this nineteenth-century tradition reveals a complexity equal to Pound's. As an aesthetic value, after all, the recondite wordiness of Swinburne or Pater certainly challenges the standard of clarity or transparency in an ur-modernist language.[53] Like Pound's *Propertius*, however, Eliot's poetry overwrites these objections and models a range of novel postures and possibilities on this otherwise troubled tradition of decadence. The local and timely context of the English war serves at once to explain and enrich this inconsistency.

"Mr. Eliot's Sunday Morning Service" presents the lexicon of decadence in a near-perfect iteration. The poem compounds its Latinate formations with a Hellenic script and shifts the possibility of coherent or easily speakable meaning into a medium as distant and mysterious as these unpronounceables:

> Polyphiloprogenitive
> The sapient sutlers of the Lord
> Drift across the window-panes.
> In the beginning was the Word.

> In the beginning was the Word.
> Superfetation of τὸ ἕυ,
> And at the menstrual turn of time
> Produced the castrate Origen.[54]

In this altogether extravagant array, Eliot stakes his critical perspective through the first, the most conspicuous, word. In keeping with the spirit of his predecessors in decadence, this location opens as a site of verbal archaeology, one that reveals the greater depth of the political moment that provokes this poem.

Does *polyphiloprogenitive* mean "loving multiple offspring"? Not even the *Oxford English Dictionary* records it. In written record, the extraordinary core formation appears most conspicuously in Robert Buchanan's mid–nineteenth century tract on the reproductive exuberance of working-class and underclass London, as "divine philoprogenitiveness." Most conspicuously, that is, because Buchanan's usage reappears, in a far less recherché setting, in the final chapter to Matthew Arnold's *Culture and Anarchy*, "Our Liberal Practicioners."[55]

The issue Arnold argues through Buchanan comprises but exceeds the testamentary laws and the attendant rites of primogeniture, which Arnold defends against the claims Buchanan presses for the sharing of inheritance by all children. What Arnold tags and typifies as "Liberal" is not merely a misguided optimism about the wise generosities of an East End London population. What *philoprogenitiveness* suggests above all to Arnold is its maker's inveterate penchant for words: Buchanan presents Liberal verbalism at its most characteristic, intense, and pernicious. The word celebrates the sordid reality of urban spawn under an idealized form of language—as the assorted offspring of some supernal logos, as the material realization of a divine logic as mysterious but potent as this vocable. This signal formation affords the ultimate instance of the intellectual and political partisanship this Liberal "practicioner" otherwise avows.

The now-legendary folly of Liberal wordiness resonates from a present location, moreover, which is Eliot's most urgent provocation. In this Liberal war, the "stupendous vacuity" of locutions like Buchanan's characterizes the lingua franca; his word sounds as an echoing exaggeration of everyday, journalistic usage in the partisan campaign. Accordingly, the rhetorical fiction that Eliot elaborates in response manifests an apparent sagacity merely (if those opening lines can be paraphrased, they propose that nothing sensible or consequential can be said: the divine Word may be doubly fertilized but the creation it engenders is lifeless, unvitalizing). The verbalism that represents the especially timely conceit of English poetic modernism is augmented thus by Pound, who counsels alterations that Eliot immediately adopts: "mensual" (a rarer, irregular form of "menstrual") and "enervate" (not an idiomatic use as an adjective, for "castrate")[56] keep the language consistently stilted, no more evidently referential or clearly propositional. The usage echoes and heckles a prevalent ideolect, one in which nominal commitment may be made to the plain logic of the war but in which the language of rationale collapses constantly into these sorts of verbal black holes in space.

The decadent identity with which Eliot consorts in these linguistic confabulations summons a double character, one that may enclose some of the complexity that attends the position attached to this label. Moral ambiguity is the one sure thing about the decadent stance. Even Robert Buchanan, who offered the prime instance of the decadent vocable in "philoprogenitive," authored *The Fleshly School of Poetry*, a piece of Victorian moralizing about sensually decadent verse so virulent that Pound could depict its author as "Foetid Buchanan," in *Hugh Selwyn Mauberley* (*P*, 189). Similarly, while a Wilde or Pater may receive the heavy imprecations of moralistic scolds like Buchanan, those writers also attain to a level of credible intensity in their evidently ethical objection to flatness of imaginative character and absence of fancy. Once cultural commentary moves into a sphere where the name of decadence is taken up for advantage, indeed, all moral coordinates in the discourse begin to shift, even to reverse, their positions. In this framework of changing values, then, the project Eliot shares with Pound reveals at once the interest of its special complexity and the evidence of its more disturbing consequences. Their echoing of the decadent ideolect of Liberal verbalism parodies the language of an established (but corrupted) class, and so advantages their access to the "purer" English tradition (their excavation of classical languages has sometimes the same motive and value), but their practices may be all too readily assigned to the rank behavior of outsiders—arrivistes with predatory methods, graspy needs. And it is in their dealing with this (assigned, anticipated) identity as interlopers that Pound and Eliot bespeak the true moral complication of their modernist project.

Under the conditions that our historical research has recovered, the poetic sensibility of the Anglo-Americans exhibits all of the defensive aggressiveness of the arriviste. This susceptibility shows itself most notably and revealingly in their need to distance themselves from other representatives of the same class. Pound and Eliot point accusingly into a mirror, where, in the starkness of some imaginative apprehension of their own worst condition, they stand revealed. This personage is not as yet the stereotypically pushy Jew, who appears soon enough for them (both) in this image. The figure emerges first in the ethnic character who shares a colonial status and so reflects back the vulnerability that

Eliot, like Pound, is attempting to cover in this lurid cartoon: the caricatured Irishman.

Sweeney appears first in the final quatrain of "Mr. Eliot's Sunday Morning Service." He edges its rites of closure with a presence wholly indifferent—

> Sweeney shifts from ham to ham
> Stirring the water in his bath

—and thus utterly different (it seems) to Mr. Eliot, whose likelier counterparts emerge in the last two lines:

> The masters of the subtle school
> Are controversial, polymath. (*IN*, 378)

Note the repetition of syllables from the first lines of the poem in these last. The "sapient *sut*lers of the Lord" echo in the "masters of the *sub*tle school," while "*poly*math" obviously recalls "*poly*philoprogenitive." Thus the poet turns a conceit of completion as masterfully subtle as these hermetic clercs could prescribe. Yet this is a pseudoconclusiveness at its sheerest. Eliot is simply imitating a ritual of closure, of enclosure, through rhyming phonemes. His poem turns a verbal circle around a center of significance that is left empty, undeveloped, undeliberated. It discovers the figure of its own speech in that astonishing trope, the "oval O cropped out with teeth," which Eliot fits into the mouth of the title character in "Sweeney Erect,"[57] where, presumably, any possibility of linguistic sense will revert likewise to sheer sound.

The ratios of quasi statement in "Mr. Eliot's Sunday Morning Service" represent with poetic accuracy the measures of pseudoreason in the language of contemporary Liberal sensibility. Yet the parody that Eliot has fashioned finds the primary agent for the mime it enacts in the grotesquely animalistic physiognomy of Sweeney. His infamously "apeneck" figure "among the Nightingales" adds to the usual cartoon of Irish colonial subhumanity a special gift,[58] which is the ambivalent facility of his inventor's own new measure: a backhanded tribute to his own capacity for simian mimicry.

Unlikely muse of Eliot's quatrain meters, Sweeney appears equally to be uninvited. The psychological complications of this project are considerable. The echoing colonial ape offers an image of this poet's basic imaginative activity, insofar as he imitates the failing mannerisms of a decaying gentry in order to accede to the cultural riches that are his primary imaginative desire. But Eliot obviously needs to ridicule the figure of the provincial's insurgent, counterconventional strength. In an inverted way, this excess sensitivity testifies to the main motive and aim in Eliot's poetic project. He seeks to legitimize his own work as the rightful custodian of "the better tradition," and he may credit his claim better by disclaiming any likeness to (other) pretenders. (To the same end, it may be said, Eliot's verbal surfaces elaborate the machinery of imitation to such a level of stylized intricacy and ingenuity that he may fashion himself superior to its claims over him, the same claims it enforces on [other] colonial apes.) The Celt will join with the Semite, then, and provide the chief points of reference for the major poems of 1918–19. This verse is heavy indeed with the matter of historical fact, the local and specific gravity of its own time, which is rife with contest and appetite, personal and international, literary and political. Within this setting, poetic modernism in England reveals at once its earliest monuments of major accomplishment and an ongoing record of its moral and political complications. The Great War for English civilization establishes the standard under which poetic legitimacy is won, and defended against (other) pretenders, and a historically informed reading of the verse may open a new critical assessment of the development it represents.

V

Poetic Modernism

"Sweeney among the Nightingales," "Sweeney Erect," "Burbank with a Baedeker: Bleistein with a Cigar," and "Gerontion": the first three of these pieces represent a culmination of Eliot's quatrain art; this developed sensibility extends in the last in the direction of a more obviously spoken poetry. Here the verbal reason that appears as the merest function of well-metered lines finds its character-in-voice in the monologue of the old man, who, as "a dull head among windy spaces,"[59] takes the resonant emptiness of Eliot's new measure to its high point of expressive pathos. As a speaking personage, the aged Gerontion is also contemporary with—and representative of—the specific generation of elderly men currently in decline. While this timely identification may be secured at length later, its major point may be taken in advance to locate this persona in the matrix of intellectual and political history. He belongs to the same generation that has authored the event that their Great War for civilization has come to represent. They have supported its insupportable cause with the old protocols of Gladstonian moral rationales. They have outlived their writ of political authority, which they have drafted in the dead hand—the dying language—of a barren rationalism. They have inscribed the lost language of the last days of Liberal England; they have authored an apocalypse of sheerly verbal logic, whose revelations include the dissolution of the speech of public reason. With the epic bleakness of the history they have effected, they have established the conditions of the modern sublime. Their great crisis has proven to be Eliot's ample poetic opportunity. He uses it to accomplish the terse and bitter eloquence of Gerontion's powers of speech, the complex monument to this long moment in Eliot's poetic development.

From its inception, this achievement requires the demise of the preceding generation. The poetics of predatory mimicry discovers its self-characterization in these verses. The imaginative action of Eliot's poetry appears in the conventionally prejudicial figures of the Jew and the Irishman. Variously, all too familiarly, these personages recall the Semite thriving opportunistically on the decay of gentile—here, liberal-genteel—culture and a provincial member of the empire aping the mannerisms of the capital. The alien likeness that the Irishman and the Jew strike to the English res is the American poet's own, which he confirms in spirit even—or especially—as he resists it so vigorously in these livid caricatures. He needs to revile the mimic (Irish) and opportunistic (Jewish) condition, even as he implements it as the enabling situation of his verse.

This embattled theme ramifies throughout Eliot's poetry of the moment. His complex and divided attitude extends into the formation and character of English literary modernism, whose main critical ideas appear at this time in testing demonstrations. The issues are now familiar: tradition and the individual talent, in the portion of this discourse that Eliot later formalized; or, closer to the quick of actual poetic activity, those rival identities of civility and savagery, the opposite models and prosodies of ceremony and shenanigans, of decorum and antic, all in all, of an established propriety being appropriated by its outlandish familiar. These divisions and tensions have generated the phenomenology of an identifiably modernist poetic practice. These concepts appear initially as principles of performance, however, which the players Eliot and Pound enact on the linguistic ground of English Liberalism at war, currently in distress. The aesthetic conception of reason that is special to English Liberalism, after all, lends itself to a parody apotheosis in a medium that admits artifice as its first rule. The mimic appropriator moves thus into attainment, displacing the current clerisy and laying claim thereby to the resources of the older English res, his most fervently desired thing. Merely instrumental, however, his identity draws its use and vantage from the very lack that compels the project. This literary personality reverts constantly, necessarily, to its compelling need and to its "darker" side, indeed to its primary and defining type: the outlandish colonial, a character without his own enabling tradition and, so, limited to mimicry. This identity reappears like the uncanny double, whether in the figures of the Irish mime or of the appropriating Jew (they are the means and end of the same process). This compound nemesis appears insistently, being at once inimical and indispensable to the project under way. Eliot's own self-division subsumes some of the core issues of modernism, then, into the personal program he plays out through this double agent. The modernist poet's campaign for legitimacy finds both its instrument and opponent in this figure of the mimic appropriator.

i

"Paint me a cavernous waste shore," goes the opening injunction of "Sweeney Erect,"

Cast in the unstilled Cyclades,
Paint me the bold anfractuous rocks
Faced by the snarled and yelping seas.

Display me Aeolus above
Reviewing the insurgent gales
Which tangle Ariadne's hair
And swell with haste the perjured sails. (*IN*, 355)

The poet's self-addressed imperatives constitute a kind of invocation manqué,
an invitation to an imaginative event that consists mainly or only of themselves.
For the scene Eliot proceeds to lay out shows virtually no relation to the framing structure he projects in the legendary prospects of the overture:

Morning stirs the feet and hands
(Nausicaa and Polypheme)
Gesture of Orang-outang
Rises from the sheets in steam.

This withered root of knots of hair
Slitted below and gashed with eyes
This oval O cropped out with teeth:
. . . .

Sweeney addressed full-length to shave,
Broadbottomed . . . (*IN*, 355)

The one echo of the mythological overture shows in the figures of Nausicaa and Polyphemus, who, enclosed jointly in parentheses, comprise nonetheless an unlikely pairing. Their only connection seems to lie in the wholly cir-
cumstantial fact that Odysseus told the story of the one-eyed giant at the court
of the nymph's father. Eliot's bracketing reads like a dramatic aside, which
lends these references a knowingness that grows emptier the more we know.
This piece of punctuational rhetoric consolidates the chief conceit of the
poem: contained (sagacious) vacancy. In one direction, this figure looks to the
hollow eye socket of the Cyclops, who, in any case, did not require the lancing
of that orb by Odysseus to render him imperceptive. And in another, the image
of the empty interior mirrors Eliot's poem itself—seen as the blank substance
of its promissory frame. He reconfigures the same motif more specifically in
"cavernous waste," the focusing image of the first line, which he replicates in
the wind-swollen canvas of the eighth line. This figure of "perjured sails" augments the visible emptiness of that windy space with the special sense of its
conventional trope. This poetic inspiration is wholly fraudulent: witness the
vacant frame of the overture now concluded in this eighth line. Eliot then de-

picts the stunt that the whole poem performs in the livid image of an "oval O cropped out with teeth"—a shape that may be deciphered, in the visual alphabet of this piece, as an exemplary emptiness of articulation.

This figure obviously depicts the vivid and impending form of Sweeney's mouth. The synergy emerging between the title character and the structural imagination of the poem shows Eliot animating in an exceptionally finessed and intricate manner to the same principle that his "Orang-outang" characterization has attributed to the "gesture" of his base-born protagonist: simian mimicry. As a poet, he merely imitates the conventional methods or expected gestures of poetic signification, opening with a frame that encloses no essential import for the poem itself. The ruse of a poetic truth resolves into its muse and model in the Irish mime, likewise (if only barely) feigning the behavior of the civilized human.

This telling identification spells itself out to greater implication and consequence in this poem's better-known companion piece. "Apeneck Sweeney spreads his knees," the scene in "Sweeney among the Nightingales" opens, where, with the primate-character's "[l]etting his arms hang down to laugh,"[60] in the second line, the poem turns immediately to the humor of an aping of human feeling and possibility. The application of simian mimicry in this poem's performance occurs subtly but, now, recognizably, indeed predictably: in the forging of closure, that is, in the art of phantom enclosure.

Eliot feigns this frame in the relationship between the epigraph and the final quatrain of "Sweeney among the Nightingales." The reference to Agamemnon crying aloud in the last stanza echoes and complements the quotation in the epigraph from Aeschylus's *Agamemnon*—ὤμοι, πέπληγμαι καιρίαυ πληγὴυ ἔσω (Look, I am struck a mortal blow within).[61] The circle the poem appears to turn converts the action depicted in the seedy bistro, the menacing gestures of its habitués and the strangely endangered situation of Sweeney, toward the type and standard of high Attic tragedy. While the contemporary scene appears clearly as an ironic animadversion of the ancient agon, the feeling of decline in the descent from the classical to the modern event is usual and conventional. The sense of diminishment in the present is as full and legitimate a poetic experience as the construction of the parallel is deliberate. Eliot seems to tend the symmetry closely. Sweeney's resemblance to Agamemnon includes the suggestion that he, too, is a returning warrior: the "zebra stripes along his jaw" (*IN*, 380) may delineate the creases of fat cut into his neck by a stiff military collar, worn with the dress uniforms of the Great War.[62] Moreover, the adventure of Eliot's plot features a murderous design on a soldier coming back, like the one imposed on the protagonist in the Attic drama. In this sense, the final stanza (below) will offer a response to the Greek epigraph in the scene it traces of mythically and heroically sacrificial deaths. This pattern affords some integral and inclusive sense as the designed meaning of the poem.

The coherence of this comprehensive structure reveals nonetheless a wholly adventitious character. The Greek epigraph appears not even in the penultimate draft of the poem. Eliot has left no space even between the title and the first line in this typescript. The absence of the epigraph, then, does not owe to the fact that his machine had no Greek. When he inserts the lettering later, moreover, in pencil, he misquotes it.[63]

The late addition of the inaccurate epigraph indicates the rather strained nature of the interpretation offered in the paragraph before last. The mythic significance that the poet seems to have ordained as the comprehensive sense of the piece appears to have been dubbed in at the last moment. At this later stage, moreover, Eliot performs a set of apparently minor revisions that may point up the complexity of aim and effect in the completed pattern. In his depiction of the doings of these subhuman personages, "the person in the Spanish cape" at first "yawns and pulls a stocking up," then "draws [it] up," and while the "silent man in mocha brown" originally "[s]its at the window sill and gapes," now he "[s]prawls."[64] A sound already occurring in the densely clustered vowel of "yawns"—and, in the next stanza, in "withdraws" and "paws"—consolidates its dominance with this addition of "draws" and "sprawls." Let the inner ear work on these imagined sounds, and the heavy pressure of the back-throat formations will nearly strangle the verbal meaning. Representation is being embedded in a sort of sublogical sensorium of bodily noises. The depicted action shifts into the realm of the inarticulate, the meaningless, even as the Greek lettering seems to lift the consideration into some sempiternity of cultural time. This disparity reenacts the reader's sense of *dis*relation between the mythic framework of the piece and the nature of its major players, who, as animal characters, seem to lack any capacity for superior meaning, let alone the cognizance of a dominant plot like *Agamemnon*'s.

The framing method of "Sweeney among the Nightingales," far from being irrelevant to the material it contains, appears indispensable to the effect of the poem. Strategically, Eliot leaves unmet the expectation this comprehensive design extends. The meaning of this overarching form lies, not in the content it organizes, but rather in the hollow gesture it represents. The ultimate piece of simian mimicry, this superstructure of potentially immense significance comes down in performance to a conventional routine, a sort of habituated trick. The *human* movement the simian Sweeney will have learned to simulate, in letting his arms hang down "to laugh," executes a behavior all too recognizable now as the meaningless mien of the poem's own superior affect, in the empty circle it turns through these concluding lines.

"[I]t is like our civilization criticized, by an orang-outang of genius, Tarzan of the apes." The praise Eliot confers on Lewis's *Tarr* nearly simultaneously, in 1918, gifts this Anglo-Canadian with a mimic facility revealingly similar to the one he displays in the "Sweeney" poems. This civilization may retain as well the full sense of its contemporary deployment as the theme word, indeed the fighting word, of English Liberalism at war. Eliot's shadowing and shamming of the normative ratios of verse decorum—the phantom frame, the bogus whole—read indeed as a critique of compatible standards in the classical, aesthetic, liberal rationalism of this cultural day. In the imaginative calculation that the Lewis review tabulates, Eliot's critical mimicry of contemporary pretense implies his intimacy with the true scale of value, a measure of propriety that comes with the property of the civilization he is claiming under the form of the idealized collective in the essay, as "our[s]."

Inwardness with the tradition is an impression difficult to resist in the accomplished fact of the poem. The references Eliot accumulates through the finale lift in a majestic cadenza; a feeling equally of closure and expansion occurs as the concerted effect of imagery, diction, and rhythm:

> The host with someone indistinct
> Converses at the door apart,
> The nightingales are singing near
> The convent of the Sacred Heart,
>
> And sang within the bloody wood
> When Agamemnon cried aloud,
> And let their liquid siftings fall
> To stain the stiff dishonoured shroud.[65]

The claims of the comprehensive design are as suasive as the changed cadence of these verses. The rhythm goes stately and fateful at the end; the coordinate conjunction that opens the final stanza lends a sense of inexorability to the progression. The poem lifts thus to the conclusion its epigraph has projected from its beginning, so it seems, as its only destination. Agamemnon's demise appears to increase its import, moreover, as Eliot moves its locale to the Nemi grove, where it gathers the aspect of a sacrificial, regenerative, potentially redemptive death. This typology exerts a magnifying effect, not only in bringing these more beneficent associations but in multiplying the heroic figure and reinforcing the sense of a precedent and pattern of heroic action, the same one in which, ironically or not, Sweeney takes his designated place. This intimation of mysterious but profound connection between past and present provides the greatest source of power to the grand finale of the poem. These rites of closure inscribe and celebrate the feeling of coherence and completeness that a continuous tradition endows and transmits, through these expansive satisfactions of rhythm and imaginative prospect. In a kind of magic lighting, a transfiguring after-clarity, Eliot catches as an atmospheric condition the improved view, the massive transformation that a sensibility privileged with the vantage of tradition can perform on a matter of modern fact as sad and apparently intractable as Sweeney.

What if the main point of light in this final vision were put out, however? It may be difficult to pin down the exact imagistic sense of these "liquid *siftings*," but the inner vowel rhymes in this two-word compound suggest the fluid acoustic of the nightingale sound. This song is lit, synaesthetically, as it sprinkles and drifts through the leaves of the trees. So, what if this incandescent song of the nightingales were really meant to have read "liquid *droppings*"? (That the hero's burial raiment displays a bird-sprinkled "*stain*," in the otherwise rinsed vision of this finale, remains as the telltale sign of that earlier stage.)[66] Runny bird turds are not the fairy filigree of a wood enchanted by the long song of tradition. Diminuendo, not pleroma, is the ending note of this penultimate draft, which still lacks the Greek epigraph as well. The poem drips away in a feeling of depletion stronger even than the pathos of heroic death, which is not highlighted by the nightingale song because that heroic death is unfocused by the (still unprovided) epigraph.

The manuscript history of the poem witnesses an equivalence between the imaginative valence of the mythic past, then, and its somewhat phantasmal powers of organization. The spell of a storied foretime, with the attendant sense of a continuous and living tradition, escalates in ratio to the distance at which this resource of literary understanding actually lies. The elusiveness of this material is what really contributes to the mood in the romantic gloaming of the final quatrain, in the finished version.

This romancing of a fugitive past or distant myth catches a main drift in modernist classicism. It demonstrates the principle that Eliot fixes in the now-famous formula of his 1923 essay on Joyce, "Ulysses, Order, and Myth." The "mythic method," which he names and outlines here, finds its advance example in his own 1919 poem. His version offers not only the obvious and essential element of parallel between the events of the contemporary narrative and those of the old mythos. In the tersely embittered eloquence of Eliot's wording in the essay, this doubling apparatus also features a means "of controlling, of ordering, of giving a shape and a significance to the immense panorama of futility and anarchy which is contemporary history."[67] Some sense of discord between the two coordinates in the temporal design is being fostered and magnified so that a shabby, indeterminate, even anarchic present will point toward the improved, disapproving view that the classical past may provide. Its better perspective lies at a distance that appears indeed as a measure and function of its irrelevance, all in all, its status as the valued and sought but elusive trove of the Anglo-American modernist's poetic legitimacy.

The attitudes Eliot expresses in the Joyce essay assumed the status of a virtual orthodoxy in modernist cultural poetics.[68] A matter of long-standing literary and critical faith, the mythic method may submit its weightier claims to the revelations made in the "Sweeney" case. Remember that the saving grace of that supernal order of myth comes into Eliot's poem as a second (last) thought. In fact, it enters from a second hand. For the crucial alteration of "droppings" to "siftings," inserted at the same stage as the epigraph to which it responds so evidently, comes from Pound (see n. 66). The same word will appear to equally charged effect in his "Envoi" to *Hugh Selwyn Mauberley*, where "[s]iftings on siftings in oblivion" mingle the "dusts" of this singer with Waller's and others', and "All things save Beauty alone" are "broken down" (*P*, 195). In an equally romantic gloaming of poetic song, in "Sweeney," the same internal vowel rhyme liquefies the progression of sound and translates its reference in the tradition to a kind of mystical precipitate, sprinkling its grace on the effort that Eliot is bringing to a perfect termination. Did Pound also suggest the *Agamemnon* epigraph? He reveals his long acquaintance with the Greek text several months later, when he writes a searching review of Browning's (to him) inadequate translation of the play.[69] Recall as well that Eliot misquotes the Greek when he inserts it in the final typescript. Is he really working from his own close acquaintance? This addition and the accompanying revision strike into the final product then a comprehensive vision that is in every sense adventitious. Yet the alien hand offers the joint signature of a single intent. Pound and Eliot sign themselves onto a literary legacy. They express their repossession of this material at a level of decorative intensity commensurate with its precariousness for them. A tradition of myth has given way to a myth of tradition. The poetics of modernist classicism finds in "Sweeney" a text that provides at once a precedent and a revelation. In turn, this poem finds a context in the Great War for civilization, which compels and accelerates an advance to the authenticity these poets seek and measure, among other places, in their command of a classicist's stance.

ii

The grander theme that this project in cultural recovery inscribes also discloses the needs of its local poetic agents. A manifold insecurity compels their quest for authenticity. The program they authorize opens thus to motive forces of unlike, and so revealing, character. In the economics of prestige literary culture, the place that Eliot and Pound assign themselves needs to be reserved from other arrivistes, doubles to whom they reveal their resemblance most clearly in reviling them so stridently. Their poetic project finds its otherwise unlikely muse, yet its most indicative image, in the cartoon figure of the opportunistic Jew.

In conventional prejudicial representation, the Jew emerges as the exploiter of misfortune. In this anxious if facile calculus, his wealth waxes on the waning fate of the gentile races and nations. He buys success, in this vindictive account, with the dirty money of commercial profits—an enterprise feeding and thriving on the sinews of its host, on the rooted, worthier, purer cultus of the domain harboring the itinerant. Not only do the conditions and syndromes of early modern anti-Semitism survive into Eliot's time. These schemes and tropes revive in virulence as the century turns through the cataclysm of the Great War. The immense strain that its expense placed on financial institutions reached the general sensibility readily, as intimately as the diminishing value of pocket change. The inveterate (albeit inaccurate) legends of Jewish usury and avarice now include fantasies of a conspiracy among weapons manufacturers and financiers.[70] The fictions of sinister mischief coalesce in imagery that depicts most vividly the underlying fear, the ramifying phobia. No raving anarchist, the Semite emerges in these cartoon pictures in the images of a bogus or stolen propriety, usually in a merely maladroit and misfit comedy look. The danger to the established order that this caricature reflects shows in the clothing—the control—he has wrested from its former, rightful representatives.

Modernist anti-Semitism is a subject sufficiently complex to require the extended and dedicated treatments it has received in Anthony Julius's *T. S. Eliot, Anti-Semitism, and Literary Form* and Robert Casillo's *The Genealogy of Demons: Anti-Semitism, Fascism, and the Myths of Ezra Pound*, which address a single syndrome in these poets. In their fashioning of the Jewish caricature, Eliot and Pound represent—and respond to—their worst fears about themselves.[71] The anxieties that the Semite stereotype deflects range considerably. The critics' lists might include one significant addition, however: the susceptibilities given into in the London of the war years. The proclivity that Julius and Casillo identify operates with a special insistence on this site, to which the determined force of background and predisposition has drawn these poets.

Sons in families that preserved an identity as American patricians of English origin, Pound and Eliot inherited many presentiments of dread. The sense of privilege had diminished with the dominance that was lost year by year to the waves of immigrants that the nineteenth century had thrown against their enislanded domain in the New World. The threat emerging from *Mitteleuropa* as well as Ireland (and the "lower" Mediterranean) precedes and provides for the unease they demonstrate occasionally about their acquired status as itinerants, an insecurity they experience particularly in England.[72] Their anxiousness about social placement intensifies and ramifies in the culture of wartime Britain. Official American indecision about involvement in the conflict accentuates and heightens their uncertainty. This incomplete connection—or disconnection—serves equally to ease their critique of English reasoning for the moral war for civilization and to compel their greater claim to the meaning of this charged and valorized term. In their imaginative calculation, they own a sense of civilization older and more venerable certainly than any its current, Liberal coadjutors could ken. Disproving the value of its current stewardship in a language of parody rationalism, they may regain control of an inheritance they designate as truly theirs. Are they repossessing the better spirit of this tradition, reclaiming it from its presently discredited defenders? Or are they merely exploiting the weakness this worthy culture currently reveals, in order to aggrandize the persons and fortunes of a group formerly regarded as inferior? These two options identify, respectively, the high ideal of their poetic project and the seamier underside of its doings. In the less-benign

Anti-Semitic cartoon, *Action*, 21 August 1937, the journal of the British Union of Fascists.

aspect, the agenda resembles the plan that a conventional prejudice imputes to
the malignant Jew. This likeness requires that one get on the authorizing side of
that stereotype. One secures one's immunity as one writes the Jew into an imagery of virulent cartoon.

Under what poetic convention could the strategy best advance? In Julius's
literary history, Eliot shows himself most open to the influence of *symbolisme*.
This modern tradition attains its greatest hold over Eliot, Julius argues, at the
same moment in which, unarguably, in the work of *Poems* (1919, 1920), he gives
intensest expression to anti-Semitic views. The crucial aspect of this Anglo-
French sensibility, Julius proposes, lies in its valuing of *la poésie pure de la
musique*, an irreducible, nonparaphrasable content. As an essentially irrational
and unspeakable animus, in this analysis, anti-Semitism submits most readily
to the scansions of a poetry resisting any dictates of common sense.[73]

The evidence of *symbolisme* in Eliot's verbal surfaces of 1917–20, however, appears as rare in occurrence as it is rarefied in aspect. What Julius calls
the "non-propositional" quality of this poetry, and so invests with the usual
attributes of *symbolisme*, shows more truly as a *pseudo*propositional quality,
which Eliot models to the provocations of the insular, Liberal war. In both of

200

these accounts of poetic statement, the dominant and correct impression is one of inconsequence. Between a precedent text in French *symbolisme* and the immediate context of English political culture, however, lies a difference in the source of Eliot's work as absolute as the disparity, in a calculation of its meaning and content, between Parnassus and Whitehall. The historicity of Eliot's anti-Semitism, and of the verse he needs to defend through his adoption of this prejudicial cartoon, is the point of difference one needs to enter into Julius's account.

To recess the expression of anti-Semitism into the prediscursive regions of a *symboliste* muse is to acknowledge its unacceptability in "polite" intellectual company. Yet anti-Semitism was a deliberated position. A quasi-scientific and cryptophilosophical legitimacy bolstered the prejudice. A conventional spectrum of intellectual disciplines offered its spokespersons a range of "reputable" idioms. Eliot does not need to hide this attitude. He expresses it in these years readily and indeed vividly. His unease lies instead in the nature and validity of his own poetic enterprise. His success requires the demise of his host and, in being achieved, concedes his adventitiousness, his own belatedness and illegitimacy. He may be expert in turning the inflated and debased verbal currency of Liberal England to his own advantage. Just so, however, he conforms to the economy of profiteering in which the Semite is feared ever to be thriving. The Jew he has fixed in the lineaments of the usual caricature will turn an oblique but severe mirror then on the poet's own motives and doings, ultimately in "Gerontion," but already also in the quatrain poems. Only glancingly, perhaps, in "Sweeney among the Nightingales," where one of its dramatis personae, "Rachel *nee* Rabinovitch" (*IN*, 380), shrinks to a diminutive familiar in the genealogical scheme that routinely features a family name in the initial position. Most conspicuously, and at sustained length, in "Bleistein."

"[W]ith a Cigar": the emblem of vulgar pretense and virulent well-being that the title adds to the name of the archetypal Semite identifies the motivating energy of the typical arriviste. Here is the usual Jew, the heading proclaims, who is dressing the part of established power and parodying its standards of grace or customary ease with this grosser token of his newfound power. Yet these stanzas "put on" the habits and manners of a traditional respectability, revealing not so much an inwardness with these materials of legitimacy as a self-advantaging appropriation. In doing so, moreover, the poet manages to turn the decorous conventions of aesthetic reason, in ratios ranging from the proportions of major form to the propositions of imaginative logic, into a sham and shadow language of artistic rationality. The literary travesty that this poem enacts requires that Eliot redress it—reviling what he otherwise revels in, as he depicts the Semitic figure in matching attitudes.

A divisional rhythm familiar from the "Sweeney" pieces emerges in the twofold scheme the full title of the poem outlines: "Burbank with a Baedeker:

Bleistein with a Cigar." In this double measure, a mythological prospect surrounds a contemporary scene. While the first section serves to introduce Burbank, this nominal figure rather disappears into the elaborate apparatus of storied allusion through which the reader must infer any particularity of character
or action. "Burbank crossed a little bridge," the poem opens,

> And Triton blew his wrinkled shell.
> Princess Volupine arrived;
> They were together, and he fell.
>
> Defunctive music under sea
> Passed slowly like the passing bell
> Seaward: the god Hercules
> Had left him, that had loved him well.
>
> The horses, under the axletree
> Beat up the dawn from Istria
> With even feet. Her shuttered barge
> Burned on the water all the day.[74]

The fourth line cites a sexual fall, but the poem overwhelms this event, at least
as a center of imaginative attention, by the accrued and mounting density of
legendary reference. Where the second line of the poem came to read as "Descending at a small hotel," thus giving explicit location to the liaison with
Princess Volupine, the first version works clearly to erase any sense of substantial occasion. Pound remarked on the second version: "if you 'hotel' this
rhythm shd. be weighted a bit, I *think*,"[75] calling for the gravity that the specificity of place requires. Eliot could not increase the weight (with a change of cadence), for the initially windy reference to the decorative and (mainly) irrelevant Triton served best his first purposes with Burbank. He did not wish to
concentrate attention on a particularized, grounded character. Uncited in the
earlier titles, even in the penultimate typescript, Burbank works mainly as an
instrumental presence, allowing a certain kind of imaginative activity to happen. A perspectivizing device, Burbank helps the poet take some angle of imaginative vantage on his real concern, that is, his original, identified subject:
Bleistein.

On this Semitic figure, Eliot builds through Burbank a vantage that takes
advantage of the associations owned by this alternative name. Its superior
mien—derived not from Burbank, California, of course, but an obviously English patronymic—provides the poet a means of diminishing the object on view
in the (twice longer) second part to the scale of a subhuman caricature. Burbank also improves—proves—Eliot's ability to do so through the erudition he
wields. He handles this recondite matter gracefully and skillfully, moreover, on
the "even feet" of these meters. This trope repeats the conceit he features in

"Mr. Eliot's Sunday Morning Service," in imaging a picture of the baptism of Jesus, in the figure of "the unoffending feet" (*IN*, 377). Eliot paces the quatrain ratios of "Burbank" to the same measure of flawlessness. Audible at once in the ruled cadence of its verses and a language of imaginative reference keyed to myth and legend, this prosody operates in consonance with the profoundest, most proper and proprietary sense of tradition.

As in the "Sweeney" pieces, however, the question of connection between the framing action of myth and the material of modern experience becomes relevant. *Dis*relation appears to be the clearest feature as the poem proceeds to its second part. "*But* this or such was Bleistein's way" (*IN*, 353; emphasis added), Eliot motions at the start of the fourth quatrain. On one hand, this initial or establishing maneuver may exclude the Jew from the better precinct the mythological references locate. On the other, however, the antithetical conjunction projects some sense of an argument under way, all in all, a rhetorical fiction of logical expostulation and response. The dialectical rhythm that Eliot traces as the syntax of the poem's greater statement—we will parse this later—yields at first reading to a feeling of *dis*continuity. This move makes the prelude appear superfluous. Potentially, it makes pointless the extensive array of imaginative learning the poet displayed there. The impostor Jew appears as a consequence in the subsequent lines, not only in the gaudy decorum of Bleistein's wealth but in the claim that the names of his tribesmen make on the titles of an older order, the entitlements of traditional privilege. Thus, with the additional stress the rhyme provides, "Sir Ferdinand // Klein" (*IN*, 354) belittles in name the respect that Bleistein might claim in keeping his company. The line and stanza break works like a trapdoor pratfall, revealing the pretense of the English knighthood as the real, giveaway name comes down with no small thud. The distinction that Bleistein's commercially dirty "[m]oney in furs" (*IN*, 353) has been splurged to earn also appears, from the viewpoint of the social order into which he seeks to buy his place, equally and wholly bogus. The forgery of social position Eliot imputes to these Jews points back, however, to the literary construction his poem has forged for itself. He has worked up the artifice of this prelude from a tradition he features really only superficially—his own version of the costume jewelry with which he festoons the Semite.

The Venice setting presents a special locale for Eliot's anti-Semitic narrative. While Jews moved through the city with a degree of relative freedom in late *medium aevum* (its commercial nexus allowed a coexistence of Hebrew, Christian, and Muslim populations), the culture of tolerance was expedient. The Jews proved especially useful in forging links with sources of material supply and centers of cultural activity in the lower and eastern Mediterranean, and contributed thus to the mercantile wealth of Venice. The money that Jews accumulated, however, only fueled the long-standing if suppressed resentment by the Christian population, especially when trade relations with the Ottoman Empire faded and individual Jewish merchants found their own points of contact and activity in that region.[76] The Jew in Venice could prompt and sustain the now-recognizable formulations of modern anti-Semitism. In its typical fictions, the wandering Jew wrests his own well-being from some general decay. The logic of this plot is reinforced, moreover, by the otherwise incidental aspects of Venetian geography and history. By means ranging from benefice to piracy, in collections variously ecclesiastical and private, the urban corporation accumulated sufficient booty in paintings and sculptures to account for its status as a museum city, a virtual repository of the material inheritance of the great cultural traditions. By virtue of its location in a marine plain, however, Venice is (perceived to be) sinking ever into the sea. Greatness in decay, its physical topography and developed conditions present the situation in which the Jew is fantasized to be thriving. It is no accident that Venice affords no shortage of "classic" anti-Semitic fictions, where the wealth and prestige attached to the older but dying institutions are seen to yield to the Jew's enterprising, adventitious designs.

How like the opportunity extended to Eliot in his own place in historical time. He has already turned this situation to his advantage, in exercises like the one he undertakes in the opening prospect of this poem. The world's mythological museum contributes, it seems, to this poem's fulsome well-being. The dubiousness of his performance, however, goes to his secret likeness to the caricature Jew, who will have exploited present decadence to foster his own new-found power. This resemblance needs to be resisted, predictably, and calls on the full force of Eliot's ability to distance it.

The Semitic character emerges oddly indeed in Eliot's initial depiction. "But this or such," the poet demurs peculiarly, "was Bleistein's way." The alternative conjunction discriminates within a trivial, incidental variation of meanings. What, after all, is the difference between a *this* and a *such*? Its indifference certainly diminishes its subject. A sham discrimination, "this or such" offers a key to a poem about discrimination. To be sure, the gesture turns the usual maneuver of normal verbal logic into a meaningless distinction. Eliot is exercising the novel ratios of his new quatrain measures. In doing so, however, he assumes a superiority to the Jew, whom he is about to accuse, in effect, of a similar travesty of convention. The cartoon figure he proceeds to feature in Bleistein may thus turn its image back on its author, in due course, as the most revealing of mirrors.

Bleistein's bodily posture, recounted through the rest of this quatrain, presents the parody character of bourgeois respectability, the grimly familiar caricature of the Semite in gentile society:

> A saggy bending of the knees
> And elbows, with the palms turned out,
> Chicago Semite Viennese. (*IN*, 353)

Sinking into a gesture that also opens the hands outward toward another, Bleistein withdraws from the social relationship on which he also imposes himself (too) familiarly. The double measure confirms his status as importunate alien. Clowning the manner of civil exchange, Bleistein makes real nonetheless the threat he represents to its values. Eliot expatiates on this danger in the main body of the poem, taking those psychological phobias into a mythological prospect at once lurid and far-reaching. Bleistein's "lustreless protrusive eye / Stares from the protozoic slime," as "[t]he smoky candle end of time // Declines." The scene of corruption expands to feature "Princess Volupine," who "extends / A meager, blue-nailed phthisic hand" and rhymes her manifest decay with that attributed to her sound-alike relative, Bleistein, whose appearance "[o]n the Rialto" discovers thus its signifying totem: "The rats are underneath the piles. / The jew is underneath the lot" (*IN*, 353–54). The rodent trope goes to Bleistein's most sinister subterfuge, which, under the Rialto bridge, touches upon a centering symbol and mainstay of Venetian economic and artistic culture. In this maligned figure, Eliot identifies the graver situation of his own creativity as a poet, thriving like the Semite he reviles on the general decay.

His prosody presents its own version of strength greatening on depletion. Twice in his rhyming pattern, Eliot redoubles the effect of enjambment with a stanza break. Thus he lands the building energies of the ongoing line on— well, oddly and inversely, on a downturn; on the cata-strophe of "Declines," of "Klein"; on a sense of shrinkage, down to the tininess that survives in the German sense of this last word; on sites that the prosodic drive obviously overpowers but, in doing so, crucially, adds to the effect and impression of its own forceful *virtù*. This stratagem typifies a poetics that draws its main strength from decay, and that aligns its contriver's motives and designs all too closely with those he caricatures so fiercely, so fearfully, now self-revealingly, in the Jew.

This complicity deepens through the poem's most remarkable word: "phthisic." This formulation, as stubbornly unpronounceable as it is (initially) unaccountable, surely affords the most strenuous exertion Eliot has made in his art of the new decadence, which builds on the old. Whereas Pater or Swinburne dwelt so evidently in the dead recesses of contemporary speech, fabricating a writerly language out of ancient and recondite *etyma*, so Eliot, working similarly in this crypt of linguistic roots and obscurities, discovers a word virtually unutterable and incomprehensible and, by this double measure, commensurate with his new poetic power. What this rare and recherché formation actually signifies, moreover, makes it all the better a demonstration of the attitudes Eliot practices through its matching vocabularies. For *phthisic* means "decayed." Dissolution generates this poet's affective force, in line with the dominant idea of modern decadence. The American poet's affiliation with this tradition also confirms his resemblance—and nuances the connection—to the figures of contumely and rebuke: to Jews turning general depletion to personal (and tribal) advantage. So Princess Volupine's hand, extended majestically in—

and over—decay, matches the poet's own, working the mortised strata of the language into a vatic splendor.

Over a now-disestablished language, Eliot takes aim as well on comprehensive logic as his point of mimic mastery. The subterfuge moves through the poem's faking of its own greater statement. The Burbank personage reemerges at the end, as though to enclose some interior coherence, so to shape and substantiate the major formulation of the poem, which swells the sense of its ending against the diminutive

> Klein. Who clipped the lion's mane,
> And flea'd his rump and pared his claws?
> Thought Burbank, meditating on
> Time's ruins, and the seven laws. (*IN*, 354)

The likely reference in this final line goes to the meditation on time that Ruskin conducted over his own *Stones of Venice*. In this light, the "seven laws" that Eliot cites so enigmatically may play for associations in Ruskin's *Seven Lamps of Architecture*. Here, as in *The Stones of Venice*, the Victorian sage subjects the cycles of cultural vitality and decline to a moralized understanding.[77] The ethical perspective that Eliot invests in Burbank at the end, however, comports oddly with the fall from grace he has undergone in the opening quatrain. This event gets overlooked, again. That this motif of decline over time is one that Burbank "thought," moreover, and so has presumably been thinking *through* the poem, adds to the problematic character of "his" moral standpoint the question of the real pressure this sensibility may exert on any thematic narrative in the poem. This nominal character has not achieved the depth and complexity needed to realize the theme with any requisite inwardness and consistency. Burbank, after all, has moved through the opening portion of the poem as a perspectivizing device mainly, in a fashion as blankly mechanical in fact as the unerringly "even feet" of its meter. Since his sin has not gained enough thematic gravity even to affect the rhythm in the initial quatrain, the improved view to which he moves at the end—not to mention the recognition and redemption on which this change depends—appears unnecessary and, accordingly, unbelievable. The moralized story is a sham. The forgery reveals an interestingly rationalistic attitude or apparatus. Recall the force of the antithetical conjunction at the transitional point of the poem. "*But* this or such" serves, so it seems, to turn the minor premise of this negative middle, as represented in Bleistein, toward the resolution this Burbank affords, bettering the fact of decadence with the grander moral-philosophical formulation imparted to "him" in conclusion. But "he" is a mirage. The ethical proposition that the whole poem coalesces to form reads in the end as meaningless, as in the middle, where its logical qualifications appear equally and sheerly verbalist.

A heuristic fiction, a character in name only, Burbank serves nonetheless as an instrument of end feeling as potent as its design is peculiarly—now recognizably—Eliot's. At the close of "Sweeney among the Nightingales," too, this poet enhances the valence of an englobing myth by the tenuousness of its hold on the narrative action. He achieves the mysteriousness of coherence again— through a coda as enigmatic in its relation to the overture of the poem as its protagonist, Burbank, remains shadowy. Meaning-seemingness assumes a now-demonstrable poetic power.

If this description reads as a formulary of modernist difficulty, so the intellectual—verbal and political—culture of Liberal England at war provides a proximate context and urgent source for such practice. In the public discourse of that recent conflict, after all, the linguistic currency of rational morality proves as worthless as its language in Burbank's poetic case. Reason-seemingness has taken over public utterance and invested it with a poetic potential as heavy as the consequences its sheerly verbal, wholly logistical sequences have wrought in history. The end feeling that Eliot's poems achieve shows in turn no aversion to working effects on a commensurate scale. No shyness or irony overrides the ceremonies of closure these poems variously intone. In their local concentrate of rhymes, in "Burbank" no less than in "Sweeney," these final quatrains enclose an acoustic sense as intense as the presentiment of some meaningful completion to the poem. The poet leaves this expectation substantially unmet, however, and so leaves the poem open to all of the associations that current English history can deliver from the failure that a Liberal's rationalistic language has manifested there. The consequences foreseen for time by a providential logic have not found their embodiment in a credible language, let alone in the provable truth of men's doings. The grand syllogism of Liberal eschatology remains at best inconclusive, in fact discredited. These are indeed "Time's ruins." This ideal scheme witnesses a coincidence in its demise in contemporary or recent history with the newly fortified strengths of Eliot's poetry, and the connection ranges all the way from this conclusion manqué to those tempos of entropy, the equally expert effects the prosodist composes through stanza and line breaks. A strength attained from decay provides his deepest point of likeness with those other opportunists of misfortune—in the Jewish caricature that Bleistein comprises with his look- and sound-alikes Volupine and Klein. The mirror scheme may be unwitting, the complicity is surely resisted, yet the firmness in the identification accounts in great part for the fierceness of Eliot's rejection of the loathed Other.

iii

The "Bleistein" poem reveals a location in the moment of Eliot's own enterprise and ambition that helps one to fix with specificity the English setting in which his "Gerontion" speaks. This insular situation emerges within an imaginative geography that is transnational or pan-European but also, most crucially and locally, post*war*. The markers of the recent conflict appear so obvious now as to be unexceptional, at least unframed. The evidence comes as a matter of imaginative and referential fact. Perhaps even that "*estaminet* of Antwerp"—where, in Gerontion's fantasy, his landlord was "spawned"—represents a word, as Hugh Kenner has suggested, that English usage has recycled from a Continental war. More clearly, in its final lines, as Kenner has also suggested, "Gerontion" extends a recognition to the famed Hall of Mirrors, the site of the recently signed Treaty of Versailles.[78] In this "wilderness of mirrors," specifically, the image and order of an older European civilization has broken into a "multipl[e] variety."[79] The unspoken but ramifying irony comprises the associations that Versailles owns from the early eighteenth century with the imperial center and symbolic capital of rational civilization. The symmetrical arrangements of this royal estate replicate in grand miniature the systematic universe of (proto-)Enlightenment science and (neo)classical logic. This sensibility has authored its Great War for civilization, which the savage ceremony of retributive rites has terminated at Versailles.[80]

While "Gerontion" expresses the revealing extreme this sensibility has reached in the most recent—the last—moment of liberal modernity, this tradition preserves a special English memory and location, too, by virtue of this poem's title. As a name, "Gerontion" (little old man) appears sufficiently general to refer to every and no one, but the word owns a conspicuous and particular association with the book-length poem that John Henry (Cardinal) Newman composed in 1865, *The Dream of Gerontius*. Its English provenance focuses most notably through the commentary its text prompted from Prime Minister Gladstone. The politician praised this meditation in old age on death fulsomely if vaguely—presumably, for the faith that Newman expressed through his speaker, which coincided closely enough with the one the providential logic of English Liberalism could foresee for its own generic man, not so old yet as he would be in 1919. Gladstone's appropriation of the poem was sufficiently forceful in its own day to be reasserted well into the next century, the correspondence being recalled and quoted in editorial forewords in reprints at least through 1907.[81]

At first sorting, then, the "little old man" of Eliot's extended monologue belongs to the senescence of contemporary Liberalism, a generation that has authored in words a war that its old men have not fought in body, and so sustains the label that the editor at the *Cambridge Magazine* affixed to them so memorably: a "garrulous gerontocracy." Eliot's Gerontion speaks for them immediately, conceding the grounds of Ogden's charge already in the second sentence of the poem. He admits his inactivity in the recent war and orients himself toward its reality in the attitudes of a verbalist rite, at once well-rehearsed and ill-performed:

> I was neither at the hot gates
> Nor fought in the warm rain
> Nor knee deep in the salt marsh, heaving a cutlass,
> Bitten by flies, fought. (*IN*, 349)

Former prime minister (and Conservative) Arthur Balfour has cotton put in his ears prior to observing a 9.2 howitzer fired. "Nor knee deep in the salt marsh, heaving a cutlass . . ."

" . . . Bitten by flies, fought."

The consonance in the second line appears odd, combining the hard referent of war in "f*o*ught" with the plush acoustic its pure vowel stretches, like a vocable membrane, across to the near rhyme in "w*a*rm." The third sentence reiterates this contradiction. A pleasance of music backgrounds the action of fighting, as "s*a*lt m*a*rsh" echoes—unobtrusively, all the more decorously and pleasantly— the "f*o*ught" and "w*a*rm" register of the preceding line. Eliot sharpens the appeal of its comfort with the piquancy the triple "e" value keys as the tonic note: "knee," "deep," "heaving." Constructed in measured words only, this war appears a good deal more attractive than it is likely to be in fact, a disparity for which this speaker offers his noncombatant status as the admitted condition. Not that Eliot allows the character-in-voice to indulge without account a wholly aesthetic apprehension of reality, which is the particularly Liberal fallacy of rationalistic language. In its support for an unseemly war, an enfeebled Liberalism has pushed the logos of reason—its own decorative protocol—to a strenuous extremity, a performance Eliot encores with the extraordinary pressure he places on the sense-making gestures of this sentence. Its clausal construction projects the progressive discriminations of verbal reason—"neither," "Nor," "Nor"—as its stipulative spirit, its motivating action. The ambitious program and plan of a thrice-suspended period turns into the wreckage its phrasal sequence actually makes of it, however. Eliot leaves his speaker gasping out his last word as the wheeze end of a deliberation, which, in this second "fought," reaches a verbal reference he cannot grace by assimilation to his seemlier procedures. The reasoning gesture that the whole construction represents rations itself out to an ugliness that is its real story—to the war it has realized, made real, and (at moments like these) recognized, as the stubborn, graceless, matter-of-bloody-fact that it is.

"After such knowledge," the speaker asks in an adjacent passage, "what forgiveness?" (*IN*, 350). The question of redemption must attend a poem read so often as a confession of the malignities of an age. But forgiveness for what, primarily? And by whose means, or by what authority? The poem expresses misgivings most intensely about a loss—or decline into superstition—of the Christian faith, from which this speaker takes no consolation, only fears of retribution in the avenging figure of "Christ the tiger" (*IN*, 349). By the measure of Eliot's own well-marked and publicly enunciated religious conversion (1927), however, one may well ask why doctrinal propriety and liturgical correctness should concern this poet's speaker as early as July 1919. Granted, the issue of membership on the right side of a religious divide will reach ultimately to the question of the Semitic presence in the poem, to be addressed shortly. And the particularly Christian dread this speaker touches may reach to the underlying anxieties of an author who has lapsed in practice. Yet the main relation between this frame of religious reference and the imaginative experience of the speaker appears really to be mythic, not credal, free and secular rather than fideist or sectarian. The appearance of

Eliot's commitment stems from his interest in the poetic uses that the story of a fall affords him.

In this scheme, the primary flaw to which Gerontion may be held accountable—as it were, the original sin of Eliot's modern man—shows as the sensibility he demonstrates in the opening moment. The vocal character he takes on at the start bespeaks the humanist hubris of rationalism. His grammar swells with the self-conceit of reasoned speech but breaks already across the war that will expose this sensibility as a pernicious fiction. The verbalist mentality will appear a year later in Eliot's characterization as specifically "liberal" (in "The Perfect Critic"), a sensibility that will have authored the war that shows a rationalistic hubris for what it is, in the mouth of this old man. Accordingly, this speaker makes a bid for forgiveness in the closing prospect. "Gull against the wind," this closing cadence rises in an attempt at an inspirational refrain,

> in the windy straits
> of Belle Isle, or driven by the horn,
> White feathers in the snow, the gulf claims
> And an old man driven by the trades
> To a sleepy corner.[82]

While the speaker clearly intimates a possibility of delivery into the open-air prospect, the image that focuses this epic perspective leads him back to the issues he realized so lividly in the beginning, to the question of the role he has played in the recent war. "White feathers" recalls the token of shame that women imposed on men not in uniform.[83] No, there are no officious patriots on patrol in the straits of Belle Isle. Just so, however, the emblem fixes the image of the speaker's evident obsession. Gerontion has earned this *blason* as his own obverse distinction—in the verbalist evasion he performs in the overture to the poem. If the rhythm of recompense expands in this visionary milieu onto the grandest scale, the memory of the offense he centers in those "white feathers" weights any attempt at redemption with the gravity of those associations.

It seems easy to read the white-on-white composition of these feathers in the snow as a visual consonance, carrying the positive connotations of a blending and resolving note. The sense of an aesthetic remedy to distress expresses an important principle, but the harder question goes to what is at stake in the reconciling action of art. A historically informed reading best addresses this question. The harmony of art: this exercise divides between the benign possibilities it extends from a traditional legacy and the perfidy it serves in recent applications. An aesthetic conception of rationality, which stresses scale or balance and harmony, presents the special conceit of English Liberalism at war. In his overture, Eliot has depicted this sensibility in rhythms that indict it openly. Indirectly but not silently, indeed forcefully, he stigmatizes it now with all the damning associations that a badge of white feathers may attach to a verbalism he refurbishes—under a still more insidious form in this finale. "[W]ind" in

"windy," "Gull" in "gulf," and "White feathers in the snow": verbal consonance blends into visual disappearance. An erasure of referential phenomena, a
suppression through words of evidence in fact, sings no high song for the principle of aesthetic—*ratio*nalistic—harmony.

"We have saved a shilling against oblivion / Even oblivious," Eliot writes
in lines for which he has substituted those five that provide the basis for the finale in the published version.[84] In each account, he exercises the same motif of
aesthetic compensation. In this earlier draft, in the orchestrations of "il–li" and
"iv–vi," he achieves a chiasmic music as intricate and sedulous as that of the
pattern he sets echoing more noticeably, in the later version. Its harmonies
rhyme with the "oblivion" that Eliot signals as his critical theme.

To give speech to the unspeakable, so to find an imaginative language for
the travesty that recent history has wrought on linguistic rationality, that is, the
major tradition of liberal modernity: these are the conditions and ambitions of
the modernist poem Eliot has authored in "Gerontion." In that final prospect,
the mixture of visual beauty and verbal terror (the meanings of words merging,
erasing their differences and canceling their ability to denominate a knowable,
controllable world) offers also the signature image of the modern sublime. The
"high" effects aimed for here suggest equally clearly the exalted place for which
an American verse is making a play—at this moment in English cultural time.

The historicity of the modernist program leaves a record whose evidence
appears now to be irresistibly (if regrettably) clear. Eliot is working within the
special distress of England at war. The crisis he has turned to the timely opportunity of his verse matches the situation in which he places the Jew of usual
caricature. "My house is a *decayed* house" (*IN*, 349), the now-predictable tale
of Semitic mischief begins, as his speaker prepares to rebuke his landlord. That
emphasized word retains the paradoxical capacity that decadence maintains as
the conceit of its tradition. Eliot, too, has taken the decay of the Liberal logos at
war as the source of his own poetic strength. However, he must shield himself
against the imprecations that attend the circumstance of such a project—his
vantage as an outlandish American on the language of this failed campaign for
civilization. Thus he blames the other, ready-made outsider, the opportunistic
Jew, not only for profiting from the decline of civilization but, by implication,
as in the "Bleistein" poem, for causing it.

The livid depiction he proceeds to feature in "Gerontion" draws a self-
portrait in a reverse mirror:

> And the jew squats on the window sill, the owner,
> Spawned in some estaminet of Antwerp,
> Blistered in Brussels, patched and peeled in London. (*IN*, 349)

The banker again observes the proprieties of punctuation. Not properly capitalized, "the jew" shrinks into the unpropertied state Eliot envisions as this
character's deserved condition. In the poem's reconstruction of current cir-

cumstances, however, the same undeserving personage has gained an improper control of London capital, of its real property and true estate. His pretense to genuineness can be authored, in this typically anti-Semitic fiction, only in the broad circumstance that the "decayed house" outlines in miniature. The apparatus in collapse images the cultural infrastructure, the varied establishments as well as the intellectual attitudes, of English civilization. In these conditions, nonetheless, Eliot has also come into *owner*ship—of a poetic voice, of an emergent place in literary culture—as shrewdly and even ruthlessly as the Jew of usual imputation. In fact, the immediately preceding sentence—"I was neither . . . fought"—reenacts in its collapsing language of rational discrimination the verbal distress of Liberal England at war, which sets the stage for his poetic performance. He will have turned the show to considerable profit. He has crumbled the structure of Liberal logic in the mouth of its old man and, in doing so, recomposed not only the intellectual agon of this moment but an emotional pathos, which is potent enough to be sustained across the length of the poem. This piece of poetic opportunism also evinces a mimic gift. If Eliot has protected himself against its worst associations in the caricature figure of the Irish mime, "[a]peneck Sweeney" reappears in the simian position to which he assigns this belittled "jew," who "*squats* on the window sill."

A bestiary of declined likenesses has replaced the gallery of acknowledged muses. Accordingly, the source of poetry shifts from the imaginative empyrean to the fury and mire of human veins. The ambition that compels Eliot's poetry is complicitous indeed with the cycles of violence driving through history. History, conceived in line with the traditions whose demise has fostered his insurgent strength as a poet, affords a suitably rich center of verse meditation, then, in "Gerontion." More than a merely nominal topic, history is an intellectual site, and it opens to a requisite complexity of attention through the archaeology of this famed passage.

"Think now," this intellectual soliloquy begins, and, in its earlier draft, continues,

> *Nature* has many cunning passages, contrived corridors
> And issues; deceives with whispering ambitions,
> Guides us with vanities. Think now
> She gives . . . [85]

What import does the word emphasized add to the deliberation that follows—before it is replaced by the now well-known "History"? *Nature* certainly furthers the sexual suggestiveness in these verbal schemes and tropes. Once the feminine gender of this figure is naturalized, those "cunning passages" recover clearly the meaning of the Shakespearean wordplay. Those genital "corridors" are "contrived" with "issues" that also recall the discharges of the Grishkin nymph, in "Whispers of Immortality," which this poet maligned as the "strong rank feline smell."[86]

Beyond the obvious misogyny and the sexual dread the wording displays, this first reading witnesses more than an attitude of contempt for the (female) flesh. "Nature" returns the personal meditation that follows to a topic that points up, now, an originating context and proximate source for the passage. The natural body, its fate and death, centers the meditation that Newman's Gerontius dreams as his dying soliloquy. The extinguishing of the several senses that Eliot's speaker records—"I have lost my sight, smell, hearing, taste and touch" (*IN*, 350)—recalls the sequence of named senses in Gerontius's monologue.[87] The title Eliot first assigned his poem strengthens the sense of some initial linkage with Newman's: "Gerousia,"[88] where *ous* remains close enough to *ius* to substantiate the echo.

Yet the significance that Eliot's speaker assumes through this parallel goes beyond the incidental similarities of situation. This memory of the older poem makes coherent the otherwise (merely) nominal alteration of topic from "Nature" to "History." This shift moves Eliot's work to a point of converging intensities, one that may be mapped now from a triangulated reference: Newman-Gladstone-Eliot. The Liberal prime minister's appropriation of that priestly preparation for a holy dying took it from the private to the public dimension, from personal biography to national destiny, from the framework of nature to the plan of history. Logic as providential and beneficent as the one Newman could speak certainly compelled the history of Gladstone's conception. The statesman's heirs expressed a special and focused faith, moreover, in the rationalistic language of English, of England. This millennial meliorism ends as the wreckage Eliot puts in the mouth of his aging Liberal, mumbling the utterance that reveals his own discredited part in the Great War for English civilization. Eliot pitches this character-in-voice now at his final climacteric, on the brink of his undoing, as he deliberates the meaning of a history he has constructed, but to a scheme of meliorist reason in which he can no longer believe.

"Think now," this disquisition begins in its finished version, "History has many cunning passages" (*IN*, 350). The bawdy pun that "cunning" yields in the first reading gives way now to the readier sense it owns as a specially tricky way of knowing. With this sense, the speaker answers the question that has prompted this response: "After such *knowledge*, what forgiveness?" (*IN*, 350). The speaker proceeds to trope this way of knowing into the figures of an intellectual maze, in which, it seems, the lady, History, works her high chicanery and wiles. Once Gerontion recovers his timely identity, however, this figure of History shows a way of knowing and speaking altogether bound up with his own intellectual character. "She" represents the typical sensibility this aging Liberal presents now in his—its—greatest distress. "She" is revealed for the "contriv[ance]" she is. The "corridors" down which the "issues" of "History" are "whisper[ed]" are those of Whitehall, yes, but also the halls of all the institutions that political Liberalism has established, in history, as incorporations of its intellectual ideals. These whispering corridors present then an echoing, heckling figure for a rectilinear discourse, for the patterns and turns of a verbal reason gone wrong.

The internal moment of the poem shows as the crisis this Liberal character-in-voice has experienced in "History," a verbalist confection Eliot undoes—redoes—at expressive length. "Think now," he proposes,

> History has many cunning passages, contrived corridors
> And issues; deceives with whispering ambitions,
> Guides us with vanities. Think now
> She gives when our attention is distracted,
> And what she gives, gives with such supple confusions
> That the giving famishes the craving. Gives too late
> What's not believed in, or if still believed,
> In memory only, reconsidered passion. Gives too soon
> Into weak hands, what's thought can be dispensed with
> Till the refusal propagates a fear. Think
> Neither fear nor courage saves us. Unnatural vices
> Are fathered by our heroism. Virtues
> Are forced upon us by our impudent crimes.
>
> These tears are shaken from the wrath-bearing tree.
>
> The tiger springs in the new year. Us he devours. Think at last
> We have not reached conclusion, when I
> Stiffen in a rented house. Think at last
> I have not made this show purposelessly. (*IN*, 350)

"Think now," "Think now," "Think / Neither," "Think at last," "Think at last": this frame sets up a rhetorical fiction of deliberated, consistent significance. This conceit proceeds to a consummate instance in those formulations near the end of the main passage. Here, in keeping with the Liberal's typical predicament, the lie that history has given to the ideal of progress turns the words of progressive and logical proposition into a composite of contradictions. How is it, after all, that an "unnatural vice" can be biologically "fathered," and a vile unreal thing begotten from a natural good? Whose "impudent crimes" are capable of generating "virtues"? These disparities, however, seem unapparent to the speaker, who talks through them with every seemliness of reasonable and coherent meaning. Not only grammatically and syntactically correct, he is logically confident, embodying the non-sense in the form of the categorical statement. The inverse ratio and particular power of this verse shows in its capacity to outsize its own rationalist measures, reaching through the sense it feigns to the illogic it really means,[89] where the emotion that is released grows in ratio to its overwhelming of an older reason. This poetry follows the critical formula of pseudostatement, which Eliot moves through a central demonstration to its defining, primary site: to the climacteric of Liberal history, the crisis of whose rationalist language provides the main opportunity for his newly matured poetry.

No, "We have not reached conclusion." The inconclusiveness suits the new muse of history, whose rationalistic language has proven to be inadequate to the end that events have reached. It is in this space—between an earlier, idealistic construction of history and the rawer, forceful actuality of these times—that the poetry of literary modernism may recover its major, shaping occasion. And, no, this is not the only modernist poetry. Wallace Stevens and William Carlos Williams, David Jones and Basil Bunting, all belong within the broader contours of this tradition. It is the special if difficult privilege of Eliot (and Pound) to have lived in the moment in which the loftiest constructions of liberal modernity came undone.[90] If an experience of breakage in that mainstream tradition affords the meaning that modernism attempts mainly to embody, the verse generated out of that catastrophic collapse owns a certain—first—claim to place in this otherwise diverse gathering of timely talents.

VI

Pound, Eliot, and the Making
of *The Waste Land*: Policing the Voices

In the labor of creating *Poems*, Eliot and Pound evolve the concepts and prosodies most readily identifiable with the tradition of high modernism. In this ideal modernism, a literary tradition affords the living depth of resource for poetry. The poet has repossessed this material to a speaking present, to a contemporary speaker, as the full ground of his identity and originality. In readily available readings, *The Waste Land* (1922) realizes these values. The formative story of the medieval waste land and grail quest tells a tale of restoration, here the recovery of a former order of physical and spiritual well-being. This legend affords a support story for the modernist poetics of repossession. The regeneration that provides aim and value in the romance narrative locates also the motive and goal of this quintessentially modernist poem, which sets out to reclaim the antique materials of its own frame of reference and refurbish this resource in its own novel designs. While Eliot's sequence projects no single, contemporary speaker clearly as the agent of this reclaiming action, the interest—and difficulty—of this imaginative task may be inferred through the most inventive dimension of the sequence: its extraordinary collage of voices. The shifting, elliptical, discontinuous character of the poem's verbal surface certainly establishes a nervy modernity as its composite personality. This startling disembodiment of poetic voice calls upon the new media of radio and telephone as its creative basis. The poem obviously sets out to do more than simulate the sensorium of modern urban existence, however.

The decentering of sensibility in the sequence recreates a state of individual dispossession. This is the establishing condition, we feel, of the whole poetic project, of a modernism that reconstitutes its current personages in terms of some underlying, abiding, unifying, and revitalizing myth of literary and cultural tradition.[91] If the reader is seeking to make this poem a charter document of high modernism, the integral coherence of the poet's speaking sensibility, deepened in its possession of the material legacy of world culture, is the value at stake—indeed, it is the protagonist.

Eliot encourages a reading that features this cause in a note he adds to the manuscript, later in 1922, in the published version of the poem. Here he describes the single figure of Tiresias as "the most important personage in the poem, uniting all the rest." The claim for major place that Eliot is making for this reporting "personage" includes an assertion that this famously blind prophet "*sees* . . . the substance of the poem."[92] What Tiresias records is the sexual encounter of the "young man carbuncular" and the "typist home at teatime" (*WLM*, 141). In the apparent depravity of these characters and the seediness of the scene, the reader also "sees," through the centering presence of Tiresias, the initiating occasion for the poem as a modern restoration quest. For this tryst instances a grimly perverted ritual of sexual fertility. As such, it can be understood as the provocation and rationale for the imaginative narrative of the poem's remaining (fourth and fifth) parts. This sequence leads through an experience of bodily purgation (IV, "Death by Water") to an intimation of mystic wisdom (V, "What the Thunder Said"), where physical existence appears to be redeemed through the application of spiritual disciplines—the twofold motive and aim of the original grail quest. With the entrance of Tiresias, moreover, the vocal medley evident in the earlier sections of the poem begins to achieve the focal intensity and definition of a single speaking character, one whose ritual dignity is consistent equally with the import of the older story and the interests and needs of the restoration quest of high modernism.

This construction needs to be probed. Although the poem Eliot publishes in 1922 responds readily to the critical fiction of an ideal modernism, a more searching interrogation of the process of *The Waste Land*'s production may expose the advantageousness of this fit. The inquiry may be aimed at the most evident point of intervention between the poem's working drafts and its finished condition: the heavy editorial labor of Pound. This work represents an event in the critical history of an ideal modernism rather like the lore of the Great War: it is *supposed* to be significant. The actual work of its archaeology, the excavation of its manuscript record, represents an effort that has been suspended under the benediction of the "usual views." Thus Pound's massive excisions, reducing the length of the poem by hundreds of lines, can be taken as the work of imagist concision—on a grand scale. Despite the relevance of such an understanding, it focuses attention too closely on the local unit—the individual line, the specific phrase, the self-contained passage. Global considerations need to be introduced through a set of critical questions that have gone largely unasked.[93] What was Eliot's original or working conception? How did Pound intercept and, arguably, reorient it? If there is a significant difference between the originating idea and the accomplished product, what may the discrepancy tell us? Might these discoveries point us back toward some of the lost origins and forgotten contexts of English modernism, those realities and provocations to which the tenets of high modernism may appear at best as secondary, attenuated formations? Among those primary locations, the most urgent, I maintain, is the setting afforded by the English war, and its bearing on *the* poem of Eliot's (and Pound's) generation may be reclaimed in due course.

Eliot signals his creative conceit in the title he assigns the working sequence: "He Do the Police in Different Voices." The wording refers to a scene in Dickens's *Our Mutual Friend*, where the cartoon personage Sloppy reads the newspaper aloud, performing its various stories.[94] Eliot's allusion cues the mélange of miscellaneous styles and discordant voices in his own talking text, where, in effect, he "do" the modern polis in multiple voices. It is to this motive that Pound aims his corrective blue pencil, in a work of extensive revision and restriction. Its aim and effect may be assessed through a review of its densest location: in the third part of the sequence, "The Fire Sermon," where, in the published version, the witnessing presence of Tiresias is established as the dominant consciousness of the poem, beginning in the scene of the grim tryst.

Eliot initially casts the meeting of the typist and the young man in a quatrain style that is, alternately, highly stylized and surprisingly awkward. A meticulous and even wearisome realism counterpoints and syncopates an otherwise elegant finish in these formalized rhymes. If Eliot "do" the quatrain in different voices (his extensive experimentation in *Poems* has opened the resourceful potentials of the four-line form), Pound objects strenuously to the macaronic character of these cadences and the mixed condition of their idioms. A key to his critical vision comes in two remarks he scribbles to the side of these typed stanzas: "*verse* not interesting enough as verse to warrant so much of it"; "inversions not warranted by any real exegience [*sic*] of meter" (*WLM*, 45). The point of gratuitousness on which these observations converge is not unwarranted: the quatrains surely "do [up]" their voices through the performative orientation Eliot brings to the language and rationale of the poem's initial conception. The excess that Pound registers, however, stems from a sense of necessity that locates his own standard and value. What determines excess, moreover, is an understanding of the essential thematic action in the poem, which is (at this stage) largely Pound's own. He is working out of some powerfully premonitory understanding of the importance of waste land mythology; this imaginative narrative exerts already for Pound the preponderant influence on Eliot's developing text. In his work on the poem's second part, for instance, he leaves nearly untouched the two scenes of sexual enervation and inertia that

Eliot initially offers: for Pound, these are both instances of a sexual fall, one that establishes the main case for retelling the myth of physical cleansing, spiritual renewal. He remains consistent to this vision in his heavy intervention in III, where, as an inventory of details and lines excised on his advice may reveal, he wishes to restrict the wording to further the purposes of this underpinning ritual myth and, ultimately, to fit out a vocal character appropriate to it.

Where originally the typist "sprawls" in "nerveless torpor" on a "window seat," waiting in a (knock-off) Japanese kimono under a Japanese print cheaply "purchased in Oxford Street" (*WLM*, 45), Pound clears out these insignia of her social location. He removes the prompt for Eliot's narrator's judgmental response, and leaves a character relatively unencumbered by concerns beyond those of the elementary drama she is about to engage in her debased version of the antique rite. Bringing "the young man carbuncular" into the simplified outline of this ritual agon requires much more work on Pound's part. The plethora of detail Eliot has used to depict this character does not dress him in the costume of primitive rites. The poet has bedecked this figure instead with all of the emblems of a (lower) clerical class push and bearing. These features converge in a character whose social position appears to be the main point of Eliot's judgmental attention. Pound, however, marks nearly all of these details for excision:

> *A youth of twentyone*, spotted about the face,
> *One of those simple loiterers whom we say*
> *We may have seen in any public place*
> *At almost any hour of night or day.*
>
> *Pride has not fired him with ambitious rage,*
> His hair is thick with grease, and thick with scurf,
> *Perhaps* his inclinations touch the stage—
> *Not sharp enough to associate with the turf.*
>
> He, the young man carbuncular, *will stare*
> *Boldly about*, in "London's one café,"
> And he will tell her, *with a casual air*,
> *Grandly*, "I have been with Nevinson today."
>
> *Perhaps a cheap house agent's clerk, who flits*
> *Daily, from flat to flat*, . . .
>
> *He munches with the same persistent stare,*
> *He knows his way with women and that's that!*
> *Impertinently tilting back his chair*
> *And dropping cigarette ash on the mat.*
>
> The time is now propitious, as he guesses. (*WLM*, 45)

The insistence with which Eliot's speaker attitudinizes the sullen vigor of the urban underclass locates this character-in-voice equally clearly on a social map. The extravagant offense he takes expresses the wishful but insecure superiority of, well, of an Eliot, that representative member of a failing patrician class. His Tiresias speaks like the consciousness of lost social dominance. The critical point in this identification lies not in a recognition of biographical content, mainly, but in a better sense of the texturing effect this complex personality achieves in a passage that marks him, no less than the young man "spotted about the face," as a socially placed personage.

Again, in lines that position Tiresias most memorably in relation to the emergent scene, Pound cuts out Eliot's speaker's (self-marking) judgment:

> I Tiresias, old man with wrinkled dugs,
> Perceived the scene, and foretold the rest,
> *Knowing the manner of these crawling bugs,*
> I too awaited the expected guest. (*WLM*, 45)

The elimination of this targeted line may be taken to typify the effect of Pound's editing on the original prosody and the complex personage it initially projected. He breaks up the multifarious command of Eliot's quatrain form, replaces its changing cadences and motley vocabulary with a much more consistent rhythm and diction, rinsing away the note of suburban bitchiness and lifting the vocal character into a single idiom of calmly solemn, ritual dignity. The scene is recast, in the published version, virtually completely in accord with Pound's view of what is proper:

> I Tiresias, old man with wrinkled dugs
> Perceived the scene, and foretold the rest—
> I too awaited the expected guest.
> He, the young man carbuncular, arrives,
> A small house agent's clerk, with one bold stare,
> One of the low on whom assurance sits
> As a silk hat on a Bradford millionaire.
> The time is now propitious, as he guesses. (*WLM*, 141)

Eliot has reduced the class markings of the male protagonist to one telling detail and thus has prepared the character for an incident whose significance is elementary, whose simplicity is chilling. What ensues is the rite of some ancient and reiterated but debased foretime, whose significance is scripted to the credible fiction of a tone now wholly ceremonial, and of a Tiresias purged of all but this liturgical personality.

This speaking identity is not imposed on the manuscript by Pound. After the encounter, Eliot's speaker makes a dramatic aside that reveals the basis for this character as liturgical observer—in the recurrent nature of the offense enacted:

(And I Tiresias have foresuffered all
Enacted on this same divan or bed,
I who have sat by Thebes beneath the wall
And walked among the lowest of the dead.*)* (*WLM*, 47)[95]

This hierophantic character represents only *one* of the personalities the manuscript projects for Tiresias, however, in Eliot's testing demonstration of the multiple, varying voices of his work in progress. Only three lines after this last excerpt, for example, as Eliot follows his base protagonist's exit, he reasserts a Tiresias of nasty (bathroom) details:

And at the corner where the stable is,
Delays only to urinate, and spit. (*WLM*, 47)

Against these lines Pound writes "probaly [*sic*] over the mark." Whose mark? The limit Pound invokes here goes to his own sense of what is proper—the proprieties of a hieratic style, the one he wishes to establish as the poem's controlling voice. Accordingly, against the parenthesized quatrain quoted just above, Pound writes "Echt" (*WLM*, 47). The approval that this German term includes as its idiomatic sense goes further, here, to raise a question asked by its literal significance: complete, total. Will Eliot turn Pound's Tiresias into the *whole* show?

The extent of the difference that Pound's editing makes in altering the vocal character of Tiresias may be demonstrated through his complementary efforts on the supporting portion of "The Fire Sermon." He cuts roughly seventy consecutive lines from the start of this section. In these excised lines, a modern "Rape of the Lock" scenario is styled to the rhymes of an eighteenth-century manner: a loosely episodic concoction of London scenes, done up (and down) in (mock-)heroic couplets (*WLM*, 23, 27). Once the casual comedy of these rhyming lines is silenced entirely by Pound, a new opening note can be struck. Pound has left the section to begin in the voice of a contemporary jeremiad: "A rat crept softly . . ." (*WLM*, 27). As it turns out, moreover, the lines that open the published version of "The Fire Sermon" are written on the back of the manuscript page from which Pound has so mercilessly purged Eliot's comic couplets. It is reasonable to presume that this overture is composed after Pound has handed back the edited pages—Eliot's handwritten addition shows no sign of having been seen by Pound. In these additional lines, Eliot has echoed and amplified the note Pound wished to privilege—in the vatic role that his persona takes up in the new opening: "The river's tent is broken . . ." (*WLM*, 24). It is most assuredly Pound who is responsible for the dominance of this vatic character in this central, orienting section of the sequence.

The fourth section of the poem witnesses a rhythm similar to the third—both in its initial configuration and its editorial revision. In manuscript, a short passage at the end that Pound lets stand will stand, in the published version, as the totality of "Death by Water." Here the body of the drowned sailor decomposes through ten lines of Eliot's highest elegiac sublime. This inviolable voice is preceded in draft, however, by a speaking character of decidedly mixed condition. An eighty-line-long story of various marine voyages is rendered through a variety of speaking styles. Eliot includes an echoing allusion to "Ulysses," for instance, but Tennyson's lyric recasting of that character's story of his last voyage (from *Inferno*) comes in and out of the gumbo tongue of some all-too-actual sea ventures (*WLM*, 63–69). Against the second line of the first holograph version of this section, Pound writes, "Bad—but can't attack until I get typescript" (*WLM*, 55). The ready offense he registers goes to qualities he will monitor and censor heavily when he gets that typescript, which will be reduced to the ten-line finale of hieratic character. What Pound values in that enigmatic tableau may be underscored by the point of the two lines immediately preceding it, which he also wished Eliot to leave in the poem:

> And if Another knows, I know I know not,
> Who only know that there is *no more noise now*. (*WLM*, 69; emphasis added)

In the published version, where Phlebas "*forgot the cry* of gulls," and where "a current under sea picked his bones *in whispers*" (*WLM*, 143), this quality of supernal quiet may now be emphasized and easily appreciated. In the manuscript version, there is too little inward consistency to fit this depiction as a single, fixed, valued destination for Eliot's voicy-noisy voyages. This mystic condition is framed as *the* end and aim of a process Pound has contoured, however. Now that the various, multifarious aspects of Eliot's original characters-in-voice have been recast in III to the narrower vocabulary and focal intensity of Tiresias as liturgical observer, the poem moves by the ritual disciplines Pound has imposed to claim this superior silence in (as) IV.

The movement from III to IV exhibits more than technical consistency, then. This process has been thematized. There is a kind of spiritual progress. While this condition of superior quiet has been abstracted from the manuscript and raised into solitary prominence by Pound, it defines the main line of value the published poem pursues—into and through the finale of part V, where the sequence proceeds to the site of early fertility religions by the Ganges River. Those rites underlie the mythic fiction of the original grail quest, to which they contribute the double significance of physical and spiritual regeneration. This ritual wisdom seems to provide for a power of newfound concentration in the poem's speaker(s): the vocal carnival of the opening parts of the sequence has given way to a Lenten abstention, showing an appropriately ceremonial singleness and consistency of hieratic voice.

Pound's approval of this movement shows clearly in the evidence he has left—or failed to leave—in the manuscript. These last pages are virtually untouched by him. Since Eliot wrote out most of this section in Lausanne in December 1921 (using some earlier material), after he left the first four sections with Pound in Paris in November, the question arises: what bearing did the editor have on the closural motion of the poem, since this last part moved so smoothly (for Pound) into execution? What significance—beyond the emblematic—may we attach to the fact that the working version of part V is typed on the foolscap paper that *Pound* customarily used? The circumstances surrounding the instigation and formation of this last section represent a topic of irrepressible conjectures.[96] The force and effect of Pound's intervention may be measured, nonetheless, with certainty.

Consider the discrepancy that exists between the shape Pound insisted on finalizing for the poem and the set of possibilities Eliot saw lying beyond "What the Thunder Said." The manuscript includes nearly a dozen additional pieces, some fragments and others complete poems. These verses range in genre from the wittily rhymed, well-formed stanzas of "Exequy" (a Laforguian revoicing of the metaphysical style), to the (somewhat too) earnest social reportage and commentary in "The Death of the Duchess," to the enigmatic "Elegy" and other elliptical, free-verse extensions of the vatic manner that appears here and there through the manuscript (*WLM*, 83–123). "The POEM ends with the 'Shantih, shantih, shantih,'" however, Pound maintains, bringing it to completion in terms he proceeds to clarify: "The thing runs from 'April . . .' to 'Shantih' without a break. That is 19 pages, and let us say the longest poem in the English langwidge [*sic*]." Hardly "without a break," the "thing" that Pound raises to the capitalized value of "POEM" shows nonetheless the qualities he has attempted to establish for the sequence as one thing, presided over by a dominant consciousness and unified by the integral concerns of the speaker he chooses to feature—the restoration quest of a waste land narrative that is compatible with the vocal character of (his) Tiresias. These are the values he uses to reduce those subsequent poems, in the same letter, to the lowercase status of "superfluities."[97] He has reorchestrated the "different voices" of Eliot's initial conception into a speaking character and imaginative narrative of concerted motive but restricted aim.

The liturgical urgency of Tiresias's voice, the narrative of the religious quest, and the transcendent dimension of the poem's ultimate values: these features are not extraneous to Eliot's working conception. The ingredients of clearly "spiritual" import represent *one* of the potential emphases in the emergent work—perhaps a preponderant emphasis, given the privileged character accorded to narratives like that, but, in the manuscript mass of the first four parts that Eliot first handed to Pound, certainly not a single line of defined emphasis. The most that can be said about the religious story in the manuscript is that it represents a sort of provisional fiction of significance, one whose chief use or value for the work in progress is the elastic, indeterminate character of its claims. It is "as if" the collocation of discordant voices could cohere in a meaning like this, the poet might be reciting to himself as he goes on generating his texts, which test and extend ever further the flexible strength of that—or any—heuristic. Under Pound's hand, however, the "as if," "quasi," or "pseudo" becomes the "as is," the "must be."

In the working drafts and original sequences, then, Eliot can be seen to be proceeding within an understanding similar to the one that I. A. Richards formulated in the critical principles of pseudostatement and the "music of ideas." In this scheme, the reasoned meaning of a poem functions mainly or only as a means of allowing the reader—in Eliot's case, the writer—to proceed. (Many readers of the published poem will share the same attitude, using the grail quest narrative just to organize their experience of an insistently bewildering poem, just to go on reading.) A significance of loosely strung, provisionally logical quality serves to appease the needs one's conditioned sensibility brings to literature, but it has little relation in the end to what the poem is "about." A rationalistic stratagem works really to free the dimensions of subtextual energy and sublogical processes that Richards wants to reclaim as the special, better provenance of poetry. It is in precincts like these that Eliot may be heard in his work of doing the polis in different voices. This newly opened zone of imaginative freedom conforms loosely but powerfully, moreover, with the new feelings rising out of the experience of recent history—in the verbal culture of the Great War. Here the limits of imperial reason and a specifically rationalistic language are lived out to an intensity of tremendous consequence, and this is registered in Eliot's ur-text. His composite of different voices and divergent motifs coheres around centers of reference that vanish, like the establishments of a nineteenth-century liberal rationalism, when looked at directly. If *The Waste Land* stands in virtually all standard literary histories as the document expressing the circumstances of the first modernist "generation," the one "lost" to the worldwide cataclysm of the First World War, its place in political and intellectual time is located with greater precision and significance by the "better maker" of its first, working drafts.

The fiction of consistent significance that Pound managed to inscribe in the sequence, however, proved to be the main point of hermeneutic appeal in the literary criticism of the next fifty or so years. This tradition of scholarly opinion witnesses a loss of historical memory in the poem, and in the literary modernism Eliot's writing typifies, which it has been the aim of the current study to recover. The history of critical misprision will be told in the appropriately full, retrospective context of the epilogue.

The interference that Pound's involvement represents in this process may be taken as the extension of a reaction formation already noted in his own career. "Perhaps be damned"; "make up yr. mind / you Tiresias if you know know damn well or else you don't" (*WLM*, 45, 47): thus Pound objects strenuously to Eliot's waffling with the contents of this personage's (still uncertain) consciousness. This complaint, and the concomitant efforts the editor makes in consolidating a dominant speaker for the poem, all go to Pound's own growing difficulty with the breakdown of individual privilege as an authoring force in poetry. Yes, Pound has animated to the same creative possibilities as the one he is attempting to repress in Eliot. He has populated the consciousness of his *Propertius* (and the renewed project of the *Cantos*) with speakers whose identities are multiple, potential. If this resource opens out of the exhaustion in the recent war of liberalism's signal value and character, of an individuality expressible in rationalistic or reliably referential language, that is a development Pound cannot countenance as an unalloyed good. It may indeed be instinct with some elementary terror. There is a presentiment of a wordless or sublogical reality here, with which a modern concept of the sublime, as we have heard, is specially conversant.

An account of these complications may produce a history of Anglo-American poetic modernism that is textured to the range and variation of its major works, a model that would need to include the reversals stemming so evidently now from early 1922. Pound's emergent work on the Malatesta Cantos will feature a play of discordant voices wholly consonant with the energy he has attempted to suppress in the different speakers of *The Waste Land*; Eliot will develop an increasingly restricted register for his own vocal identity as a poet, escalating into ritual dignities as his subsistence idiom. As a function of the experience that the two poets underwent together in the war, however, they share an understanding of the extraordinarily novel possibilities it opened for literature, possibilities to which both poets responded—amply, concurrently, diversely, and if, in the end, divergently, this opposition represents an assumption by each of the position formerly held by the other. Theirs is a body of writing whose fully complex dimensions may be restored with a new understanding of the historicity—the historical origins, provocations, and implications—of the enterprise they joined in forming.

Ford

The problems and opportunities that the culture of the Liberal war extends to the conventions of prose fiction are considerable. It could be argued (the argument will be rehearsed later) that models of progressive time, which define a main line of value in the world view of liberal modernity, are intrinsic equally to the temporal consciousness of the (modern) novel, which, in its idealized form at least, follows plot and sequence to logical consequence. The genre of the novel consolidates its dominance in literary history, one may also propose, in rough synchronicity with the founding and establishment of the intellectual standards of modern liberalism. To its idealized series, then, the Great War uttered a disruption that locates equally a point of immense distress and a site of potential innovation. The levels of experiment and discovery range from the propositional logic of the narrative plot (the additive meaning of its serialized incidents) down to the fundamental template of the directed statement, the individual sentence, that primary form of ratiocinative formulation and conclusion. The ambitious risks that these several areas define need to recover some dimension of the challenge they originally represented: by the end of the twentieth century, after all, the ethic and method of the antinovel has conventionalized the energies of most earlier deflections. If the difference that the experience of the Great War represents in the history of liberal modernity also presents the main staging area and proving ground for literary modern*ism*, moreover, the exceptional status that suffix confers may realize its meaning best through a reading of the fiction that witnesses the true difficulty of the disruption. This is a literature written by a figure fixed ambivalently, but indicatively, between the moderns and the modernists.

Ford Madox Ford is so situated. His series of war novels, *Parade's End* (1924–28),[1] holds a severe and searching mirror up to the political stratagems, the linguistic strategies and policy logic, of the partisan war. The literary initiatives stemming out of this circumstance are certainly evident to Ford, and at signal moments in the sequence he locates the possibilities whose realization will constitute the major accomplishments of literary modernism in England. As a "Condition of England" novel (a genre including Wells's *Mr Britling Sees It Through*), *Parade's End* also belongs to a fictional convention of social history, which seems to mark the more traditional aspects of its author's literary imagination. Out of this sensibility he resists the initiatives to which his modernist acquaintances have enkindled. His affiliation with the energy they represent, however, makes him go on noticing the openings he has to keep closing down. Beyond the historical documentation that this literature of astute record affords, the value of Ford's somber chronicle of Liberal folly includes a measure of the difficulty—and, arguably, the value—of other writers' dedicated attempts to turn these circumstances into the basis of a new imaginative literature.

Ford catches the national character at war in a political comedy of full dimension. To his protagonist and (sometime) counterpart, the déclassé English aristocrat Christopher Tietjens, Vincent Macmaster appears as the exemplary antagonist. He is the type character in Ford's lampoon of a timely Liberalism. The political fortunes of this aspirant M.P. rise in proportion to his capacity for manipulating traditional Liberal principles to fit the exigencies of war. Identified as "Whig," an aspirant member of the party clerisy and a would-be commentator on belletristic literature, Macmaster "had very early decided on the career he would make." While he begins the series in the typical Liberal position of denying the imminent outbreak of war, his conversion is swift, complete, and much to his benefit. By the end of the first novel, he has been knighted,[2] and by the beginning of the third, Sir Vincent Macmaster has become "Principal Secretary to H. M. Department of Statistics."[3] The *triumph* that Vincent Macmaster realizes as the unsubtle, doubled significance of his name has been won along the standard Liberal way: his work in the Department of Statistics, for chief instance, echoes to the background sound of falsified reports, pseudologic, and sham rationale that characterized partisan apologias for the war effort. The verbal milieu of the Liberal war seems to be understood in these novels, presumptively, as a medium of reversal, deceit, and compromise. An equally timely record of England's condition might be expected, then, in a verbal register that echoes or inflects the present state of the national language.

Certainly the great achievement in Ford's *The Good Soldier* (1915) will have been to strike a tone remarkably consonant with the war milieu in its second year. The baffled rationalizations of John Dowell, straining to make the outrageous behavior of his English acquaintances seem morally coherent and reasonable, echoes suggestively and plaintively to the dominant sounds of the Liberal times, for which it seems to discover new depths of imaginative feeling.

Yet "The Saddest Story" (the original title of the novel) had in fact been substantially completed before the onset of war. This title occurred to publishers as too dispiriting in 1915, however, in view of their readership's already sagging morale. Beyond that change, the only bearing of the war on the text of this novel appears in the date of the recurring annual disaster, which Ford shifted—to 4 August, the day England entered the war—in revisions he completed in weeks after the outbreak of war.[4] If this date has served to encourage readers to confuse Ford's fiction with a war record, the resonance that *The Good Soldier* discovers with the language of current political culture seems all the more noticeable as a tone wholly missing, and a literary initiative entirely forgone, in *Parade's End*. Ford takes the decision of imaginative conscience *not* to further the work of that conceit in the linguistic fabric of his fiction. He repeats this decision with a revealing insistence.

"The compartment smelt faintly, hygienically, of admirable varnish," goes the opening of *Some Do Not*, the first novel in *Parade's End*, where, in the high summer of 1914, the "train ran as smoothly—Tietjens remembered thinking—as British gilt-edged securities. It traveled fast."[5] The reversal Ford is preparing turns on the deep conceits that attend this imagery, clichéd or not, of liberal time. Linear and progressive history promises a dividend, the return on a "gilt-edged" bond, where the innocence that the liberal mind usually assumes for the perfectible human sounds the ironic off-note to the *guilt* that humanity will reveal for its part in the war about to erupt. Yet the derailing catastrophe toward which Ford has launched his story is less remarkable for such prescience—he foresees a historical future that has already occurred—than for its technical possibility. It locates the kind of breakage that may open a new or different order of fictional time. Thus Ford extends himself the same opportunity he has already taken up in *The Good Soldier*, where he magnifies the impact of Dowell's most shocking recognitions through the manipulation of memory and the fracturing of narrative continuity. The invitation that the war novel's opening extends for a comparable invention, then, is all the more striking in being declined. Ford makes nothing of it in the new book, which he never derails from its rather conventional narrative track (the few flashbacks and time shifts are predictable, mainly undramatic, and routine, all in all, an affirmation of normative, reasonable, cause-and-effect sequences).

The refusal gains significance in view of the opportunity Ford goes on identifying. His insistence in this respect seems equal to his steadfastness in turning down the offer. In the opening moments of the several novels in the war series, he repeatedly features this idea of progressive time in crisis—a predicament with no future, however, in Ford's prose.

Take the extraordinary promise he records in this early prospect in the second novel, *No More Parades*. A junior officer, recently out of university but already too long at the front, rehearses a Marxist argument for the fulfillment of historical time in an egalitarian state:

The young captain leaning over the table began a long argument as to relative seniority. He argued with himself, taking both sides in an extraordinarily rapid gabble. . . . He began to talk, faster than ever, about a circle. When its circumference came whole by the disintegration of the atom the world would come to an end. In the millennium there would be no giving or taking orders. Of course he obeyed orders till then.[6]

The improvements this speaker predicts for the historical future reveal their determining force in language, particularly in its rationally gradualist capacity, in the narrator's cagy paraphrase. The "when . . . then" progression Ford sets out realizes the promise of history as the premise of a proposition that shows a standard grammatical logic only. It moves to conclusion, not on the basis of any empirically reasoned sequence of causal facts, but under the momentum of syntax alone: the ordering force of serial clauses in a sheerly linguistic time. The wild tropology of circles and circumferences reveals the writing of reason for the fantastical lexicon it is. The creative opportunities that attend its striking demise may comprise schematic hallucinations like this speaker's, but they also exceed that sort of obvious, broadly drawn comedy of intellectual madness. The business-as-usual insanity that Ford draws into his cartoon anticipates some of the intensities that the author of "A Press View" achieved. Consorting with a logic it was also constantly dissolving, the "View" pushed through to novel areas of experience and effect. The credences given to the weirdly reasonable scenes imaged there were as disturbing, certainly, as its oddest prospects. While Ford intimates a similar dimension of unexpected potential, he moves immediately and instinctively to silence it. "The fellow was not drunk. He talked like a drunkard, but he was not drunk. In ordering him to sit down Tietjens had . . . ,"[7] well, had taken orders from his officer-author, Ford. The novelist will subdue any enthusiasms like those in his fictional prose.

A similar rhythm of opportunity and refusal appears in the opening paragraphs of the third novel in the series, *A Man Could Stand Up*. Valentine Wannop, lover to Tietjens and emergent heroine of the story, hears a telephone ringing on the morning that the war has ended. The day of "Destiny" (in Ford's capitalization) toward which Liberal eschatology has oriented itself in the course of the war, this ending is also the conclusion to which Duration has moved in the gradualist, rationalist fashion of partisan historiography. "Slowly," goes the first word of the novel,

amidst intolerable noises from, on the one hand the street and, on the other, from the large and voluminously echoing playground, the depths of the telephone began, for Valentine, to assume an aspect that, years ago it had used to have—of being a part of the supernatural paraphernalia of inscrutable Destiny.

The telephone, for some ingeniously torturing reason, was in a corner of the great schoolroom without any protection, and called imperatively, at a moment of considerable suspense, out of the asphalt playground where, under her command ranks of girls had stood electrically only just within the margin of control, Valentine with the receiver at her ear was plunged immediately into incomprehensible news uttered by a voice that she seemed half to remember. Right in the middle of a sentence it hit her:

". . . that he ought presumably to be under control, which you mightn't like!"; after that the noise burst out again and rendered the voice inaudible.

It occurred to her that probably at that minute the whole population of the world needed to be under control; she knew she herself did. But she had no male relative that the verdict could apply to in especial. Her brother? But he was on a mine-sweeper.[8]

The destined end of rational history has been awaited with the same patience it takes to get through the first sentences. Ford's mimicry is intricately seditious. In the initially conspicuous figure of two-sided sound, he repeats the to-and-fro scheme, the dialectical pattern to which the officer-intellectual in *No More Parades* chanted his parodic rationale for advance to the millennium. At the start of this (originally) final novel, then, Ford gathers the antiphonal noises of material history toward their resolving note, their ideally conceived synthesis. The promised conclusion proves to be nothing more than a thrumming telephone. The voice sounding to the armistice, in effect the conclusion to the Liberal syllogism of history, finds no clearness of superior or triumphant reason but breaks up into incomprehensible static. Sheer sound preserves the noisy residue of time's older, now-ruined mythology. The stuff of some new (dis)order of verbal time lies nonetheless in this raw acoustic material. To this novel possibility, the linguistic mimicry of Ford's prose seems to quicken almost irresistibly—in the extraordinary performance of the novel's second sentence, which stretches through most of its second paragraph. The specially elaborate effect hinges on the ambivalence Ford builds into the verbal construction "called": the noun ("Valentine") it modifies as participial adjective stands so far out in the sentence (and on the far side of such a dense warren of phrases and clauses) that "called" keeps turning back to find, in the "telephone" nearer to hand, the subject it might thus activate as main verb. The forward movement of linguistic time, so syncopated, offers its own sort of comic contretemps, a rhythm rising relentlessly but uncertainly and standing thus as the verbal record and match of an older model of rational progress—once confident in language and history both—now out of joint, unutterably. Its disappointments may be performed with the same quirky, mischievous brilliance now routine in Ford's preludes, but he is playing in advance of a show that ends, in effect, just after it has begun. The language and style revert by the end of this opening vignette into the regimen of serviceable prose that the author will feature as the novel's staple measure.

"There won't be any war, Ford. Not here. England won't go into a war." So the novelist Mary Borden pleaded wishfully on a high summer weekend, the first of August 1914, at the country house to which she had invited Ford, Violet Hunt, and Wyndham Lewis. Twenty-five years later, Lewis recalls the response:

> Ford thrust his mouth out, fish-fashion, as if about to gasp for breath. He goggled his eyes and waggled one eyelid about. He just moved his lips a little and we heard him say, in a breathless sotto voce—
> "England will." . . .
> "England will! But Ford . . . England has a Liberal government. A Liberal government cannot declare war."
> "Of course it can't," I said, frowning at Ford. "Liberal governments can't go to war. That would not be liberal. That would be conservative."
> Ford sneered very faintly and inoffensively: he was sneering at the British Government, rather than at us. He was being omniscient, bored, sleepy Ford, sunk in his tank of sloth. From his prolonged sleep he was staring out at us with his fish-blue eyes—kind, wise, but bored.[9]

Prescient, but inert, Ford preserves this temperamental posture in the opening moments of the novels in the war series, where, in effect, he foretells impassively the same reversals of intellectual and political history that, in 1914, others cannot yet countenance. The same taciturn temper attends his refusal to pursue in these novels the consequences of the accidents he has plotted so carefully from their openings. Does this disinterest stem only from some inveterate sense of the official lie? Or is there some positive coherence to this resistance, all in all, a value system the rejected initiatives oppose?

"One could have fought with a clean heart for a *civilisation*," Tietjens proposes, lodging in the tense of a past and foregone condition the word and value the Liberal government likewise emphasized in its war campaign. But "as long as we did it in a decent spirit," he continues, "it was just bearable."[10] The charged and valorized word is "decent." The manifold irony of its application in the work of the current war comes to a single point as Ford continues, when Tietjens recalls his initial position in the Ministry of War Information. "One could keep at one's job—which was faking statistics against the other fellow— until you were sick and tired of faking and your brain reeled." The enterprise plays its evident indecency through the moral delirium that Tietjens is describing and that he takes next into a presentiment of its due retribution. "It was probably impolitic to fake—to overstate!—a case against enemy nations. The chickens would come home to roost in one way or another, probably. Perhaps they wouldn't. That was a matter for one's superiors."[11] Punctuated thus, "to overstate!" exclaims its mock surprise at the practice it enacts as well as characterizes: euphemism, the linguistic equivalent for the faking of data, and a reminder of the verbal culture of pseudologic that attended and complemented the official disinformation Tietjens is engaged in disseminating. With the silent but reliable irony of that exclamatory mark, Tietjens also expresses his author's feeling of moral indignation at all of this deceit and hints Ford's own reproof of its sedulous untruth—in terms no more unsure than the genuine longing Tietjens expresses for accountability and ultimate justice. It is this reprieve from indecency—from the specious reasoning as well as fraudulent figures of the government's official publications—that Ford seeks equally as a verbal artist. He steers the linguistic and narrative artifice of his fiction against this current drift and the ethical outrage it represents to him. "Decency" provides the gold standard against which moral frauds—and verbal counterfeits—are recognized and devalued.

Ford's ability to withstand those blandishments calls upon resources he invokes in response to an opposition he names more specifically, in another vignette in *No More Parades*. Tietjens's senior officer explains a practice of verbal deceit as the convention of a new but regrettable day. "What is language for?" his commander asks,

> "What the *hell* is language for? We go round and round. I suppose I'm an old fool who cannot understand your modern ways. . . . But you're not modern. I'll do you *that* justice. . . . That beastly little McKechnie is modern. . . . Do you understand what your little beast did? He got leave to go and get a divorce. And then he did not get a divorce. *That's* modernism."[12]

"Modernism" refers the detested McKechnie's behavior to a range of associations this term has accumulated already by the mid-1920s. Within the religious communities of the Anglican and Roman churches, at the turn of the (last) century, the term *modernism* served to name and censure an energy of rational analysis and skeptical inquiry into those various Catholic orthodoxies. While the "divorce" the officer references in relation to McKechnie might seem to be the likeliest site to which a force of religious liberation would be applied, it is, instead, on the elementary level of language itself, in particular in lying, that the officer finds the "modernist" quality at its characteristic work. Recall as well that the "modernist" impulse in early twentieth-century religion was linked with a practice of "free reason," thus in name and in spirit with a tradition of "liberalism." On the evidence equally of recent history and the representation in these war novels of Sir Vincent Macmaster and his partisan likes, political Liberalism has committed itself as well to verbal deceit, to a language of the merest reason-seemingness. "Modernism" reappears two years later in the title of *A Survey of Modernist Poetry* (1927), where Laura Riding and

Robert Graves will identify as "modernist" some of the same qualities our historical researches allow us to understand, now, as extensions (and animadversions) of this Liberal debility in wartime. (The formulations of Riding and Graves will be assessed in the epilogue.) The several-leveled reference of recent political and cultural history thus compresses a sense for modernism in Ford's pages that is at once urgently current and richly problematic. These are the fostering conditions of a literary art in England that is specifically modernist, and it will earn this (obverse) distinction by entering into transactions with the Liberals' rational mendacity and by forging a verbal currency out of that linguistic material.

Ford responds to the provocation that will trigger the major literature of modernism in England by intensifying his allegiance to its opposite quality. Possibly, Ford Madox "Hueffer"'s Anglo-German background contributes to a feeling of precariousness when any adversarial possibility is extended to him. His need to adhere to the true (Tory) blue of an English national character may derive from this same sensitivity, and this need compels some regrettably intense expressions of anti-German polemic over the course of the war.[13] Yet any construction of Hueffer-Ford as the alien of excess vulnerability does not cover this author's skillful willingness to satirize the majority party of England at war. The threat he registers in his special unwillingness as a writer lies instead in the challenge these recent developments in political and intellectual culture have posed to the deep mainstream of the traditional novel—the ethic and episteme of temporal progressivity, in historical as well as literary and linguistic time. The vigor of his resistance testifies in its own inverted way to the nerve and dare of an enterprise that ignites to those counterconventional energies. His example affords a most specific and telling pretext, then, for the work of a novelist who takes the challenge Ford declines as the main incentive for her mature career.

4

Woolf, Among the Modernists

In 1928, near the end of a decade that has witnessed her emergence as a major writer, Woolf recalls an early moment in the intellectual culture of postwar England. In the semiwhimsical, semifictional reminiscence of *A Room of One's Own*, she tells the story of her recent sojourn to an Oxford college, as she attempts to account for the feelings of unease that a standard scene in collegiate life has stirred. The source of her disquiet lies, in a mildly Wordsworthian way, in the memory of an earlier visit, which she locates, lightly but decisively, some time before the war. What changed between 1913, say, and 1919 (or 1928) shows—subtly but unmistakably, elusively but urgently—in the tone of things. Tonality grows out of the attitudes and practices she apprehends, in her most highly charged imagery, as that "more profound, subtle and subterranean glow, which is the rich yellow flame of *rational intercourse*." Equipped beforehand to savor the pleasures of its methods and consensus understandings, she must ask instead, in "listening to the talk," "what was lacking, what was different." The change she intimates in this "rational intercourse" becomes the point of further interrogation and, by the end, her own searching disillusionment:

> I had to think myself out of the room, back into the past, before the war indeed, and to set before my eyes the model of another luncheon party held in rooms not very far distant from these; but different. Everything was different. Meanwhile the talk went on among the guests, who were many and young, some of this sex, some of that; it went on swimmingly, it went on agreeably, freely, amusingly. And as it went on I set it against the background of that other talk, and as I matched the two together I had no doubt that one was the descendant, the legitimate heir of the other. Nothing was changed; nothing was different save only—here I listened with all my ears not entirely to what was being said, but to the

murmur or current behind it. Yes, that was it—the change was there. Before the war at a luncheon party like this people would have said precisely the same things but they would have sounded different, because in those days they were accompanied by a sort of humming noise, not articulate, but musical, exciting, which changed the value of the words themselves.[1]

Who put music, once, into the rhythms of the speech of reason? What supplied the tonic value for the cultivated language of those earlier days? The conceit of that special, particularly *aesthetic* conception of "rational intercourse," of harmonic logic, came as the signature measure of L. T. Hobhouse's (specifically English) *Liberalism*. This sensibility has lost its expressive power, however, its effective strength and credibility. Woolf's attempt to account for the difference fixes it no more casually than accurately: in the war. The sordid illogic of that enterprise, needing to be set to reason's tune to be put right, has called upon and exhausted all of the resources of that majority concept. This single but immense eventuality accounts for all that has gone wrong, the off-note now in the undertone of things, in the institutional music of English intellectual culture.

Listening to the whispery difference, Woolf proves her acuteness as auditor and her special inwardness with the mysteries of this tradition. As Virginia Stephen, she was born to receive this legacy from Sir Leslie Stephen, a dean of Victorian liberal intellectualism. If the patrimony needs to be sorted out into its assets and liabilities at a later stage of this consideration, its recipient certainly expresses an ambivalent attitude in her response to this college scene. Its demise coincides with an opportunity as obvious as the one represented by the mingling of sexes on this privileged site. This development appears sufficiently familiar by now to be noted as a matter of welcome fact. Accordingly, a further reference to Victorian love poetry, sung as it were to the older music of rational intercourse, points up the welcome silence one finds now in these halls: its representation all too evidently limited a woman to the romantic interest.[2] Nonetheless, the former order's passage into memory clearly leaves behind a feeling of diminishment and regret. Nostalgia obviously softens the prospect. The coherence one used to experience in social and intellectual dimensions reached indeed to the somatic, cellular level of the civic creature's thinking life. The feelings of gain and loss nearly equal out.

This ambivalence positions Woolf especially promisingly as a literary sensibility of the first postwar moment. Out of the ruins of a once-established language of reason, she may forge a new imaginative idiom. Her identity as a writer hinges nonetheless on her membership in a social class, and her own genetic memory makes hers one of the most indicative and expressive records of the loss on which her newfound power relies. The cultural history that provides context and explanation for the production of English literary modernism finds through Woolf its most inward and urgent telling. She is working in the remains of a civilization, one to which her genealogy (if not gender) has encouraged her to expect access. The special intimacy that her background gives her with the fundamental assumptions of the liberal tradition makes her work the fully dimensional representation of this moment. She will offer the most extended demonstration—and realization—of its literary potential.

I

Voyaging Out

The moral rationalism of late Victorian liberalism massed most critically in the young writer's experience. This sensibility appeared at its most wicked and insidious in the figure of her half brother, George Duckworth. "He smoothed out the petty details of the Victorian code," Woolf recalls in 1939, "with his admirable intellect, his respect for reason":[3] the protocols of logic met those of social and ethical behavior. George Duckworth is preserved in literary memory, however, as the violator of his half sister's late childhood and early adolescence. His sexual predation certainly gave the lie to the code of high propriety, which any Victorian liberal's "respect for reason" had invested with moral as well as intellectual and social importance. Virtually from the start, then, Virginia Woolf was positioned at an acutely critical angle of relation to this set of values.

Within the same framework of ethical rationality, however, Leslie Stephen labored with an intensity more than equal but, it appears, wholly earnest. If this irascible Victorian has dropped out of most accounts of his daughter's intellectual makeup, since his excesses of personal temperament seem to move him to the furthest fringe of credibility, the substance of this genuine legacy needs still to be taken into account. To a contemporary, Leslie Stephen represented "the very type, or mould, of so many Cambridge intellectuals."[4] A specifically rational agnosticism coalesced with a scholarly passion for the eighteenth century, as the Age of Reason. His main determination, as it developed over a long career, was to separate morality from religion and establish it instead on the basis of right reason. This ambitious program directed his aims to the development of a sensibility that might be labeled "manly logic."[5] Its intellectual character, however, showed vivid deficiencies to his daughter, at least in the representation his own behavior gave it:

> Give him a thought to analyse, the thought of Mill, Bentham, Hobbes; and his [mind] is (so Maynard [Keynes] has told me) acute, clear, concise: an admirable model of the Cambridge analy[tical spirit]. But give him life, a character, and he is so crude, so elementary, so conventional, that a child with a box of coloured chalks is as subtle a portrait painter as he is.[6]

If Leslie Stephen was attempting to extend the instruments of reasoned thought, as a spiritual lead or moral guide to the vagaries of human life and feeling, this was a sphere of experience of which he knew nothing.

Again, in the routine crisis of midweek, on the day their household accounts were tallied. Virginia's father had shifted this responsibility onto her older sister (in 1895, after their mother's early death), Vanessa, who, "on Wednesdays, was the recipient of much discontent that he had suppressed; and her refusal to accept her role, part slave, part angel of sympathy, exacerbated him so that he was probably unconscious of his own barbarous violence."[7] Financial balances present the circumstance in which Leslie Stephen might demonstrate his manly ratio in exemplary, emblematic fashion. He fails again in this signal instance. Yet his youngest daughter's effort to explain—perhaps to forgive—extends even at this late date with the reflex of original instinct. She expresses an ideal form of the intellectual disposition he bequeathed her. Liberal not only in tolerance or accommodation, she allows above all for the specific unfreedom with which an "unconscious" compulsion like his is consistent. "*Barbar*ous violence," moreover, calls up from its roots the first and urgent sense of savage *babble*, speaking at this level to a fear as primary as the liberal belief in the articulate reason of the civilized individual.

The moment that the composition of this memoir encloses tells heavily on the sympathies and positions it maintains: under the gathering and breaking storm of the Second World War. The better part of her paternal legacy represented the best hopes humanity held onto in the analogous situation of twenty-five years earlier. This tradition subsists in the most urgently topical piece of writing she composes at this later moment: *Three Guineas*. Closely argued, densely and empirically reasoned, this antiwar treatise is massively and even wearisomely buttressed with its apparatus of scholarly citation and case-making, syllogism and proof.[8] Its passionate rationality stands as strikingly at odds with the cooler and suaver manner of her accomplished style, moreover, as it reveals the underlying, abiding strength of that intellectual faith. If those protocols of documentary logic appear overprepared, their excesses preserve a memory of what they attempt to correct: the errors of insufficiency to which an overconfidence amounted in 1914. Reason seemed so self-assured then that its demonstrations could remain a function of progressive words alone, of sequences sheerly verbal. Now, in the rational management of fact, she sets the liberal intelligence she has inherited to its necessary, better work.

Nonetheless, these same exertions express a desperation. The earnestness of first principles meets the lesson that the extremity of current circumstances repeats: the inefficiency of reason's appeal to history. In the late 1930s, she is revisiting—or awaiting—the disappointment that her father's failed example first instanced. His failure to realize his intellectual ideals will provide a model and form for her understanding of subsequent events, especially those superintended in 1914 by the (somewhat) younger men of his own aging generation of Liberals.

Working already from the precedent of her father's obvious contradictions, Woolf's critical intelligence could register the official reasoning of the 1914 war clearly and, so, discredit it readily. While she appears to be prepared then to inscribe the Great War as the demise of the high ideal of liberal rationality, this main point of intellectual reference identifies a center of emotional gravity as well. In her previous experience, this tradition has been modeled by characters hardly so compromised beforehand.

Thoby Stephen, her older brother, brought into an intense and refreshing configuration the major attributes of their father's intellectual personality. A passion for Swift and the Age of Reason, a sensibility given to strong opinions and convinced in particular of the irrelevance now of Christianity, fiercely moral but committed to logic rather than faith as the basis of correct action, his rational atheism stemmed identifiably from Leslie's root. From the values they shared he cultivated and stylized his own version of the one type they comprise: the liberal autodidact, a persona formed to the standard of mental freedom they both esteemed as the first and necessary condition of valid (inductive) thought. If Leslie had become resentful and hidebound, however, Thoby was optimistic and spontaneous. His energies were contagious. He magnetized a cast of characters to himself at Cambridge, and reconvened them in London, in 1905, as the intellectual company of the first days of Bloomsbury.

More particularly, these were the followers ("the apostles," in their own nomenclature) of their Cambridge professor and mentor, Henry Sedgwick, a devotee of the moral philosopher G. E. Moore. His recently published *Principia Ethica* (1903) established an intellectual standard as well as a practical value for their gathering. While Moore's emphasis on the importance of personal friendship extended its blessing on the intimacies of their group, his logician's insistence on the truth of reason moved in directions especially compatible with the artistic orientations of their membership. His tough, Socratically rational attitudes added a stress on the importance—the necessity—of beautiful objects. In the idealist calculus of the *Principia*, these artifacts conform in the appeal of their proportions to the ratios of the deeper rationality, where balance or harmony may be perceived and appreciated as an artistic quality, which is also an absolute intellectual value. In principle, Moore rehearses the aesthetic conception of reason, which Hobhouse consecrates at the end of the same decade in *Liberalism*. The concord this idea esteems provides an encompassing category of value, whose activities in early Bloomsbury range from the ratiocinations of propositional thought to the harmonizing of personal relations.[9] While Moore's own focus would remain close to his chosen concerns as philosophical aesthete and discriminating friend, nuancing the register of artistic perceptions and improving the work of intimate acquaintances, this apparently private sensibility could identify its like in the public sphere of political and partisan Liberalism, which, ideally at least, witnesses a commitment to similar principles of equity.

The Liberal agenda for the 1906 election expressed a sort of philanthropic egalitarianism in an ambitious program of social welfare. The party triumphed mightily. When Woolf recalls the several members of the new fellowship going out with her in January 1906 to Trafalgar Square to celebrate the landslide victory,[10] she preserves some sense of connection between their identifiably private or even exclusionary intensities and the directions of contemporary history. A millennial expectation seemed fully credible for these young intellectual partisans; the century ending the current thousand-year period was beginning on a visionary premise.

Scheduled to go up to the bar in the late autumn of 1906, acceding in everyone's expectations to a legal and political career of exceptional brilliance, Thoby Stephen took a summer holiday in advance, on the continent. He and his younger brother Adrian traveled rather daringly by boat down the Dalmatian coast, then on horseback through Montenegro. By plan they met up with their sisters in mid-September in Greece, at Olympia. What had promised to be an itinerant romance through classical antiquity, however, was afflicted from the beginning with illness. Vanessa developed appendicitis, while the strain of travel, coupled with the frustration of being confined to the role of nurse and attendant, led Virginia into a bout of heavy depression. Thoby had to travel back to London ahead of them. When, in mid-November, they finally arrived in the city, they found their brother severely ill. He had contracted typhoid on the return journey. On 20 November, Thoby died.[11]

What persisted in his younger sister's memory she clarifies and magnifies through the imaginative lens of *Jacob's Room* (1922). Certainly the character of Jacob Flanders matches Thoby Stephen's in many evident respects, including their student careers at Cambridge and their immersion in the university culture of liberal intellectualism. In the recasting of the events of that fateful summer of 1906, Woolf moves the parallel to its major revelation. In the historical fiction of the novel, she reconfigures the pestilence infecting her brother as the disturbance sweeping out of the eastern Mediterranean in the midsummer of 1914, that is, the war, which eventuates in Jacob's death.[12] The cultural order that Jacob and Thoby represent together presents the imperiled value. The rational capacity, which Thoby had brought into such an exceptionally promissory form, locates the range of possibility and loss in which Jacob's death resonates.

The disestablishment of rationalist language in the Great War provides the instigating condition of considerable verbal invention for London modernists. What Pound and Eliot apprehend as the failing strength of an intellectual and political institution, however, Virginia Stephen has experienced ahead of time as personal loss. In the manifold reiteration of the 1914 moment in her fiction, this prepossession marks her individual difference. Her biographical circumstances help her to render the event with all of the immensity of its potential of feeling concentrated and intensified.

Woolf moves toward the war with the readiness this preparation affords, but her interests in the questions it presents also took literary expression earlier. In this period the major work is *The Voyage Out*. Begun in 1908, substantially completed by 1913 (its publication was delayed until September 1915), her first novel carries the imprint of her family background. The early mentorship of her new brother-in-law, Clive Bell, has reiterated and strengthened this influence. His affiliation with the Cambridge apostles and their subsequent reembodiment in Bloomsbury extended most crucially to a belief in Moore's philosophy of art.[13] Thus the standard of aesthetic reason—its manifestation as beautiful truth, more specifically, as musical and harmonious rationality—represents a value and practice that her fiction addresses, but not simply or single-mindedly. This body of concepts stands as a possibility, which her imaginative language tests. This intellectual structure also encompasses and confines her protagonist. Woolf's resisting reciprocity with the tenets of this tradition identifies already the conflicted status of its main positional attitudes for her. The critical sensibility she reiterates through this test develops and aims her then toward the major crises of Liberalism in August 1914. Her early effort may be read most profitably with this later end in view.

i

The voyage out in the novel of this title belongs at first sorting to the narrative conventions of the feminine *Bildungsroman*. The plot of its transatlantic journey and South American adventure promises a romance of expanding possibilities for its heroine. Initially, at least, the story conforms. In the deflection and frustration of these expectations, however, the novel begins to generate its author's counterconventional energy and interest. For *The Voyage Out* extends to a revealing extremity the particularly English sensibility that Woolf has invested in Rachel Vinrace. In the protracted crisis of its last part, the author exposes the limitations of her protagonist's frame of reference, not as a censure of this character's personal shortcomings, rather as a searching interrogation of the forces and values that have gone into Rachel's making. Woolf exhibits the deforming constraints of the system in the contortions into which Rachel's experience throws her, in her response to the radical novelty these new and strange lands will present. Nor, ostensibly, has her author traveled completely successfully as yet beyond British insularity and similar circumscriptions. Yet the novel encloses a drama that provides the best record from these early years of Woolf's contested relation to the culture impinging on the formation of her own imaginative intelligence. The full and elaborate *Weltanschauung* of Liberal imperialism encompasses this novel. Its recognizably institutional attitudes show on board and *en voyage* through the persons of ostensible authority.

Of these figures the most notable is Richard Dalloway. The character going by this name is better known in Woolf's fiction from his subsequent appearance as the husband of Clarissa, *Mrs. Dalloway*. In that novel, however, he emerges as a shadowy personage. A reverse prominence of public and private roles, in the 1925 text, puts him in a diminished position; throughout the narrative Clarissa backflashes an emotional history, which relegates Richard to a sort of tender ineffectualness. In 1908, however, he assumes a substantial reality. His density and pressure come from the matter of historical fact that Woolf catches up in the career she represents in him.

In the political culture contemporary with the novel's composition, the partisan interests and ideological energies that meet in Richard Dalloway present a most local and timely point of convergence. "In one word—Unity," he begins his somewhat mottoed and sloganeering response to Rachel's request to express his "ideal." "Unity of aim, of dominion, of progress. The dispersion of the greatest ideas over the greatest area." He expatiates:

> "[W]hen I consider my life, there is one fact I admit that I'm proud of; owing to me some thousands of girls in Lancashire—and many thousands to come after them—can spend an hour every day in the open air which their mothers had to spend over their looms. I'm prouder of that, I own, than I should be of writing Keats and Shelley into the bargain!"[14]

Political Liberalism owned as its intellectual property the "progress" Richard has named as the meliorist ideal of his domestic agenda. By official subscription, however, Richard stands as a Conservative M.P., and not in name only. The "dominion" over foreign races that he establishes as a major and equal value in his personal campaign represents an interest favored traditionally by the party to which he belongs. The merging in his person of attitudes conventionally opposed runs true to the main point of balance and power in the long political moment of the novel's composition. Richard locates the centrist coalition that Liberal imperialism maintained, variously in public and *in camera*, from the time of the 1906 election, when the domestic program that the party was elected ostensibly to serve was augmented powerfully in chambers with the imperial interests and global designs of Asquith, Grey, and Haldane. The open-air confidence this joint philosophy shows in Dalloway's testament reflects best the hegemony it actually enjoyed.

A like alliance of rival ideologies appears in the less conspicuous but equally significant figure of the ship steward, Mr. Grice. While the interests he serves appear inseparable from the adventuring motives of the commercial empire, the buccaneering business in which he assists yields first place in his affections to the plight of the urban underclass, specifically, the English underfed. The provisioner for the transatlantic voyage configures in his role and person the concern for material well-being that the 1906 election has renewed as the social conscience of a Liberalism ranging otherwise in its enterprises so widely across the globe. The greatest vulnerability of his position shows at its point of greatest stress, where Mr. Grice needs to find intellectual coherence for his dual career as imperial factor and millennial agent. The pressure point lies in his personal library, where the self-educated ideologue stocks the authors that express a progressivist ethic, on which an ideology of expansionist improvement like his, or Dalloway's, might rely. He references his meliorist ideals to the major names of T. H. Huxley, Herbert Spencer, and Henry George (*VO*, 54). Predictably, Clarissa Dalloway hears in Grice a kind of plain-man evangile for her husband's Liberal imperialism, hailing the steward as a "philosopher and poet" (*VO*, 54). To Rachel, however, "the lean person of Mr. Grice," prone to vent the "tirade of a fanatical man" (*VO*, 53), is only a "bore" (54). The intellectual respectability he seeks so desperately drains equally noticeably from the position Woolf stakes in him.

When the intellectual sensibility that Grice represents enters Rachel's ken in the person of Dalloway, however, her resistance diminishes. This politician reveals the same tradition with a reality more substantial, an enhanced gravity if not an increased appeal. Dalloway brings one strain in the liberal mind into the close focus of his own compelling personality. Progressive logic represents a value common not only to those writers in Grice's library. Leslie Stephen thought and wrote out of the same tradition of optimistic rationality, at least in his early days, when "manly logic" still owned (for him) the more cheerful *virtù* of such a term. Undiminished in the quasi-paternal figure of Dalloway, masculine reason appears in this character's mien. With the full force and complexity that the legacy presents to her, Woolf tropes a machine scheme into his representative speech, where the mechanical factor catches the ruled, programmatic quality of rational language:

> Mr. Dalloway rolling that rich deliberate voice was even more impressive. He seemed to come from the humming oily centre of the machine where the polished rods are sliding, and the pistons thumping; he grasped things so firmly but so loosely; he made the others appear like old maids cheapening remnants. Rachel followed in the wake of the matrons, as if in a trance. (*VO*, 47)

The phallic imagery clearly identifies the male character of this speech. Woolf reiterates its gendered identity in the feeling of self-conscious unlikeness and alienation that it fosters among these "maids" and "matrons." The attraction it manages to exert for the protagonist appears at once problematic and powerful. The "trance" he creates in Rachel locates a substantially negative force in the plot of her story, all in all, a sort of productive impediment in the developing interests of the feminine *Bildungsroman*. Against Mr. Dalloway's conventional sensibility, then, the rhythms of liberation are expected to rise.

Specifically English, the disposition that Richard Dalloway typifies represents a limitation in cultural as well as personal terms. If the narrative of

Rachel's far-flung adventure promises some delivery beyond his insular domain, the Dalloways' taking their leave from the ongoing expedition at the midway point seems to assist in this process. This reinforcement occurs, however, in no simple or mechanical fashion. An incident that immediately precedes their departure needs to be considered: the sexual violation Rachel undergoes at Richard's whim (*VO*, 76). Unforeseen, even desperate in the uncontrol he shows, the kiss recalls the lengthier, more invasive attentions that George Duckworth paid to Woolf. The panic this incident triggers initially for Rachel reaches back into the anxieties that Duckworth's behavior prompted as the intense and constant distress of Woolf's mid–late adolescence. In the experience she presents through her character, however, the episode begins to live soon afterward as a locus of interest and energies formerly unknown, indeed, as a growing point of novel possibilities. "You're peaceful," goes the character's attempt to compose herself in a mood that will steady her movement in this new terrain:

> She became peaceful too, at the same time possessed with a strange exultation. Life seemed to hold infinite possibilities she had never guessed at. She leant upon the rail and looked over the troubled grey waters, where the sunlight was fitfully scattered upon the crests of the waves, until she was cold and absolutely calm again. Nonetheless, something wonderful had happened. (*VO*, 76–77)

Rachel reconstructs the trauma the sexual offense has occasioned for her in a way that gives power and agency to its victim. The heroine may forget the sins that romance like this transfigures and forgives. Where Rachel turns the terror of potentials formerly unknown into the pleasure of expected and manageable conventions, these attitudes appear to be the focus and aim of Woolf's intent to display a compensatory behavior. In the account of Rachel's progress, nonetheless, Dalloway's action also visits discredit on the systems of thinking that Rachel is attempting to leave behind. He works thus to further her story, so to serve the purpose of the main thematic interest. In the precedent text of Woolf's own life, after all, the whole code of Victorian moral reason broke down through George Duckworth's offices, so to expose its incoherence and, inevitably if painfully, open some sense of the possibilities it could not covenant. A range of alternative, counterconventional outlooks begins to appear within the broadening compass of *The Voyage Out*.

As in the prospect of the dream Rachel experiences on the night of the event. The immediacy of this reaction testifies to the relevance of the figure that the nightmare projects so strikingly, disturbingly:

> She dreamt that she was walking down a long tunnel, which grew so narrow by degrees that she could touch the damp bricks on either side. At length the tunnel opened and became a vault; she found herself

trapped in it, bricks meeting her wherever she turned, alone with a little deformed man who squatted on the floor gibbering, with long nails. His face was pitted and like the face of an animal. The wall behind him oozed with damp, which collected into drops and slid down. Still and cold as death she lay, not daring to move, until she broke the agony by tossing herself across the bed, and woke crying "Oh!"

Light showed her the familiar things: her clothes, fallen off the chair; the water jug gleaming white; but the horror did not go at once. She felt herself pursued, so that she got up and actually locked her door. A voice moaned for her; eyes desired her. All night long barbarian men harassed the ship; they came scuffling down the passages, and stooped to snuffle at her door. She could not sleep again. (*VO*, 77)

Whether or not we understand that Dalloway's behavior has stirred the dormant forces of Rachel's sexuality, the figures of "desire" haunting her testify less evidently to the strength of these physical presentiments than to the intensity of their cultural proscription. Eros in exotica, the imagery she generates clearly reflects the estrangements that a woman raised to her station will have suffered: libido lives in alien lands, fearsomely. Yet the threat she registers depicts a danger more than specifically sexual. A whole system of cultural values is imperiled, and the resistance Rachel puts up to this menace brings one of the most prominent of these standards into play.

The higher ideals of late Victorian imperialism appear in this scene in the reiteration of its mission statement. This ideology assigns an embodiment of colonial savagery its symbolic place, on the bestial floor. The dream works equally to concede the proscription (in order to allow the dreamer to proceed) and, ultimately, to subvert and transgress it. Richard Dalloway has just belied this conventional sensibility's superior, overweening truth. Opportunist of inconsistency like this, the dreamer maneuvers for advantage, restoring to unlike potency the forces Dalloway and a system now discredited have repressed. In place of reason's civilizing speech, she hears a creature "gibbering" his own insurgent, adversary theme.

And counterappeal? In the elementary oppositions of the dream, the image overwritten with the heaviest prohibition may locate, of course, the point where the dreamer brings the greatest pressure to bear. The most forbidden interest seeks most forcibly the freedom of release. The insistence of a figure appearing twice in this vignette suggests the dreamer's densest presentiment, her intensest energy, as her half-awake thoughts respond to the provocation of that outlandish character in the dream itself. These "*barbar*ian men" answer his "gibbering," then, from the echoing depths of this marked word. These *babbling* savages repeat the motif of a sheerly creaturely speech. The attraction that the sound exerts seems equal to the force of the system it opposes. To test the potential of words heard mainly or only as sound, so to establish a vocabulary that may tap resources of feeling or sensation previously unheard, to contest thus the hegemony of a rationalistic language, so to challenge the protocols of masculine logic and break the spell its verbal ceremonies have cast as her subservient "trance": the novel of this woman's personal development moves to issues specifically—and primarily—linguistic. With the light of an irony inquiring finely into her own nurture, Woolf sets her character searching for liberation in a quest that needs to sail against Liberalism, in particular against the manifold constraints that the speech of reason has talked her into accepting.

ii

Rachel's response to novel linguistic possibilities evolves to the major station she marks in her reading of *Decline and Fall of the Roman Empire*. Monument to the encyclopedic spirit of the Enlightenment, Gibbon's work embodies the logic and language of classificatory rationalism, not only in the majestically designed proportions of its organization, but through the exact and exacting ratios of its sentences. An exemplary record of the eighteenth-century sensibility that Leslie Stephen so revered, its estimable effort establishes a center of attention he might not have predicted, let alone approved, for his daughter's character:

> With a feeling that to open and read would certainly be a surprising experience, she turned the historian's page and read that—
>
>> His generals, in the early part of his reign, attempted the reduction of Aethiopia and Arabia Felix. . . . The northern countries of Europe scarcely deserved the expense and labour of conquest. The forests and morasses of Germany were filled with a hardy race of barbarians, who despised life when it was separated from freedom.
>>
>> Never had any words been so vivid and beautiful—Arabia Felix—Aethiopia. But those were not more noble than the others, hardy barbarians, forests, and morasses. They seemed to drive roads back to the very beginning of the world, on either side of which the populations of all times and countries stood in avenues, and by passing down them all knowledge would be hers, and the book of the world turned back to the very first page. (*VO*, 174–75)

Unfixed on maps she knows, Arabia Felix and Aethiopia live for Rachel as "vivid" and "beautiful" names, not as places but as words, mainly as imaginary locales of sound. This sensory register also enhances the semantic valence of those "hardy *barbar*ians." The sense that its Greek etymology preserves of *babble*—a speech received by the "civilized" as sheer sound—stirs with the enthusiasm that the music of the Latin language has activated in Rachel. The welcome she extends measures a substantial advance in her developing awareness. She has overridden the proscription that the same nominal value of the babbling savage drew in her earlier dream, which was monitored still by the rationalistic conscience of an Edward Gibbon (or a Leslie Stephen). "[T]o drive roads back to the very beginning of the world," so to turn "the book of the world" back "to the very first page," marks a conversion of the imperial project into an intellectual adventure, which Rachel's author maps as a homing approach to some ultimate, originary tongue.

Going native? Not merely. Edenic and millennial equally, Rachel's vision projects as its potential a usage unencumbererd as yet by the plot of a history already elapsed. The prospect exerts for the young woman the appeal of a new beginning. Its Word speaks the promise of a knowledge unlocked for her like a *mysterium*, from a language only as magical in fact as it may prove at last useful. The key to this trove and resource appears nonetheless to have been cut to a design as secret for Rachel as the speech of Gibbon's *lingua antiqua*. The task that its discovery sets her establishes the narrative motive and deeper interest in her story, where, the reader expects, her spirit will expand in response.

The outgrowing of older notions of verbal logic takes Rachel on a voyage of adventure, self-invention. Woolf furthers this process initially by the development of a love interest with the young writer, Terence Hewet. Into this character, Woolf has blended Clive Bell's mentoring presence for herself and the romantically standard Other. Woolf was already attempting to approach areas of imaginative awareness beyond the ken of Bell's sensibility, however, and so the chief feature of Hewet's appeal shows in his difference from that model. While the understanding that Bell presented conformed to those conceptions of linguistic reason that the liberal mind of contemporary England afforded him, the attraction that Hewet exerts for Rachel comes through the challenge he mounts to those conventions. "'I want to write a novel about Silence,' he said; 'the things people don't say. But the difficulty is immense'" (*VO*, 216). This enterprise defines the limitation of a rationalist idiom specifically, and especially for Rachel. Her feeling for Terence proceeds through the knowledge and compass of reasoned speech and extends through Woolf's representation into some sublogical or pararational language. Rachel attempts to move into some supraverbal dimension of sheer sensation and impression:

> She was conscious of emotions and powers which she had never suspected in herself, and of a depth in the world hitherto unknown. When she thought of their relationship *she saw rather than reasoned*, representing her view of what Terence felt by a picture of him drawn across the room to stand by her side. This passage across the room amounted to a physical sensation, but what it meant she did not know. (*VO*, 224; emphasis added)

"Moreover, none of the books she read, from *Wuthering Heights* to *Man and Superman*, and the plays of Ibsen," goes this list of insufficiencies, "suggested from their analysis of love that what their heroines felt was what she was feeling now. It seemed to her that *her sensations had no name*" (*VO*, 223; emphasis added). Even the more adventuring attempts of earlier and recent literature to present a similar experience offer themselves as verbal conventions merely, being emptied of the substantial originality and reality of a vivid, "physical sensation" like hers. Wordlessness like this, Rachel's author allows her to aver, consists of a novel reconnaissance on the possibilities of human feeling.

The energy that Woolf invests in these possibilities mounts to the prominence of crisis and climacteric in the novel. The action in the final third of the book rises and falls around an expedition to a distant jungle site, which positions at its extreme and emblematic verge the exchange that takes place between Rachel and Terence. Where even the sounds of human speech have grown strange, so the conventions attending these two conversants show an equal potential to be unmade, remade. Here then is Rachel's Arabia Felix, her own Aethiopia. A locale of words freed it seems from previous inscriptions, the place locates the uncharted strength of a native instinct, her own promissory genius.

iii

The language odyssey that evolves with Rachel's advance to this distant locale, however, stops at that destination. Woolf undermines its visionary possibilities insistently, indeed fatalistically. From the outset of this last venture, in fact, her protagonist (not easily distinguishable in this respect from her narrator) demurs. Rachel's worst intimations are borne out, moreover. The expedition will eventuate in her death, an outcome linked suggestively but internally and essentially to the awareness she has touched in the jungle deeps, at the core or promised origin of a new speaking order. Divided thus against its own ideal, stymied just where its ambitions might begin to be realized, *The Voyage Out* reads in the end as the novel of a development that does not occur, a story of hopes undone—in a diminuendo that includes as well a hermeneutic of their undoing.

"They seemed to be driving into the heart of the night," the narrator warns, as the river venture turns toward the inner recesses of the jungle. The feeling of mysteriousness gains its particular pressure and density in its effect on human speech. With the closing in of the background sound, talk between members of the party becomes strange:

> The great darkness had the usual effect of taking away all desire for communication by making their words sound thin and small; and, after

walking round the deck three or four times, they clustered together, yawning deeply, and looking at the same spot of deep gloom on the banks. Murmuring very low in the rhythmical tone of one oppressed by the air, Mrs. Flushing began to wonder. (*VO*, 265)

The wearing away of customary manners and meanings in their spoken exchanges begins to alter the orientation of human language. The speakers seem increasingly to address the natural noises surrounding them. The response these answering echoes represent rises in an antiphonal rhythm more and more antic, to a sort of creaturely heckling that makes of its own meaninglessness a louder and stronger sound:

> At one point Hewet read part of a poem aloud, but the number of moving things entirely vanquished his words. He ceased to read, and no one spoke. They moved on under the shelter of the trees. There was now a covey of red birds feeding on one of the little islets to the left, or again a blue-green parrot flew shrieking from tree to tree. . . . Again he read from his book:
>
> > Whoever you are holding me now in your hand,
> > Without one thing all will be useless.
>
> A bird gave a wild laugh, a monkey chuckled a malicious question, and, as fire fades in the hot sunshine, his words flickered and went out. (*VO*, 267)

These acoustic effects thicken with the atmosphere as the party progresses into the forest. The menace emerging in the narrative report also underscores the sense of adventure now quickening in Rachel, who, as she pairs off with Terence, proceeds it seems to her promised end in this novel of possibilities:

> As they passed into the depths of the forest the light grew dimmer, and the noises of the ordinary world were replaced by those creaking and sighing sounds which suggest to the traveler in a forest that he is walking at the bottom of the sea. . . . Terence and Rachel hardly spoke.
> . . . They heard the flapping of great wings; they heard the fruit go pattering through the leaves and eventually fall with a thud. The silence was again profound.
> "Does this frighten you?" Terence asked when the sound of the fruit falling had completely died away.
> "No," she answered. "I like it." (*VO*, 270–71)

The hegemony any male voice earlier enjoyed now falls away, and, at least momentarily, Rachel can respond affirmatively to the question of her courage to grasp the main chance. This reply seems consistent with the instinct and energy the entire novel will have framed as the primary site of its ultimate story, as the opening moment of the self-creation Rachel has been attempting to begin.

The disappointment seems as subtle as it is quickly apparent:

> She repeated "I like it." She was walking fast, and holding herself more erect than usual. There was another pause.
>
> "You like being with me?" Terence asked.
>
> "Yes, with you," she replied.
>
> He was silent for a moment. Silence seemed to have fallen upon the world.
>
> "That is what I have felt ever since I knew you," he replied. "We are happy together." He did not seem to be speaking, or she to be hearing.
>
> "Very happy," she answered.
>
> They continued to walk for some time in silence. Their steps unconsciously quickened.
>
> "We love each other," Terence said.
>
> "We love each other," she repeated. . . .
>
> "We love each other," Terence repeated, searching into her face. Their faces were both very pale and quiet, and they said nothing. . . .
>
> "Terrible—terrible," she murmured after another pause. (*VO*, 271)

The temporary suspension of existing conventions has left these speakers with nothing new to say. The major motive that this novel of feminine adventure has disclosed—to redress the inequities inherited with the existing linguistic system—reverts to an older idiom, its usages wholly unrenewed. Hewet simply reproduces the familiar locutions of romantic love (speaking for *both* of them), which Rachel echoes accordingly.

The reverse turn this development represents reaches further through the "terror" Rachel "murmurs" in the after-hush. In this landscape of alien and unknown noises, the double syllable of *mur-mur* recovers the significance it originally owned as a nonce word for meaningless sound. A hope to reclaim the potent stuff of a new gnosis in the primary material of speech shows now as a fear of unmeaning phonemes, as a horror of primitive beginnings. In the representation of this last passage, after all, human speech limits itself to the mainly mimic facility of animal sounds.

When Terence and Rachel repeat this scene at a second landing, and attempt to give their sentiments a new footing and a fresh expression, the failure recurs. His conventional romantic address and her mechanical answer represent no advance in the visionary project of the novel. The ambition to recover in the sheer material of sound the content of a new language dissolves, in fact, to a nightmare prospect. A sensorium of sheer noise devolves a physical convulsion on Rachel as well as a bizarre hallucination, in a phantasmagoria whose bewildering effect is commensurate with its considerable length:

Voices crying behind them never reached through the waters in which they were now sunk. The repetition of Hewet's name in short, dissevered syllables was to them the crack of a dry branch or the laughter of a bird. The grasses and breezes sounding and murmuring all round them, they never noticed that the swishing of the grasses grew louder and louder, and did not cease with the lapse of the breeze. A hand dropped abrupt as iron on Rachel's shoulder; it might have been a bolt from heaven. She fell beneath it, and the grass whipped across her eyes and filled her mouth and ears. Through the waving stems she saw a figure, large and shapeless against the sky. Helen was upon her. Rolled this way and that, now seeing only forests of green, and now the high blue heaven, she was speechless and almost without sense. At last she lay still, all the grasses shaken round her and before her by her panting. Over her loomed two great heads, the heads of a man and woman, of Terence and Helen.

Both were flushed, both laughing, and the lips were moving; they came together and kissed in the air above her. Broken fragments of speech came down to her on the ground. She thought she heard them speak of love and then of marriage. Raising herself and sitting up, she too realised Helen's soft body, the strong and hospitable arms, and happiness swelling and breaking in one vast wave. When this fell away, and the grasses once more lay low, and the sky became horizontal, and the earth rolled out flat on each side, and the trees stood upright, she was the first to perceive a little row of human figures standing patiently in the distance. For the moment she could not remember who they were.

"Who are they?" she asked, and then recollected.

Falling into line behind Mr. Flushing, they were careful . . . (*VO*, 283–84)

Left behind as inexplicably as it was lapsed into, leaving the reader as perplexed as the character was overwhelmed, this interval presents in effect the long moment of the novel's suspended hopes and absconded possibilities. The case that this *Bildungsroman* has made for the rebuilding of language from the base and the recovery of some novel foundational order finds Rachel now not as its agent but as its casualty.

The derangement she enters presents a foretaste and forewarning of the disorder from which she subsequently suffers and ultimately dies. Thus, on their return to the hotel, as Hewet reads aloud to her a passage from Milton's *Comus*, a density of references to legendary figures and locales presents a lexicon so unknown to her ears that it seems wholly musical. Where Terence's remarks also direct her to appreciate this sheerly acoustic quality, her response coincides with the next stages of her fatal illness:

Terence was reading Milton aloud, because he said the words of Milton had substance and shape, so that it was not necessary to understand what he was saying; one could merely listen to his words; one could almost handle them. . . . Rachel at any rate could not keep her attention fixed upon them, but went off upon curious trains of thought suggested by words such as "curb" and "Locrine" and "Brute," which brought unpleasant sights before her eyes, independently of their meaning. Owing to the heat and the dancing air the garden too looked strange—the trees were either too near or too far, and her head almost certainly ached. (*VO*, 326–27)

While the intensification of these symptoms takes the narrative through Rachel's final decline, the spasm she manifested earlier clearly began the process. Her condition links back, associatively and powerfully if not clinically, to the overpowering stimulus that Woolf has instanced in sounds like these. In the disturbing echoes of "Locrine" and "Brute," she has set in reverse the resonant splendor of Rachel's promised Aethiopia, her much-desired Arabia Felix.

The demise of those fresh, apparently valuable, even visionary initiatives presents thus the major interpretive problem in the novel. Contemporary postcolonial attitudes may address this perplexity and read in Woolf's text the revenge tragedy of a late imperial age. Thus the romancing of "primitive" conditions from the protected vantage of a "civilized" capital meets its just and fated end in the unspeakable, insurgent Otherness of that intransigent locale. Some timely parallels ratify this critical description. Woolf's acquaintance E. M. Forster draws an analogous situation in *Passage to India*: the mystic syllables that Mrs. Moore hears in the caves of Malabar hold a potency so disturbing to her English preconceptions that they leave her, in the end, fatally disoriented. Rachel's "terror" may also own an origin with the "horror" that Conrad's *Heart of Darkness* has found on the outward verge of a commercial empire. The whispered dismay of the adventurer Kurtz is likewise twice-told: "Terrible—terrible"; "The horror—the horror."[15]

Woolf's narrator proposes an understanding in terms closer to the protagonist's experience. In the last paragraph of the chapter preceding the expedition, the narrative locates a motivating interest and promissory aim in the insufficiency of conventional speech, revealed to Rachel's ears as a diminished version of some ultimate, better potential. "Aimless, trivial, meaningless, oh no—what she had seen at tea made it impossible for her to believe that. The little jokes, the chatter, the inanities of the afternoon had shriveled up before her eyes" (*VO*, 263). What opens in turn as a prospect of promissory renewal is a topos equally mythic and contemporary, a historicized Eden, one in which the garden of novel possibility holds as well the serpent of its undoing:

Underneath the likings and spites, the comings together and partings, great things were happening—terrible things, because they were so great. Her sense of safety was shaken, as if between twigs and dead

Studio portrait of Virginia Woolf, 1925

leaves she had seen the movement of a snake. It seemed to her that a moment's respite was allowed, a moment's make-believe, and then again
the profound and reasonless law asserted itself, moulding them all to its
liking, making and destroying. (*VO*, 263)

In this "moment's respite," Woolf's premonitory account offers a poignant
sense of the suspension from existing rules that the jungle expedition represents. Against the potential this adventure extends for some new or renewed
community of speech, however, the author sets the more than equal ballast of
that "profound and reasonless law" that (re)"asserted itself." She is sacrificing
those benign possibilities in advance to a force or fate that is not *ir*rational, not
even *un*reason*able*, but "reason*less*." In the emptiness that this suffix designates
she represents an elementary void. Her novel has launched its heroine into this
terra incognita, which she has attempted to map and make compatible with her
own best interests. Yet the resistance that Woolf configures and the failure she
forecasts also confirm in the wording through which she asserts this terror the
sanctuary she wishes to preserve. By the reverse logic of its ultimate term, "reasonless" cedes some ultimate value and substantial reality to reason itself.
Fairly, too. When, after all, does the language of this narrative exceed or depart

from the rationalistic standards that the author seeks otherwise to challenge and surpass? The reassurance such conventions offer may increase with the force Woolf brings to contest them. To shake their sedulous hold on her, she will need a disruption closer to home, a defiance more sizable by far than the one she has imagined into this distant locale.

The depth and extent of the connection between Woolf and the experience of the Great War affords the substance of a growing body of critical literature, led by Karen Levenback's *Virginia Woolf and the Great War*, which establishes not only the immediacy of the author's exposure to events but their persistence in her memory. Levenback is extending the premises of Alex Zwerdling's *Virginia Woolf and the Real World*, which helped in the early days of the Woolf recovery to question the construction of her literary character as the fugitive aesthete and establish a record of sustained engagement with social issues in the imaginative fabric of her fiction.[16] Woolf's perception of the war as a political event reveals an intellectual discrimination, however, which draws specifically and necessarily on her intimacy with the attitudes and practices of English Liberalism. This focus provides the growing point of a body of work that preserves the density of a private, writerly interaction with the public material of her craft and art. How she appropriates the crisis of rationalistic language in the policy wars as an opportunity to develop a new literary idiom is a story of the gestation and (re)birth of the major novelist of English literary modernism, one that begins, not inauspiciously, on the smallest scale.

II

Shorts

In a quasi-Socratic dialogue, situated within the elegant pretense of "The Evening Party" (July 1918), Woolf allows two speakers to exchange conventional views—about customary usage and its shortcomings, about the reality that the language of habit and common sense must fail to grasp:

> "See what comes of trying to say what one means! Nonsense!"
>
> "Precisely. Yet how sad a thing is sense! How vast a renunciation it represents! Listen for a moment. Distinguish one among the voices. Now. 'So cold it must seem after India. Seven years too. But habit is everything.' That's sense. That's agreement. . . . It's all compromise— all safety, the general intercourse of human beings. Therefore we discover nothing; we cease to explore; we cease to believe that there is anything to discover."[17]

The failure of the language of common sense seems to occur even—or, in the sense of the opening wordplay, especially—with the best of intentions, when one tries to be most "precise." The next move in this conventional minuet might include an allusion to this proverb fragment of Heraclitus:

> People are deceived, [he says], in the recognition of things that are obvious in much the same way Homer, who was wiser than all the Greeks, was deceived. For he was deceived by the words spoken to him by some boys killing lice: "What we saw and caught we leave behind, while what we did not see or catch we take [away with us]."[18]

While Woolf's speaker makes the conventional complaint about the limits of conventional expression, the ancient fable reasserts the power of the elusive. This fugitive presence exerts the full force of its appeal here, too, in the image bewitching the next turn of the exchange. "Speech is an old torn net," the first conversant resumes, "through which the fish escape as one casts it over them" (CSF, 99).

What swims through the mesh of idiom and consensus values leaves the trace of an inventive, counterconventional energy. This sensibility flourishes, around the July 1918 date of this story's composition, in the shorter fiction Woolf drafts between 1917 and 1920. In this work she cross-talks the "compromise" language that a "general intercourse of human beings" settles on for "safety," so to engage a range of resonance that is dangerous, perhaps, certainly unexpected. She converts the conventional sense of words, all in all, a common language of measured meanings and reasonable exchange, into its constant opposite. The sequences of verbal logic lead the discourse to a result similar to the one the first speaker achieves as the consequence of her efforts in the same direction, to a "non-sense" equivalence. The regret this speaker expresses initially shifts too, in the due course of Woolf's development over these years, to the sort of value she includes in the numinous image of those elusive fish.

These creatures flash like the totem animals in another tribal dialect, an alternate speaking community, a new literary attitude and practice. They appear as the leading spirits of London literary modernism, a gathering in which Woolf's first experimental work finds its company, its context, and its resonance. At the same moment, Pound and Eliot also confabulate the language and habits of rationalistic compacts. A speech that appears reasonable at least—or at most—on its verbal surface reverts to its opposite and reaches a new depth of evocation. Swimming through the apparatus of conventional syntax and grammatical logic are linguistic fish as strange, after all, as the deep-water incomprehensibilities of superfetation, of phthisic, of polyphiloprogenitive.

How to account for this concurrent turn in Woolf's career presents a question that goes to the motivating interests of her mature oeuvre. What brings her to the heckling and incendiary echoing of reasonable speech in particular? While the question admits her likeness to the Anglo-American poets, the inquiry needs to concede the possibility of an alternate origin from theirs in her specific biographical circumstance and, so, a differing explanation. While

Pound and Eliot obviously echo the provocations of Liberal reason in distress, could Woolf's version not be the hyperlogical language that "madness" may adapt? Is this not a vocabulary and manner that the successive and progressive breakdowns she underwent between 1913 and 1915 led her to manipulate, initially perhaps as its unwitting victim, ultimately as its master strategist? Leonard Woolf's descriptions of her demeanor in these periods feature several instances of rationalistic insanity.[19]

Any psychological hypothesis involves the sort of comprehensive categories of evaluation that Louis A. Sass offers in his *Madness and Modernism: Insanity in the Light of Modern Art, Literature, and Thought*. In this phenomenology of schizophrenia and its bearing on a specifically modern(ist) art, the illogic of extreme reason appears frequently as a descriptive conceit. Certainly, the paradox of rationalistic insanity catches the spirit of post-Enlightenment reason at its climacteric and crisis. An inwardness with this intellectual history gives an interior coherence to Sass's record of the extremity it attains at this last turn of the modern age, which is the moment of artistic modernism. Liberal reason, speaking at the apparently contradictory extreme of madness, obviously marks some final stage for the dominant episteme of the preceding centuries. This formulation only verges on being made, however, in Sass's account,[20] which instances the same deficiency that Pippin suggests is the shortfall in Nietzsche's own record of the philosophical problem of modernism. The intellectual dilemma of the Enlightenment is left looking for the one historical event that makes this crisis real. Thus, Sass, too, leaves the end game of liberal modernity oddly unsituated. Reason's struggle with itself in the Liberal London of the war years is a setting that goes wholly missing in Sass's account. His consequent reduction of the major figures of English literary modernism—Pound and Eliot as well as Woolf—to subjects of glancing or summary reference suggests a need,[21] not to modify his model, but to clarify, then to locate its most exemplary demonstration: in the London of the war years. This critical placement may restore to the writing being examined a specificity—as well as an extremity—of instance. This awareness also serves in Woolf's case to recover the historicity of her most distinctive work. It helps an assessment as well to exceed any narrowly private pathology in the behavior it explains and to regain for her imaginative language, spoken as the last word of liberal modernity's ultimate struggle, the status of the response it represents to the discourses sounding around her.

Relative to other modernists, moreover, she comes incomparably close to this political idiom. Through the war years, Leonard moved carefully and successfully through the journalistic culture of political London. The Fabian Society that Beatrice and Sidney Webb had convened included him already before the war, and, by the time conflict began, he was serving in an important editorial capacity for their weekly, the *New Statesman*. On its pages the range of opinion on the Liberal government's cause- and case-making was probably at its greatest. A partisan replication of official rationales met equally steadily with skeptical and informed dissent. Leonard's own orientation to this verbal culture formed strongly in accord with the positions of E. D. Morel's Union of Democratic Control. If the socialist values that Leonard shared with the Webbs led him in Morel's direction to begin with, the same radical vantage drew his attention now to the language of Whitehall and its established cause: to the rationales for the moral war for civilization, which Morel exposed for the ruse they constituted. The members of the Bloomsbury group tended to reiterate this critical temper, which they stylized variously.[22] Their resistance to the war and its apologias ranged from diffident snobbery to the public courage of Bertrand Russell and, ultimately, Lytton Strachey.

The record that Virginia Woolf leaves in her diary of the political war and its hortative words is elliptical, usually cynical, sometimes penetrating. In the offhand way that an ongoing exposure to the official ideolect might predict, she writes on 3 January 1915, on her return from a concert at Queen's Hall. "I think patriotism is a base emotion," she reports. She clarifies: "By this I mean . . . that they played a national Anthem & a Hymn, & all I could feel was the entire absence of emotion in myself & everyone else."[23] The next day, casually but tellingly, she documents the language upon which this voice of national cause draws. In an instance as representative of the journalistic war as it is indicative of the army's own specially rigorous absurdity, she cites the dominant, nonsense logic. "Philip [Woolf] . . . told us tales of military stupidity which pass belief." She specifies: "They found a man guilty of desertion the other day & sentenced him; & then discovered that the man did not exist."[24]

Woolf leaves no further record in her diary until the summer of 1917, as a result of the breakdown she suffered in February 1915, although she began to reengage by the end of 1915. By the spring of 1917, she is writing short fiction, responding concurrently with the first efforts of other London modernists. The resumption of her diary report, moreover, shows an alertness to the verbal culture of the war, whose literary potential may be taken to focus her engagement.

This "talk of peace," she observes on 4 January 1918, "comes to the surface with a kind of tremor of hope once in 3 months; then subsides; then swells again. What it now amounts to," she cautions, "one doesn't even like to guess," but "one can't help feeling something moving," so that, in this presentiment of the common expectation, "one may wake to find the covered murmur proclaimed in every newspaper."[25] The elevated idiosyncracy of the diction goes to a possible source in Shakespeare. In the opening lines of the prologue to the fourth act of *King Henry V*, the chorus anticipates the battle of Agincourt: "*creeping murmur* and the poring dark / Fills the wide vessel of the universe." (ll. 2–3). If the Shakespearean echo is active, as Woolf's editor suggests, its forward allusion to the imminent event at Agincourt serves certainly to deflect any wished-for development of peace, at least in the near term. Even if the English victory at Agincourt stands as a marker in historical time of English hegemony in Europe, Woolf's text extends no welcome prediction of a pax Britannica. And the phrasing of this allusion indicates the special density of Woolf's perception of her present circumstance. Indeed, the worked and enigmatic intricacy of her wording reflects the sort of literary potential that the verbal circumstance of the war affords her. Thus the "covered murmur proclaimed" in current journalism appears to her ears in a way that these three words coalesce to suggest: in their close and almost unpronounceable proximity. The clotting of these vocables conspires in mimic effect, in particular, to suppress any easy or coherent meaning. The nonsense that *mur-mur* preserves in the double syllable of its onomatopoeic beginnings brings this memory to a precise—and paradoxical—location in the newspaper culture of Woolf's war. It is blah-blah of this radical kind, as the topic covered, that is the subject of voluble and confident proclamation. In these contemporary and timely constructions of opinion and popular consciousness, then, Woolf hears the new consensus of non-sense.

Woolf's diary turns her searching view again on these political circumstances. "A cold dismal day," the entry for 13 April 1918 observes, responding at first to the large (final) offensive the Germans have launched in France, "& very bad news in the newspapers." This journalism affords the primary medium in which the political war was waged, as the subsequent report rather mournfully recalls. Still at this time the press of a majority Liberalism, its stubbornly dominant culture appears in its representative figures—its well-worn issues and passwords, its timeworn personages:

> Stout red-faced elderly men are visibly perturbed. And Ireland has Conscription. If one didn't feel that politics are an elaborate game got up to keep a pack of men trained for that sport in condition, one might be dismal; one sometimes is dismal; sometimes I try to worry out what some of the phrases we're ruled by mean. I doubt whether most people even do that. Liberty, for instance.[26]

Liberalism's fading strength shows clearly in the state of the Irish Question. The Home-Rule initiative, which the main portion of the party supported before August 1914, has given way to the holy war that the Continental enterprise represents—a sacred campaign for which no compulsion should seem to be required. While Ireland never had to submit to conscription,[27] Woolf's mistake goes to the deeper truth of Liberalism's current distress. Not only have partisans failed Ireland in that long-standing effort at independence; Irish men should not need to be conscripted in a campaign for which they should see the reason—and need—to enlist. Woolf envisions Liberalism thus at its present extremity. This decline may be aligned with the fact that it is a party of "elderly men," in other representations as well as in Woolf's. In a fashion characteristic equally of her inwardness with its embattled tradition and the concision this affinity affords her record of its critical condition, Woolf locates the problem of that partisan enterprise in the theme word of Liberalism itself. The discrepancy she scores into "Liberty"—a token promising freedom also rules individuals—presents a contradiction which, if only nominal, goes all the more accurately to the source of the unsureness she registers. This doubtful counter catches in its signal instance the sort of verbal uncertainty—and a trace of the linguistic trickery—that English Liberalism has come to feature as its distinctive ideolect.

This instigation, the main provocation of London modernism, has already worked its way into her literary texts. Her earliest effort in this new direction appears to be "The Mark on the Wall," written in the spring of 1917 as the first work undertaken since her 1915 breakdown. The scene of a speaker narrating the impressions she receives from a mark on the wall seems to stage an advance example of Woolf's major later work in the novel of consciousness. She frames and informs this interior moment, nonetheless, with a strong sense of extrinsic location, which she draws in the striking finale:

> Someone is standing over me and saying—
> "I'm going out to buy a newspaper."
> "Yes?"
> "Though it's no good buying newspapers. . . . Nothing ever happens. Curse this war; God damn this war! . . . All the same, I don't see why we should have a snail on our wall."
> Ah, the mark on the wall! It was a snail.[28]

The wider enterprise that "this war" presents circles around the main speaker in the form of its written record. A culture of journalism, which this second personage represents as a medium equally unreliable and irresistible, impinges vividly—not to say profanely—on the main speaker. At the defining moment of the piece, as it proposes its (last) answer to the visual riddle of the title figure, it also exposes itself most noticeably to its own moment in political history. The interior keep of its private speech, which locates the area of Woolf's main subsequent development and marks also her most readily identifiable modernist provenance, opens into a public idiom as noisome as the vulgar tongue appears to be. This is a conversation that needs to be reconstructed from the pages of Woolf's story, where, in effect, she situates the poetics of her own emergent modernist enterprise in relation to the language and circumstance of contemporary history.

"And the novelists in future will realise more and more the importance of these reflections," that is, of self-reflection, goes the discourse of the narrator's mind. This narrator muses on the content of literary expression in "The Mark" in particular, which opens anew to the myriad possibilities that a record of self-involved consciousness may promise: "for of course there is not one reflection but an almost infinite number; those are the depths they will explore, those the phantoms they will pursue" (*CSF*, 85–86). As in the dramatic finale of the story, however, when the private voice of the dominant consciousness is interrupted by a sound from outside, Woolf is setting up the ostensible preference in her fictional poetics—an apparently autonomous interiority—for cross-talk with history. She scores the noises that current events are making into the awareness that the "novelists in future" will pursue, as she foresees them

> leaving the description of reality more and more out of their stories, taking a knowledge of it for granted, as the Greeks did and Shakespeare perhaps—but these generalisations are very worthless. The military sound of the word is enough. It recalls leading articles, cabinet ministers—a whole class of things indeed which as a child one thought the thing itself, the standard thing, the real thing, from which one could not depart save at the risk of nameless damnation. Generalisations bring back somehow Sunday in London, Sunday afternoon walks, Sunday luncheons, and also ways of speaking of the dead. (*CSF*, 86)

"Generalisations," Woolf's acquaintance Arnold Bennett has demonstrated in the classic analysis of September 1914, present the new ideolect of total war, a context that "the military sound of the word" specifies clearly. In reports censored to maintain secrecy on military details and bolster civilian morale for the efforts of mass war, generic counters stand instead of particular referents. Those vacuous abstractions and ballooning platitudes present themselves as a record of encouraging evidence. Pound's "outweariers of Apollo" pronounce their own "Martian generalities," in a figure contrived in the same season, in his verbal image of a public logic worn out in the work of war. Where Pound listens to public speakers wearied with their own eager but specious appeals to the god of reason, Woolf hears an equally meaningless language in official rationales, in policy documents and partisan briefs, in those "leading articles" of "cabinet ministers." She represents the Word and clerisy of a political and intellectual Liberalism, and she registers its discredit with an intimacy and familiarity that signal her main point of difference from Pound's jocoserious plaint. In one sense, this development represents the welcome decline of a patrician class long corrupted in its moral and intellectual blood. The voiding of authority in the father's language, however, stirs in the linguistic initiative it encourages as a most complex, difficult benefice. From the perspective of securities formerly maintained, a venture of this tradition-defying type leads to nothing less than "nameless damnation," which spells out, indeed, the damnation of namelessness. Rachel Vinrace has taken this risk with her voyage to the silence at the center of things. Her ambition fails, arguably, with her author's nerve. While Woolf may have sacrificed Rachel to a Stephen ideology, to which her own fealty bound her still, this older gnosis dissolves in front of us in the passage above. The intellectual history that this passage limns witnesses the disintegration of the Liberal episteme in the work of the current war. The cautious confidence Woolf pronounces for the new attitude she professes as a novelist reflects the circumstances of her own difficult rebirth as a writer.

These conditions may be seen now to foster the comprehensive conceit of the story—its serious caprice. To dedicate lengthy and even recondite attentions to the microscopic spot on the wall entails a sort of archly matter-of-fact outrageousness. A strange reason-seemingness provides the performative pretense of the piece. This is an attitude familiar to contemporary Liberalism, too, in a partisan journalism to which Woolf alludes in the closing note of the story.

An intensity of connection between this political usage and Woolf's new practice carries the provocation into the echoing, respondent form of her sentences. Mock-logical, quasi-propositional, a novel prosody takes the syntax into sequences and permutations like the following, beginning in the first deliberation on the identity of the mark. "If that mark was made by a nail," the proposition overtures, with a restraint the subsequent phrases will not abide by for long,

> it can't have been for a picture, it must have been for a miniature—the miniature of a lady with white powdered curls, powder-dusted cheeks, and lips like red carnations. A fraud of course, for the people who had this house before us would have chosen pictures in that way—an old picture for an old room. That is the sort of people they were—very interesting people, and I think of them so often, in such queer places, because one will never see them again, never know what happened next. (*CSF*, 83)

The initial conditional clause positions the speaking intelligence in the attitude of a cautious hypothesis, restricting the consideration that follows, or so the gesture promises, to the limited topic of its particular possibility. A subsequent abundance of verbal energy runs a surplus of words over the ratios that a specifically rationalist grammar establishes. Woolf anticipates the rhythm that the whole passage instances in her movement through the several clauses of this lead sentence. Where the opening proposal shifts into the negative stipulation of the second clause ("it can't have been"), this syntax predicts some further refining of a line of reasoned, dialectical inquiry ("it must have been"). To its narrowing lead, the mind of the sequence steers next, however, to an equal and extreme degree of freedom. The miniature painting depicts a figure ("white powdered curls" and so on) wholly imagined by the narrator. Fancy turns to ruse with the judgmental statement of "[a] fraud *of course*." This emphatic phrase assumes for the deliberation it concludes some process of (logical) course. The winking admission of the author manipulating a piece of transparent strategy offers this circumstance of deliberated thinking, then, as the real subject of fraud; we have, after all, seen nothing *of* (such a) *course*. Note as well that the narrator links the fraudulence of the object to the taste of those former tenants, who chose it "in that way—an old picture for an old room."

Matching the times and styles of the painting and the chamber, however, has nothing inherently fraudulent about it. "[F]or the people who had this house before us would have chosen pictures in that way": suspicion of fraudulence falls instead on "for," on the conjunction of reasoned explanation and, by the end of the passage, on the language the rationalist weaves with such specious ease. Protocols of logic as hollow as those being offered in the "leading articles" of the Liberal press, in the policy documents and "generalisations" of the war party's "cabinet ministers," may be heard—and called now—to account for the new style Woolf features. Her method curves back into a frame of reference and resonance graver by far than the apparently insubstantial fancies of this isolated narrator.

Behind this new practice lies the coherent motive and style of pseudostatement. Woolf clarifies its forceful appeal through an appreciation of its local adept. This is the poet who enters her ken, only four days after the signing of the armistice, to leave the verses she has already read carefully, by the time of this diary entry, in her new labor as typesetter for the Woolfs' fledgling efforts at the Hogarth Press. He leaves an impression in person, which she references, suggestively but searchingly, to the effects his recent quatrains have contrived:

> Mr Eliot is well expressed by his name—a polished, cultivated, elaborate young American, talking so slow, that each word seems to have special finish allotted it. But beneath the surface, it is fairly evident that he is very intellectual, intolerant, with strong views of his own, & a poetic creed. I'm sorry to say this sets up Ezra Pound & Wyndham Lewis as great poets, or in the current phrase "very interesting" writers. He admires Mr Joyce immensely. He produced 3 or 4 poems for us to look at—the fruit of two years, since he works all day in a Bank, & in his reasonable way thinks regular work good for people of nervous constitutions. I became more or less conscious of a very intricate & highly organised framework of poetic belief; owing to his caution, & his excessive care in the use of language we did not discover much about it. I think he believes in "living phrases" & their difference from dead ones; in writing with extreme care, in observing all syntax & grammar; & so making this new poetry flower on the stem of the oldest.[29]

This newcomer tricks out the polities and rituals of conversation, which he follows in order to reveal nothing of himself. His work in verse observes the conventions of its own traditions equally meticulously, only to withhold disclosure as well. She appreciates this reticence about the revealing statement in the contrast she draws, in early December 1918, with the poetry of John Middleton Murry. Not to be preferred, Murry's work shows her "a plethora of words; his poem is intricate & involved & as thick as a briar hedge," but "he does his thinking aloud; not making you fetch it from the depths of silence as Eliot does."[30] Paradoxically, this American's verse conforms to the rules in the formation and expression of thought, adhering in its appearance to "all syntax & grammar" in Woolf's perception, and so looks no less worked on its surface with the verbal artifice of ratiocination than Murry's. Its primary difference and ultimate appeal, however, lie in the "depths of silence" that underline its final effect, its last Word. The suavely inconsequential structures in Eliot's periodic quatrains would confirm her reading. How does an apparatus of rationalistic language reverberate to purposes so far out of line with its nominal or conventional values of achieved and articulated meaning? This particular inconsistency goes to the riddle that I. A. Richards poses, in the critical notion of pseudostatement, as the nascent strength of the new poetry. Woolf marks her own distinction in the preference she expresses for this contemporary poetics. Its contrivance strikes a respondent chord in her, and not only on account of its timeliness. It speaks so powerfully to her because she has attempted to implement a similar conception in her own work, beginning a year and a half earlier in "The Mark." The appreciation she conveys of Eliot gauges the special pressure, moreover, of her imminent efforts—the gestation of a piece she has begun to write by 26 November 1918.[31]

"Solid Objects" tells the story of a young man abandoning a favored career as a junior M.P. Its fiction reenacts a loss of faith in the political endeavor that coincides, in November 1918, with the still-living memory of the war just ended. This background comes into focus for the story best through Woolf's diary record of (the first) Armistice Day:

> Monday 11 November
>
> Twentyfive minutes ago the guns went off, announcing peace. A siren hooted on the river. They are hooting still. A few people ran to look out of windows. The rooks wheeled round, & were [wore?] for a moment, the symbolic look of creatures performing some ceremony, partly of thanksgiving, partly of valediction over the grave. A very cloudy still day, the smoke toppling over heavily towards the east; & that too wearing for a moment a look of something floating, waving, drooping. We looked out of the window; saw the housepainter give one look to the sky & go on with his job; the old man toddling along the street carrying a bag out [of] which a large loaf protruded, closely followed by his mongrel dog. So far neither bells nor flags, but the wailing of sirens & intermittent guns.[32]

The conclusion to the Liberal's grand syllogism of history finds its ritual celebrant in these oddly hierophantic crows, who superintend the arbitrary incidents of any old day.

Long discredited now, the motivating interests and methods of the policy war appear in the opening prospect of "Solid Objects"—in a perspectivizing critique that reads perhaps as their truest witness. Woolf's political characters perform argumentative *gestures* only. Their vivid but empty ritual of debate shrinks into a minimal, even trivial configuration, as the long-range view depicts what appears to be a knot of ratiocinating insects. "The only thing that moved upon the vast semicircle of the beach," the vision begins,

> was one small black spot. As it came nearer to the ribs and spine of the stranded pilchard boat, it became apparent from a certain tenuity in its blackness that this spot possessed four legs; and moment by moment it became more unmistakable that it was composed of the persons of two young men. Even thus in outline against the sand there was an unmistakable vitality in them; an indescribable vigour in the approach and withdrawal of the bodies, slight though it was, which proclaimed some violent argument issuing from the tiny mouths of the little round heads. This was corroborated on closer view by the repeated lunging of a walking-stick on the right-hand side. "You mean to tell me . . . You actually believe . . ." Thus the walking-stick on the right-hand side next the waves seemed to be asserting as it cut long stripes on the sand.
>
> "Politics be damned!" issued clearly from the body on the left-hand side . . . (*CSF*, 102)

The single audibility in the exchange pronounces a censure on the political endeavor, whose ideal of reasoned exchange has declined into an idiom of empty gesticulation, a language of postural forms only. The pantomime argument is repeated: "They flung themselves down by the six ribs and spine of the black pilchard boat. You know how the body seems to shake itself free from an argument" (*CSF*, 102).

The protagonist's action in the last frame of the opening scene—"John, who had exclaimed 'Politics be damned!' began burrowing his fingers down, down, into the sand" (*CSF*, 102)—takes him in the direction that the story projects as the destination of his lapsed career. He reaches after one of those buried collectibles, the "solid objects" that now obsess his attention. These pieces find their signal position as paperweights on his mantelpiece, where they serve to hold down the documents—at one time, presumably, the rational language—of his now-abandoned campaigns. Over and against those "addresses to constituents, declarations of policy, appeals for subscriptions, invitations to dinner, and so on" (*CSF*, 104), his enthusiasm moves to the dense, impenetrable obscurity of these new beauties: "The finest specimens he would bring home and place upon his mantelpiece, where, however, their duty was more and more of an ornamental nature, since papers needing a weight to keep them down became scarcer and scarcer" (*CSF*, 105). In this configuration, the written logic of an older political prose offers a fading pretext only for the decorative display of these favored, weighty objects.

Woolf registers the shift, moreover, in her own imaginative language. She moves further toward a savoring of words themselves, as denser drops of solid matter. She follows this lead into the textures of the lengthy sentence I left unfinished above. "'Politics be damned!' issued clearly from the body on the left-hand side," this paragraph begins, pronouncing a loss of faith in partisan propositions and opening the space of this alternative usage:

> and, as these words were uttered, the mouths, noses, chins, little moustaches, tweed caps, rough boots, shooting coats, and check stockings of the two speakers became clearer and clearer; the smoke of their pipes went up into the air; nothing was so solid, so living, so hard, red, hirsute and virile as these two bodies for miles and miles of sea and sandhill. (*CSF*, 102)

The rule of linguistic hypotaxis certainly diminishes in these verbal constructions. No complex subordination, not even a cogitating syntax with propositional content, a rhythm of inventory and list dominates the verbal consciousness. In the pairing pattern, the words coalesce as nominal objects, in linkages that materialize increasingly as the two-part rhythm repeats. This linguistic thinginess rings in voluble and now obvious response to the silencing of logical—and ideological—words, to the discrediting of the political ideolect that Woolf registers so cannily in the opening prospect.

This development extends to far-reaching consequence in Woolf's work. Feminist critics theorize it to a degree of equal import. Hélène Cixous and Luce Irigaray recognize that this practice represents no simple indulgence of the verbal sensorium. An appreciation of linguistic "texture" for its own sake takes back a dimension of language proscribed by the father's language and recovers it as the substance of a specifically "feminine writing."[33] Their emphasis on its gendered interest and import, however, needs to be augmented by some understanding, in Woolf's work especially, of its forcing historical circumstance. This new usage emerges with all of its immanent promise as a response to the failing language of the state—as represented in the opening vista. A historical content of most local depth and particular implication may be discerned in this usage.

The scene that presents the signature instance of this impulse comes later, in *Mrs. Dalloway*. An airplane writing letters in the sky leaves an advertisement in a drifting and shifting calligraphy, which, in effect, spells out the organic character of the script. This unfixity also assures the indeterminacy of its message. "[A] thick ruffled bar of white smoke . . . curled and wreathed upon the sky in letters. But what letters? A C was it? An E, then an L?"[34] The onlookers' labored pronunciation of these formations further underscores their mouthful realities. "'Glaxo,' said Mrs. Coates in a strained, awe-stricken voice" (*MD*, 20). While these features characterize accurately the poetics of *l'écriture féminine*, Woolf draws a texture and complexity of feeling into this usage from the historical circumstance that has fostered it, and this context may be redrawn with this enriched appreciation in view.

What needs to be remembered from this model representation is the signal imagery of its own local moment. For the airplane remains in the early 1920s as an emblem of eventualities as shocking as the consequences this instrument wrought, in the new airborne campaigns on civilians in the Great War: "The sound of an aeroplane bored *ominously* into the ears of the crowd. . . . *Dropping dead down* the aeroplane soared straight up" (*MD*, 20; emphases added). The linkage between the recently ended war and the enterprise of skywriting was in fact well established already in 1922, when the practice began—under the official and published encouragement of the Air Ministry, which argued that skilled pilots could be kept thus in training, and at no cost to the state. The aerial spectacle represented thus a restaged memory of the Great War, and it is accordingly no accident that the most acute auditor on the ground below Woolf's sky prospect is the war veteran Septimus Warren Smith, into whose interior monologue the sound provides a transition. Woolf proclaims this connection, moreover, through the background sound she affords the aerial prospect: a church bell tolling the hour of eleven. The recent war, which ended officially on the eleventh hour of the eleventh day of the eleventh month, still owns this number by rights of association as heavy as those ritualized, already annually ceremonialized memories. The Great Silence that was observed at the signal moment in these liturgies of remembrance is recast as the backdrop and counterpoint to the tolled hour of eleven in Woolf's text:

> All down the Mall people were standing and looking up into the sky. As they looked the whole world became perfectly silent, and a flight of gulls crossed the sky, first one gull leading, then another, and in this extraordinary silence and peace, in this pallor, in this purity, bells struck eleven times, the sound fading up there among the gulls. (*MD*, 20–21)

In its dignified sublimities the passage offers some register of the vast transformations Woolf has wrought on the history occasioning it.

The fresher recollection of November 1918 establishes a connection between historical event and literary practice that is less ceremonialized, less evident then to our contemporary retrospect, but for all that still comprehensive and intense in its demonstrations. The visceral idiom of Woolf's newly corporeal Word represents a response to the same provocations she graphs so vividly in the cartoon depictions of her initial vista in "Solid Objects": the speech of political reason has argued itself into meaninglessness, and the sheer materiality of language presents a resource of novel, plastic stuff. This understanding restores a historicity to each of Woolf's two new initiatives and lends to the program they comprise the full import of the one answer it represents. To consolidate verbal things, as in "Solid Objects"; to disembody the logic of proposition, as in the opening moment of "The Mark on the Wall": these two maneuvers represent complementary options in a literary engagement with the current

The Great Silence, 11 A.M., 11 November 1920, for the unveiling of the cenotaph and funeral of the Unknown Warrior.

state of the language, where a statement being made holds a formal import only, and the gestures advancing it serve to further an appreciation of the material character of language itself.

Even as a pair, however, these initiatives reveal a sphere of clearly limited application. The mock-propositional impulse seems to move to the scale of the individual sentence, by the rule of (pseudo)sententiousness. A sensory perception of language inheres to an even briefer unit of measure, insofar as these sensible instants need to be detached from comprehensive structures of verbal logic. The experience of fictional continuity goes missing with these new initiatives. Local intensities supplant the conventional representations of narrative time and replace its customary satisfactions—as realized, for instance, in the fairly standard progressions to which Woolf submits the romance adventure of *The Voyage Out*. The new writing does not feature event and consequence, or sequence and eventuality, as its main attraction. Woolf organizes it at first, accordingly, in the form of the short story. This genre seems to work for her in lessening expectations for the major incident, in dissolving the dominant logic of plot, and so in allowing the energy of the text to work within those local moments of verbal improvisation. By contrast, the novel she undertook to write in these same years—the now little-read *Night and Day*—situates its fictional action before the war. It reverts to those devices of linear plot and romance interest that her war-forged sensibility could no longer countenance with any degree of intellectual responsibility, let alone imaginative interest.[35] Her major development in this respect may be taken to represent her response to the main provocation the war has constituted for her.

What the mind of Liberal England at war reveals to a detailed appreciation is a discrediting, suffered in the ultimate form of the absolute proposition, of the meaning of time. The grand syllogism of history has withered into the insignificance of its own sad parody of itself. The rationales that Liberal apologists have extended for the war are now recognizably sham, the better destiny of progress a phantom. Where the means of reason reach ends as insupportable as those of the recent war, whose closure Woolf opens to the unceremonious blank this finale draws in her diary entry of that day, so the interim experience of sequence and time proceeds with no appeal to that superior logic, the conduct of whose propositions offered once an ideal or promissory form for temporal process itself. The improving mirror these schemes of meliorist reason turned on the representation of temporality in fiction clouds over now and dissolves chronology into the sheer plod of one damn thing after another, the merely serial quotidian. Unsolved, this problem of inconsequence also offers an opportunity for the modeling of alternative, even multiple conclusions—small but constant consolidations in the temporal medium (recall those points of repeated coherence that Pound fashions, in *Sextus Propertius*, in the reiteration of the *gen* syllable). A design of this kind compels the major project of Woolf's subsequent work in the narrative art of the novel. If this prescription reads as a description of the possibilities that modernist fiction in general will have realized by the end of her career, her version of this enterprise takes its first turn, it is essential to recognize, out of the immediate and local circumstances of the culture of the political war. She preserves this memory—along with the struggle its title bespeaks—in "An Unwritten Novel." This story represents the last effort undertaken before she begins her major work in the new direction, in her novel *Jacob's Room*, in January 1920.

"An Unwritten Novel" opens by situating its narrator, who is its protagonist, in front of its nominal subject—a female personage encountered in the facing seat of the evening train.[36] Her visage emerges from a collage of "[f]ive faces opposite," a medley of equally indiscriminate phenomena: "Marks of reticence are on all those faces: lips shut, eyes shaded, each one of the five doing something to hide or stultify his knowledge" (*CSF*, 112). The scene appears reminiscent (in advance) of the typical and enabling predicament of the modernist novel. External circumstance may no longer be relied upon to provide the sufficient interest of conventional character and the ready incentive of end-driven plot. The new sort of story forges ahead then—the narrator focuses further the silent inquiry—as she shifts the gaze between the singled-out face and the headlines of this signal day:

As if she heard me, she looked up, shifted slightly in her seat and sighed. She seemed to apologise and at the same time to say to me, "If only you knew!" Then she looked at life again. "But I do know," I answered silently, glancing at *The Times* for manners' sake: "I know the whole business. 'Peace between Germany and the Allied Powers was yesterday officially ushered in at Paris—Signor Nitti, the Italian Prime Minister—a passenger train at Doncaster was in collision with a goods train. . . .' We all know—*The Times* knows—but we pretend we don't." (*CSF*, 112)

The allusion to the formalization of the Versailles "peace" treaty injects a frame of temporal reference of a model, comprehensive kind. The historical narrative seeking completion in this closural event reaches for some ideal sense of an ending. The main story of recent years moves to a conclusion that is consummate, at least promissory. Woolf has glimpsed this ultimate moment in advance, in her diary entry for the first Armistice Day, when the rituals claiming an integration of the drear experience of the previous four (and more) years appeared intentionalist at best, and so disintegrated into the random observations of that bland day. Similarly, now, she suspends the sense of an ending that Versailles extends with a reference to an event that represents, well, a catastrophic deflection from its projected destination: a train wreck. The image of linear movement (confounded) calls up an equivalent figure at the beginning of Ford's war sequence, which presents its own powerful augury of the violence that the imminent event will do to models of rational and systematic progress. Recent history has visited a contretemps on the established plan of time, which Woolf reconfigures as the problem—and opportunity—of her current situation as a novelist.

The memory this passage preserves also extends to the formulations of an essay that stands as Woolf's main treatise on her modernist poetics. "Character in Fiction" (1924) also centers its attention on the task of writing a novel about a chance encounter on a passenger train with a Mrs. Brown, a personage better known to subsequent readers under the title Woolf affixed to an earlier (1923) version of the same piece, "Mr. Bennett and Mrs. Brown." This Mrs. Brown is a character whose drabness of visible aspect leaves at once an impression of uneventful circumstance and a challenge for the narrator to weave some story of coherent motive and meaningful realization. In the essay, moreover, Woolf presents her dilemma as the energizing circumstance of a literature whose exemplars include not only herself, but also Eliot and Joyce. In the later essay, she attempts in addition to draw a line through literary history and establish the difference between an "Edwardian" sensibility, manifest, say, in a Bennett or a Galsworthy, and an imaginative consciousness she calls "Georgian" but understands—most ostensibly, in the examples she selects—as modernist.[37] The main area of imaginative engagement and speculation in both attempts lies in her consideration of what makes character significant; in this new calculation, a Mrs. Brown or her forerunner may mount to prominence. Her most searching interrogation, however, goes to her repeated concern with imaginative consequence, all in all, to alternative models of sequence and completion or closure.

Thus, in the later essay, she observes that Edwardian fiction seeks an ending in a medium of real action, of timely resolve and actual consequence: "In order to complete [the books of Wells, Bennett, Galsworthy] it seems necessary to do something—to join a society, or, more desperately, to write a cheque."[38] Woolf seeks to leave this sort of resolution aside; Edwardian fiction represents to her a set of conventions that are drawn in an entirely different kind of imaginative time. What has changed so profoundly between the first and third decades of the century is this feeling that things can make sense and achieve completion in the dimension of external history. The major experience of the intervening years makes for the difference in this imaginative apprehension. A once-beneficent syllogism of history, moving at its end into the grim and menacing conclusion that Versailles represents, comprises a now-antiquated ideal of time.

The beginning of Woolf's career as a writer of fiction that is modernist by standard accounts coincides thus, in her own designation, with a decisive moment in political history. The novel she writes alongside the short fiction of the late 1910s tells the absolute character of the difference the Great War made in her imaginative apprehension of time. Situating its story in the years before 1914, *Night and Day* proceeds as an Edwardian romance, à la mode: the manifold complications of its plot exist mainly in order to be worked out, in good time. The novel's anachronistic project attempts to confirm a sense that events may—should—develop to the sort of conclusion that the marriage finale (or promise) of romantic comedy typically signals and celebrates.[39] Woolf cannot substantiate this intimation in a text that references itself to a postwar reality.

The discrepancy between *Night and Day* and the short fiction she writes in the same years indicates at once the main problem and major opportunity of her mature career, as modernist. She needs to unmake and remake the model of imaginative temporality in which the novel is set by precedent convention. This task defines the crisis that other writers of prose will have identified, but failed to use as an opportunity. The difference between Ford (among others) and Woolf lies in this respect in a daring advantage, taken. The enterprise represents nothing less than a recognition that older modes of historical and narrative time have ceased to cohere. This intensified awareness of time, of her own moment in history in particular, establishes the modern*ist* consciousness of her work, where this suffix designates a heightened sense of temporal specificity, a condition coinciding as well with some fundamental rupture in the previous structure of time.

Woolf has come to this critical moment gradually, in fact, organically. Her convention-altering energies work first on the level of the sentence. A novel prosody of syntax undoes the credible logic of words, substitutes the material reality of language for any encompassing proposition, and achieves at moments a sententiousness of splendidly expressive emptiness. While this limitation seems to confine the initial realization of her inventive impulse to the smaller scale of the short story, it also points to the local source, the most immediate and provocative model for this echoing response: the degraded statements that Liberalism has set as the new standard of public reason and speech. How to parlay the specific intensities of this initial stimulus into the larger temporal dimensions of the novel? How to achieve a feeling of imaginative import equal in degree to the history occasioning it? *Jacob's Room* takes these timely questions and ambitions as a linked initiative—a project at once linguistic and narratological. Its modernist identification may include an adequate acknowledgment now of the formative event that the Great War has afforded.

III

Jacob's Room

The one story that *Jacob's Room* tells through the several decades of its family history is the long advent and quick consequence of the war. "'So of course,' wrote Betty Flanders, pressing her heels rather deeper in the sand, 'there was nothing for it but to leave'" (*JR*, 7), the novel opens, situating its action some time in the mid-1890s. Calling in 1922 through this character's family name to one of the most charged sites of the recent conflict, the reference presages, in the mass grave of Flanders fields, a destination that Betty's son Jacob will have attained—by these final lines:

> "Jacob! Jacob!" cried Bonamy, standing by the window. The leaves sank down again.
> "Such confusion everywhere!" exclaimed Betty Flanders, bursting open the bedroom door.
> Bonamy turned away from the window.
> "What am I to do with these, Mr. Bonamy?"
> She held out a pair of Jacob's old shoes. (*JR*, 176)

"So of course": a novel that opens with a gesture of logical conclusion includes in its beginning a sense already of an ending—the imminent fate that Jacob's name ensures he will claim. The future memory of a history that has already happened allows Woolf to develop the core story of the war as a matter of forward premonition. The prophetic references with which the verbal fabric of the narrative teems (these will be sighted shortly), however, coalesce in nothing resembling a consistent or consecutive process. Like this initial instance, the allusions are momentary, disjointed, and coded. These signal details need to be retrieved from the narrative by a sensibility attuned to their meaning, so to recover from their dense and heavily elaborated welter of contingent circumstance and alternative dramas the focal reference they (supposedly) compose. Even then the elliptical and discontinuous character of this (putatively) salient narrative keeps it disappearing from view, at least from prominence. Which is to say, the main story is not a main story, unless or until one looks at things from the particular and partial vantage that hindsight entails. The dubiousness that any conclusion thus assumes represents a feeling Woolf stirs from the first words of *Jacob's Room*, when any final—and finalizing—idea seems premature, in the extreme.

The Great War presents the stimulus and condition I have advanced as the formative circumstance of English literary modernism. *Jacob's Room* preserves this special pressure as an incentive for an enterprise and design that appear modernist in a critical description of readily recognizable, established kind. Consider the import that initial gesture might acquire—within a standard narrative of world cultural history. The unembodied consequence with which the novel begins throws over an older notion of cause-and-effect sequence. The promise of consistent process seems to have been belied, right (wrong) from the start. The opening disposes of the expectation that a single destination will be attained in time: the end point in Betty Flanders's process of thinking, as a writer, locates the starting point for ours, as readers. Positions of instigation and termination appear as the result of perspective only. Frameworks of temporal reference seem as provisional or arbitrary as the places from which they are staked. These are the tenets of the relativist, Einsteinian cosmos, where a specificity of location determines the radical particularity of one's temporal orientation. These conditions appear as the forcing circumstance of a new narrative art: the novel of modernism.

The importance that the war assumes in Woolf's affiliation with this literary energy shows in a novel that unfolds as an intensifying awareness of that Great War, an event she decenters as she orients us toward it through markers that appear chancy, partial, or arbitrary, all in all, just a trick of perspective. Moment by moment, fragment by fragment, its episodic structure creates and intensifies a feeling of being encapsulated in a given instant of temporality, one that reads nonetheless as no absolute reality. Any number of narratives are occurring simultaneously but independently, the reader senses, and Woolf strengthens this impression of relativism by attaching to these divergent stories a subtly variegated range of stylistic manners and linguistic practices.

William Handley appreciates some of these features, but in a different critical context, in "War and the Politics of Narration in *Jacob's Room*." While Handley does not address the question of Woolf's modernist identity, at least in his major category of analysis, he attributes these technical initiatives to the prevailing circumstance of the war, which affords the determining context for novelties that are modernist by standard account. The importance he accords to the war goes to the resistance it stimulates in Woolf's new methods of presenting events and, mainly, characters. The disjoining of serial plot into single, vignette-like instants accrues to an effect of discontinuity that leaves, increasingly, a feeling of incompleteness in the reader's understanding of and relation to Jacob. Appearing piecemeal, glimpsed in instants that fit into no consistent or consecutive fiction, this elusive personage remains a fugitive, in Handley's story, from those forms of knowledge that Woolf associates with the work of war. Thus, in Handley's understanding, a definition of individual character presents a limitation or objectification that allows the entity it contains to be appropriated to the uses of political institutions, most notably those of the Ministry of War.[40]

In this construction, the novelist opposes the diminishments that existence suffers under the conditions of political history. Thus she reiterates the premise of radical, absolute subjectivity. Virtually timeless, this subjectivity emerges in Handley's critical prescription as a wholly potentialist energy—as incomplete in the realization of Jacob as it must be unbounded by the nominal objectivity of this title figure. While Jacob does become engulfed in the war story as a historical character, Handley concedes, the values of elusiveness and indeterminate subjectivity continue to be implemented through Woolf's narrator (this personage manages somehow to avoid the limitations—the fate—of other individual subjects):

> The narrator's profound opposition to objectification detaches her from the objects of her aesthetic eye and heightens the consciousness of her own status as a subject. This defiantly random and personal narrator becomes the subjective point of interest within a world of regimented, dehumanized objects. Woolf's aesthetic project—her need to "get at" reality differently from the Edwardian novelists, whose treatment of human beings as objectlike is homologous to their uses and abuses by socially hegemonic authority—is a fighting response to the war, to the hierarchical structure, culture, and rigid psychology of a society that pulls itself toward this destructive end.[41]

The formal and technical qualities identifiable otherwise as modernist align themselves in this reconnaissance with the work of an opposition to the benightedness of older times and traditional ways. Handley's Woolf answers her own moment with an antiphon of vital challenge, which sounds to a critical preconception of modernist literature, the one Stephen Dedalus sets up (in standard accounts like Handley's) as the staging area of the modernist project. The "nightmare of history" scene in *Ulysses* casts the author in the role of committed adversary to present necessity,[42] offering through resistance to the dead legacy of the past or the murderous work of historical institutions an alternative estimable, in Handley's claim, in ethical as well as aesthetic applications.

My main disagreement with Handley—and the critical tradition (n. 42) he represents at its best—goes to the quality and significance of the relationship he defines between the local circumstance of the war and the attitudes and practices of the respondent novelist. He conceives Woolf's attitude as one of resistance to her current circumstance, and he represents this resistance in terms that are moralized, universalized, not at all historicized. The difference in our views involves the historical consistency of her work. For *Jacob's Room* becomes at once historically representative and technically inventive—important as a modernist novel—in the reciprocity it reveals with the verbal culture of the war. This situation witnesses an immense disruption in the prevailing order of linguistic time and affords accordingly the context and impetus for the really new work of which a modern*ist* literature needs to consist.

Recall the logistics to which the Liberal Word reverted, in the days immediately preceding the outbreak of hostilities. The notion that the speech of superior reason could not only cogitate the logic of proper action but direct the development of events suffered the great casualty. The language of proper, internal, moral rationality was collapsing, in the terrified presentiment of one writer, into "the logic of events beyond our control," by which, day by day, country by country succumbed to the law of some primitive necessity. Currently, already even in these hours immediately preceding England's declaration, "'conversations'" (between the major powers) enclosed the work—the hope—of words within the tersely dismissive gesture of those inverted commas.[43] In those silent and silencing rejoinders, the penmen registered the premonition that the world could slip the bond of the Word. Woolf reclaims this intimation as the condition of the language that the war leaves her—most evidently and urgently in her representation of the onset of that event.

"And then, here is Versailles" (*JR*, 128), goes the whole of a one-sentence paragraph in the midst of a representation of Jacob's continental tour. Woolf situates his expedition in the early summer of 1914. Surely, the forward import of this allusion lies in a future that this instant in narrative historical time cannot be expected to contain. As a name and place, nonetheless, "Versailles" cannot help but stir an immense range of associations for a reader with any historical memory, in 1922 and after. The unspokenness of those meanings—indeed, their unspeakability—lies as the most expressive dimension of this citation. Between this single word and the extent of accumulated and suggestive reference it releases is a disproportion that accords with the status of rationalistic language. Measured and reasoned speech cannot comprise the range of meanings and feelings its words have picked up from the history they have failed to regulate. This shortfall gains all of its apposite volume and resonance through the particular reference that Versailles represents—not only in the particular frame of the recent war but as the monument this royal estate constitutes, in its scheme of reasoned and metered degree, to an earlier Age of Reason. This disparity presents the real source of readerly emotion in the text and, for a historically informed reading, the truest replication of the moment being augured—in retrospect. It captures most accurately the fate that a rationalistic language will meet, increasingly, as the summer of 1914 draws on.

Not saying it: for a sensibility formed in accord with the Liberal belief in the speakable reason of things, the most expressive record of the meaning of this war lies in the failure of language. In this inverse ratio, where the expressive potential of words grows in proportion to what they withhold from disclosure, one reads the rubric of a poetics acknowledging at once its own novel power and a content as somber as the history it cannot name. Thus the historical narrative of late summer edges its references to the imminent event with a reticence that speaks the Liberal's unspeakable distress:

> Now the agitation of the air uncovered a racing star. Now it was dark. Now one after another lights were extinguished. Now great towns—Paris—Constantinople—London—were black as strewn rocks. . . . The salt gale blew in at Betty Flanders's bedroom window, and the widow lady, raising herself slightly on her elbow, sighed like one who realizes, but would fain ward off a little longer—oh, a little longer!—the oppression of eternity. (*JR*, 160)

The breeze blowing into Betty Flanders's bedroom from the East is salted with the menace of events moving in England's direction from *Mitteleuropa*. The "extinguish[ing]" of the "light" coincides with the onset of war,[44] imaging in particular the slippage of those powers of "civilization" for which the Liberal campaign would be nominally fought. Woolf's paragraph reproduces and embellishes the opacity to which this partisan usage actually fell. The tropes turn away from the historical event she portends. The uncertainty of verbal reference coalesces with the immensity of what (every reader knows now) is not being said. Thus she recovers the feeling most immediate to the moment in English Liberal time that the narrative occupies. The unspeakability of that imminent event is, indeed, having its language prepared. This linguistic and stylistic art quickens as well with the unpurged terror of the original wordlessness. Woolf leaves the silence of the undeniable at the end of her sentences—the trepidation Betty Flanders feels about some impending but unnamed fate comes from the same place—and draws from this resource a manifold of unforetold power.

The main source of historical feeling in this text lies then in the limitations of its language of conventional reference. This conceit works with all of the force and import of Woolf's own recent experience, so that it shows even in her most direct citation of the war, earlier in the narrative. "And now Jimmy feeds crows in Flanders" (*JR*, 97), she startles thus into the account of events occurring in 1911 (or so). Projecting an event at least several years beyond the place its representation takes in the historical narrative, she matches this piece of narrative anachronism with a corresponding anomaly in language. The event centering this forward reference appears so unaddressable that she must disrupt the usual or customary movement of discourse in order to countenance it in words. The use of the coordinate conjunction in the initial position of the sentence referencing the war signals, in the linkage upon which "And" insists, the actual disconnection in the verbal logic of the paragraph and the reasoned sequence of its sentences. As the narrative resumes, then, the habits of fictional and linguistic process reestablish themselves. Accordingly, the war begins to disappear from any ready or vivid verbal view,

> and Helen visits hospitals. Oh, life is damnable, life is wicked, as Rose Shaw said.
>
> The lamps of London uphold the dark as upon the points of burning bayonets. The yellow canopy sinks and swells over the great four-poster. Passengers in the mail-coaches running into London in the eighteenth century looked through leafless branches and saw it flaring. (*JR*, 97)

From the specified directness of "crows in Flanders" in the opening citation, the reader's attention shifts through verbal formulations of the war that appear increasingly generalized and oblique. These "hospitals" might be anywhere, Rose Shaw's adage applies (from its first voicing, early in this paragraph) to a prewar circumstance, and the appearance of martial hardware in the subsequent vignette turns on the slanted and refractory angle of its own trope away from the scene this figure decorates. The narrative imagination of the passage follows this trajectory in a similar direction, all the way to the eighteenth century. Steadily, inexorably, the mind's eye takes its gaze and its language further and further away from the primary, obvious, once unignorable atrocity of the war. The linear and sequential element in a standard rationalistic language coincides, it is fair to say, with strategies of aversion or deflection. The intrusiveness that the war constitutes in the initial depiction may be smoothed over; the logic of solid grammar may appear to accommodate that shock; the progress of conventional and comprehensible plot seems even to assimilate the outrage. Conversely, however, in the reader's inner ear, this reasonable regularity becomes complicit with an act of suppression. What is not said grows thus in expressive power.

The unspeakability of this war engages the main energy of Woolf's verbal inventiveness in *Jacob's Room*. Beginning in the threat the war addressed to conventions of contemporary understanding, its legacy as a verbal record remains in a steady unrepresentability, or in a representation thus unsteadied. In balancing the unsayable with the unforgettable, she poses again the dilemma that a contemporary sensibility met, in addressing a circumstance for which one had no apposite language. Her response to those developments in political and intellectual history represents no moralistic riposte, of the sort later critics may impute to her. Rather, the sound of these recent times shows the agon and pathos of its war of words in the expressive inarticulateness of her own. This collaboration represents an enterprise as disturbing, potentially, as it has tended to be missed in critical constructions that are preconceived, ethically and conventionally. The problem that her work presents, then, goes to the first question of its motivating force. Why consort as a verbal artist with the worst perfidies history has to offer? The issue may be developed through some of the more extended and provocative demonstrations Woolf affords that language of the Liberal war.

Several of the epic perspectives Woolf sets up in her narrative of the early summer of 1914 dramatize the characteristic paradox of Liberal verbalism:

> The battleships ray out over the North Sea, keeping their stations accurately apart. At a given signal all the guns are trained on a target which (the master gunner counts the seconds, watch in hand—at the sixth he looks up) flames into splinters. With equal nonchalance a dozen young men in the prime of life descend with composed faces into the depth of the sea; and there impassively (though with perfect mastery of machinery) suffocate uncomplainingly together. Like blocks of tin soldiers the army covers the cornfield, moving up the hillside, reels slightly this way and that, and falls flat, save that, through field-glasses, it can be seen that one or two pieces still agitate up and down like fragments of broken match-stick. (*JR*, 155–56)

The unthinkable proceeds with a machinelike reasonableness in these sentences, which submit their various sets of military personnel to deaths as readily acceptable, it appears, as the unimpeded sequence of their own syntax. Recall the characterization of programmatic, mechanical (male) rationality in the voice of Mr. Dalloway, in *The Voyage Out*. In *Jacob's Room*, this reasonable speech feigns saneness in the face of incipient chaos. Thus Woolf regains the feeling of Liberal reason at its daily brink in the imminent war. Leaving the war unmentioned directly in this narrative moment of mid-July 1914, moreover, Woolf compounds the oddness of its all-too-logical atrocity with the eeriness of that preview.

She repeats these procedures in a one-sentence, last-paragraph performance in chapter 12. Raised to the prominence of its ominous site (chapter 13 will relate in its elliptical way the outbreak of war), this passage conveys in the leisurely advance of its grammatical period the same faith in the logic of progress that it espouses as its vision of human destiny. The linguistic premise of Liberal time sets the tempo to which history conforms, in this ritualized sentence:

> Sunlight strikes in upon shaving-glasses; and gleaming brass cans; upon all the jolly trappings of the day; the bright, inquisitive, armoured, resplendent, summer's day, which has long since vanquished chaos; which has dried the melancholy mediaeval mists; drained the swamp and stood glass and stone upon it; and equipped our brains and bodies with such an armoury of weapons that merely to see the flash and thrust

of limbs engaged in the conduct of daily life is better than the old pageant of armies drawn out in battle array upon the plain. (*JR*, 163)

Ironic foreshadowing aside, Woolf's inwardness with the tenets of Liberalism
contributes to a coherence equally visionary and linguistic. The party of
progress has given the issue of evolution the meliorist spin she replays, as she
coopts the possibility of some residual savagery and turns it to the work and
purpose of these later, more useful days. A partisan faith in the powers of language underwrites this apparent mastery. Thus the reduction of warfare and its
instruments to the figurative term of an extended metaphor bespeaks a verbal
control over such unwelcome reality. The martial tropes serve compellingly
nonetheless to turn the gaze forward in the historical time of the narrative. The
imminence of the event this Liberal sensibility could not predict, let alone master, awaits the completion of the syntactic period—in the event of Woolf's next
chapter. Future memory sets the untoward eventuality of war against the sequence and episteme of verbal reasoning like this, revealing it for the artifice of
rationalistic language that it is, and turning its character-in-voice from the con-
fidante of logic's promise to the clown too confident by far in the methodical
processes of old ways. High farce, or low tragedy, the drama of optimal possibility that reason's dream of history will have projected through verbalist
schemes like these plays itself out and resonates in the advance awareness of
what has already happened to it.

The seriocomedy in this verbal prospect bespeaks a rather grave exhilara-
tion. This mood of rueful humor includes at once a sense of historical tragedy
and an intimation of novel possibilities. Her reasons for complying with this
usage, that is, comprise but exceed the appeal this new prosody may exert as a
register of timely intensities. The sensibility she puts on reveals a gendered dimension. Woolf clearly associates a superior confidence in verbal logic with the
identifiably male institutions of intellectual and political Liberalism. In a prose
that echoes and accentuates that partisan distress, then, she witnesses and intensifies developments that serve her certain purposes as a female writer. In due
course, she may take this occasion as the opportunity and instigation for the
forging of an alternative order of literary speech.

The historicity of this feminist initiative shows elsewhere in the elaborate
historical fiction of the novel. *Jacob's Room* includes as one of its constitutive
stories an account of recent English Liberalism. An in-depth setting in this respect serves at once to situate the formation of its title character and to lay out
the conditions prevailing in Woolf's own growth into womanhood. Those masculine conventions establish the values and attitudes she will manipulate in her
reverse-echo demonstrations.

In this historical fiction, Jacob matriculates to Cambridge at a highly
timely date: October 1906. The great political victory the Liberal party enjoyed
earlier in this year coincides with a movement on the title character's part into

the headiest of its partisans' intellectual environments at the university. Woolf focuses this environment into Jacob's experience in the person—and library—of his primary mentor, Professor (Mr.) Plumer:

> Cold grey eyes George Plumer had, but in them was an abstract light. He could talk about Persia and the Trade winds, the Reform Bill and the cycle of the harvests. Books were on his shelves by Wells and Shaw; on the table serious sixpenny weeklies written by pale men in muddy boots—the weekly creak and screech of brains rinsed in cold water and wrung dry—melancholy papers. (*JR*, 35)

"Shaw and Wells and the serious sixpenny weeklies!" (*JR*, 35), the narrative exclaims in reiteration, and again, to emphasize the pervasiveness of this triple-figure presence: "Wells and Shaw and the serious sixpenny weeklies" (*JR*, 36). The two most popular authors that literary liberalism could offer join in this refrain with an evocation of the more elite media of partisan thought. Its ideology comprised an equally widely working force. Where the narrative memory extends through Plumer's to Gladstone's Reform Bill of 1884, Woolf recalls a precedent and legacy for the programs of social welfare that the party will advance as the progressive agenda of 1906. The sidelong allusions to "Persia and the Trade winds," however, bring into view the interests that an imperial Liberalism has already pursued in the Boer War and continued into the present century. Plumer's study and speech thus convene the centrist coalition the party will maintain from 1908. The intellectual demeanor that Plumer features, moreover, models the means by which Liberal ideologues will reconcile those apparently opposite values of global dominion and domestic attention. "Cold grey eyes" that ignite with the fire of "an abstract light" portray a passion that, in its interest in theoretical deliberation, and under the revealing light of the literature arrayed around it, identifies the rationalist's aspect. Those unlike notions of domestic progress and global development (under English auspices) conformed to the one scheme of meliorist reason, which modeled onto history a plan and ideal sequence originating in a rationalistic conception of language on which Liberals typically relied.

Woolf gives these attitudes their characterizing voice in a historical fiction she situates at the same moment, in *The Voyage Out*. Recall the machine trope she works through Mr. Dalloway's vocal personality. This figure expands to the visionary dimensions of her imaginative assessment and critique of linguistic reason. It is powerful. It is male. It is the engine of "advance" (carried into his own advance, on Rachel). It turns back from mid-Atlantic to regard the island's social history, which, in Dalloway's selective and self-satisfied remembrance, he has rewritten to the better logic and improving plot of material progress. It moves forward on this voyage out to the coterminous extent of the empire. At this farthest degree, it seeks to realize the ultimate validation of its logical episteme, a conclusion to be attained in space as well as in time. This masculine order of rationalistic language extends its empowerment to Jacob through the university that institutionalizes these values. This conferral occurs in the ceremony of closure to the Cambridge chapter, in its last paragraph, where, on an otherwise typical night, Jacob

> went out into the court. He buttoned his jacket across his chest. He went back to his rooms, and being the only man who walked at that moment back to his rooms, his footsteps rang out, his figure loomed large. Back from the Chapel, back from the Hall, back from the Library, came the sound of his footsteps, as if the old stone echoed with magisterial authority: "The young man—the young man—the young man—back to his rooms." (*JR*, 46)

The sense of entitlement this "young man" acquired through his matriculation at the school of liberal reason enters the expressed and measured pace of its own ideal time. The cadence to which his steps conform only confirms the ratios of an authority established, passed on: rational, male. Arbitrarily constituted as a matter of stylized timing, Woolf dumbs it down, subtly but audibly, in the echoing repetition her narrator extends in the third sentence: "He went back to his rooms, and being the only man who walked at that moment back to his rooms . . ." In an awkwardly word-poor way, she replaces the general or expected feeling of munificence with a sense of verbal shortage. Thus she indicates the point of resistant play that the masculinist manner will afford her. In the historical fiction, nonetheless, male authority sounds as inarguable, at least immovable, as the stones that effect, in their echoing testimony, some sense of legitimacy and permanence. History will be spoken to meters equally reasonable, by men as well prepared in the rationalist's academy to take on the heavy but regular (and progressive) work of ideal time, which the clocklike rhythm projects as its promise into the historical fiction. The future belongs to the grammar and syntax of a matching pattern in language, and the recessional to the Cambridge experience leads this representative "young man" toward it.

The future arrives on the "[f]ive strokes Big Ben intoned." While this sound echoes back to the end of the Cambridge chapter, it plays just ahead of events transpiring on an afternoon early, evidently, in August 1914, when the legacy invested in Jacob comes to its momentous term. The rationalistic balance it invokes goes to a standard—once prevailing, now collapsing—that Woolf uses to center her epic perspective on this world-shaking moment:

> Nelson received the salute. The wires of the admiralty shivered with some far-away communication. A voice kept remarking that Prime Ministers and Viceroys spoke in the Reichstag; entered Lahore; said that the Emperor travelled; in Milan they rioted; said there were rumours in Vienna; said that the Ambassador at Constantinople had audience with the Sultan; the fleet was at Gibraltar. The voice continued,

imprinting on the faces of the clerks in Whitehall (Timothy Durrant was one of them) something of its own inexorable gravity, as they listened, deciphered, wrote down. Papers accumulated, inscribed with the utterances of Kaisers, the statistics of ricefields, the growling of hundreds of work-people, plotting sedition in back streets, or gathering in the Calcutta bazaars, or mustering their forces in the uplands of Albania, where the hills are sand-coloured, and bones lie unburied.

The voice spoke plainly in the square quiet room with heavy tables, where one elderly man made notes on the margin of typewritten sheets, his silver-topped umbrella leaning against the bookcase.

His head—bald, red-veined, hollow-looking—represented all the heads in the building. His head, with the amiable pale eyes, carried the burden of knowledge across the street; laid it before his colleagues, who came equally burdened; and then the sixteen gentlemen, lifting their pens or turning perhaps rather wearily in their chairs, decreed that the course of history should shape itself this way or that way, being manfully determined, as their faces showed, to impose some coherency upon Rajahs and Kaisers and the mutterings in bazaars, the secret gatherings, plainly visible in Whitehall, of kilted peasants in Albanian uplands; to control the course of events. (*JR*, 171–72)

The clock bearing a man's name pronounces in this public space the memory of the echo it presents of Jacob's cadence at Cambridge, whose metronome moved him already in the direction of masculine command. Men's time comes thus into its fullness, measured and prepared long in advance to the patterns that an academic rationalism will have fostered in its teachers and students. Its representatives in 1914 are contemporary with the Plumer generation, which finds in this moment the particular crisis of a patrician Liberalism which is attempting to implement into history the moral rationalism of its Victorian (Gladstonian) gnosis. Woolf makes evident the conflict between its faith in the ethical reasonableness of policy, bespoken with the "inexorable gravity" of its old men's efforts "to control the course of events," and the imminent riot of *Mitteleuropa*, configured as the incomprehensibility of those barbarous tongues. These "sixteen gentlemen, lifting their pens or turning perhaps rather wearily in their chairs," appear nonetheless "manfully determined . . . to impose some coherency" on this incipient mess. In the fatigued zeal that this masculine episteme brings to its self-appointed task, they display the pathos that the language of Liberal England's last days has left as its lasting memory. So what, beyond the lead Woolf follows in plotting the thwarted syllogism of partisan history, does she make of these remains of history—as it was conceived and spoken through the now-failed language of Liberal rationalism?

Cross-talking the grammar of male reason in an intricate counterpoint and riposte, her play stirs with the possibility of an alternative character-in-voice.

She signals the singular import of this project already on the first page of the novel, in a not-so-oblique depiction of its writing scene. That picture of a woman writing augurs her own drama of composition in this novel and, accordingly, needs to be redrawn at length:

> "So of course," wrote Betty Flanders, pressing her heels rather deeper in the sand, "there was nothing for it but to leave."
>
> Slowly welling from the point of her gold nib, pale blue ink dissolved the full stop; for there her pen stuck; her eyes fixed, and tears slowly filled them. The entire bay quivered; the light-house wobbled; and she had the illusion that the mast of Mr. Connor's little yacht was bending like a wax candle in the sun. . . .
>
> "Where *is* that tiresome little boy?" she said. "I don't see him. Run and find him. Tell him to come at once." ". . . but mercifully," she scribbled, ignoring the full stop, "everything seems satisfactorily arranged, packed though we are like herrings in a barrel, and forced to stand the perambulator which the landlady quite naturally won't allow. . . ."
>
> Such were Betty Flanders's letters to Captain Barfoot—many paged, tear-stained. Scarborough is seven hundred miles from Cornwall: Captain Barfoot is in Scarborough: Seabrook is dead. Tears made all the dahlias in her garden undulate in red waves and flashed the glass house in her eyes, and spangled the kitchen with bright knives, and made Mrs. Jarvis, the rector's wife, think at church, while the hymn-tune played and Mrs. Flanders bent low over her little boys' heads, that marriage is a fortress and widows stray solitary in the open fields, picking up stones, gleaning a few golden straws, lonely, unprotected, poor creatures. Mrs. Flanders had been a widow for these two years. (*JR*, 7–8)

The conclusion that leads off the novel positions the logical process it summarizes at the high relief of its own conspicuous oddness. In this sensibility, Woolf depicts the primary antagonist of a woman writing. The single statement that the sentence comprises thus stymies her with its own rationalized finality. She struggles against "the full stop" of reason's period, but as a productive impediment. She dissolves the obstacle it constitutes with the ink whose flow it has stimulated. Under this resistant pressure she opens into a zone of emotion that represents, in effect, the insurgent counterappeal of this woman's address to a language of masculine rationalism.

The reprieve Woolf's female realizes thus leads her to the freedoms of the final paragraph in this first vignette, where a usage new to the author aligns itself recognizably already with those features that the critical prescriptions of *l'écriture féminine* will have assigned to women's writing. In the free indirect speech of Betty Flanders, Woolf expands into a syntax that is paratactic, generously but also ingeniously so. Rhythmical, sensual rather than blandly abstract and propositional, teeming indeed with a representation of diverse emotions, loose and cumulative but not conclusion-oriented, the sequence turns on conjunctions that coordinate rather than subordinate the clauses in series, letting its main lines of feeling rise in apparent defiance to the constructions of rationalistic language. How salient is this manner in the novel, however? And what kind of preemptively "feminine" identity may be attached to the composite product of her work on its verbal surfaces?

In a searching archaeology of the manuscript history of this book, Kate Flint has shown that Woolf's process of revision features no increase in those linguistic and stylistic traits that are, for Cixous and Irigaray, prescriptively "feminine." Instead, as Flint shows in a number of demonstrations, Woolf's rewriting coincides with a growing focus on the social topography of her characters' experience, of the necessary if difficult interaction between genders. In a critical description of a representative instance, Flint observes summarily:

> [I]t can be noted that cultural relations have taken the place of private, maternal ones. It is superficially tempting to describe the alternating fluid and broken rhythms, the associationism, the oral and exclamatory qualities of the manuscript passage as an attempt to develop a distinctive "feminine voice" in writing which would accord neatly with Luce Irigaray's description of women's language and which appears to illustrate Julia Kristeva's brief description of Woolf as "haunted by voices, waves, light, in love with colours—blue, green—and seized by a strange gaiety." But Woolf ultimately chooses to replace intimate, uncertain fears and desires, the two barely divisible, with images belonging to a fragmented London social world. These suggest a preoccupation with lacunae in cultural communication between classes, between women, as well as between the sexes.[45]

The problem of communication between the genders has emerged as a concern to replace Woolf's earlier experiment with a method and mannerism identifiable (potentially) as feminine. For Woolf, in Flint's convincing investigation, the social differentiation of consciousness and language for men and women presents the emergent interest and theme of her work. Accordingly, in Flint's demonstration, there is an interaction among several idioms in Woolf's verbal field, where the interplay between the abstracter rationalism of a putatively "masculine" command and some subversive, assignably "feminine" riposte is supplemented by the subtler differences of other, divergent tongues: of social class, of generation, and so on. The weave that Woolf's text effects in its realized complexity presents the evidence of its author's critical entrance into a full variorum of conditioned ideolects, into history.

Before the war, in Woolf's perception, the language of history was owned by men who promised "to control the course of events." "'So of course,' wrote Betty Flanders," inscribing in that out-of-place conclusion a striking sign of this masculinist history, gone awry. Between ideal and eventuality, as between the nineteenth and twentieth centuries, a difference falls that also defines the place Woolf primarily occupies as a writer. A woman's incentive may have launched her incursion into this space; female interests do not encompass the full range of possibilities that mark her accomplishment. The instant of difference that she inhabits so intensely and expressively also marks a characteristically, paradigmatically modernist moment. Among its main representatives, her major place is richly earned.

IV

Mrs. Dalloway's Insubordinate Clause

Why does Woolf's place in this modernist company need to be earned? Because the public language through which she records the significant difference of her own moment in history is not hers by conferred right or prior entitlement. She needs thus to re-earn her access to this public tongue continually. An ongoing concern in her career as a female author lies in the difficulty of the public utterance.

The language that female writers must put on in the political condition replays the drama of its construction in *Mrs. Dalloway*, in the personage of Lady Millicent Bruton. Writing a letter to the (London) *Times*, in this indicative instance, Lady Bruton encounters the impediments that her gender has met in an approach to this medium of political exchange. To her assistance, she has summoned a company of men. They serve, in effect, to maintain a masculine command over the language of civil discourse—so long as her weakness appears not so ingenious as her author's highly strategized, archly ironic presentation of this "feminine" debility:

> After a morning's battle beginning, tearing up, beginning again, she used to feel the futility of her own womanhood as she felt it on no other occasion, and would turn gratefully to the thought of Hugh Whitbread who possessed—no one could doubt it—the art of writing letters to the *Times*.
>
> A being so differently constituted from herself, with such a command of language; able to put things as editors like them put; had passions which one could not simply call greed. Lady Bruton often suspended judgment upon men in deference to the mysterious accord in which they, but no woman, stood to the laws of the universe; knew how to put things; knew what was said; so that if Richard [Dalloway] advised her, and Hugh wrote for her, she was sure of being somehow right. (*MD*, 109)

The men's lesson spells itself out thus:

> Hugh began carefully writing capital letters with rings round them in the margin, and thus marvelously reduced Lady Bruton's tangles to sense, to grammar such as the editor of the *Times*, Lady Bruton felt, watching the marvelous transformation, must respect.... [A]nd Hugh went on drafting sentiments in alphabetical order of the highest nobility, brushing the cigar ash from his waistcoat, and summing up now and then the progress they had made until, finally, he read out the draft of a letter which Lady Bruton felt certain was a masterpiece. Could her own meaning sound like that? (*MD*, 110)

Whitbread's "grammar" of "sense" proceeds as a linear, alphabetized sequence to some "sum[mary]" point that Lady Bruton is encouraged to regard, if from afar, as a "masterpiece." What has been mastered, of course, is "*her own* meaning," which has been given away in this unequal exchange with the word and logic of the dominant consciousness. The gestures of subjection that Lady Bruton makes, however, are offered with the slyer obeisance of her author's compliance with reverential attitudes toward masculine command. A reverse mastery of cross-talked convention emerges as the subtler conceit of this piece.

If Woolf subverts thus the attitudes of male control, in what language might she speak "her own meaning"—in response at least to those political issues in which men enjoy the mastery of an established, indeed exclusionary, usage? While it may be gratifying to suppose that the practice of "writing the body" and indulging the ritualized privacies of *l'écriture feminine* might offer some tonic riposte to the woes and maims that mark men's political history, the fact remains that the public character of the major themes resides in large part as a function of the customs, the discussions, in which these issues have been inscribed. Woolf needs to negotiate "her own meaning," in other words, in relation to the language of institutionalized attitudes, entitled ideologies, endowed powers. The considerable difficulty of this transaction appears in the vivid instance of another scene in the novel, where the Dalloways, gathered around the morning papers, are cued to begin a conversation that is keyed to "the public-spirited, British Empire, tariff-reform, governing class spirit." Clarissa's grievance speaks *in oratio obliqua*, but her author forgoes indirectness: "With twice his wits, she had to see things through his eyes— one of the tragedies of married life. With a mind of her own, she must always be quoting Richard—as if one couldn't know to a tittle what Richard thought by reading *The Morning Post* of a morning!" (*MD*, 76–77). "[Q]uoting Richard" quoting the words of the journalistic day leaves Clarissa, indeed, with a good deal unsaid. The authorial complaint erupts into the narrative discourse in a way that provides its own witness, inadvertent or not, to this point. Convention, literary or political, does not accommodate a woman's opinion; "her own meaning" gets deflected into outbursts easily dismissible as overreactive emotion.

Feminine repetition may reiterate the particular idiom of the Liberal war to some significant difference, however. The language of rational command has already suffered its own discrediting. This war matériel, this amalgam of verbal plastic, might be adapted to a diversity of expressive purposes—including the meaning of recent history, the profounder feeling of reason undone. This range of imaginative possibilities begins to emerge in Woolf's work around the figure who stands as a mirror complement to Lady Bruton.

Lady Bexborough occurs first in Woolf's work in "Mrs. Dalloway in Bond Street," the 1923 story that presents the novel in draft miniature. Clarissa remembers her registering the news of the death of her son in the war. "But if Dick were to die tomorrow," Clarissa muses, using this possibility to sound out the customary explanations and consolations for death, "as for believing in God—no, she would let the children choose, but for herself, like Lady Bexborough, who opened the bazaar, they say, with the telegram in her hand—Roden, her favourite, killed—she would go on. But why, if one doesn't believe? For the sake of others, she thought, taking the glove in her hand."[46] Obliged by her nobility to hold the official line, Lady Bexborough reinscribes in her attitude and bearing the defining marks of her patrician class. Clarissa's perception of her injects a more particular emphasis, however. Not believing in the proceedings, which she must conduct otherwise with the full decorum of formal protocol, Lady Bexborough manifests a capacity for paradox, all too reminiscent of the public idiom of the Liberal war. Proceeding reasonably, but for reasons increasingly specious, or at best unconvincing; seeing it through, even when one sees through it: a language of rationale mainly or wholly ceremonial echoes through the equivalent disposition of this official figure. Nonetheless, Clarissa intimates some profound significance in this instance. Is this variation on the Liberal's typical scene just the human content, on the personal and local scale, of the universal drama? The specific gravity of particular suffering can hardly have its value gainsaid, especially in so exemplary a demonstration. In its very representativeness, however, this depiction reiterates the bigger critical question. If Lady Bexborough merely echoes the usual attitude of the masculine war, should it not be a good deal less moving, at least from a female author's point of view? Should not Lady Bexborough, and Clarissa Dalloway, and their author, each be asking: could her own meaning really sound like *that*? Or is the masculine attitude being reproduced in some fundamentally, substantively altered way—by (the fact of) a woman expressing it?

Proving equality in men's work was one of the mottoes spoken to endorse women's collaboration in the efforts of the domestic war.[47] If contemporary necessity represents one of the concessions that a feminist ethic needs to make, Woolf's own political (and literary) sensibility reveals a historicity that is not exempt from those contingencies. Unlike the leadership (and some of the membership) of the Women's Social and Political Union, however, Woolf remains uncoopted by the dominant gnosis of the political war. A skeptical temper allows her participation in the language of that campaign to maintain as her own authorizing condition a perception of its enfeebled state. She makes the language of rational command resonate on her pages, but not in its heroic *virtù*, rather in its tragic pathos. This tonality ranges from the somber folly of the "sixteen gentlemen" attempting to legislate the logic of a prodigal history in *Jacob's Room* to the estimable sadness of a peeress registering this one effect of their failed effort, in a spirit of seemly reason equal or better indeed in its embittered dignity.

Where Woolf takes over this ideolect in its delinquent condition, then, she seeks to rehabilitate it to the degree of its expressive potential, as this last passage anticipates. A deeply considered development of the initiatives that the political and historical moment has opened appears in the following prospect, in *Mrs. Dalloway*, where Lady Bexborough will reappear:

> But what was [Clarissa] dreaming as she looked into Hatchard's shop window? What image was she trying to recover? What image of white dawn in the country, as she read in the book spread open:
>
>> Fear no more the heat o' the sun
>> Nor the furious winter's rages.
>
> This late age of the world's experience had bred in them all, all men and women, a well of tears. Tears and sorrows; courage and endurance; a perfectly upright and stoical bearing. Think, for example, of the woman she admired most, Lady Bexborough, opening the bazaar. (*MD*, 9–10)

The "image" Clarissa intimates is rich with an expressive power that Woolf conveys indirectly but, now, recognizably. Consider her weavery in the verbal, lexical frame. As "[w]hat" moves into the look-alike difference of "white," the capacity of language to discriminate and ration out such differences seems to disappear. The optical prospect, if it can be glimpsed at all, rhymes visually with a whiting out. This is a minimal but significant instance of the modernist sublime. Familiarly, now, the instrumental rationality of language has collapsed into some profounder apprehension of the indistinguishable, the unreasonable, the unspeakable—under the irresistible pressure that recent history has placed on the standards and practices of an older rationalistic grammar. As with Pound's and Eliot's, then, Woolf's version of this new usage points in context to the war moment as its founding or shaping occasion. The consonance that her response reveals with theirs carries a signal insistence, moreover, that she is registering history and representing its significance in a language of imaginative expression that marks her equality in this endeavor with the men who gave her the occasion and, for that matter, with the male modernists who reacted to its provocation in the same way. "[A]ll, all men and women" have taken the weight of recent historical experience. In practice, most important, Woolf renders the sadness of "[t]his late age of the world's experience" with a *gravitas* that bespeaks her equality in that formative ordeal. Not that she needs to submit to the conditioned ideolects of history or necessity any more than Pound or Eliot. Woolf's character-in-voice takes up a position at the expressive off-angle to the conventions under which the war and its suffering were processed and rationalized. "[A] *perfectly* upright and stoical bearing" strikes more than a slight dubiety into this record of otherwise estimable strength. The irony reads as the condensed, realized, and worldly-wise record of that experience. Like Pound's and Eliot's, then, and unlike Lady Bruton's, Woolf's is a mimicry with a signifying difference. This critical edge makes the language of a masculine establishment speak a "meaning" of "her own."

A meaning most clearly *not her own* appears in the lettering of her expected usage, in the sentence following directly upon the extraordinary accomplishment of the Bexborough passage. Here, as Clarissa peers through the bookstore window, she assembles a list of "feminine" reading, for a woman confined to her sickbed: "There were Jorrocks' *Jaunts and Jollities*; there were *Soapy Sponge* and Mrs. Asquith's *Memoirs* and *Big Game Shooting in Nigeria*, all spread open" (*MD*, 10). The idiot alliteration of "Jorrocks' *Jaunts and Jollities*" sets the register for a literature of the ridiculous (the novel by R. W. Surtees is a minor classic in its own subgenre, however, turning in its jolly way through the fox-hunting society in the north of England). These additional items range thus from the caricature image of *Soapy Sponge* to the distracted entitlements of the rich in Africa and center on the author—and genre—of "*Mrs*. Asquith's *Memoirs*." The discredit that *Mr*. Asquith and his partisan spokesmen have brought to the rational language of masculine command—re-echoed in the language of Woolf's adaptation in the preceding sentences—has also released for speech a sub- or antilogical freedom, which a female sensibility may be supposed to seek as a long-sought reprieve. Point for point, the style and energy of a writing assignable to the poetics of *l'écriture féminine* inscribe themselves in this second instance: an acoustic *jouissance*, a resizing of the ratios of importance, so that the domestic, somatic, and incidental acquire a priority too long denied by a proprietary control of the public sphere of speech by men. And if the next-to-last item Woolf cites represents a reference to Lady Asquith's compendious, two-volume *Autobiography* (1920), it is telling that Woolf retitles not only the book but its author, who appears on the book jacket and title page as "Margot Asquith."[48] "*Mrs*. Asquith's *Memoirs*" aligns the work and the sensibility it expresses with the social roles imposed on it. "Mrs." Asquith views the political scene from a vantage nominally but already and identifiably secondary. This reduction seeks and discovers its level in the literary company that the prime minister's wife is made to keep. This reduction also carries with it a judgment on the unpublic tongue to which women revert, by the compulsion of convention. The separate space that a "female writing" occupies as its assigned domain is what Clarissa Dalloway seems to be locating, after all, as she assembles this reading list in her head for Evelyn Whitbread, confined to her sickbed.

Woolf presents this literature as a sign of the same restriction she may gainsay, otherwise, in forging an alternative order of public speech. A juridical view, it emerges in the necessary friction of Woolf's own strenuous, counterconventional effort: to transcend the secondary condition she depicts as the second (habituated) nature of women. She will take the opportunity the war affords to access the political language, which has debarred her in the past, as the matériel of her own innovative usage.

This appreciation shifts the bearing of the war in Woolf's text from the evident or expected frames of reference. The same novel offers its readers the psychologically tortured veteran of war, Septimus Warren Smith, and, in the unfortunate Anglo–German, Doris Kilman, a fugitive relict of pan-European conflict. Understandably, these two personages have focused the attentions of a critical literature that attempts to assess the historical content and timely significance of Woolf's novel. Even the most casual reading of the novel must pause on the expressive pathos of Smith. Equally compellingly, the condensed and bitter vindictiveness of Kilman reads as the grim warrant and promise for future strife. Should Woolf's readers' attentions really shift then from the evident centers of historical gravity to those stylistic high points, which comprise indeed a high-wire act of rarefied type and, arguably, lighter-than-air performance? Conversely, more searchingly, does the most experimental work in the novel's verbal imagination offer an answer, some ultimate (if not tonic) response to the conflict that Woolf has depicted so vividly as the condition of these two characters' historical existence?

To posit a problem-reply model is to re-embody the composite personage of Smith-Kilman in a triangulated pattern already established in the novel. Dr. (Sir) William Bradshaw emerges out of the political-intellectual culture of Liberal England at war to offer the resolving formulations of that tradition to the war veteran Smith and, implicitly, to the war victim Kilman. Despite the physician's attempted interventions, of course, Smith proceeds to take his own life, while Kilman's estrangement from the institutions over which Bradshaw retains authority remains unrelieved. The manifest inadequacy of the official physician's mottoes goes not only to disprove the rule of his nominal authority, already ruined anyway in the campaigns of the verbal war, which he will be heard to echo. The imperviousness of Bradshaw-talk to the suffering it will have helped to induce locates the ample space of Woolf's intervention—and invention—as a writer. She works against—and within—his particular idiom of privilege, a single ideolect of power, one presumptive construction of verbal authority. In her echo and riposte to his institutional usage, Woolf moves into a position of curial power fully commensurate with his majority consciousness. In her imaginative grammar, that is, she makes sense of the woes and maims of the history that she has inscribed in the joint figure of Smith-Kilman, whose status as victims has compelled the attentions of a critical tradition (as noted earlier) whose terms of analysis and commentary are moralized, not historicized. In her answer to the failing language of Bradshaw's masculine command, moreover, Woolf engages with the linguistic condition of English political history and generates a meaning of her own.

"Proportion," Dr. (Sir) William Bradshaw counsels as the universal cure—for the misfit humans and (now) unfit soldiers submitted to his psychiatric care. A knighted man of science, a figure laying claim to high and representative importance in the broadest compass of the professional classes, Bradshaw focuses a frame of social reference that Woolf knew through the cultural gentry of her own acquaintance. "Proportion," moreover, resonates to those notions of balance or harmony in ratio that Hobhouse's *Liberalism* has signatured as the motto and creed of that intellectual partisanship, among whose members Bradshaw's medical program most volubly qualifies him:

> To his patients he gave three-quarters of an hour; and if in this exacting science which has to do with what, after all, we know nothing about— the nervous system, the human brain—a doctor loses his sense of proportion, as a doctor he fails. Health we must have; and health is proportion; so that when a man comes into your room and says he is Christ (a common delusion), and has a message, as they mostly have, and threatens, as they often do, to kill himself, you invoke proportion; order rest in bed; rest in solitude; silence and rest; rest without friends, without books, without messages; six months rest; until a man who went in weighing seven stone six comes out weighing twelve. (*MD*, 99)

The "rest cure" Woolf endured during her illness of 1915 placed her in the same relation to Bradshaw as the one this physician patronizes in his presumptive attitude of good sense.[49] The sphere of personal experience that she references in this aggrieved allusion adds vehemence to the coherence of her critique.

Clearly, this tonic concept of "proportion" prescribes and endorses a structure of power. This verbal counter includes among its synonyms a sense of comparative scale, relative masses, and graduated importance. In the Liberal England that Woolf represents through Bradshaw's verbal ritual, this theme word preserves the echo and refrain of an ideology of hierarchy. This idea of social echelon discovers a further validation, moreover, in the root meaning— as well as derived uses—of "*ratio*nality." Schemes of degree assign the preemptively masculine agents of rationality, like himself, the pride of highest place in an economy of gendered qualities. Bradshaw's fixation goes to a cluster of assumptions that functions thus as the mainstay of his own majority claims. Moderation has obviously gone prodigal in his hugely out-of-balance devotion to the goddess of proportion, and Woolf extends her exposé equally to areas of political attitude and verbal practice:

Proportion, divine proportion, Sir William's goddess, was acquired by Sir William walking hospitals, catching salmon, begetting one son in Harley Street by Lady Bradshaw, who caught salmon herself and took photographs scarcely to be distinguished from the work of professionals. Worshiping proportion, Sir William not only prospered himself but made England prosper, secluded her lunatics, forbade childbirth, penalised despair, made it impossible for the unfit to propagate their views until they, too, shared his sense of proportion—his, if they were men, Lady Bradshaw's, if they were women (she embroidered, knitted, spent four nights out of seven at home with her son), so that not only did his colleagues respect him, his subordinates fear him, but the friends and relations of his patients felt for him the keenest gratitude for insisting that these prophetic Christs and Christesses, who prophesied the end of the world, or the advent of God, should drink milk in bed, as Sir William ordered; Sir William with his thirty years' experience of these kinds of cases, and his infallible instinct, this is madness, this sense; in fact, his sense of proportion. (*MD*, 99–100)

The minority status that Lady Bradshaw assumes in her husband's picture of proportionate things looks for its clarifying analogy and formative model to the verbal record of his representation—his character speaks indirectly but unmistakably in these sentences. Structures of subordination in grammatical composition witness the double principle of dominance and subsidiarity as a function of language itself. This rhetorical fiction projects his own writ of authority. Thus, in the second sentence of the first paragraph quoted, a series of dependent formations, variously result and appositive clauses, bears out the portioning force of the speaker. The rationalist of language is the rationer of status. Bradshaw measures out the relative values of autonomy and reliance—physician and patient, health and sickness, freedom and seclusion—from the position of an authority he deploys through a strategy of syntax, with the force of the habit that assumes this advantage. His appositive phrases also bespeak graded relations: "as they *mostly* have," "as they *often* do." These sizing ratios repeat the scaling action that the speaker carries out in the subordination of clauses and fit him thus in a posture of control as accustomed and comfortable as the ease these gestures display.

His parentheses also lower their contents to peripheral or subsidiary positions, most suggestively in the sequestering reduction of Lady Bradshaw's domestic and maternal duties. This form assigns privacy to the substance of her experience and so assumes the same attitudes that the masculine rationalist takes on in his role of portioning authority, which reserves to itself the function of the public utterance. These parentheses mark the place of a woman's deprivation, of no political account, and, as such, image the site of Woolf's own primary struggle as a writer.

The restriction imposed on women involves and results in their exclusion from the political idiom of a civil—still masculinist—tradition. Historically (necessarily) understood, Woolf's attempt to enter this discursive space finds a language that all too apparently lacks "her own meaning." Her poetics of liberation, as it were, the first language of social participation, is spoken as the *un*-control of the older logos. Her critical and interpretive mimicry reveals not only an intimacy with the ideolect of cultural privilege and the language of political history, and more even than a cognizance of its folly and absconded power. His prosody of logic has gone into obvious distress, and Woolf shapes and accentuates these cadences as the vocabulary of her own converse mastery. To the hierarchical order that a relation of main to dependent portions articulates, that is, she brings the insubordinate force of clauses refusing to be borne, we will see, into the authority of those older proportions.

"I remembered that I had certain grievances against [Mary Carmichael]. She had broken up Jane Austen's sentence." The notion that Woolf introduces in *A Room of One's Own* to describe a novel initiative in literature gives way, in this account, to the logical extension and consequence of that rupture. "Then she had gone further and broken the sequence—the expected order." Whatever complication the ironically raised eyebrow of Woolf's essay style may afford here, it is clear that the disruption that this presumptively female writer offers stands as a pattern and plan for Woolf's own initiatives as a female author. These several opportunities—the sentence, the sequence—are covered later as well by Rachel Blau DuPlessis, more or less at the same pace. She motions toward the promissory form of the disrupted sentence but finds its motive interest in liberation poetics realized most clearly in the extended dimensions of narrative time, where gendered conventions may be unmade, remade; where, for chief instance, the marriage conclusion of the plotted romance may be deferred or replaced.[50] Nonetheless, the insurgent, reverse-precedent energy works first within the frame of the individual sentence, a construction Woolf understood as a function of her personal background and historical experience. Its model—and dominant—form comes from the English Liberal idiom. This sentence is parsed to the rationalist grammar and, within this scheme, reveals its ideal coherence. The disintegration of this intellectual and linguistic tradition in the Great War opens the rationalist's sentence as the zone of Woolf's first, most urgent opportunity. The rescaling of the ratios of this model proposition comes thus with the echo and resonance of the historical experience of the war. If this connection becomes fully audible by the last example in the following inventory of her new usage, the ordaining occasion—and its awful import—may be sensed to begin with in minimal, even (apparently) trivial instances.

Her rearrangements appear typically in sentences like these, already in the third and fifth paragraphs of her text, where a nominal subordination of clauses conceals—and reveals—their really indomitable quality. Unobtrusively, to begin with:

> For so it had always seemed to her, when, with a little squeak of the hinges, which she could hear now, she had burst open the French windows and plunged at Bourton into the open air. (*MD*, 3)

Cause, temporal location, and relative reference: three clauses—limited under their given conditions to support and subsidiary functions—are massed unusually forward in the sentence. The effect is to block the reader's view on—and movement to—the unit of putatively main, independent status, which never appears. The structure outsizes any claims to primacy, expressly and substantially, so that a new sort of equity is engendered, suggestively but effectively. More provocatively, and noticeably:

> For having lived in Westminster—how many years now? over twenty,—one feels even in the midst of the traffic, or waking at night, Clarissa was positive, a particular hush, or solemnity; an indescribable pause; a suspense (but that might be her heart, affected, they said, by influenza) before Big Ben strikes. (*MD*, 4)

Under the sounds that Big Ben intones as the measure and ethic of some normative ratio and portioning masculine authority, the sentence forms itself, in discordant concord. The main consequence of the initial subsidiary clause disappears as the sequence leading to the promised completion interrupts itself, first in the self-questioning interjection of Clarissa's monologue, then by the appositive "Clarissa was positive." Instead of an end-directed momentum, this periodic sentence generates an energy of attention to these separate phrases along the way. Each of these competes equally for the preponderance Woolf strategically withholds, letting them settle among themselves to a level scale.

That this conceit is the growing point of a novel prosody and style might be shown by any number of examples, most appropriately, say, in the expansive ratios of a sentence like this next. The dominance that the first clause promises dissolves progressively, sizably, volubly. The leading idea loses itself as the syntax moves into the new rule of its former subordinates:

> She began to go slowly upstairs, with her hand on the bannisters, as if she had left a party, where now this friend now that had flashed back her face, her voice; had shut the door and gone out and stood alone, a single figure against the appalling night, or rather, to be accurate, against the stare of this matter-of-fact June morning; soft with the glow of rose petals for some, she knew, and felt it, as she paused by the open staircase window which let in blinds flapping, dogs barking, let in, she thought, feeling herself suddenly shriveled, aged, breastless, the grinding, blowing, flowering of the day, out of doors, out of the window, out of her body and brain which now failed, since Lady Bruton, whose lunch parties were said to be extraordinarily amusing, had not asked her. (*MD*, 30–31).

A preponderance of insubordinates moves not to one but *as* one majority premise. The discrepancy that the whole sentence effects so majestically—between the original import of the initial clause and the insubordinate force of every other, accumulating phrase—reads in its elegant and confident disproportion as the formal reordering of the Bradshaw authority.

So, if Woolf's new poetics takes its leveling aim on that rational attitude and rationing practice, why hold on so persistently to the framework of the older echelon? Why not just slide into the style that prescribes an equality of degree as the implication of the name it (already) carried and as the meaning of a work already diversely achieved under its heading: the "stream-of-consciousness" method? Compare the "inward monologues" of Woolf's Dalloway with those of Joyce's Bloom, for signal instance, and their differences on this point of rationalist language become tellingly apparent. Bloom's verbal consciousness proceeds most characteristically as a series of sublogical responses, as disjointed as the stimuli (and avoidance processes) that prompt him.[51] Clarissa's speaking personality is forming always in relation to the evident pressure of a rationalist syntax. This apparatus may come undone, but its coming undone forms an important portion of its expressive power. The unraveling of a rationalist syntax in the fabric of Woolf's fiction reenacts the disestablishment of this institutional language in the culture of Liberal Britain, in its Great War. This historical memory—in all of the expressive potential we have learned to recognize in it—lives on in the witness and record of her imaginative writing.

The figure associated most closely with the war—Septimus Warren Smith—suggests most movingly perhaps the origins of Woolf's modernist prosody in the political discourses of the war. He waits at the end of this sentence, which features Clarissa sorting, shopping:

> And as she began to go with Miss Pym from jar to jar, choosing, nonsense, nonsense, she said to herself, more and more gently, as if this beauty, this scent, this colour, and Miss Pym liking her, trusting her, were a wave which she let flow over her and surmount that hatred, that monster, surmount it all; and it lifted her up and up when—oh! a pistol shot in the street outside! (*MD*, 13)

The veteran Septimus, it turns out, registers simultaneously the motor car explosion that this closing phrase invokes. For him, the noise echoes to the background—now surround—sound of his trench experience. The holocaust that Smith's response embodies as a physical memory consummates the logic of Liberal reason in history, which, like this sentence, will have failed to achieve its completion. Into the unraveled syntax of that master language, into the disheveled remnant of that majority tradition, Woolf has concentrated a representative instance of her new usage and a resonant memory of the history occasioning it.

V

Unbracketed

[A shell exploded. Twenty or thirty young men were blown up in France, among them Andrew Ramsay, whose death, mercifully, was instantaneous.][52]

The bracketing action that the narrative of "Time Passes" performs on this character's death in battle reenacts the strategy shown in the framing of this central section of *To the Lighthouse*. The war is parenthesized, contained as an interlude: the life of the Ramsay family goes on, in the domestic circumstance of their summer house on the Isle of Skye, in the first and third parts of the novel. Where the conventional representation of family experience in the Great War tends to surround the intimate, interior coherence of the home with the encircling menace of world conflict,[53] this composition reflects the threat that the new international frame of reference presents to those older economies of local feeling. As Woolf switches these primary and subsidiary positions, her novel also suggests a formal statement. Does her gesture not recall the portioning measures of Dr. Bradshaw? Is she lowering the miseries of war into this enclosure? Or does she edge this gesture with the pressure of a resistant irony, with some canny calculation of what *out*sizes its scaling action?

The critical theme that James Haule stresses in his record of discoveries made in exploring the manuscript sources and compositional process of this section emphasizes points of authorial perspective and imaginative restraint. Going back to the text Woolf drafted earlier in 1926 and published in Paris, in the magazine *Commerce*, Haule has recovered the original English typescript of the French translation and found a tone and persona at moments remarkably different from those struck only a year later in the published novel. A voice of strident antiwar statement and a vocabulary of livid if figurative indictment of masculine responsibility supply an intermittent but insistent pressure, enough to make the difference significant when, a year later, the piece that reappears as the middle section of the novel shows virtually nothing of this editorializing attitude.[54] While the specific instances of wording and polemical reference in this early version are interesting and even compelling on their own, the salient issue in the process that Haule documents goes to the evolved consciousness of the novelist and the conception of aesthetics to which, in effect, the finished version leaves a testament.

The elimination of strongly expressed opinions and the rinsing away of those more aggrieved figures of political position, Haule proposes, show, as second thoughts, the better "artistic" sense of the novelist. For Haule, this revision is undertaken "for *artistic* reasons." In that rawer, earlier version, he proposes, the representation was "too intense" for Woolf, and so, he stipulates as he continues, aesthetically inadmissible: "it was *not art*" (Haule's categories need to be given their emphatic due).[55] The point of proper compositional process, in Haule's reading, lies in the purging of those impurities of political conflict and historical turmoil. The imaginative vocabulary that Woolf attains thus bespeaks a tranquillity coincident, in Haule's reading, with the healing motive and distancing intent in her art of the parenthetical bracket. For him, this punctuation serves as an emblem of the central section and as an instrument of its consistent motive: to sequester the ordeal of war in this middle period of the book and lower the violence of Andrew Ramsay's death, within this bracketed language, into the discrete silence of a parenthetical aside.[56]

I rehearse Haule's reading at length because his approach presents a well-intentioned, wholly representative mistake. He accepts the premise of some universal abstract language for art, a lexicon in which the parenthesis may assume a steady meaning and constant valence. A historically informed reading, however, reaches back through Woolf's previous writing to the cultural ground that forms and informs those parenthesizing gestures. She repeats the same proportioning and rationing measure that Dr. (Sir) William Bradshaw extended so strenuously, from the Liberal gentry he typifies, to the resistant incident of the war. She is recycling the tired form of a partisan gerontocracy and using it to represent the crisis of a dying ideolect. In the pathos of its manifest inadequacy to the actuality of that experience, moreover, the brackets express the immense pressure of the events that their gesture has failed to deter or, now, assuage. "[M]ercifully": the consolation that this adverbial qualifier extends in the report of the battle casualty conspires with the usual improvement of euphemism, like the putatively "instantaneous" death. A recognition of the conventionalized idiom that Woolf replicates also brings with it some sense of the typicality—the immensity—of the incident she depicts. She reenacts an attempt through language to take the human loss this war has produced in unprecedented scale and rationalize it, so to put it in the measuring perspectives of the "rational" attitude, the portioning and reasonable spirit. *Representing* this improving attitude and intimating its limitations, not using it to serve the purposes of emotional composure, Woolf puts it in the display frame of her own parenthesizing gesture. The brackets present an image of the special exception and betterment of experience that agents like Bradshaw aimed at an event that outsized him, them. The rest is, indeed, history.

Woolf represents the limitations of a rationalist language in a conceit she repeats strategically through "Time Passes." She tropes the historical reality of the war into figures of natural discord and upheaval that serve, first, to conceal that referent, ultimately to reveal their own concealments. Her initiative in this direction begins in the second vignette, and the practice expands to include prospects as vast as these:

> The nights now are full of wind and destruction; the trees plunge and
> bend and their leaves fly helter skelter until the lawn is plastered with

them and they lie packed in gutters and choke rain-pipes and scatter damp paths. Also the sea tosses itself and breaks itself, and should any sleeper fancying that he might find on the beach an answer to his doubts, a sharer of his solitude, throw off his bedclothes and go down by himself to walk on the sand, no image with semblance of serving and divine promptitude comes readily to hand bringing the night to order and making the world reflect the compass of the soul. (*TL*, 128)

So with the house empty and the doors locked and the mattresses rolled round, those stray airs, advance guards of great armies, blustered in, brushed bare boards. (*TL*, 128–29)

Night after night, summer and winter, the torment of storms, the arrow-like stillness of fine weather, held their court without interference. Listening (had there been anyone to listen) from the upper rooms of the empty house only gigantic chaos streaked with lightning could have been heard tumbling and tossing, as the winds and waves disported themselves like the amorphous bulks of leviathans whose brows are pierced by no light of reason, and mounted one on top of another, and lunged and plunged in the darkness or the daylight (for night and day, month and year ran shapelessly together) in idiot games, until it seemed as if the universe were battling and tumbling, in brute confusion and wanton lust aimlessly by itself. (*TL*, 134–35)

If this highly figurative idiom does not reference the war directly, the wording takes the distant but irrepressible impress of that reality. The artistry insists on *disparity* between what the words appear to designate and what they must be taken to signify. We know what is meant (meaning *is* as historically determined as readership), the words are not saying it, and the discrepancy itself is the expressive and significant theme. This calculated mismatch of language and reality catches, reiterates, and amplifies the subtle but truest motif in the ordeal that recent history has featured.

While Haule reads Woolf's verbal indirections as the work of the (properly) aesthetically minded novelist, a historically informed understanding sees the artistry of a critical, highly time-mindful sensibility. Woolf recognizes and represents the failing grasp of an older rational language, portioning its verbal measures to a reality that no longer comports with those once decorous measures. She pitches her idiom at the furthest point of current intellectual and political crises. Her representations do not emanate from some preserve of private sensibility, either in the narrower constructions of *l'écriture feminine* or in the "artistic" refuge that Haule sees in the turns of poetic tropes like these. In the disparity between their ostensible meaning and their ultimate reference lies the irreducibility of history to the order and schemes of reasoned speech, to language itself. The ground of this sensibility lies in the shaking earth of the Great War. This space in historical time locates the staging area of the literary art of the generation in whose midst Woolf functions at her optimal powers. Where verbal logic opens into the abyss of its own irrelevance, she enters the realm of a special sublimity. She shares this area of imaginative awareness with the other major writers of English modernism.

A Memory for Modernism,
the New Critical Constructions, and This
Awful Truth of Pseudotruth

The critical books that I. A. Richards wrote in the 1920s generated a considerable volume of commentary through the next several decades. Of these treatments, one of the most searching comes in 1934 from Wyndham Lewis in *Men without Art*. Lewis not only confronts the major tenets of *Science and Poetry*, *Principles of Literary Criticism*, and *Practical Criticism*. He also addresses their relevance to the productions of an emergent literary tradition, one that gives primacy already to Eliot and that will be recognizable by midcentury as English modernism.

"There is one main subject to be studied in connection with anything that can be described as Mr. Eliot's critical system," Lewis proposes in the framing statement of "T. S. Eliot: The Pseudo-Believer," and then specifies, emphatically, "namely the whole question of *sincerity*, in all its ramifications. That notion, with all the values attaching to an actual doctrine of *Make-Believe*, has gradually become for Mr. Eliot, as for Mr. Richards, the central affair."[1] Where Lewis uses this issue of sincere belief to focus his interrogation of Eliot's work, he is responding most obviously to the poet's gradual, by now adamant detachment of his verse sensibility (and prose temperament) from the core formulas of Richards's critical books.[2] The most notable of these were the principles of pseudostatement, which manifested a merely grammatical rationality of language, and pseudobelief, where, similarly, a sheerly formalistic iteration of traditional religious ideas could inspire a *feeling* of belief, some vague (because outdated) spiritual sensation. This most profoundly agnostic prosody and doxology must challenge Eliot's claim for place in the various faith communities of his famous (later) self-identification, as a "classicist in literature, royalist in politics, and anglo-catholic in religion."[3] Lewis visits this contradiction unremittingly, perhaps with the invidious insistence of the increasingly *un*favored member of the same literary generation, but also with the moral force of an avenging fury.

For Lewis is observing Eliot with the correctness of memory. This is the author, after all, whose *Poems* (1920) and original work (we can now say) on *The Waste Land* implemented the major principles of Richards's critical vision in representative, indeed exemplary demonstrations. Lewis frames this disparity between Eliot's earlier poetry and later criticism and magnifies it with a clarity of detail and implication that is unmatched elsewhere. His consideration serves not only to reflect some inconsistencies in the career that the older Eliot has constructed so carefully. Lewis identifies a split in Eliot's literary character that matches a division in the subsequent criticism of the poet's work and the "modernism" of which it was, initially, a defining representation.

Lewis aims his exposé most penetratingly at the later Eliot, whom he accuses of covering or attenuating the energies that animated the early verse. The defensive or reactionary formations that he identifies in the "critical system" of Eliot are framed, moreover, as the tenets of a new critical tradition, which are, in fact, the origins and premises of the New Criticism. Lewis's contrarian vantage thus offers a staging area for a wider, summary view. He points up the blind spots in the early responses to modernist poetry in the first of these new critics. He also reveals the pressure points that Eliot's early initiatives represented in a framework of contemporary cultural values. For Lewis is himself a representative of the embattled standards of prewar Englishness. In the intense record of his censure and rebuke, we may find the beginning of a long story of critical avoidance, suppression, or rejection of the menace that this early modernist poetics truly constituted—a threat better assessed now that the historical sources of this sensibility have been restored to understanding. In the same way, we find some of the reasons why the work of this current study had to be undertaken still, at so late a date.

Lewis pays his most heated and revealing attentions to the effect that the Richards-Eliot sensibility has, for him, on an older "masculine" identity. Where the merest feeling of a creed will suffice, or the sheerest procedure of argument will appease, this "make-believe" truth emerges in Lewis's depiction in the cartoon images of intellectual or spiritual emasculation. "Here we see it, in Mr. Richards's account," he emphasizes,

> as a sort of *impotence to believe*. These "means for inducing and promoting it" smack of specifics for more enterprising virility, Pelmanism, or other props for the will or fillips for the senses proper to a shell-shocked society. . . .
>
> That "the being oneself" should be the fundamental difficulty hit upon by Mr. Richards is instructive. For manifestly the *pseudo* technique must tend to undermine the vigour of this all-important selfhood to a peculiar degree. (*MWA*, 88)

This "shell-shocked society" presents the status quo post of a state whose young men, once in rude health, set out on the adventure that wore off that blush. To this diminished circumstance, Lewis attributes the pseudoist initiative and its delusive but representative appeal: where was once a confident *virtù* of statement and belief, he complains, a feeble seemingness now prevails. The "vigour of this all-important self-hood" bespeaks a conception of masculinity that Lewis attempts to preserve in the image of conditions prevailing before the war. In aim and orientation, this nostalgia is composed of those qualities we recognize now as the manifold casualty of that event. The "manly logic" of Sir Leslie Stephen came to its last pass in that campaign. In a language of rational morality, this generation invested a putatively masculine authority, which, in its debilitated postwar condition, Woolf could depict as the febrile exertions of those "sixteen gentlemen lift[ing] their pens." In the somber folly of their own inconsequence, they attempted thus "to control the course of events." Odd accomplice that Lewis might otherwise appear to be with this cohort, he emerges nonetheless as an apologist for those institutions of "male reason" (the gender is presumed with the power to assign it), variously intellectual and national.

These embattled values tend to be presented in the mood of rhetorical rebuke, here in a piece of eloquent contumely. "There you have it," he summarizes the pseudoists he reduces thus to this juridical cartoon, "the agreeable, the life-giving, lies that we tell ourselves must be cut off from all embarrassing logical entanglements, and erected into autonomous systems" (*MWA*, 86). That the Word of the rationalist logos might be embodied in the world, so to "control the course of events," is an aspiration to which Lewis subscribes and that he underwrites with a "vigour," more specifically and tellingly, with a "virility," that is equivalent, given the full historical condition, with the real desperation of its case, of its own outdatedness. The manifest extremity he represents serves the certain use of situating the objection he typifies in a status quo ante bellum. Much of the subsequent critical resistance to the same initiatives may be assigned to the same location, staked in varying sets of terms.

Lewis's resistance is situated in a discursive field he builds out of the opposition between classicism, an absolute value in his construction, and decadence, in his representation a wholly objectionable phenomenon. By "classicism," he means sincerity, transparency of language, all in all, the earnest command of the world through a reasonable Word—the ideal scheme to which (the later) Eliot professes (to Lewis) his insincere, unbelieving, and unbelievable fealty. "Decadence," in turn, captures the ruse and disguise in which Lewis has fixed this poet—insofar as Eliot's "true" values represent a lapsed or decayed version of the better standard, which classicism represents. Not only a category of judgment, decadence also locates for Lewis a moment in cultural history, one that is familiar to us now through the refrains of Pound's own sound-alike association: it rhymes suggestively but powerfully with the "decade" of the 1890s. In a signal passage, Lewis assimilates Eliot to those naughty 1890s under the rubric of Richards's own salient value and practice of pseudostatement. Thus (Lewis's) Eliot, extending the regrettable legacy of the most notorious personage of that earlier decade,

> has built up a great reputation as a critic of the art he has successfully practised, and that system is balanced, in a feat of very peculiar equilibrium, upon a notion of *insincerity*, in essence not so dissimilar to the theory advertised by Oscar Wilde in *The Decay of Lying*. "Insincerity" and "lying" are not of course used here with any of the popular stigma attached to them, but only as we find them employed in the works of Oscar Wilde or of Mr. I. A. Richards or of Mr. Eliot himself. The Naughty 'Nineties were nothing if not socially snobbish: and *all* the moral values, of "honest," or of "good," necessarily came into contempt. (*MWA*, 81)

Although Lewis asserts that his evaluation has nothing to do with conventional morality, insofar as he imposes nothing like a "popular stigma" on " 'insincerity' and 'lying,' " he belies the claim in the closing appeal, as he comes to the rescue of those distressed standards of the "honest" and the "good." In its totality, the passage serves at once to measure the threatened status of those conventional categories and, with an equivalent force, to assert them. With the considerable pressure of the reactionary, that is, Lewis delineates a position of endangered norms. From this initial resistance, indeed, a tradition of critical resistance to Eliot's early—and major—initiatives will spring readily into place.

This resistant sensibility expresses itself simultaneously, in 1932, in F. R. Leavis's *New Bearings in English Poetry*. Leavis's work witnesses the subsistent strength in English literary criticism of "the moral tradition." From Matthew Arnold, this line of commentary descends to Leavis from the mid–late nineteenth century, when, no less than in the twentieth, it represents a rejection of decadence—in the linguistic representations as well as the ethical dimensions of this temperament. Not that Leavis's readings are easily attitudinized as reaction formations or transparent passéism: his critical temper gains its durable strength and lasting appeal through his highly intelligent praise for those traits in the early poetry of Eliot (sometimes Pound) that are, by the most obvious signs, modern*ist*. "Poetry matters because of the kind of poet who is more alive than other people," Leavis asserts, making the case for the special condition of modernity in this kind of writer, who is *"more alive in his own age*. He is, as it were, at *the most conscious point* of the race *in his time*. ('He is the point at which the growth of the mind shows itself,' says Mr. I. A. Richards.)"[4] A poet's self-consciousness about writing in a present that is *the* present, not just any (old) moment in modernity; an imaginative activity animating to a sense of its absolute singularity in history: it is all here, as the limiting and distinguishing condition of a writing that gives the suffix in modern*ism* its readiest meaning.

Richards offers one sign of his importance in the early calculation of this modernist literature, moreover, when Leavis calls upon him to provide that endorsement, perhaps even the trumping validation, for his own formulation of the essential temper of the new poetry. Yet Richards is being implicated otherwise in a critical project he might barely recognize. For the Richards who factors into Leavis's appraisal emerges in no evident or significant way as the codifier of the pseudoist principle. In Leavis's initial instance of the defensive misprision, the values and practices that Wyndham Lewis has characterized as decadent are rewritten to the standard and plan of their corrector—what we will recognize eventually as a "classical" modernism. In this wise, the long critical story of "rehabilitating" poetic modernism takes its first turn. For Leavis's tensely eloquent evangile will provide a powerful model for subsequent constructions of modernism. (To several generations of British academics, his standards will be definitive, and they will prove equally influential in transatlantic passage.)

Leavis's reading of "Gerontion" consolidates the achievement he esteems in *Poems* (1920), that breakthrough volume of poetic modernism. Accordingly, he emphasizes the timeliness of the poem's colloquial tone. Equally, in a matching poetic activity, he appreciates the already characteristically modernist effort of "making it new"—specifically, in Eliot's refurbishing the words of literary quotation through the richly various texture of his own verse. Within this model of dominant or obvious modernist qualities, he holds the poem in his own summary view:

> Instructions how to read the poem (should anything more than the title and epigraph be necessary) are given in the last line:
>
> > Tenants of the house,
> > Thoughts of a dry brain in a dry season.
>
> It has neither narrative nor logical continuity, and the only theatre in which the characters mentioned come together, or could, is the mind of the old man. The Jew who squats on the window-sill could not hear the old man even if he spoke his thoughts aloud, and the field overhead in which the goat coughs has no geographical relation to the house. All the persons, incidents, and images are there to evoke the immediate consciousness of the old man as he broods over a life lived through and asks what is the outcome, what the meaning, what the residue. This seems simple enough, and the transitions and associations are not obscure. (*NB*, 72–73)

Whose "immediate consciousness" may this be? This vocal character responds to the questions he—Leavis—"asks," that is, "what is the outcome, what the meaning, what the residue." What is the moral of this man's experience, Leavis is asking of his "Gerontion." The ethical imperative he senses as the unifying energy of the piece shows its effort most clearly in this conception of the speaker, who, as a "comprehensive and representative consciousness," directs the meditation he centers to a statement whose range and import may, like himself, be generic or universal.

Thus, while Leavis needs to concede that the poem shows "neither narrative nor logical continuity," he detects, crucially, no *pseudo*logical quality. The challenge that historical circumstance has set to the standards and practice of a rational language and its moral elaborations is one that Leavis's poet seems to ken from afar, but to which his Eliot forms a response substantially unaltered by this crisis in Leavis's own ethic and episteme. For the insincerity that Wyndham Lewis imputed to the method of (Richards's) Eliot certainly interrupts the work of discursive earnestness that Leavis's poem needs to perform. Accordingly, where Richards takes the final lines of "Gerontion" as the proffer of a rhetorical fiction (only) of deliberated thought (as "an excuse," that is, just "a kind of disguise"),[5] Leavis needs to make these same lines frame the poem as a consistent, sustained statement. No pseudostatement, no pseudobelief for Leavis's Eliot, whose characterizing labor is "a striving after a spiritual state based upon a reality elusive and yet ultimate," all in all, the "attainment of a difficult sincerity" (*NB*, 98). Leavis takes the major influence that Richards's critical initiative locates in the production and understanding of modernist literature and writes it out of the account.

Leavis's reading of *The Waste Land* extends the deflections he enters into Richards's orientations on (earlier) modernist poetry. His recasting appears most clearly in his application of Richards's critical principle of "musical organization." The "music of ideas" that Richards heard first in "Gerontion" offered his hermeneutic for a loose, really *pseudo*discursive motion in that poem: a sort of theme-and-variation format, which played its intellectual content, as it were, more to appease the reader's need for (an appearance of) meaning than to adduce the solid concepts of a deliberated, directed sequence of thought. Leavis realigns this critical conceit, however, with his own preference for some overriding and defining idea in the poetry.

Alluding in a note to "Mr. I. A. Richards," who "uses the analogy from music in some valuable notes on Mr. Eliot" (*NB*, 81), Leavis applies the plan to *The Waste Land* in a reading that features the ordaining role of Jessie Weston's *From Ritual to Romance*. Her work helps Eliot in his "difficult problem of organization" (*NB*, 81). In Eliot's appropriation, in Leavis's account, "*From Ritual to Romance* . . . provides a background of reference that makes possible something in the nature of a musical organization" (*NB*, 81). This schematized intelligence bespeaks the real "unity" of *The Waste Land*. The poem's coherence is "that of an inclusive consciousness: the organization it achieves as a work of art is of the kind that has been illustrated, an organization that may, by analogy, be called musical" (*NB*, 87). This "*inclusive* consciousness," like the one Leavis hears in "Gerontion," stakes the critic's major claim for the later sequence. He reclaims *integral* significance, which he hears in the words of this representative but single consciousness, who serves in turn to harmonize the relation between theme and speech, the mythological apparatus of the poem and its dramatic realization. Thus Leavis's *Waste Land* accomplishes its music of ideas in the moment-by-moment expressions of its speakers. Its readers may take from it a suitably complex but nonetheless comprehensible demonstration of the themes that Weston helps the poem to feature, that is, to repeat in a richly varied musical organization: fertility and waste, potency and decay.

Leavis reworks these motifs into his own critical ideolect. Fertility and potency stand against waste or decay as moralized metaphors. Not that Leavis's sequence is, even euphoniously, preachy. Nonetheless, physical decay locates a topic of proscribed associations for Leavis; it is synonymous with ethical degeneracy and, so, with decadence. This judgmental term reveals its negative charge for Leavis in the remarkably one-sided, simplistic reading he gives Pound. Leavis presents the single achievement of this poet's career as the resistance he exhibits in *Hugh Selwyn Mauberley* to the aesthetic myths of decadence, which have otherwise dominated his (unfavored) career.[6]

Accordingly, Leavis's critical commentary on Eliot's poem represents an obliquely but highly pitched battle to preserve this work from the corruptions of decadence. The critic's undeclared but evident foe is the pseudoist principle, to whose operations Wyndham Lewis is currently imputing the label—the stain—that Leavis needs to keep off this major poem of modernism. The primary channel of these decadent effects lies in an aesthetic form typified by the music of ideas in "Gerontion," where, in Richards's reading, the poem belies the ideas arranged on its surface with the emotional undertones and subcurrents that this (mere) rhetoric of reason stirs. In Richards's *Waste Land*, similarly, a medley of voices is organized loosely and even opportunistically within a heuristic fiction that came late in the poem's compositional day and that has virtually nothing to do with what the poem really means. But not for Leavis, not for his Eliot, who could tolerate no such disparity, which would be synonymous with decadent insincerity.

"There is no great distance in time and no gulf of any kind," Leavis concludes further on, "between the poet of *The Waste Land* and the critic who associates himself with 'a tendency—discernible even in art—towards a higher and clearer conception of Reason, and a more severe and serene control of the emotions by Reason'" (*NB*, 95). The "distance" Leavis shrinks between *The Waste Land* and subsequent works, and the formula he uses to bridge the difference between Eliot's earlier and later periods, serve really to place its poet and his prevailing attitudes further back by far in time, in a sort of status quo ante bellum. A poet responding with any artistic (or moral) sentience to the provocations of the history intervening between 1914 and 1922 could hardly countenance the proposition of some model, compositional logic that would capitalize Reason and make it the center and agent of the rationalist's imperium. The poet of the major modernist work, Leavis's Eliot represents the construction of an English critic who is possessed by a profound and powerful if unacknowledged nostalgia for conditions existing before the war. Indeed, "The Situation at the End of the First World War," the long historical chapter in *New Bearings* (*NB*, 29–65), makes no comprehensive or pointed formulation about the event he signals in his chapter heading. Leavis's account of English literary history runs essentially continuously from early Yeats to current Bridges.[7] Not that Leavis grants every poet's right to exist. The conditions for writing poetry, however, have not substantially altered.

The January 1926 date of Eliot's statement about artistic "Reason" situates it near the time of his overt subscription to organized religion,[8] an event whose implications Leavis obviously wishes to retrofit as the relevant, ordaining conception of the earlier work. This writing includes not only *The Waste Land* but its adumbrations in the volume that marked the major new turn in Eliot's career: *Poems* (1920). If Leavis is admitting no impediment to this true marriage of the older and younger—the one true—Eliot, it is a union that Wyndham Lewis also witnesses, but with the reverse emphasis of his special objection. The same traits that Leavis is saying were never really important for Eliot—those belonging to the decadence he deplores no less intensely than Lewis—dominate the whole career of Lewis's poet. The one program being established—for and against this signal instance of modernism, at the moment when the movement first enters the intellectual formations of literary criticism—is the absolute value of classicism, whether it is represented by Leavis's Eliot, conforming to those values of harmony, balance, and ratio that are recognizably or conventionally classical, or by Lewis's Lewis, being himself. That Leavis's Eliot won the decision in the history of subsequent understandings and critical modelings of modernism is a point that need not be contested. What may be recognized now, however, is that the classical value system helps Leavis to suppress the evidence—and Lewis the merit—of its contrary quality, which both commentators align with the pseudoist principle of Richards and to which they animate in (sometimes fascinated) aversion: decadence. They form jointly into a first line of response to modernist poetry that is, in effect, a resistance position. They represent a rejection of the energies that connect literary modernism with the event that proved to be so tumultuous a development in their circumstance and status as Englishmen.

One measure of the importance that this principle of pseudologic owns in the development of a recognizably modernist poetry comes in the first book of literary criticism to use this term in a deliberated, conspicuous position: *A Survey of Modernist Poetry* (1927) by Laura Riding and Robert Graves. Modernism retains its adversarial status from its former place in the religious controversies of turn-of-the-century Britain and France. The standards that the poetic modernism of Riding and Graves defines itself against are identified as those of the "plain reader." This personage expects a readily discernible sense in verse, all in all, some rationally paraphrasable meaning. The modernist poetry these authors prefer does not simply leave this expectation unmet. The poem they offer as a most indicative instance of modernist verse toys with those conditioned expectations, playing along with and pulling against the manifest drift of an apparently rationalistic syntax and grammar:

> The rugged black of anger
> Has an uncertain smile-border.
> The transition from one kind to another
> May be love between neighbour and neighbour;
> Or natural death; or discontinuance
> Because so small is space,
> The extent of kind must be expressed otherwise;
> Or loss of kind when proof of no uniqueness
> Strikes the broadening edge and discourages.
> Therefore and therefore all things have experience
> Of ending and of meeting,
> And of ending . . .

Alternative, causal, and summary conjunctions work in consort with the dominant punctuational mark of the semicolon, indicating some linkage of subsidiary parts in larger, more complex statements. Yet, as Riding and Graves observe, the "impression that the poem gives of being didactic" is likely to generate "antagonism" for the reader, for whom "the reaction of blank incomprehension will be commonest."[9] The perversity with which the (sheer) appearance of reasonable meaning is conveyed may be suggested by the repetition of "therefore and therefore," which, as a reiterated gesture of logical conclusion, leads up doubly to (and from) nothing readily comprehensible at all.

The poem is Riding's "The Rugged Black of Anger," which she published under that title in 1928. As it moves freely through its conceit of reason-seeming meaning, it suggests some level of conventionalized address in its implementation of the poetic concept and prosody of pseudostatement. Its echoes may be heard in contemporary work, say, in the opening verses of a poem that W. H. Auden composed in April 1929:

> The strings' excitement, the applauding drum
> Are but the initiating ceremony
> That out of cloud the ancestral face may come.
>
> And never hear their subaltern mockery,
> Graffiti-writers, moss-grown with whimsies,
> Loquacious when the watercourse is dry.[10]

If the first tercet works as overture, this purpose is discernible only a good deal later in Auden's career, when he supplied the initially untitled poem with the label "Family Ghosts"—these are the figures being summoned, evidently, through the "initiating ceremony" he traces in these opening lines. Whatever logic this first tercet promises, however, its rationalist syntax of stipulative statement and result clause is followed in the second tercet with a collapse into parataxis and a steadily denser accretion of trope and epithet. What, after all, is the import, determined or not by the title, of the figures in the last two lines? The affective dimension of the poem has detached itself wholly from the sense-making gesture, the propositional syntax, of the first tercet. The space between the two stanzas locates one of the major growing points of modern poetry, opened up by the experimental work we have surveyed in the verse of wartime and postwar modernism.

The poetic initiative that Auden shares with Riding (despite the dislike she and Graves express for this poet) shows a consciousness that is novel but confident, evolving with an assurance that contrasts interestingly with the position she stakes in relation to the same impulse, as a critic, with Graves. The "'obscurity'" that these two commentators assign to the modernist poem's defiance of plain sense is a little apologetic. Even inside the framing and distancing gesture of those inverted commas, "obscurity" allows the standard it opposes to dictate the term of description, which is really one of evaluation. Their defensiveness in this respect compels an attempt elsewhere to disconnect the energy they esteem from the label of "Decadence," at least to detach that brand from themselves through a vigorous diminishment of the attitudes and postures attached to it.[11] A word edged with the heaviest imprecation that a conventional temperament can address to the new usage, that is, still measures the difference between practice and acceptance, between poetry and criticism, between literary imagination and social attribution.

The reaction of Leavis and Lewis takes its place then as an early instance in a series of readings, which may be represented fairly as a history of omission, or forgetting, or suppression. The generation of critics they anticipate—some of the lines of genealogical descent are evident, direct, others submerged—recycles those tenants and conventions to fit the tradition of modernism firmly in its classical mold, even in an ostensible attempt to discern what is new, or renewed, in this verse. These are the American new critics. While these writers have no real memory of the war to suppress, their lack of this experience allows them to assert the presence and power of a classic rationality in the poetry. This estimation often emerges so overtly at odds with the evidence in the verse as to measure, with the inverse ratio of their willful insertion, the real importance and power of its absence as an imaginative capacity in this literature. The appropriation of Richards by the new critics witnesses this fascinating and (now) historically significant resistance to his signal principle, as a movement through this map of misreading may, by the end, fully attest.

I

"Discussion of the new criticism must start with Mr. Richards. The new criticism very nearly began with him."[12] The distinction that John Crowe Ransom attributes to Richards in the opening sentences of *The New Criticism* (1941) maintains a reservation, however, which he intimates in the subtitle of his first chapter: "I. A. Richards: The *Psychological* Critic" (emphasis added). Specifically, "the idea of using the psychological affective vocabulary in the hope of making literary judgments in terms of the feelings, emotions, and attitudes of poems instead of in terms of their objects" represents to Ransom one of "those specific errors of theory" by which "the new criticism is damaged" (*NC*, xi). Ransom further specifies—he emphasizes—his objection: a "bias has governed Richards' conception of poetry" from the outset, and "its bias is deeply *nominalist*." What he means, he proceeds to stress in detail, is that Richards's sensibility appears "very alert to the possibility that a word which seems to refer to the objective world, or to have an objective 'referent,' really refers to a psychological context and has no objective referent" (*NC*, 5). This model of cognitive disjunction operates not only on the referential level of individual words, Ransom observes further. The separation he indicates reappears in the propositional function of language, in its "discourse," all in all, in its statement-making capacity, which, Ransom complains, Richards has split to iterate a difference between the emotional, poetic, or "evocative" and the knowledgeable, scientific, or "symbolic." This division appears as false to Ransom as the terms of his rhetorical question are heckling: "How does Mr. Richards know that one discourse is symbolic, and furnishes knowledge, while another discourse is evocative, though it may look symbolic, and furnishes only emotion?" Ransom answers himself, immediately and predictably, by asserting the impertinence of the issue: "I cannot see the ground of his zeal in urging the distinction" (*NC*, 11).

Thus, while Richards will figure significantly in Ransom's codification of a new critical poetics, the sensibility that the American features already forgoes what is probably the most important principle in the English critic's literary intelligence. Their differences turn around the worthiness of the poetic process that Richards drew into the formula of pseudostatement. This is a discourse that, to the degree that it "may *look* symbolic," knowledgeable, or logical, and insofar as these appearances deceive, operates as a coadjutor to the feelings that it is poetry's special and privileged place to claim. What Ransom does with the awareness Richards has worked into his theorem is to pay it an oblique or inverted tribute. The American acknowledges the dichotomy of science and poetry, of empirical reason and imaginative feeling. He rewrites the English critic's response to these conditions, however, in reactionary reverse. Thus Ransom's formula of poetic structure sets itself forth in terms of a "logical discourse," which, far from being subservient in the management of the ultimate poetic effect, dominates the experience. His poet stimulates the sublogical or pararational activities of feeling through incidental measures like rhythm, which Ransom relegates to a secondary dimension of literary intelligence and which he labels "poetic texture."[13] What this texture achieves, all in all, is a variation on the main theme. The stuff of local color, it offers a sort of divergent interest from the main statement, which, in being used to subdue the wealth of proliferating detail, maintains and even increases the appeal of some comprehensive, even proverbial and old-fashioned sense.

These two opposite responses to the one problem represent a dissent of great range and implication. Their difference goes to a fundamental divergence of attitude, a discrepancy of formative orientation, insofar as the historical basis of Richards's formula is unknown to Ransom. The challenge to the standard of rationalistic language that Ransom apprehends is one he calculates thus within a world cultural, world historical framework, so that the problems he encounters—and the answer he offers—retain a level of generic nonspecificity. "The *peculiar* plight of the moderns" (*NC*, 38), he motions to open a reconnaissance on Richards's consideration of the knowledge-emotion dichotomy: the emphasis added here may underline the absence of anything particular or new at all in the subsequent discussion and formulation. Whereas "Richards has defined [this plight] several times, and discussed it intensively in his little book, *Science and Poetry*," this is a work of intensive specification, Ransom is compelled to concede, "from which I offer no quotations" (*NC*, 38). Ransom's failure to engage in word and detail (let alone implication) with the work of major and sustained relevance to the issue at hand induces a formulation that reduces Richards's own complex and textured understanding to a truism: the dilemma, in Ransom's understanding of Richards's modernity, is one of "nervous strain" (*NC*, 38), an anxiety syndrome that grows out of the discrepancy between an older culture of religious creed and newer systems of scientific knowledge. This foreshortening gestures in one direction to the readiness of the cure: through an effort of the rational will, Ransom's poets will (re)assert their imaginative reason and maintain a proper dominance of "logical structure" in their verse. This prescriptive understanding points in the other direction, moreover (as plainly as Ransom's admission about what he is not dealing with), to all that it has missed: the historicity of Richards's critical sensibility. The American writer confronts the disruption of reason's older sequences, but in the ideal time of the optimal subjunctive: in this framework, his poets can reverse errant impulses and rewrite regrettable inflections. The English critic has experienced the dissolution of reason in its worldly institutions, however, in the closely local infrastructure of English Liberalism. The war Richards lived through unspelled the grand syllogism of history to the sense—and immensity—of its own negative conclusion, that is, in no negotiable terms. This was the *terminus ad quem* for an older rationalistic language, which might be reintroduced into verse, but only opportunistically, strategically, so to provide in its own inadequacy the emotions associated with its recent and complete undoing.

The reassertion of this English dimension of Richards's literary intelligence may serve not only to reclaim the urgent and timely source of the formulations for which I have tried to recover an original historical content and depth. The specificity of his placement accounts for an intensity in Richards's address to the main issues. This is a quality we are in a position now to appreciate in some of its full volume and resonance, so that the American new critics' inability to take its measure may become to an equal degree significant.

"Man's prospects are not at present so rosy," Richards ventures in the opening words of *Science and Poetry*, establishing in that otherwise odd combination of portentousness and homeliness a tone that catches the exact note of the crisis he is about to define: all-encompassing but familiar, even intimate. The prospect shows an apocalyptic quality that is constituted almost wholly of close-up shocks, all in all, a revelation of some new and brink condition that appears most urgently in the experience of everyday living. Thus Richards's "Man"

> has recently made a number of changes in his customs and ways of life, partly with intention, partly by accident. These changes are involving such widespread further changes that the fairly near future is likely to see a complete reorganization of our lives, in their intimate aspects as much as in their public. Man himself is changing, together with his circumstances; he has changed in the past, it is true, but never perhaps so swiftly. His circumstances are not known ever to have changed so much or so suddenly before, with psychological as well as with economic, social and political dangers.[14]

These wide-ranging changes may have occurred "partly with intention," and may be associated then with the gradualist sequencing of progressive history. What interests and compels Richards most of all, however, is the novelty or surprise factor in the current condition, which will have come about "by accident." The disaster he invokes goes of course to the grand contretemps that the war represents in the model logic of an older progress, and this reference establishes the main point of orientation in the subsequent formulations of cultural history.

"*The average educated man is growing more conscious,*" Richards emphasizes as he rounds the manifold fracture of this recent moment into a summary of presumptions now undone. This is "an extraordinarily significant change. It is probably due to the fact that his life is becoming more complex, more intricate, his desires and needs more varied and more apt to conflict. And as he becomes more conscious he can no longer be content to drift in unreflecting obedience to custom."[15] If one doubts that the war initiated the complex benefit of this change, Richards describes the "custom" undone by this event in a way that reiterates that point of instigation:

310

In the past, Tradition, a kind of Treaty of Versailles assigning frontiers and spheres of influence to the different interests, and based chiefly upon conquest, ordered our lives in a moderately satisfactory manner. But Tradition is weakening. Moral authorities are not as well backed by beliefs as they were; their sanctions are declining in force. We are in need of something to take the place of the old order. Not in need of a new balance of power, a new arrangement of conquests, but a League of Nations for the moral ordering of the impulses; a new order based on conciliation, not on attempted suppression.[16]

The innovations for which Richards hopes equally in the social history and psychological life of postwar Europe locate in Versailles no promissory monument. The edifice represents instead a defining milestone, a turning point, in effect a staging area for awarenesses building out of the values with whose dissolution this structure is now identified. The war that was fought to such a bitter and bloody end at Versailles marks this temple of the Age of Reason as a ruin, one that stands nonetheless as the basis of a new attitude. Richards keeps the structure in view, then, partly as a memory that provides the incentive for social renovation, but mainly as a reference that textures the sensibility of a fresh poetic experience, which is the most sustained and explicit consideration of his book. Verse that uses the meters and sequences of traditional reason, but mainly to disappoint its (now-discredited) expectations and ends, may regain some due sense of the historically momentous. The formulas that Richards proposes are of his own recent moment, and the sensibility he delineates in his model concept of pseudostatement reveals an equal attention to timeliness.

"[R]ecently," "swiftly," "so suddenly": the temporal markers these adverbs supply (in the first of the two extracts) intensify a sense of the contemporary with a feeling of accelerated change, really an altered perception of the process of time. This sense of unexpectedness comes from an experience of interruption. The recent war has precipitated this apocalypse of Now, this revelation of an interval of difference, which marks itself off as a more intense present; some excess or aggravated awareness of disruption edges and magnifies this sense of the hour. The paradigmatic moment of modern*ism*, it is constituted by Richards with a feeling of novelty equally self-conscious and consequential. A historicized reading of Richards serves thus to locate a main prognostication and a specific prescription for English modernist literature. English modernist poetics reveals equally the unavailability of reason, at least and especially in a dress recognizable in any way as conventional. The "logical structure" that Ransom sets out to reclaim from Richards and to assert as a dominant and living tradition in poetry represents thus an attempt to rebuild Versailles. Ransom would impose this outmoded coherence on a poetry as resistant now to those structures as postwar, postlogical Europe. An absence of this historical awareness in Ransom allows him to establish for himself, and the American new critics succeeding him (even in their variety and particularity), an already collapsed standard of value. When this model is imposed on modernist poetry in particular, it instances a misprision as rich with implication as the emphasis it so consistently misses.

Ransom displays his own tendentiousness in this respect in his account of Eliot's 1919 essay on Ben Jonson. In this paraphrase of Eliot's understanding of Jonson, Ransom misses the dramatic, developmental character of the essay itself. Eliot's piece recreates the code of a comprehensive logic, as embodied in the doxa of the humors, but proceeds by the end to undo it, reenacting in this way the demise of equally reasonable and ideal schemes in his recent historical experience. Ransom's lack of knowledge in this regard is the obvious and ramifying absence in his reconstruction of Eliot, who, as a poet and even sometimes as a critic, needs equally to erect and dismantle the apparatus of rational adequacy, so to capture the resonance or depth significance of his own moment of time.

Failure to catch this disparity and apprehend its exact meaning manifests itself variously in Ransom's report. One result is an imputation of "confusion" to Eliot, insofar as the poetry and criticism witness to this commentator a duplicity, or a divergence. To Ransom, Eliot's verse runs sometimes on energies that the author of the essay on Jonson would need (according to Ransom) to proscribe (NC, 136). Further, the standard to which Ransom holds the sensibility of Eliot's criticism accountable does not remain intact and valid, he concedes, even in the present essay. The appreciation of Jonson veers dangerously near, he admits, to a validation of Shakespeare's own characteristic imaginative action, which features a play of creative difference between appearance and meaning, between a surface of verbal reason and a depth of unspoken significance. Here, to Ransom's momentary dismay, Eliot comes appallingly close to that loathed "doctrine of logical irrelevance in poetry" (NC, 173). If this concession gestures toward the more intense dimension of the paralogical or quasi rational in Eliot's literary imagination, its work in the verse and prose stems from a range of lived experience that Ransom does not understand and so cannot accommodate or acknowledge. One measure of the threat it presents, a sure testament to the revolutionary value it constitutes, shows in Ransom's heavy effort to rescue his chosen poet from it. "[Eliot's approach to the sublogical] is not quite so near as Richards comes in his analysis" (NC, 173), he counters immediately, and so, by benefit of the rationale of the greater evil avoided, reclaims Eliot. This salvaging action points up all too clearly his presentiment of the menace with which he is otherwise unable to engage—and this disengagement measures the limitations of his (American) understanding.

He attempts similarly to rehabilitate Richards in The New Criticism, but to the image and ethic of the pedagogue. Richards assumes this identity through Ransom's reading of Practical Criticism, a book whose explicit occasion—a number of specimen poetic texts are set before students at Cambridge, and their responses are collated and analyzed—places Richards most readily at the head of a classroom. Never mind the fact that Richards usually declines the office of mentor and guide, holding instead to his customary interest and course: he remains focused on the psychology of these readers' responses; he is examining the interaction between the statements the poetic texts appear to be making and the wide and often wild variety of reactions—emotive, juridical, fantastical—these wordings trigger.[17] Instead, Ransom sees a Richards he has redressed, in effect, to fit the dignity of the schoolmaster's occasion. This figure gives himself over to the practical task of imparting an appreciation of verse and improving the response of students. This work serves equally to simplify and to clarify (really, to dispense with) his usual psychological "apparatus" and to reorient his attentions. Thus Richards emerges as an "astute reader" of verse, one whose "contribution to intensive reading" leads him, under Ransom's approval, to look "much more closely at the objective poem than his theories require him to do. His most incontestable contribution to poetic discussion, in my opinion, is in developing the ideal or exemplary readings, and in provoking such readings from other scholars" (*NC*, 45). The now-welcome absence of the theoretical dimension in Richards's consideration—his otherwise insistent interest in the pseudoist illusion of reason and the concomitant reality of the illogical quality of the imagination—leaves for Ransom "the *objective* poem." This artifact seems to invite and sustain the sort of virtuoso reading that Ransom values not only as a performance of its own but as a representation of what is *really* there—now that the play of difference, which any individual reader's imaginative mind and suggestible psyche might provide, has been dismissed from school.

This revision leaves an entity presentable in the distinctly teachable terms of Ransom's own critical predilection. The preferred poem features "the structural principle which we call the 'argument,' 'idea,' or 'thesis' of the poem—the one we represent in abbreviated form by some well-turned 'paraphrase'" (*NC*, 62). The "logical structure" that dominates Ransom's earlier definition of the ideal poem reappears in this guise as Richards's own. The provocation that any logical quality in the statement provides for the *psycho*logical activity of the English critic, however, has been gainsaid entirely in favor of this "objective" thing. Ransom has written out of consideration Richards's most important critical contribution.

A similar reorientation shows in the appropriation of Richards's work by Kenneth Burke, a figure usually—if loosely—grouped among the new critics. In this company, Burke's intellectual stature is certainly unsurpassed. He emerges as a sensibility who articulates the tenets of that movement at once independently and representatively, revealing equally their coherent motives and special limitations.

In *Permanence and Change: An Anatomy of Purpose* (1935), Burke rehearses a set of concerns consistent with the major issues that Richards has addressed in *Science and Poetry*: the place that rational statement may take in relation to motives or interests that remain private, in one sense unconscious and in the other unpublic. Over the greater part of the book, Burke appears to be preparing a validation of Richards's major formulations, which he will address directly in his last chapter; along the way, he displays a generalized assent to Richards's special premises. He recognizes, for instance, "the differences between [a writer's] private way of following his thoughts and the order in which he presents them to others. Consider all the logical modulations which one adds in the attempt to socialize his point of view." "[C]onsider" specifically, Burke indicates, "how spontaneously [this writer] puts forward, as his grounds for belief, many points and progressions of thought which had never even occurred to him until he sat down to the business of motivating his argument for his public."[18] The grammar and vocabulary of rationale may be common to a social population, in other words, but it seems extrinsic to the inner rhythms and covert motives underlying one's expression. Burke witnesses a division similar in every respect to the one Richards has taken as the main tension in his idea of pseudostatement. Indeed, Burke's most cogent and closely argued researches go directly to the contrary measures of motivation and rationalization, and he provides an understanding of the problem in a historical dimension that is at once comprehensive and succinct. "[W]hen the rational schema of classification had come into full flower," he observes as a historian of ideas, "[p]oets, whose logic is rooted in experience, were now faced with a contrary logic wholly the product of rational speculation, and their bewilderment was considerable."[19] The conflict between reasonable speech and empirical knowledge intensifies thus for Burke, who raises its drama into a cosmic prospect:

> Perhaps because we have come to think of ourselves as *listening* to the universe, as waiting to see what it will prove to us, we have psychotically made the corresponding readjustment of assuming that the universe itself will abide by our rules of discussion and give us its revelations in a cogent manner. Our notion of causality as a succession of pushes from behind is thus a disguised way of insisting that experience abide by the conventions of a good argument.[20]

Where Burke's universe outsizes one's rationality, it works to the same ratios Richards intimates in the discourses of the Liberal war, where, too, the prosodies of logic operate mainly or only to express their own irrelevance. Richards takes this disconnection with the severe finality of its historical occasion. Closing off the appeal of reason, shutting down the prospects of rational gradualism, he turns verse away from the destinations of logical progress and hears its most expressive measure in the sentences of pseudostatement, an echoing resonance of the severe meaninglessness of reason in history. These are last words, at least when heard in a historically grounded understanding. Alternatively, however, Burke proposes that humans not only make pseudostatements all the time but do so in a sort of experimental, forward-looking, trial-and-error methodology. In the ongoing interaction between a "recalcitrant" world and an adaptable language, he insists, the practical rationalist will work out a piece of verbal reason that is coherent and real, all in all, a representative statement. (Burke's is the underlying and abiding faith of an American pragmatist, who will continue to tune the verbal proposition more and more finely, until it becomes a satisfactory proposition of the actual.) "And in the end," he concludes, finding triumph in conclusiveness, "our *pseudo-statements* may have been so altered by the revisions which the recalcitrance of the material has forced upon us that we can now properly refer to them as *statements*."[21]

Burke's negotiations with Richards show him taking over the notion of pseudostatement in a fashion uninformed by its shaping English occasion.[22] He does not understand how a failure of trust in the speech and episteme of public reason underlies Richards's theorem, nor how the end of liberal modernity recurs in the poetry to which this critical theorem responds. He cannot recognize that, beyond this pseudostatement, no conclusion is sure. He has not lived through the undoing of rational certainty in the Great War.

II

The literary principle of pseudostatement is one that a historicized understanding enriches, then, with the significance of its own formative days. It is the defining idea of a critic who was pressed into service under other circumstances, however—on another continent, in the years following the *next* world war. In the American academy, in the 1940s and after, Richards was used to frame a new critical understanding of a poetic and literary tradition that came under the general heading of "modernism." In this application, his critical idiom began to echo wholly—and significantly—differently. His sensibility lost its original, specific, historical gravity. To tell the story of this systematic reorientation, this organized forgetting, is necessary. Omission and revision in these subsequent years solidified the construction of a modernist literature that reveals now a sort of empty center, or an alternate, invented center. Its representatives affirm the validity and significance of what they miss by the insistence with which they look away.

W. K. Wimsatt's 1950 apology for "Eliot's Comedy: *The Cocktail Party*" defends the merit of the verse in this drama (against the charge of its vitiation in the later career). He asserts that "[t]he most remarkable thing about Eliot's meters has *always* been their heavy reliance on the logic, the word repeated and modulated (the *traductio*, the 'turn'), the phrase paralleled and contrasted, the analogies of overflow from line to line—against these the prosody in the sense of syllables or stresses often seeming at a sunken level."[23] The emphasis I have added to *always* goes to the questionable extent of this claim. A priority of obviously logical content may be claimed in the later poetry but not in the earlier verse—at least not without a rather twisting retrofit (of the kind Leavis has already evinced for us). In the specific terms of his appreciation of *all* of Eliot's work, moreover, Wimsatt is projecting an oddly—but now recognizably—revised model of the critical concept of pseudostatement. As for Ransom, in his double structure of logical statement and poetic texture, the "prosody" of "syllables or stresses" that consolidates the sphere of feeling operates for Wimsatt "at a sunken level," that is, beneath those various manifestations of rational and neoclassical balance. As for Ransom, these well-arranged statements stand for Wimsatt as the express value of the poem's dominant consciousness. Sublogical music obviously serves for this critic only to counterpoint and augment the better work of a rationalist grammar and not, as for Richards, the other way around. An analogous moment occurs when an explorer, crossing the equator, finds the needle of a magnetic compass reversing direction. Transatlantic passage produces the same effect on the indicators of Eliot's (and Richards's) major poles of value.

A similar reorientation shows in Cleanth Brooks's "T. S. Eliot as 'Modernist' Poet," a relatively late (1972) contribution to the new critical construction of Eliot but one that shows in the marked word of his title the newly expanded and now-valorized category of this understanding. The "modernist" project involves for Brooks a repossession of rational order, an agenda he works out by turning some of Eliot's descriptive understandings of poetics into prescriptive statements. Thus Brooks's poet takes properly—correctively—in hand the "dissociation of sensibility" that the critic Eliot has discerned as the post-Renaissance legacy of modernity. Brooks's Eliot restores the balance between reason and feeling in a feat of neoclassical equilibrium that reveals its commitment to proportion, in effect, to the traditional and even ritualized ratios of rationality. What is most telling in this respect is the main locus of Brooks's poetic evidence, the staging area of his "modernist" program: not, say, in *Four Quartets*, where the poet's discursive and semiliturgical rhythms may intimate statements of the greater divine logos, but in the main in the quatrain stanzas of *Poems* (1920), in particular in "Whispers of Immortality" and "Sweeney among the Nightingales."[24] Some profounder recognition evidently compels Brooks to the place where his own values and standards are most substantially challenged—even as the procedures he esteems appear, at least superficially, to be working as the stable regulators of the verse. If he can save ratio here, Brooks might be saying to himself, the literary history of modernist poetry might be set going, in his critical reconstruction, right—not wrong—from the start.

The critical concept that Brooks evolves as his major contribution to new criticism is doubtless "poetic tension." Under this heading, he presents the verbal artifact as an idealized mirror of historical experience: the real discrepancies that the world presents between value and actuality, say, enter the order of literary feeling as irony or paradox, where balanced antitheses can resolve those contradictions and discomforts. Harmony and equanimity abide equally too in this neoclassical construction of modernism. Brooks formed his thinking in this respect, he claims in an acknowledgment made late in his career, in reading the texts of Richards. The debt he cites in this respect, however, reveals more about the edited and selective nature of this formative reading. Brooks's Richards is not the author of *Science and Poetry*, where the English critic witnesses a fundamental disruption between the languages of empirical reason and aesthetic feeling. The later, attenuated version of that division in *The Philosophy of Rhetoric* is the one Brooks invokes as the major influence on him. The core formulas of the earlier (here unmentioned) book are relegated to the status of a regrettable, now happily superseded "psychological machinery," whose equally disreputable "psychological terminology" proved "irrelevant to *our* interests" (emphasis added).[25] Speaking for new criticism as an institution, Brooks reiterates a shared inability to get Richards's English measure.

This critical and literary sensibility is not readily teachable, at least not without the work of historical archaeology. Thus the emphasis on pedagogy that new criticism reiterates will prove instrumental in perpetuating the history of forgetting that Richards's once-timely witness will suffer subsequently. In the years following World War II, a generation of teachers would need to make poetry available to students who were not usually equipped with a readiness to attend to historical explanations of literature. These readers were presumed by the standards of democratized education to possess a power to analyze mainly or only what was right in front of them. Even if their instructors understood the political backgrounds to Richards, the historical sources and intellectual implications of *Science and Poetry* would find no favored place in a curriculum of (what was coming to be known as) modernist literature. These teachers tended instead to adapt the classroom apparatus in *Practical Criticism*, a volume Brooks cites in the same essay as a welcome instance and prized implement for poetry's "powerful educative force."[26] What he means by this accolade is the reducibility of poetry to a logically organizable content, a readily available—teachable—rationalism. That is most certainly *not* Richards's intellectual interest in this model volume. Modernist poetry, moreover, will have flown this standard of value upside down, turned Brooks's schoolroom inside out, and placed at its center the salient value of the *un*speakable, the *un*reasonable. This dimension may reveal the import of its real challenge, then, in the consistent effort that the new criticism expends in suppressing it.

Emblematic site of American new criticism, the rationalist's classroom works to a degree of salient importance in the construction of literary modernism that Wimsatt reflects in his long essay "Horses of Wrath: Recent Critical Lessons." Containing passages drafted between 1956 and 1962, this comprehensive piece represents an effort undertaken over the long heyday of the new criticism in the American academy. Wimsatt witnesses the philosophical proclivities of this school most indicatively in his depiction of Richards, a critic committed in this presentation to the "quieter kind of affectivism, the equipoise, the beautiful harmony of impulses." The "harmony" or balance that Wimsatt champions goes to a root value, the radical valence of rationality. Ratio subsists in (Wimsatt's) Richards's system as a tradition of Enlightenment reason so irrepressibly strong that it has mutated only superficially through several centuries. Thus Wimsatt finds this better rationality of Richards "connected with utilitarian ethics during the nineteenth century. J. S. Mill's two essays on poetry, for instance, show how this eighteenth-century heritage might get into criticism; they echo the way it had already done so in Wordsworth and Coleridge."[27] A standard of applicable reason thus appears for Wimsatt, as for Brooks and Ransom, as the underlying, abiding, unbroken line of value in the poetics of Enlightenment modernity.

Wimsatt's preference reaches its revealing limit when he attempts to extend it to the literature of English modernism, as framed by Richards's critical ideas in particular. The effort bespeaks the import of the loss Wimsatt cannot admit. He attempts to realign Richards and the modernist temper this critic reflects with those foregone orders, all in all, with the standards of rational balance and equanimity whose collapse provides the occasion and meaning of English modernism. Thus Richards's "equipoise" offers Wimsatt

> a new witness for something like a classical disinterest or detachment. With all its up-to-date paraphernalia of verbal analysis, Richardsian aesthetics was readily available or at least convertible for purposes of cognitive literary talk, and for that reason Richards became a venerable name in the schools and among analysts and grammarians, persons who recognized their business to be not the fanning nor the feeding and watering of emotions but the explication of the sources of emotion in the uses of language.
>
> All this connected of course readily enough with "neo-classicism." I have been delaying only through purposes of climax and emphasis, not through absentmindedness, to say that looking around the critical landscape of that now remote period, one notices too the conspicuous figures of Pound and Eliot. . . . Impersonality, craftsmanship, objectivity, hardness and clarity of a kind, a union of emotion with verbal object, a norm of inclusiveness and reconciliation, and hence a close interdependence of drama, irony, ambiguity, and metaphor, or the near equivalence of these four—such ideas made up a new system as it worked its way into practical criticism about 1935 or 1940.[28]

The title of Wimsatt's piece derives from Blake's aphoristic fragment, "The Tygers of Wrath Are Wiser than the Horses of Instruction," a source that points up some of the complex motivation lying behind this critical construction of modernism. Wiser or not, Wimsatt's instructors are wroth indeed with a feeling of disestablishment. What has lost dominance is the rationalist standard of the academy, which Wimsatt and his teacherly colleagues have attempted to reestablish as the singing school for verse. The reactionary animus in this project may testify in its own inverted way to the credible and even threatening presence of an alternative, insurgent tradition, whose reality Wimsatt acknowledges in his very opposition to it. His need to erase its antithetical reality leads him, in the exemplary indiscretions of this last passage, to the really drastic oversimplification he makes of Richards and the equally unrepresentative balances he sets up in English modernism. These are the representative misprisions of an American new criticism.

These alternate orientations are so profoundly embedded in the national character of the new critics, however, that even an attempt to identify their mistaken apprehension of Richards ends up repeating the error, revealingly. The illuminating case is offered by Gerald Graff in his 1967 essay, "The Later Richards and the New Criticism." What will strike one initially in reading this lucid piece is the fact that Graff gets Richards—really, the *early* Richards—completely right. Graff identifies "his deep-seated dislike of the intellectually formulable, the 'mere' doctrine" as the espoused content of poetry. In Graff's report, however, this system of values shows up in Richards's descendants, in the American new critics, as a set of preferences ostensibly unchanged. In "their own dogmatically posited dichotomies," he avers, "[t]he widespread tendency to define poetry in terms of various kinds of non-propositional, non-logical, non-discursive modes, the tendency to say that poetry is not propositional but 'dramatic,' not statement but 'gesture,' 'icon,' 'the dancing of an attitude,' or the 'play' of conflicting 'tensions,' 'ironies,' or 'ambiguities,' etc., can be traced directly to Richards's opposition between scientific and emotive statement, and has the same philosophical basis."[29] We must now counter by asserting that the new critics hardly abjure the presence—indeed, the priority—of logical content, plain statement, rationally paraphrasable meaning. In reading Richards's American legacy, that is, Graff gets his English source right and his American derivation wrong.

On the crassest level, perhaps, the motive in this misreading goes to a younger critic's need to clear the space for his own revisionary program. He conveys its major aim and adamant value in the summary judgment of this rhetorical question, really a rebuke. "If the 'unique mode of knowing' which poetry is supposed to offer is incomprehensible in rational terms, as Tate, Brooks, Wimsatt and others are constantly saying, then can these critics legitimately claim to have defined a poetic truth any more objective and capable of verification than the 'truth[e]' accorded by Richards to emotionally gratifying non-assertions?"[30] Graff demands a model of poetic knowledge that stands the test of logical content and provable truth; he asks for a critical poetics that manages fact adequately, rationalistically (a task he takes up in other writings of the

319

same period in his career).[31] Even if the younger critic has fabricated a difference from his elders on this matter of values, it is nonetheless telling in the extreme that he advocates so passionately for this absolute, unnegotiable standard of rationalist language in poetry. The strength (and reflex nature) of this progression measures his own—and, *malgré lui*, the new critics'—resistance to the significance of Richards's primary historical experience: the demise of the Enlightenment ideal of meliorist reason in the prosecution of the English war. Confined in their lived experience to American history, Graff and the new critics witness a sensibility unseasoned equally by the conditions impinging on Richards's formulations and by the possibilities consequent to this exposure. This limitation may be assessed, in a concluding demonstration, to measure the true import of what is missed.

III

As a young poet-intellectual, Ransom wrote *God without Thunder: An Unorthodox Defence of Orthodoxy* (1930). Here he attempts to repossess the conditions under which an older religious dogmatism found its power. In this milieu, in Ransom's reconstruction, an undivine humanity saw its own helplessness in the image of a God whose force was absolute, and in whom faith was founded on the rock of doctrine, not on the optimism of human logic. This vision exerts for Ransom the appeal he reveals in the terse eloquence of his own apologia. "Jewish theology was not rationalistic," he expatiates, "but perhaps it was something better: it was realistic."[32] His "defence" of this sensibility is "unorthodox," however, insofar as the current, reigning orthodoxy features the high priesthood of science, which commits its ministers to the method and value of empirical, meliorist reason. Thus Ransom's defense aims its attack on the dominance of positivist logic. The members of this modern church reveal to Ransom the weakness of their special hypocrisy, most notably in the gestures of reconciliation they purport to make with that older, recalcitrant God.[33] This new "God without Thunder" is a deity whose limitations provoke Ransom's fiercely focused grievance. What this dominant model disallows in human experience is the reality of the suffering that the Old Testament writers clarified and inscribed so powerfully. "(Our own opportunities in this respect have been nothing like so rich.)"[34] The inadequacy of modern rationalistic language speaks most clearly to the poet-critic, even through the discrete space his parentheses enclose, where he reveals the deep appeal of an experience that would give the lie to that false god's ideology.

The wish Ransom expresses was granted all too amply in England's Great War of 1914–18. Framed by the discourses of progressive reason, the ongoing ordeal of the war wore out this idealizing scheme and challenged its rationalis-

320

tic language. The American Ransom has not heard its Word. He replicates the incident the war represents, nonetheless, in the image of his own intellectual and imaginative desire. He longs for a crisis identical with the one the war constituted, in Britain in particular.

That catastrophe bespeaks the immensity of its poetic potential, moreover, in the detailed comprehensiveness with which Ransom recounts the history and values of the modern secular faith. Rationalism represents to him the established standard of a modernity he specifies as "liberal," a mind-set he takes back to its nascent days at the start of the Protestant Reformation and connects accordingly with the prepotent creed of free reason. This spirit works diversely and widely in Ransom's view but always under the optimal possibilities of independent rational inquiry, logical tolerance, and the prospect of communitarian progress.[35] He wishes to press this episteme of meliorist and empirical reason to the point of critical mass and revelatory intensity that the apocalypse of the war has already afforded. He wants to catch it out. As a young man, Ransom speaks the same need that (Pippin's) Nietzsche reveals in his search for the one event that realizes—that makes real as an actual experience—the overturning of those dominant models of liberal Enlightenment modernity. He expresses thus the deeper need of a poet's imagination, not only to work in the elemental clarity of those facts, but to live intensely in this instant of history, that is, in the lengthened moment of the end of the modern age. The kind of disruption he covets, we now realize, locates the defining moment of English modernism. The interruption that the discourses of the Liberal war uttered and entered into the ideal sequences of meliorist reason clearly opens as a space of irresistible poetic possibility for the young Ransom. His desire underscores the profounder appeal of the meaning the war offers, not as a wished-for consummation of human bodies but as a *terminus ad quem* that is also a *terminus a quo*, both an end feeling and a staging area.

Missing the triggering incident of the war, however, Ransom fails in consequence to take the measure of its effect, that is, to take in the real gravity and finality of its impact. He manifests this superficiality in the development of his complaint against meliorist reason. The youthful southern agrarian voices this objection first in *God without Thunder*, but, in due and short course, he alters this jeremiad to the call for "logical structure" in verse, the quality he puts in a privileged place in poetry in *The New Criticism*. Ransom needed to have been in Liberal England and heard the language of its last days to understand that he really could not take back that first wish.

The preferences that the younger poet expressed—in his not quite adult-age rebellion against the standards of the rationalist establishment—are reversed as well in the transatlantic passage of Richards's critical ideas. The reception of his signal principles by the American new critics records nothing less than a loss of modern memory. In their reorientation of Richards and their subsequent constructions of modernist literature, moreover, the New World critics void this body of work of its testamentary strength, its historical content, and its achieved significance—its reenacting of the end of Old World values, attitudes, and practices. This timely writing may now begin to recover some of that daunting import.

NOTES

Prologue

1. In T. S. Eliot, *Collected Poems 1909–1962* (1963; rpt. London: Faber, 1974), 40, 41. Eliot mentions the poem as "this new one, 'Gerontion,'" on 9 July 1919 in a letter to John Rodker, in *The Letters of T. S. Eliot*, vol. 1, *1898–1922*, cd. Valerie Eliot (London: Faber, 1988), 312. The working manuscripts of the poem will be referenced in the closer reading and commentary of chapter 3.

2. Eliot, *Collected Poems*, 39.

3. Ibid., 40.

4. Paul Fussell, *The Great War and Modern Memory* (1975; rpt. New York: Oxford University Press, 1981), 174. Recent attempts to situate the work of literary modernism in relation to the Great War include Trudi Tate, *Modernism, History and the First World War* (Manchester, England: Manchester University Press, 1998), and Allyson Booth, *Postcards from the Trenches: Negotiating the Space between Modernism and the First World War* (New York: Oxford University Press, 1996). Tate adopts a pan-European and transatlantic perspective and gains in comprehensive prospect what she forgoes in grounded accounts of particular national histories. Booth focuses interestingly and correctively on the relation between the specific details of the military experience and its representation in "civilian" texts, for example, on the novel phenomenon of the "missing" soldiers—corpses unreturned for burial, because of the disintegrating effects of high explosives. Like Tate's, her account includes a long and diverse bibliography of imaginative literature under the heading of "modernism." This term remains unquestioned and undeveloped as a category and so organizes its referents at a level of generality that I set out to restrict and return to the specificity of one of its earliest and most influential circumstances. A good account of the material experience of the war in Britain and its impact on a broadly based literary culture comes from Samuel Hynes, *A War Imagined: The First World War and English Culture* (New York: Atheneum, 1991).

5. I take the term and concept from James Campbell, "Combat Gnosticism: The Ideology of First World War Poetry Criticism," *New Literary History* 30 (1999):

203–15, which identifies the main judgmental and interpretive principles in the critical tradition exemplified by Fussell.

6. Fussell, *Great War and Modern Memory*, 313–14.

7. Jay Winter, *Sites of Memory, Sites of Mourning: The Great War in European Cultural History* (Cambridge: Cambridge University Press, 1995), 3–5, 29–53, 178–203, 221.

8. J. A. Hobson, *Democracy after the War* (London: Allen & Unwin, 1917), 17. A helpful overview of Hobson's background and place in relation to a Liberal intelligentsia comes from Sylvia Strauss, in her introduction to Hobson's *Towards International Government* (1915; rpt. New York: Garland, 1971), 5–13. Positioned on the radical wing of partisan activities, Hobson maintained an affiliation with the British Labour party and, at the outset of war, with E. D. Morel's Union of Democratic Control, discussed in chapter 1. Hobson's dissent from the logic of Liberal war policy does not remove his text from the influence of that broader political discourse.

9. Charles W. Hayward, *War and Rational Politics* (London: Watts, 1915), 61. The gruesomely cartooned quality in this depiction recurs throughout the monograph. See 7, for example, where a depiction of "the cart of civilisation," running (as it were) on the "linch-pin of rationalism," meets the "rude jolts and bumps from careless or drunken drivers," while the "international diplomatic axle" also helps to steer the cart awry. The insistence on maintaining some line of polemical argument (a good deal more obscure in its original iteration than in this paraphrase) through such a dense warren of tropes and fantastical figures provides its own measure of the distress of reason in the current circumstance.

10. Virginia Woolf, *The Voyage Out* (1915; rpt. San Diego, Calif.: Harcourt Brace Jovanovitch, 1990), 9. The novel, the writing of which was undertaken in 1908, would be accepted by the publishing house of Gerald Duckworth on 12 April 1913, but various circumstances, including Woolf's illness and the outbreak of war, postponed its publication until 1915. The situation is recounted by Hermione Lee, *Virginia Woolf* (London: Chatto & Windus, 1996), 326–27.

11. Virginia Woolf, *Jacob's Room* (1922; rpt. San Diego, Calif.: Harcourt Brace Jovanovitch, 1990), 7. The first mention of *Jacob's Room*—as "a new novel"–occurs in Woolf's diary on 26 January 1920; she cites it under its title on 10 April 1920. See *The Diary of Virginia Woolf*, vol. 2, *1920–1924*, ed. Anne Olivier Bell (New York: Harcourt Brace Jovanovitch, 1978), 13, 28.

12. In *Personae: The Shorter Poems of Ezra Pound* (1926; rev. ed., ed. Lea Baechler and A. Walton Litz [New York: New Directions, 1990]), 90. "A Pact" appeared originally in *Poetry*, April 1913.

13. In Pound, *Personae*, 185. Pound writes to Scofield Thayer on 7 June 1920 of "H. S. Mauberley": "he was done in Dec. and Jan." Unpublished letter, *Dial* archive, New York Public Library.

14. In Eliot, *Collected Poems*, 18, 19. The poem is dated from manuscript evidence by Christopher Ricks, the editor of T. S. Eliot, *Inventions of the March Hare: Poems 1909–1917* (New York: Harcourt Brace, 1996), 331. Its publication in Eliot's *Prufrock and Other Observations* (London: Egoist, 1917) was preceded by an appearance in 1915 in the magazine *Others*.

15. In Eliot, *Collected Poems*, 39.

16. John Rawls, *Political Liberalism* (1993; rpt. New York: Columbia University Press, 1996), esp. xxiv, xxvi–xxviii, xxx, 47–59, 212–27. Rawls undertakes an exacting distinction between "the reasonable," which he understands in terms of a body of doctrine held in common, which imposes fair and equitable demands for the purposes of cooperative existence, and "the rational," which pertains to a capacity for calculation normally or mainly self-interested in quality.

17. Jonathan Parry, *The Rise and Fall of Liberal Government in Victorian Britain* (New Haven, Conn.: Yale University Press, 1993), 131, 4, 90.

18. Ibid., 223, 169.

19. Ibid., 231ff., esp. 253–54, 258, 260. Parry argues that Gladstone's personal style and the "cult of the Leader" philosophy he evolved represented a sharp deflection from the parliamentary Liberalism of the party's Whig precedents. See also T. A. Jenkins, *Gladstone, Whiggery, and the Liberal Party* (Oxford: Clarendon, 1988), and Jenkins, *The Liberal Ascendancy, 1830–1886* (New York: St. Martin's, 1994).

20. Dora Marsden, "England and Ireland," *The Egoist: An Individualist Review*, 1 June 1916, 81. The provocation for Marsden's article is the Easter Rising in Ireland, but the target of her remarks is the Liberal style, which she analyzes over the course of the war. Her commentary will be treated at length in chapter 1.

21. Rawls dates "the modern" from the beginning of the Reformation in *Political Liberalism*, esp. xxiv, xxviii. This chronological marker is adopted as the basis of Jacques Barzun's monumental compendium on the history of the "modern" age, *From Dawn to Decadence: 1500 to the Present: 500 Years of Western Cultural Life* (New York: Harper-Collins, 2000), esp. 3, 48.

22. Helpful accounts and analyses of these developments come from Clyde F. Crews, *English Catholic Modernism* (Notre Dame, Ind.: University of Notre Dame Press, 1984), and Lester Kurtz, *The Politics of Heresy: The Modernist Crisis in Roman Catholicism* (Berkeley: University of California Press, 1986).

23. See Barzun, *From Dawn to Decadence*, 125, where he follows the term and concept of "the modern" as it evolves its sense from "the present" to a self-defining distinction from the past.

24. Robert Pippin, *Modernism as a Philosophical Problem*, 2d ed. (Oxford: Blackwell, 1999), esp. xiv, xv, 29, 31, 44.

25. Pippin, "'Nihilism Stands at the Door': Nietzsche," in ibid., 78–113, 152.

26. Hugh Kenner, *The Pound Era* (1971; rpt. Berkeley: University of California Press, 1974). For a rationale and a methodology of new historicism, see Stephen Greenblatt, "Towards a Poetics of Culture," in *The New Historicism*, ed. H. Aram Veeser (New York: Routledge, 1989), 1–14.

The mix of ingredients in the cultural texts examined in a new historicist approach is sampled fairly in the promised contents of *American Modernism across the Arts*, ed. Jay Bochner and Justin D. Edwards (New York: Peter Lang, 1999), 1: "The work that follows relates photography to fiction, poetry and advertising, rhythm to science, music and ethnicity, Modernist formalism to autobiography, anarchy, and the weather, film to streets, malls and baking, sexual identity to street theater, ethnicity and native myth." The consequent sense of a mass-based production of modernism is augmented thus, 2: "[W]e have begun a demonstration of [the] breadth and hidden corners [of American modernism]. Our definition, if we had one, would be wider than any previous, as we enlarge the corpus, rewrite forms and origins, and increase contacts. . . . We want to provide an antidote to the unitary and decontextualized critical myth which invented 'High' Modernism. . . . We propose to readjust the horizons."

The extension of the concept and category of the "literary" that is effected in the new historicist approach is framed in the introduction to *Seeing Double: Revisioning Edwardian and Modernist Literature*, ed. Carola M. Kaplan and Anne B. Simpson (New York: St. Martin's, 1996), xv: "Following trails blazed by recent criticism—by feminism, by gender studies, by cultural studies, by New Historicism, and by post-colonial theory—we enter into the current dialog [*sic*] of our discipline. This dialog is complicated and enriched by calling into question traditional literary categories and judgments, by attempting to redefine the concerns and objects of literary analysis, by including formerly marginalized perspectives, and by encouraging previously silenced minorities to cultivate their own voices." The aim of this collection of essays is to discredit the "specialness" of modernism as well as an older concept of "the literary"; the "major" works of English modernism are thus set in continuity and contiguity with a range of Edwardian texts, which are read as evidence and expression of a popular culture that provides the generative basis of work in the two eras. The relation of modernist projects to the work of popular culture is asserted further in Michael Tratner's *Modernism and Mass Politics: Joyce, Woolf, Eliot, Yeats* (Stanford, Calif.: Stanford University Press, 1995), e.g., 2, where Tratner promises to "show that many modernist literary forms emerged out of efforts to write in the idiom of the crowd mind. Modernism was not, then, a rejection of mass culture, but rather an effort to produce a mass culture, perhaps for the first time, to produce a culture distinctive to the twentieth century, which LeBon called 'The Era of the Crowd.'"

A further turn in this argument asserts the complicity of modernist motives and aims with the work of a literary marketplace that, being understood as a nexus of commercial interests and popular consciousness, was formerly (supposedly) assumed to lie off-limits to the superior sensibility, say, of Eliot, Pound, or Woolf. A representative instance is *Marketing Modernisms: Self-Promotion, Canonization, Rereading*, ed. Kevin J. H. Dettmar and Stephen Watt (Ann Arbor: University of Michigan Press, 1996), 3, which claims as its "dual trajectory" an attempt "both to reconsider the critically suppressed relationship between canonical modernists and the commercial marketplace, and to provide a metacommentary on the exclusionary and political effects devolving from such a pristine conception of modernist poetics, its dense and mysterious 'purity.'" Whether the consciousness of modernism addresses a marketplace outside of itself, or is constituted by the conditions and circumstances of a mass-based readership, is a question that needs clarity of definition and exploration. In *Modernist Writers and the Marketplace*, ed. Ian Willison, Warwick Gould, and Warren Chernaik (London: Macmillan, 1996), the essays are presented as attending particularly to the "developing *relationship* between modernist authors and the marketplace," more specifically, to "the *rapprochement* between modernist writers and the marketplace" (xiii, xv; emphases added).

27. Modris Eksteins, *Rites of Spring: The Great War and the Birth of the Modern Age* (Boston: Houghton Mifflin, 1989). These passing and occasional references do not amount to any consistent positioning of a group sensibility.

28. Ibid., esp. "Sacred Dance," 192ff. The doctrine of EMANCIPATION provides a capitalized motif in Barzun's history of Reformation and post-Reformation liberalism, in *From Dawn to Decadence*. For an account of the relation between political nationalism and avant-garde aesthetics, see Paul Peppis, *Literature, Politics, and the English Avant-Garde: Nation and Empire, 1901–1918* (Cambridge: Cambridge University Press, 2000), esp. "'Surrounded by a Multitude of Other Blasts': Vorticism and the Great War," 96–132, which develops the complexity of the journal's position in relation to the nationalist discourses of the current war. The focus falls mainly, appropriately, on Lewis: "Confronted with the tumultuous realities of war's opening, Lewis was pulled, like his ambivalent protagonist [in "The Crowd Master"], by the competing claims of self and nation, dissent and patriotism, nonconformity and collectivism," 113. The dissent from current conventional expressions of patriotism represents to Lewis (and the avant-garde temper) the necessary or better sensibility of "patriotic dissent," 114, a nationalism that reserves as its essential condition the validating and authorizing force of the exceptional individual. For Peppis's commentary on Ezra Pound's relation to "the Vorticists' ideal of engaged dissent," 129, see 128–29.

29. The most comprehensive formulation of avant-garde aesthetics at this time comes from Marjorie Perloff, *The Futurist Moment: Avant-Garde, Avant-Guerre, and the Language of Rupture* (Chicago: University of Chicago Press, 1986), which focuses mainly on prewar activity on the Continent but follows the legacy of futurism in the postwar poetry of Pound and Eliot.

30. George Dangerfield, *The Strange Death of Liberal England* (1935; rpt. New York: Putnam's, 1980), viii. Dangerfield maintains that the war's importance lay in the distraction it offered to the insurgent energies of three forces of unrest in domestic and imperial politics: the women's movement, workers' organizations, and Ulster.

Chapter 1

1. The most extensive account of L. T. Hobhouse's place in English political culture comes from Stefan Collini, *Liberalism and Sociology: L. T. Hobhouse and Political Argument in England, 1880–1914* (Cambridge: Cambridge University Press, 1979), esp. "Radical Journalist," 79–120, and "New Liberal Theorist," 121–46.

2. Background to the problems centering the attentions of Liberal consciousness in the Edwardian decade is set out usefully by Collini, *Liberalism and Sociology*, "Individualism and Collectivism," 13–50.

3. L. T. Hobhouse, *Liberalism* (London: Williams and Norgate, 1910), 127–28.

4. Ibid., 129–30.

5. Ibid., 23.

6. Ibid., 123.

7. Gustave LeBon, *The Crowd: A Study of the Popular Mind* (1960; rpt. New York: Viking, 1967), e.g., 61–62: "The ideas suggested to crowds present themselves then in the guise of images and are only accessible to the masses under this form. These image-like ideas are not connected by any logical bond of analogy or succession, but may take

each other's place like the slides of a magic lantern which the operator withdraws from the groove in which they were placed one above the other. This explains how it is that the most contradictory ideas may be seen to be simultaneously current in crowds." See also 41, 60.

8. Arnold's original (1869) text was "expurgated" for the 1875 edition. The earlier version, with the correction of evident errors, is restored by J. Dover Wilson, ed., *Culture and Anarchy* (1932; rpt. Cambridge: Cambridge University Press, 1969), esp. 166–70. Arnold's long-standing involvement—engagement and debate—with the principles and procedures of the Liberal party provides a pervading topic of consideration for Lionel Trilling, *Matthew Arnold* (New York: Norton, 1939), esp. 223–24, 254. Arnold's embattled affiliation with the Liberal party is summed up thus by Park Honan, *Matthew Arnold: A Life* (New York: McGraw-Hill, 1981), 336: "Calling himself 'a Liberal tempered by renouncement,' he edited Burke's *intelligent* Irish speeches, and refrained from party loyalties himself but supported M.P.s who lacked blind partisan feeling." The internal quotation is referenced to William Robbins, *The Ethical Idealism of Matthew Arnold* (London: Heinemann, 1959), 55.

9. Arnold, *Culture and Anarchy*, esp. "Hebraism and Hellenism," 129–44.

10. Hobhouse, *Liberalism*, "Gladstone and Mill," 102–15, esp. 104: "The Gladstonian principle may be defined by antithesis to that of Machiavelli, and to that of Bismarck, and to the practice of every foreign office. As that practice proceeds on the principle that reasons of State justify everything, so Gladstone proceeded on the principle that reasons of State justify nothing that is not justified already by the human conscience." Hobhouse's main proposition is that Gladstone represents an advanced consciousness in the Victorian era, the growing point of promissory developments in Hobhouse's own day, e.g., 105: "[Gladstone] was before his time."

11. Ibid., 221. See also 106, where Hobhouse aligns Campbell-Bannerman specifically with the "better" tradition of Gladstonian moral "Sense." A useful overview of the partisan situation and Campbell-Bannerman's relation to the imperialist wing comes from George L. Bernstein, "Sir Henry Campbell-Bannerman and the Liberal Imperialists," *Journal of British Studies* 12 (1983): 105–24. See esp. 112ff. for Bernstein's account of the "methods of barbarism" speech, which was delivered on 14 June 1901.

12. The relation of Grey to the imperialist wing, variously on the Boer War controversy and the emerging situation of 1906–14, is recounted and analyzed by Keith Robbins, "Sir Edward Grey and the British Empire," *Journal of Imperial and Commonwealth History* 1 (1973): 213–21. The struggle that English Liberalism underwent in reconciling the pressures of imperialists to the domestic agenda of the party may be followed in George L. Bernstein, *Liberalism and Liberal Politics in Edwardian England* (Boston: Allen & Unwin, 1986), "The Challenge of Liberal Imperialism," 27–46, and "Liberalism and External Affairs," 166–96.

13. F. W. Hirst, J. L. Hammond, and Gilbert Murray, *Liberalism and the Empire: Three Essays* (London: Johnson, 1900), xvi. For commentary on the organized resistance of Liberals to the Boer War, see John W. Auld, "The Liberal Pro-Boers," *Journal of British Studies* 14 (1975): 78–99, esp. 86–88.

14. "England's Duty," *Manchester Guardian*, 3 August 1914, 9. The signatories include Hobson and Hobhouse as well as Hammond and Hirst. The writers profess belief

in the government's statements that there are no "unpublished agreements" that would bind England to France's side in the event of a European war.

15. Gilbert Murray, *The Foreign Policy of Sir Edward Grey 1906–1915* (Oxford: Clarendon, 1915). In the introduction, Murray claims that the letter published in the *Manchester Guardian* had been drafted more than a week before it was published—the collection of signatures occasioned the delay—and that the interim revealed that "[t]he statesman whom I had suspected as over-imperialist was doing everything to preserve peace: the Power whose good faith I had always championed was in part playing a game of the most unscrupulous bluff," 10–11. Murray's change of view is based on the case presented by the British White Paper, which he uses as the basis of his chronicle of this period in the short chapter, "Diary of the Twelve Days," 13–28.

16. "How We Stand Now," an address to the Fight for Right League, March 1916. Printed in Gilbert Murray, *Faith, War, and Policy: Addresses and Essays on the European War* (Boston: Houghton Mifflin, 1917), 128.

17. Herbert Butterfield, *The Whig Interpretation of History* (1931; rpt. New York: Norton, 1965), esp. "The Underlying Assumption," 9–33, e.g., 12: "Working upon the same system the whig [*sic*] historian can draw lines through certain events, some such line as that which leads through Martin Luther and a long succession of whigs to modern liberty; and if he is not careful he begins to forget that this line is merely a mental trick of his; he comes to imagine that it represents something like a line of causation. The total result of this method is to impose a certain form upon the whole historical story, and to produce a scheme of general history which is bound to converge beautifully upon the present—all demonstrating throughout the ages the workings of an obvious principle of progress, of which Protestants and whigs have been the perennial allies while Catholics and tories have perpetually formed obstruction."

18. Ibid., 46. While "the whig historian sometimes seems to believe that there is an unfolding logic in history, a logic which is on the side of the whigs and which makes them appear as co-operators with progress itself," 41–42, "the result of [proper] historical study is precisely the demonstration of the fallacy of our arm-chair logic," 72.

19. Ibid., 61.

20. Ibid., 13–14.

21. Butterfield returns constantly to the figure of Luther and follows the concept of progress evolving out of the subsequent representations of this historical character.

22. L. T. Hobhouse, *Questions of War and Peace* (London: Fisher Unwin, 1916), 129–30.

23. Ibid., 173–74.

24. "The New Austrian Panic," *New Statesman*, 25 July 1914, 486–88. The article is signed "Plinthos."

25. "War," *Daily News and Leader*, 3 August 1914, 6.

26. "Events of the Week," *Nation*, 1 August 1914, 653.

27. E.g., "England and the European Crisis," *Manchester Guardian*, 28 July 1914, 8, where this writer, while objecting to the balance-of-power doctrine, also makes the point that a war fought to the advantage of Russia would tilt the balance in the wrong direction: "And as though the disturbance of the balance of power—the foul idol of our foreign policy, as BRIGHT once called it, that has done incomparably more mischief than

any worshiped by the heathen—were not likely to come from the other rather than the side of Germany." Again, in "Our Duty," *Daily News and Leader*, 31 July 1914, 4: "It is suggested that interest, our interest in 'the balance of power,' commits us to support Russia. No man has given substance to that hollow and disastrous phrase, but nothing is more certain than that the surest way to destroy any balance in European affairs would be to help Russia to crush Germany and Austria."

28. The rising plaint in these days included an avowal of Grey's and Asquith's statements that no binding tie would require English involvement in a war on France's side. Thus "Keep the Peace," the main editorial in the *Daily News and Leader*, 1 August 1914, 6: "[W]e have the explicit and repeated assurance of the Government that we are free of all ties, pledges, and obligations to go to war in support of Russia or France. . . . It is our duty not only to keep out of the war should war come, but to announce here and now our rigorous neutrality. . . . Why does not Mr. Asquith or Sir Edward Grey make that simple announcement of our neutrality?" Again, in "War," *Daily News and Leader*, 3 August 1914, 6: "We are under no obligations to defend against all and sundry the neutrality of Belgium by force of arms, and if there is a political case for doing so it has not yet been presented, nor do we believe it can be made out." Thus, too, in "England's Duty," *Manchester Guardian*, 1 August 1914, 8: "We are, therefore, absolutely free; there is no entanglement in Belgium. Is any further argument needed?" The same paper expressed disquiet on the same issues, however, in "England's Danger," 30 July 1914, 8: "We care as little for Belgrade as Belgrade for Manchester. But, though our neutrality ought to be assured, it is not. Mr. Asquith speaks with a brevity natural, perhaps, if we were directly concerned, but quite unnatural if it were certain, as it ought to be, that we should not be involved. Sir Edward Grey walks deliberately past opportunities of saying that we are and will be neutral in the quarrels of Europe. From the Admiralty we have ominous rumours of naval concentrations." On 1 August 1914, in "England's Duty in a European War," 9, the *Manchester Guardian* also provides a history of quoted ministerial statements for the nonexistence of any "unpublished agreements."

29. "On the Brink," *Manchester Guardian*, 3 August 1914, 6. The case for the German move into Belgium is made thus, 6: "Germany's position is graver than it has been since the days of Frederic [*sic*]. With the genius and the brilliancy of France on the one flank and the overwhelming numbers of Russia on the other she felt herself fighting against odds for her very existence."

30. "England and the European Crisis," *Manchester Guardian*, 28 July 1914, 8: "This is mediation with the shirt-sleeves rolled up. It is something far more serious, for it seems to mean that if Russia, Germany and France start fighting we must start too. The whole future of England depends on the suppression of that spirit. It is war to the knife between it and Liberalism. Either it kills us or we kill it."

31. "Politics and Affairs: The Part of England," *Nation*, 1 August 1914, 657. The accommodation of the war by its erstwhile opponents shows the same devious facility in the case of Christabel Pankhurst, as appraised by her sister E. Sylvia Pankhurst, *The Home Front: A Mirror to Life in England during the First World War* (1932; rpt. London: Cresset, 1987), 66: "Her speech was wholly for the War; light, dialectic, as though of some academic political contest; no hint appeared of the appalling tragedy." Christabel Pankhurst had returned to England from her exile in France on the "Suffragette con-

spiracy charges" and, with her mother, Emmeline, had undertaken a campaign in support of the war. The opportunities of war-related work for women contributed to this shift in position for the leading figures in the Women's Social and Political Union.

32. While the sense of an Anglo-German liberal fraternity was attested by expressions like the one referenced below (n. 33), the separate histories of political Liberalism in England and Germany may be underlined to clarify the need on the part of English partisans to attest this international community. A comprehensive assessment of a pan-European liberalism and its varying national emphases and precedents is provided by Ernest Haas, *Nationalism, Liberalism, and Progress*, vol. 1, *The Rise and Decline of Nationalism* (Ithaca, N.Y.: Cornell University Press, 1997), which, under the heading of (Weberian) "rationalism," compares and contrasts the evolving values and practices of the major nation-states. Haas's historical overview stresses the difference between the relative stability of political Liberalism in Britain, with a legacy extending back to 1688 and a convention fairly established by the early–mid nineteenth century, and modern Germany, whose confederation in 1870 coincided with an increase in measurements of rationalization (modernization, urbanization, and industrialization), but whose political traditions were insufficiently established to provide reliable embodiments of liberal values. See Haas, 62–90, 222–37. The "reversion" in the Germany of the subsequent decades is studied closely by Dieter Langewiesche, "German Liberalism in the Second Empire, 1871–1914," in *In Search of a Liberal Germany: Studies in the History of German Liberalism from 1789 to the Present*, ed. Konrad H. Jarausch and Larry Eugene Jones (New York: Berg, 1990), 217–35, which examines the shift of the political majority in the Reichstag to the conservative parties in these years but stresses the ongoing, lasting impact of original, liberal values in a proliferating infrastructure of social services. In effect, then, the recent political and social history of Germany presented English Liberals in 1914 with two distinct images: fellow travelers, lapsed companions. Each of these could be turned to the purpose of an English commentator; inevitably, perhaps, but remarkably swiftly, the second of these gained sway in the days after 4 August.

33. "England's Duty: Neutrality the One Policy," *Manchester Guardian*, 3 August 1914, 10.

34. "On the Brink," *Manchester Guardian*, 3 August 1914, 6. The earlier phrase in quotation marks comes from a *Times* editorial.

35. H. W. Massingham, "The War and After: What We Are Fighting For," *Daily News and Leader*, 10 August 1914, 4.

36. "The Peasant Nation," *Westminster Gazette*, 28 July 1914, 4: "Servia, indeed, has been aptly described as the Peasant State of Europe."

37. Seppings Wright, "What Can Servia Do?" *Westminster Gazette*, 31 July 1914, 1–2.

38. The main work of exposition comes from E. D. Morel, *Truth and the War* (London: National Labour Press, 1916). In "Denials and Avowals," 35–41, Morel surveys the repeated denial by Grey and Asquith of any "secret treaties" and presents these public statements as the proximate cause of war, insofar as these assurances led Germany to believe that Britain would not interfere on France's side. See esp. 39–41, where Morel shows that the "conversations" with France, to which Grey and Asquith admit-

ted, actually entailed military plans, a global strategy that would be activated in late July and would result not only in the removal of the French fleet to the Mediterranean but in the preparation of a 135,000-man contingent of the British Expeditionary Force. The evidence indicating these secret agreements is presented in "The Betrayal of the Nation, 1906–1911," 273–85, and "The Betrayal of the Nation, 1912–1914," 286–300.

39. The text of the speech is presented with the least evident editorial intervention as "Sir E. Grey's Speech," *Manchester Guardian*, 4 August 1914, 7–8. The major point about England's freedom to decide is reiterated insistently through the speech, e.g., 8: "as regards our freedom to decide in a crisis what our line should be, whether we should intervene, or whether we should abstain, the Government remained perfectly free, and, *a fortiori*, the House of Commons remained perfectly free."

40. Ibid., 8. The quotation from Gladstone, with some variation of punctuation that owes to the report of a spoken text, matches the wording in *Hansard's Parliamentary Debates*, as cited.

41. "Sir E. Grey's Speech," 8: "Let us suppose that the French fleet is withdrawn from the Mediterranean, and let us assume that the consequences, which are already tremendous even to countries at peace, . . . let us assume that out of that come consequences unforeseen which make it necessary at a sudden moment that in defence of vital British interests we should go to war, and let us assume . . ."

42. "Peace or War," *Manchester Guardian*, 4 August 1914, 6.

43. "A Dramatic Scene: The House and Sir Edward Grey's Statement: Logic of Events," *Westminster Gazette*, 4 August 1914, 10.

44. Ibid.

45. "Comments," *New Statesman*, 1 August 1914, 513.

46. "Mr. Asquith's Appeal: Britain's Case and Her Duty Now: Memorable Guildhall Meeting," *Manchester Guardian*, 5 September 1914, 7. The full text of the speech is also provided as "The Call to Arms: Mr. Asquith and Britain's Honour: A Crime to Stand Aside," *Manchester Guardian*, 5 September 1914, 8.

47. "The Greatest Need of All," *Manchester Guardian*, 9 November 1914, 6. Asquith's speeches were collected in a three-penny pamphlet, "The War: Its Causes and Its Message" (London: Methuen, 1914).

48. "Why Did We Go to War?" *New Statesman*, 24 October 1914, 53.

49. An informative summary of government policy and practice is provided by Hynes, *A War Imagined: The First World War and English Culture* (New York: Atheneum, 1991), in "The War against Dissent," 78–87, esp. 79: "DORA gave the State unlimited power to control the instruments of communication and the transmission of information, and to define what was meant by those terms." Where DORA aimed "to prevent the spread of reports likely to cause disaffection or alarm," 80, its targets included the expression of antiwar views, in private or in public, as well as the publication of unfavorable accounts on the progress of military affairs. A comprehensive history of the censorship of war news in the press is provided by Martin J. Farrar, *News from the Front: War Correspondents on the Western Front 1914–18* (Stroud, Gloucestershire, England: Sutton, 1998), which outlines a three-phase history of control. From August 1914 until May 1915, correspondents were officially forbidden entry to the front and were expected to recycle and "stylize" reports controlled by the Press Bureau of the War Office;

between May 1915 and April 1917, correspondents were admitted to the general theaters of operations, but their copy was still closely monitored by the press officer in the field and the War Office in London; from April 1917 until the end of the war, a new openness allowed greater specificity of detail in the accounts of military engagements, but the tendency to report events in a way favorable to British interests had now become firmly established. A close account of the kind of obstacles correspondents faced (until late in the war) is provided by Nicholas Hiley, "'Enough Glory for All': Ellis Ashmead-Barlett and Sir Ian Hamilton at the Dardanelles," *Journal of Strategic Studies* 16 (1993): 240–64, which documents the conflicts between the reporter and the military authorities.

50. Arnold Bennett, "Public v. Censor," *Daily News and Leader*, 22 October 1914, 4. The expressed intent of the article, which does not oppose the British war aim, is to preserve intellectual validity in that military campaign.

51. "Towards Victory," *Daily News and Leader*, 29 October 1914, 4.

52. "The Great Battle in France," (London) *Times*, 9 September 1914, 9.

53. "A Week of the War" ("By a Student of War"), *Manchester Guardian*, 1 July 1916, 8.

54. "Comments," *New Statesman*, 14 April 1917, 26.

55. Ibid.

56. Edward Bellamy, *Looking Backward, 2000–1887* (1888; rpt. Boston: Houghton Mifflin, 1926).

57. "Looking Backwards: A Fragment," *Nation*, 10 March 1917, 758. The ellipses with which the piece begins simulate the condition of a "fragment," as does its unnamed author.

58. "Lucian," *1920: Dips into the Near Future*, 2d ed. (London: Headley, 1918), 5. This second edition carries a preface, dated December 1918. The early postwar moment allows the writer to drop the guard of mock argument and maintain: "Satire seemed the only means of exposing a mind of bottomless credulity" (n.p.).

59. Ibid., 43, 45.

60. "A Press View," *Nation*, 2 November 1918, 128–29.

61. "Power of Satire," *Nation*, 30 March 1918, 788: "His invention consists in attributing to [these militarists] a practice which is ideally [logically] consistent."

62. George Bernard Shaw, *Common Sense about the War* (November 1914); the essay is reprinted, with a representative sampling of the responses it prompted, in *Current History of the European War*, vol. 1, *What the Men of Letters Say* (New York: New York Times, 1914), 11–61. The main points of Shaw's argument consist of his identification of the military Junkerism in England as well as Germany, 12–15, the tendency of the British public for an "intellectual laziness," 18–19, which allows them to accept the government's "case," and the irrelevance of the issue of Belgium, 25–30. The essay appeared initially as a pamphlet published by the *New Statesman*. The placement of the review (n. 63) in the same journal does represent an implementation of the principle of amicable dissent and reasoned exchange.

63. "On Controversy," *New Statesman*, 5 December 1914, 218.

64. "The Faithfulness of Belgium," *Nation*, 4 March 1916, 787.

65. Gilbert Murray, "Democratic Control of Foreign Policy," in his *Faith, War, and Policy: Addresses and Essays on the European War* (Boston: Houghton Mifflin, 1917), 93.

This review appeared initially in the *Contemporary Review*, February 1916. Ponsonby's book was published in 1915.

66. "Atrocities," *New Statesman*, 29 August 1914, 634.

67. "Is the Tide Turning?" *Daily News and Leader*, 9 September 1914, 4.

68. "The Phantom Army," *Daily News and Leader*, 16 September 1914, 4.

69. Havelock Ellis, "The Future of Socialism," *Nation*, 13 October 1917, 62. The recent events in Russia, the abdication of the czar in March and the October rising, evidently led Ellis to read these other positive consequences of the war.

70. "The Ethics of Lying," *New Statesman*, 17 June 1916, 248. Cf. Oscar Wilde, "The Decay of Lying: An Observation" (1889; rev. 1891), in *Literary Criticism of Oscar Wilde*, ed. Stanley Weintraub (Lincoln: University of Nebraska Press, 1968), 165–96.

71. Good accounts of Fabianism, the relation of Fabianism to British political culture, and the local environment of the *New Statesman* may be found in Margaret Cole, *The Story of Fabian Socialism* (London: Heinemann, 1961).

72. H. G. Wells, *Mr Britling Sees It Through* (1916; rpt. London: Hogarth, 1985), 339.

73. Ibid., 284ff., 296.

74. One of the most striking examples comes in the combat memoir of C. E. Montague, *Disenchantment* (1922; rpt. London: Chatto & Windus, 1934). Montague's earlier career as a leader writer for the *Manchester Guardian* affords him an intimacy with the idiom of Liberal policy and rationale. "There's reason in everything" echoes throughout this account—194, 196, 205—as Montague's mocking riposte to the partisan rationales for the war. He exposes the verbal perfidy of Gilbert Murray in an extended demonstration (190ff.) in his chapter "Our Moderate Satanists," which is titled in evident memory of Matthew Arnold's "Our Liberal Practicioners." He is eloquent in his rebuke. His disapproving review in *Disenchantment* censures in particular the discursive conventions of *contemporary* Liberalism, an outgrowth in his view of the intellectual and verbal culture of wartime England. "During the war the art of Propaganda was little more than born," this member of the party's foregone intellectual community mourns. "Yet for more than three years since the Armistice our rulers have continued to issue to the Press, at our cost as Blue Books and White Papers, long passages of argument and suggestion almost fantastically different from the dry and dignified official publications of the pre-war days," 120. Oddly straightened logic, daffily rationalized statistics, bizarre novelties of argument and case-making: these features have established themselves as a matter of weekly expectation in the Blue Books and White Papers in the *New Statesman*. The "digni[ty]" of Liberal reason in its earlier and better manifestations exerts the more powerful appeal of nostalgia, however. The full account witnesses some profounder gravity of attraction to a status quo ante bellum. If reason has gone prodigal, that is, its deviants need not be indulged or encouraged but should be brought home to repentant correctness. An older ideal of Liberalism exerts an influence that is undiminished, being enhanced despite—or because of—its recent disproofs. This is a faith that Montague maintains in the searching interrogations of his own supremely reasonable style.

75. Irene Cooper Willis, *How We Went into the War: A Study of Liberal Idealism* (Manchester, England: National Labour Press, 1918), "The Holy War," 86–141, esp.

86: "It is largely due to the Liberal papers that the war came to be fraught with higher than material aims. . . . If the *Times* had been the sole spokesman, it might have contented itself with asserting the identity between our vital interests and the cause of right and honour. . . . It was the Liberal aversion to war, the extreme Liberal dissatisfaction with the vital interest argument, combined with their final submission to the fact of war, which made this war different from previous ones and consecrated it from the outset as a war on behalf of civilisation. The birth of the Holy War was in this wise." Willis's attention, like mine, concentrates on salient articles from the early months of the war in the dailies most obviously aligned with the Liberal party, the *Manchester Guardian* and the *Daily News and Leader*, and on the partisan literary weeklies, the *New Statesman* and the *Nation*, where the tone of the intellectual campaign was struck. *How We Went into the War* becomes the first piece in a triptych gathered by Willis as *England's Holy War: A Study of English Liberal Idealism during the Great War* (New York: Knopf, 1928), which reprints the 1918 text under the heading "Going into the War" and joins it with "Getting on with the War" and "Coming out of the War." The perceptions in the first part remain the most fresh and original. Willis's affiliations with the International Labour party and the Union of Democratic Control are noted by Marvin Swarz, *The Union of Democratic Control in British Politics during the First World War* (Oxford: Clarendon, 1971), 100. See also interchapter 2, n. 4.

76. Willis, *How We Went into the War*, 134.

77. Ibid., 138–39. Willis is responding to an editorial in the *Nation*, 3 October 1914.

78. Marsden is situated in English political culture and her relation to the Women's Social and Political Union (in particular, her developing differences from the Union on the suffrage question) is set out by Bruce Clarke, *Dora Marsden and Early Modernism: Gender, Individualism, and Science* (Ann Arbor: University of Michigan Press, 1996), "The *Freewoman*: Dora Marsden's Methods," 47–93, and "The *New Freewoman*: Abandoning the Phrases," 95–136. Clarke formulates Marsden's successive positions thus, 11–12: "Her transformations may be traced from a residually social-democratic rallying around a shared and shareable gender conception—the prophetic call to a body of freewomen—to the androgynous anarchism of the egoist, an individualistic formula usually appearing in the singular."

79. Dora Marsden, "Views and Comments," *Egoist*, 1 April 1914, 123–26, esp. 126; "Authority: Conscience and the Offences," *Egoist*, 1 August 1914, 281–84, esp. 281: "Gods and other authorities are soft cushions of words placed near the vague rim where power fringes off into limitation."

80. Dora Marsden, "Quid Pro Quo," *Egoist*, 15 August 1914, 301.

81. Dora Marsden, "England and Ireland," *Egoist*, 1 June 1916, 81.

82. Dora Marsden, "Views and Comments," *Egoist*, 1 September 1914, 324. The general topic of this piece is "cant," 323–25, which she centers in the emergent discourse of the Liberal war.

83. Dora Marsden, "Views and Comments," *Egoist*, 15 September 1914, 344.

84. Advertising notices for meetings of the UDC appear regularly in the *Cambridge Magazine* from the autumn of 1915 until the autumn of 1917, when the general tenor of the advertisements takes a more commercial turn. At the earlier moments, however, sizable—quarter-page—notices for the meetings, including information about agendas or

who will preside, are provided. The most comprehensive account of Morel's organization is Swarz's *Union of Democratic Control*, which documents the first meeting of the UDC at Cambridge in early March 1915, with Morel as speaker, 64; Swarz also records the prohibition on meetings by the council of Trinity College, Cambridge, on 19 November 1915, "although thirteen fellows (and two ex-fellows who were regular members of the high table) were members of the local branch," 113. The presence at Cambridge of two notable members of the UDC, Bertrand Russell and G. Lowes Dickinson, helped to direct the organization's attention to the university; see 30.

85. See n. 38.

86. Morel, *Truth and the War*, 284–85.

87. Adelyne More [C. K. Ogden], "The One Thing Needful: A Suggestion to Members of Parliament," *Cambridge Magazine*, 29 January 1916, 240.

88. Ibid.

89. "The Duty of Suicide—Fiat Justitia Ruat Caelum," *Cambridge Magazine*, 18 November 1916, 143. Ogden's pseudonym for this piece is "Idealist." The emphases are his.

90. Adelyne More [C. K. Ogden], "What the Public Wants: The Right Words in the Right Order," *Cambridge Magazine*, 26 February 1916, 339. The emphases are Ogden's.

91. I. A. Richards, *Science and Poetry* (New York: Norton, 1926), 21–22: "The minor branch we may call the intellectual stream; the other, which we may call the active, or emotional, stream, is made up of the play of our interests. The intellectual stream is fairly easy to follow; it follows itself, so to speak; but it is the less important of the two. In poetry it matters only *as a means*; it directs and excites the active stream. It is made up of thoughts, which are not static little entities that bob up into consciousness and down again out of it, but fluent happenings, events, which reflect or point to the things the thoughts are of. Exactly how they do this is a matter which is still much disputed."

92. Ibid., 67–68, 70.

93. The several oblique indications in *Science and Poetry* of the war's bearing on the formulation of Richards's critical concept of pseudostatement will be reviewed in the epilogue. It is a testament to the immensity of this influence and its overpowering impact on the rationalist standards of Richards's own academic life that it is not apprized directly.

94. C. K. Ogden and I. A. Richards, *The Meaning of Meaning: A Study of the Influence of Language upon Thought and of the Science of Symbolism* (London: Kegan Paul, 1923), 89. A large number of subsequent editions, many with substantial revisions, leave this earliest version the one closest to the historical context of some of their critical ideas. The circumstances of the Ogden-Richards collaboration are set out helpfully by John Paul Russo, *I. A. Richards: His Life and Work* (Baltimore, Md.: Johns Hopkins University Press, 1989), 97. Richards later claimed that "the book was the 'joint product of two widely differing temperaments looking together—like two eyes'"; he insisted likewise that "among the sentences" in the book "there were few of any theoretical consequence in which we didn't both take a shaping hand." Russo reveals, however, that the long chapter on "Word Magic," which provides the critical basis for the commentary on "musical discourse" or "affective resonance," was written earlier by Ogden; also, "the chapter on the theory of signs and the appendices on context and grammar" had been drafted previously by Richards (97, 709–10, n. 31, n. 32).

95. Ogden and Richards, *Meaning*, 91–92. If, on the basis of the disclosures made by Russo (n. 94), it becomes possible to hear the negative measure being supplied to this passage by Ogden and the indulgent by Richards, the composite effect of resistant reciprocity comprises the full complexity (in historical context) of the poetic use of musical reason-seemingness.

96. This 1926 essay by Richards, "The Poetry of T. S. Eliot," appears as appendix B in his *Principles of Literary Criticism*, 2d ed. (1928; rpt. New York: Harcourt, Brace & World, n.d.), 293.

97. Ibid., 290: "We can, of course, make a 'rationalisation' of the whole experience, as we can of any experience. If we do, we are adding something which does not belong to the poem. Such a logical scheme is, at best, a scaffolding that vanishes when the poem is constructed. But we have so built into our nervous systems a demand for intellectual coherence, even in poetry, that we find a difficulty in doing without it."

98. Ibid., 293–94: "The peculiarity of Mr. Eliot's later, more puzzling, work is his deliberate and almost exclusive employment of ["the music of ideas"]. In the earlier poems this logical freedom appears only occasionally. In 'The Love Song of J. Alfred Prufrock,' for example, there is a patch at the beginning and another at the end, but the rest of the poem is quite straightforward. In 'Gerontion,' the first long poem in this manner, the air of monologue, of a stream of associations, is a kind of disguise, and the last two lines,

> Tenants of the house,
> Thoughts of a dry brain in a dry season,

are almost an excuse. The close of 'A Cooking Egg' is perhaps the passage in which the technique shows itself most clearly. . . . 'The Waste Land' and 'The Hollow Men' (the most beautiful of Mr. Eliot's poems, and in the last section a new development) are purely a 'music of ideas,' and the pretence of a continuous thread of associations is dropped."

99. A good account of Ogden's editorial project is provided by W. Terence Gordon, *C. K. Ogden: A Bio-Bibliographic Study* (Metuchen, N.J.: Scarecrow, 1990), 28–38. The series included the first edition of Richards's *Principles of Literary Criticism*, the posthumous collection of T. E. Hulme, *Speculations*, Bertrand Russell's *The Analysis of Matter*, and Ludwig Wittgenstein's *Tractatus Logico-Philosophicus*. Before the war, Wittgenstein had studied with Russell at Cambridge, where he began the work that culminated in the *Tractatus*, which he finished in the summer of 1918, following his service in the Austrian army. For the effect of this military experience on the training in logical analysis that he received at Cambridge, in particular on his emerging conception of the unsayability of certain essential things, see the carefully contextualized reading by Marjorie Perloff, *Wittgenstein's Ladder: Poetic Language and the Strangeness of the Ordinary* (Chicago: University of Chicago Press, 1996), "The Making of the *Tractatus*: Russell, Wittgenstein, and the 'Logic' of War," 25–48, esp. 38–41, 43, 45.

100. Hans Vaihinger, *The Philosophy of "As If": A System of the Theoretical, Practical and Religious Fictions of Mankind*, trans. C. K. Ogden, 2d ed. (1935; rpt. New York: Barnes & Noble, 1966), xli, "Autobiographical: The Origins of the Philosophy of 'As If,'" which Vaihinger supplied for the English translation (published in its first edition

in 1924). While Vaihinger pays no great amount of attention to the linguistic dimension in his theory of fictions, Ogden is impelled to assert the indispensability of the linguistic consideration to Vaihinger's subject, in his prefatory note, vi: "For those that hold that Vaihinger's monumental work laid insufficient stress on the linguistic factor in the creation of fictions, the next step would have been to make good this omission—had not that step already been taken by Bentham a century earlier. 'To language, then—to language alone—it is that fictitious entities owe their existence; their impossible, yet indispensable existence.'" This insistence on the linguistic basis measures a pressure specific to Vaihinger's English translator and, arguably, to the English circumstances contributing to Ogden's interest in the "as if" principle. Vaihinger exerted only limited appeal in prewar England, whether or not the lack of translation was accountable. The one review of the 1911 publication of *Die Philosophie des "Als Ob"* comes from G. R. S. Mead, "The Philosophy of 'As If': A Radical Criticism of Human Knowledge," *Quest* (1913): 459–83. The *Quest* was the journal of the Quest Society, which represented, in effect, an institutionalization of English interest in the philosophy of (American) pragmatism. The relation of Vaihinger to pragmatism, indicated later in this chapter, is discussed helpfully in the context of the Quest Society by Patricia Rae, *The Practical Muse: Pragmatist Poetics in Hulme, Pound, and Stevens* (Lewisburg, Pa.: Bucknell University Press, 1997), 80–98.

101. Vaihinger's main attentions in this respect are concentrated in "The Linguistic Form of the Fiction," in *Philosophy of "As If"*, 91–95, esp. 91; see also 11.

102. William James, *Pragmatism* (1907), in *Pragmatism and Other Writings* (New York: Penguin Putnam, 2000), e.g., 58: "We saw in the last lecture ["Some Metaphysical Problems"] that the pragmatic method, in its dealings with certain concepts, instead of ending with admiring contemplation, plunges forward into the river of experience with them and prolongs the perspective by their means," and 113: "The import of the difference between pragmatism and rationalism is now in sight throughout its whole extent. The essential contrast is that *for rationalism reality is ready-made and complete from all eternity, while for pragmatism it is still in the making, and awaits part of its completion from the future.*" Vaihinger, *Philosophy of "As If"*, addresses the relation of his philosophy to pragmatism briefly, in his preface to the English edition, viii: "Pragmatism, too, so widespread throughout the English-speaking world, has done something to prepare the ground for Fictionalism, in spite of their fundamental difference. Fictionalism does not admit the principle of Pragmatism which runs: 'An idea which is found to be useful in practice proves thereby that it is also true in theory, and the fruitful is thus often true.' The principle of Fictionalism, on the other hand, or rather the outcome of Fictionalism, is as follows: 'An idea whose theoretical untruth or incorrectness, and therewith its falsity, is admitted, is not for that reason practically valueless and useless.'"

103. Vaihinger, *Philosophy of "As If"*, 11.

104. Vaihinger, *Philosophy of "As If"*, "Nietzsche and His Doctrine of Conscious Illusion," 341–62, esp. 356, an analytical paraphrase of writings posthumously collected: "The human intellect, with its fixed forms, particularly its grammatico-logical categories, is a 'falsificative apparatus'—and yet man makes use of it consciously. . . . Thus it has come about that these errors have made man inventive: and that is why the 'cult of

error' is necessary: indeed a 'joy in illusion' develops the 'will to illusion,' for we recognize 'the value of regulative fictions, e.g., the fictions of logic.'" The quoted phrases are referenced by Vaihinger.

Interchapter 1

1. "The Irish Disturbances," (London) *Times*, 26 April 1916, 7.
2. "The Message of Anzac Day," (London) *Times*, 26 April 1916, 7.
3. Homi Bhabha, "Of Mimicry and Man: The Ambivalence of Colonial Discourse" (1983), reprinted in *October: The First Decade, 1976–1986*, ed. Annette Michelsen et al. (Cambridge, Mass.: MIT Press, 1987), 318.
4. "[T]hat form of difference that is mimicry—*almost the same but not quite*—will become clear," Bhabha proposes in ibid., 322, in the opposition he emphasizes thus, 322: "*Almost the same but not white*: the visibility of mimicry is always produced at the site of interdiction. It is a form of colonial discourse that is uttered *inter dicta*: a discourse uttered at the crossroads of what is known and permissible and that which though known must be kept concealed; a discourse uttered between the lines but as such both against the rules and within them." The "insurgent counter-appeal" that Bhabha hears as the underlying motive and aim, 323, is amplified and categorized as a wholly disruptive function, 323–24: "[T]he fetish mimes the forms of authority at the point at which it deauthorizes them. Similarly, mimicry rearticulates presence in terms of its 'otherness,' that which it disavows. . . . The ambivalence of colonial authority repeatedly turns from *mimicry*—a difference that is almost nothing but not quite—to *menace*—a difference that is almost total but not quite."
5. T. S. Eliot, "Ulysses, Order, and Myth," *Dial*, November 1923, 480–83; Ezra Pound, *Make It New* (London: Faber, 1934).
6. Robert Crawford, *Devolving English Literature* (Oxford: Clarendon, 1992), "Modernism as Provincialism," 216–70. While Crawford maintains the double identity of savage civility in literary modernism as his composite construction, 218–19, his emphases in the subsequent discussion tend to underline decisively the element of "the barbaric." See esp. 219, 221, 223, 234, 235–37.

Chapter 2

1. The transition is followed by Noel Stock, *The Life of Ezra Pound*, 2d ed. (San Francisco: North Point, 1982), 53ff. The most thoroughly grounded account of Pound's London years comes from Humphrey Carpenter, *A Serious Character: The Life of Ezra Pound* (Boston: Houghton Mifflin, 1988), 97–371.
2. The statement is part of Pound's prospectus for a "College of the Arts," which he appends to a letter to Harriet Shaw Weaver, 12 October 1914, in *Selected Letters of Ezra Pound, 1907–41*, ed. D. D. Paige (1950; rpt. New York: New Directions, 1971), 41, n. 2.
3. References to Pound's periodical publications will include the information relevant to initial appearance and the volume and page numbers in the invaluable compendium *Ezra Pound's Poetry and Prose: Contributions to Periodicals*, 10 vols., arranged by Lea Baechler, A. Walton Litz, and James Longenbach (New York: Garland, 1991), cited as *EPPP*; these volumes are organized chronologically and feature facsimile re-

productions of the first publications. Thus Pound's impassioned exercises in defining the concept of the vortex, elaborating its artistic principles as well as its visual images, may be found in "Vortex: Pound," *Blast* 1, June 1914, *EPPP*, I:259-60; "Wyndham Lewis," *Egoist*, 15 June 1914, *EPPP*, I:251-52; "Vorticism," *Fortnightly Review*, 1 September 1914, *EPPP*, I:275-85; and "Affirmations (II): Vorticism," *New Age*, 14 January 1915, *EPPP*, II:4-5. See also "Affirmations (III): Jacob Epstein," *New Age*, 21 January 1915, *EPPP*, II:6-8. Pound's role in the formative stages of vorticism is recounted in the retrospective headnote he provides to the reprinting of the "Vorticism" essay from *Fortnightly Review* in Pound, *Gaudier-Brzeska: A Memoir* (1916; rpt. New York: New Directions, 1970), 81.

4. "The Renaissance (II)," *Poetry*, March 1915; *EPPP*, II:29. This three-part series ran from February to May 1915.

5. The opposition between English "civilisation" and German *Kultur* was framed early in the war. A good account is provided by Samuel Hynes, *A War Imagined: The First World War and English Culture* (New York: Atheneum, 1991), "The War against Culture," 67-78, esp. 67-72, where Hynes follows the shift in reference and implication for *Kultur* from a sophisticated urban culture to a primitive cultus of blood violence and tyranny.

6. "Patria Mia (I)," *New Age*, 5 September 1912; *EPPP*, I:77. This series appeared in eleven installments between 5 September and 14 November 1912.

7. Letter of 28 March 1914, from London, to Harriet Monroe, in Pound, *Selected Letters*, 35.

8. "Patria Mia (I)"; *EPPP*, I:77.

9. "Through Alien Eyes (III)," *New Age*, 30 January 1913; *EPPP*, I:116. This series appeared in four installments between 16 January and 6 February 1913.

10. "Through Alien Eyes (I)," *New Age*, 16 January 1913; *EPPP*, I:114.

11. "American Chaos (I)," *New Age*, 9 September 1915; *EPPP*, II:108. The series appeared in two parts, on 9 September and 16 September 1915.

12. "American Chaos (II)," 16 September 1915; *EPPP*, II:109.

13. See the material referenced above, n. 5.

14. "The Non-existence of Ireland," published as "Affirmations (VII)," *New Age*, 25 February 1915; *EPPP*, II:20. This series (with topical subtitles) appeared in seven installments between 7 January and 25 February 1915.

15. "Provincialism the Enemy (IV)," *New Age*, 2 August 1917; *EPPP*, II:252. The series appeared in four installments between 12 July and 2 August 1917.

16. "The Revolt of Intelligence (V)," *New Age*, 8 January 1920; *EPPP*, IV:6. This series appeared intermittently in ten installments between 13 November 1919 and 18 March 1920.

17. As punctuated by Pound in his letter from London of 15 November 1918, in *The Selected Letters of Ezra Pound to John Quinn, 1915-1924*, ed. Timothy Materer (Durham, N.C.: Duke University Press, 1991), 167.

18. Ibid., 168.

19. Thus the concentration of Scottish texts in the earliest examples in the *OED* entry, which labels *glamour* a "corrupt form" of "GRAMMAR; for the sense cf. GRAMMARYE [Grammar; learning in general]." *Glamour* is established in literary language by the

time of Scott (1805, 1830), when it has acquired the meaning of charm, magic, or even deception. The example from Robert Burns (1789) plays between the related meanings of the "corrupt" and "standard" forms: "Ye gipsy-gang that deal in glamor, / And you deep read in hell's black grammar, / Warlocks and witches."

20. "Provincialism the Enemy (III)," *New Age*, 26 July 1917; *EPPP*, II:234.

21. "Provincialism the Enemy (I)," *New Age*, 12 July 1917; *EPPP*, II:231–32.

22. "The Backbone of the Empire," in "Studies in Contemporary Mentality (X)," *New Age*, 25 October 1917; *EPPP*, II:288. This series appeared in twenty installments from 16 August 1917 to 10 January 1918.

23. "Our Contemporaries," *Little Review*, July 1918; *EPPP*, III:132. For background on "the statistic Webbs" and the "worn out theories" of Shaw and Fabianism, see chapter 1, n. 71.

24. "The Beating Heart of the Magazine," in "Studies in Contemporary Mentality (VIII)," *New Age*, 11 October 1917; *EPPP*, II:284.

25. "'The Strand,' Or How the Thing May Be Done," in "Studies in Contemporary Mentality (V)," *New Age*, 13 September 1917; *EPPP*, II:271.

26. "The 'Spectator,'" in "Studies in Contemporary Mentality (IV)," *New Age*, 6 September 1917; *EPPP*, II:269.

27. Stock, *Life of Ezra Pound*, 207, finds the initiative behind this poem in a letter from Pound to Iris Barry on 27 July 1916. Pound "said that if she could not find any decent translations of Catullus and Propertius he supposed he would have 'to rig up something.' It was the same letter in which he had spoken of the Roman poets as 'the only ones we know of who had approximately the same problems as we have. The metropolis, the imperial posts to all corners of the known world'" (Pound, *Selected Letters*, 90). In view of the fact that the poem was not published until 1919, Stock asserts, but on no evidence, that "although the work was dated by the author 1917," it "was probably not finished until the middle of 1918 at the earliest." Citing the same letter to Barry as the origin of the project, J. P. Sullivan, *Ezra Pound and Sextus Propertius: A Study in Creative Translation* (Austin: University of Texas Press, 1964), asserts, 4: "The *Homage to Sextus Propertius* was the result, and it was completed in 1917." Again, no evidence is presented for the assigned date of completion. Carpenter, *A Serious Character*, 324, quotes an unpublished letter to Pound's father of 3 November 1918: "Also done a new *oeuvre* on Propertius," and so assumes a recent completion date. It seems advisable thus to project a time frame for the whole process of composition from midsummer 1916 into the autumn of 1918, the second half of the war.

28. The fables are joined with other exercises in prose, and represented as experiments in evolving a more complex tonality (including urbanity, irony, and so on) in Pound's emergent project of the *Cantos*, by Ronald Bush, *The Genesis of Pound's "Cantos"* (1976; rpt. Princeton, N.J.: Princeton University Press, 1989), 161–66, where the terms of consideration remain internal to Pound's literary biography.

29. "Irony, Laforgue, and Some Satire," *Poetry*, November 1917; *EPPP*, II:296.

30. Jules Laforgue, *Moral Tales*, trans. William Jay Smith (New York: New Directions, 1985), 87, 91. Cf. the original French text in *Moralités Légendaires* (Paris: Mercure de France, 1925), 143, which presents a phrase to which Smith's translation comes closest: "l'Ordonnateur-des-milles-riens."

31. "Our Tetrarchal Précieuse (A Divagation from Jules Laforgue)," by "Thayer Exton," *Little Review*, July 1918; *EPPP*, III:126.

32. Laforgue, *Moral Tales*, 109; cf. Laforgue, *Moralités Légendaires*, 173, where Laforgue writes the final reproof in a French to which Smith's translation is again close: "[Salome a] voulu vivre dans le factice et non à la bonne franquette, à l'instar de chacun de nous."

33. As punctuated in "An Anachronism at Chinon," *Little Review*, June 1917; *EPPP*, II:209.

34. "Aux Étuves de Weisbaden [*sic*] A.D. 1451," *Little Review*, July 1917; *EPPP*, II:224.

35. Pound disclaims "An Anachronism" thus in a letter to Margaret Anderson, editor of the *Little Review*, on 17 July 1917; in *Pound/ The Little Review: The Letters of Ezra Pound to Margaret Anderson: The Little Review Correspondence*, ed. Thomas L. Scott, Melvin J. Friedman, and Jackson R. Bryer (New York: New Directions, 1988), 93.

36. The identification of "philology" with the mind of *Kultur* and the German university system, in Pound's eyes with the dehumanization of learning, is developed with special virulence in "Provincialism the Enemy (I)," *New Age*, 12 July 1917; *EPPP*, II:232.

37. Letter of 28 December 1918, from London, in *Selected Letters of Ezra Pound to John Quinn*, 170.

38. Letter of 24 January 1931, from Rapallo, Italy, to the editor of the *English Journal*, in Pound, *Selected Letters*, 231. The correspondence emerges from a recent exchange with Harriet Monroe about the negative review the poem received in *Poetry* in 1919 by William Hale, who faulted Pound's "mistranslation."

39. These opening lines of the first poem in the sequence are taken from *Personae: The Shorter Poems of Ezra Pound* (1926; rev. ed., ed. Lea Baechler and A. Walton Litz [New York: New Directions, 1990]), 205, cited parenthetically hereafter as *P*. Various (numbered) sections of *Homage to Sextus Propertius* appeared in *Poetry*, March 1919, and *New Age*, 3 July 1919, 31 July 1919, 14 August 1919. Poems I, III, and VI, which appeared originally in *Poetry*, were reprinted in *New Age*, 19 June 1919, 17 July 1919, 28 August 1919. The poem (in twelve parts) was published in October in *Quia Pauper Amavi* (London: Egoist, 1919).

40. There is a steady tendency in the critical literature to read the poem as ahistorical, at least apolitical. Thus Stock, *Life of Ezra Pound*, 207, reads "a personal statement, by Pound's Propertius or by Pound, which places the joys and trials of female company and the inspirations to be derived from love, above imperial police-work." That the most provocative element in the poem is Pound's refusal to engage with the matter of current political fact is the assertion of Donald Davie, *Ezra Pound: Poet as Sculptor* (New York: Oxford University Press, 1964), 85: "For an expatriate American to tell London, after the Flanders trenches had endured three years of hideous futility, that the poet had the right and sometimes the duty to turn his back on all affairs of state and national destiny, in order to celebrate his love affairs with witty cynicism—this was a very perilous enterprise. And it was doubtless this (though also, one may suppose, common decency of feeling) that caused Pound not to print the sequence until the war was over." It is in the main the relation of Sextus Propertius to the culture of literary politics in Augustan Rome, not Pound's understanding of contemporary England at war, that

provides the focus for discussion about "political attitudes," in Sullivan, *Ezra Pound and Sextus Propertius*, 58–64, 75–76. The parody Sullivan attributes to Propertius's echoing of Virgil and Horace is repeated by Pound, Sullivan asserts, but only at the expense of Virgil and Horace (and the Augustan court), not in relation to any local political culture of Pound's own.

41. The texts of Propertius's Latin and the Loeb translation are provided by K. K. Ruthven, *A Guide to Ezra Pound's "Personae" 1926* (Berkeley: University of California Press, 1969), 102, 104; cited parenthetically hereafter as *GD*.

42. Published originally as "Dogmatic Statement concerning the Game of Chess: Theme for a Series of Pictures," *Poetry*, March 1915; as "Dogmatic Statement on the Game and Play of Chess (Theme for a Series of Pictures)," *Blast* 2 (War Number), July 1915; and in *Lustra* (1916) as "The Game of Chess: Dogmatic Statement concerning the Game of Chess." The relevant wording preserved in the title of each version is "dogmatic statement," the sense of which is not forgone in the texture of the poem. The argument lies in the vehement analogy that Pound draws between the lines of force on the chess board and those of the vortex; see *P*, 124.

43. This tradition finds a clear treatment in Marcia L. Colish, *The Mirror of Language: A Study in the Medieval Theory of Knowledge*, 2d ed. (Lincoln: University of Nebraska Press, 1983).

44. Pound provides major statements of these aims in "The New Sculpture," *Egoist*, 16 February 1914, *EPPP*, I:221–22; "Troubadours: Their Sorts and Conditions," *Quarterly Review*, October 1913, *EPPP*, I:165–79; and "Vers Libre and Arnold Dolmetsch," *Egoist*, July 1917, *EPPP*, II:222–23. Good discussions of literary vorticism come from Timothy Materer, *Vortex: Pound, Eliot, and Lewis* (Ithaca, N.Y.: Cornell University Press, 1979), and Reed Way Dasenbrock, *The Literary Vorticism of Ezra Pound & Wyndham Lewis: Towards the Condition of Painting* (Baltimore, Md.: Johns Hopkins University Press, 1985); and of the musical tradition from Stuart McDougal, *Ezra Pound and the Troubadour Tradition* (Princeton, N.J.: Princeton University Press, 1972), and Peter Makin, *Provence and Pound* (Berkeley: University of California Press, 1978). For an account of the rival values that the visual and aural dimensions of poetry acquire in Pound's early practice, see Vincent Sherry, *Ezra Pound, Wyndham Lewis, and Radical Modernism* (New York: Oxford University Press, 1993), 43–89.

45. Bush, *Genesis of Ezra Pound's "Cantos,"* 167ff., carefully dates the resumption of work on the earlier Cantos and relates it to the (ongoing) project of *Propertius* as well as to the growing influence of Remy de Gourmont, T. S. Eliot (*Prufrock and Other Observations* [1917]), and Jules Laforgue. Vincent E. Miller, "The Serious Wit of Pound's *Homage to Sextus Propertius*," *Contemporary Literature* 16 (1975): 452–62, follows a continuity between *Propertius* and the resumed (and revised) Cantos as a consonance, which involves similar attempts to relate and entwine the quotidian and trivial with the sublime and transcendent (Miller's main models are the Provençal troubadours and the Roman elegists). See also Hugh Kenner, *The Poetry of Ezra Pound* (Norfolk, Conn.: New Directions, 1951), 163, where the "shifts of texture and tone" that are "central to Pound's mature poetic practice" are derived mainly from the exercise in *Propertius*, 162–63. Here the irony of the modern poet commenting on the ancient text provides a lightening, distancing effect on the materia poetica.

46. Early ("ur-")versions of the first three Cantos appeared as "Three Cantos, I, II, III" in *Poetry*, June, July, August 1917. These texts are provided as appendix I, "Three Cantos 1917," to Pound, *Personae*; ur-Canto I, 231–32.

47. *The Cantos of Ezra Pound* (1970; rpt. New York: New Directions, 1986), 7. The opening lines of Canto II preserve those of "Three Cantos, I." This Canto II, which consists largely of material Pound wrote in May 1922 (numbered then as VIII, to be resequenced by 1925 as II), develops the form of the journey chronicle in "Three Cantos, I" into this fully dimensional mythos of the epic voyage. The passage I have quoted is discussed by Bush, *Genesis of Ezra Pound's "Cantos,"* 241ff., as an example of the dominant tone and style of the post-1922 Cantos.

48. "April," *Poetry*, November 1913, *P*, 92–93; "Gentildonna," *Poetry*, November 1913, *P*, 93; "The Encounter," *Smart Set*, December 1913, *P*, 113; "Liu Ch'e," *Des Imagistes* (New York: Albert and Charles Boni, [2 March] 1914), *P*, 110–11; "In a Station of the Metro," *Poetry*, April 1913, *P*, 111.

49. In "Vorticism," *Fortnightly Review*, 1 September 1914; *EPPP*, I:281.

50. "The Coming of War: Actaeon," *Poetry*, March 1915; *P*, 109–10. The poem is situated helpfully by James Longenbach, *Stone Cottage: Pound, Yeats, and Modernism* (New York: Oxford University Press, 1988), 123–25, as an observation of British troops holding maneuvers on the heath before Stone Cottage, in Sussex, where Pound was staying with Yeats.

51. In "Illustrations on Sublimity," for example, in *Dissertations Moral and Critical* (1783), James Beattie writes: "When Macbeth (in Shakespeare) goes to consult the witches, he finds them performing rites in a cave; and, upon asking what they were employed about, receives no other answer than this short one, '*A deed without a name.*' One's blood runs cold at the thought that their work was of so accursed a nature, that they themselves had no name to express it by, or were afraid to speak of it by any name. Here is no solemnity of style, nor any accumulation of great ideas; yet here is the true sublime; because here is something that astonishes the mind." The specifically rationalistic character of language, which it is the mark of the sublime to defy and exceed, is the substance of a subsequent point by Beattie: "It may now be remarked in general, that the sublime is often heightened, when, by means of figurative language, the qualities of a superior nature are judiciously applied to what is inferior. Hence we see in poetry, and in more familiar language, the passions and feelings of rationality ascribed to that which is without reason, and without life." Both passages quoted in *The Sublime: A Reader in British Eighteenth-Century Aesthetic Theory*, ed. Andrew Ashfield and Peter de Bolla (Cambridge: Cambridge University Press, 1996), 189, 191. Among its several uses, this collection gathers the evidence of a varying and wide-ranging discourse on the subject in the eighteenth century and, correcting the dominance of visual and pictorial elements in subsequent reconstructions, restores the importance of the rhetorical and linguistic dimension in the considerations of those first contributors, summarized thus in the introduction, 10–11: "Samuel Holt Monk's thesis [in *The Sublime: A Study of Critical Theories in Xviii-Century England* (Ann Arbor: University of Michigan Press, 1960)] distorts the eighteenth-century debate through its devaluation of rhetorically centered discussions of the sublime," which mark, in this recovery, "a departure from another

classical authority, Aristotle, whose analysis of catharsis is to a great extent supplanted in the eighteenth-century tradition by the turn towards Longinian sublimity."

52. "Jules Romains" appears as the final section of Pound's extensive review and sampler, "A Study in French Poets," *Little Review*, February 1918; *EPPP*, III:51. An overview of Romains's poetics and the relation of theory to practice may be found in P. J. Norrish, *Drama of the Group: A Study of Unanism in the Plays of Jules Romains* (Cambridge: Cambridge University Press, 1958), esp. "The Concept of Unanism," 3–22, which Norrish relates, 11, "quite as much to a social ideal, extending to a practical doctrine, as it is to pure theory," and which Norrish regards as being in place by 1911.

53. "[A Review of] *Odes et Prières*, par Jules Romains," *Poetry*, August 1913; *EPPP*, I:149.

54. In the opening words of "Vortex: Pound," *Blast* I, *EPPP*, I:259, Pound writes: "The Vortex is the point of maximum energy." His concentration on the apex or focal point of the vortex equates associatively with the figure of the single, individual artistic intelligence. Thus in "Wyndham Lewis," *Egoist*, 15 June 1914, *EPPP*, I:251, he appreciates the designs of "Timon" as the "sullen fury of intelligence baffled, shut in by the entrenched forces of stupidity" (a phrase he varies through this period). Thus in February 1918, in "Jules Romains," *EPPP*, III:50: "[V]orticism is, in the realm of biology, the hypothesis of the dominant cell."

55. The first three prose fables appear in the *Little Review* in May, June, and July 1917, and the fourth in July 1918; Eliot's French exercises, discussed in chapter 3 as the extension of the same sensibility, appear in July 1917; Eliot's major extensions of this initiative lie in his quatrain poems, three of which ("Sweeney among the Nightingales," "Whispers of Immortality," and "Mr. Eliot's Sunday Morning Service") appear in September 1918.

56. Letter of 29 May 1917, from London, in Pound, *Selected Letters*, 112.

57. A good discussion of this development is provided by Stephen Kern, *The Culture of Time and Space 1880–1914* (Cambridge, Mass.: Harvard University Press, 1983), "The Cubist War," 303. Kern indicates as well the official status of camouflage units and their association with well-known artists: "By the end of the war camouflage sections employed three thousand *camoufleurs* (including such prominent artists as Forain and Segonzac) to dissimulate the big guns and other conspicuous objects. Their insignia was a chameleon."

58. "'Dubliners' and Mr. James Joyce," *Egoist*, 15 July 1914; *EPPP*, I:264.

59. A superb presentation of this situation is provided by Kern, "Temporality of the July Crisis," in his *Culture of Time and Space*, 259–86, which conveys the sense of unprecedented urgency that the new communications technology injected into the more decorous pace of older diplomacy. The ultimata and deadlines that issued from the various capitals were the result, Kern plausibly suggests, of the escalation that was brought about by the telegraph and the telephone.

60. "The Glamour of G. S. Street," *Egoist*, 1 August 1914; *EPPP*, I:272. The writing character of Street may be fairly sampled by the title, *Books and Things: A Collection of Stray Remarks* (London: Duckworth, 1905); the pieces collected here certainly show the spacious ease, elegant or not, that Pound discerns in Street.

61. "Affirmations (II): Vorticism," *New Age*, 14 January 1915; *EPPP*, II:4.

62. David Weir, *Decadence and the Making of Modernism* (Amherst: University of Massachusetts Press, 1995), "The Definition of Decadence," 1–21. The "making" of "modernism" locates Weir's content and aim, insofar as his main focus falls on mid–late nineteenth-century literary culture.

63. Cassandra Laity, *H. D. and the Victorian Fin de Siècle: Gender, Modernism, Decadence* (Cambridge: Cambridge University Press, 1996), "The Rhetoric of Anti-Romanticism: Gendered Genealogies of Male Modernism," 1–28. To the tendencies set out in this consideration, Laity follows H. D.'s development, in subsequent chapters, as response and reorientation.

64. "The Renaissance (III)," *Poetry*, May 1915; *EPPP*, II:84–85.

65. "Mr. Yeats' New Book [*Responsibilities and Other Poems*]," *Poetry*, December 1916; *EPPP*, II:185. The Yeats-Pound exchange on the 1890s between 1913 and 1916 is followed by Longenbach, "Tragic Generations," in *Stone Cottage*, 156–76, esp. 165–66.

66. Letter to Eliot's mother from Vivien Eliot, 30 April 1917, in *The Letters of T. S. Eliot*, vol. 1, *1898–1922*, ed. Valerie Eliot (London: Faber, 1988), 178: "Only when he began to be more bright and happy and boyish than I've known him to be for nearly two years, did *I* feel convinced—and only when he has written *five*, most *excellent* poems in the course of one week, did Ezra Pound and many others believe it possible."

67. "Drunken Helots and Mr. Eliot," *Egoist*, June 1917; *EPPP*, II:206–7.

68. Letter of 3 May 1916, from London, in *Pound/Lewis: The Letters of Ezra Pound and Wyndham Lewis*, ed. Timothy Materer (New York: New Directions, 1985), 35. Letters of 1 June 1916 and 29 February 1916, from London, in *Selected Letters of Ezra Pound to John Quinn*, 75, 64.

69. The prevalence of this conception of death-in-birth might be measured by the prominence given it in a near-contemporary account by Holbrook Jackson, *The Eighteen-Nineties: A Review of Art and Ideas at the Close of the Nineteenth Century* (1913; rpt. Atlantic Highlands, N.J.: Humanities Press, 1976). While the end of the century weighs on the mind like a memento mori, in Jackson's picture, these same years also stimulate feverish activity. The contrary signs of the time are the autumnal flourish, the hectic red of imminent death. The approaching end has force-ripened these youthful careers, bringing them to an early perfection—pristine but exhausted, already consumed at the moment of its first flush. The paradox finds its signature image in Aubrey Beardsley, whose surplus of boyish energy seemed to hasten his death. He appears thus in the first paragraph of Jackson's book, already making real the conceit Jackson will repeat frequently. "The Eighteen-Nineties were at their meridian," Jackson opens, "but it was already the afternoon of the Beardsley period"—an age that ended as it began, he continues, "in the evening of its brief day," 17. It is 1895; Oscar Wilde, who has just reached his zenith with the production of *The Importance of Being Earnest*, falls in disgrace. Through this most conspicuous and public example, 79–90, Jackson brings the decade to early termination at its apex; the fin de siècle collapses at its center, its summit. See esp. 89: "Dandy of intellect, dandy of manners, dandy of dress, Oscar Wilde strutted through the first half of the Nineties and staggered through the last." For repetition of the death-in-birth theme, see, for example, 18: "a quickening of life in the last years" and "a compound of feverish restlessness and blunted discouragement"; the conceit is

applied with special frequency to Beardsley, 95–96. The same theme recurs in Yeats's depictions of Ernest Dowson and Aubrey Beardsley, in "The Tragic Generation," in Yeats, *Autobiographies*, 2d ed. (1955; rpt. London: Macmillan, 1970), 303, 330.

70. In the early printings of the poem, the age that Pound attributes to his poetic character follows the numerical adjective of the French (but not the exact phrasing) in Villon's original verse: *Dial*, September 1920, *EPPP*, IV:88; and *Poems 1918–21* (New York: Boni and Liveright, 1921), 53. Cf. "En l'an de mon trentiesme aage," *Le Testament*, in *The Poems of François Villon*, trans. Galway Kinnell (Boston: Houghton Mifflin, 1977), 26. Pound's alteration in subsequent editions is referenced below, n. 72.

71. The opening of the poem is translated thus by Kinnell, *Poems of François Villon*, 27: "In my thirtieth year of life / When I had drunk down all my disgrace / Neither altogether a fool nor altogether wise / Despite the many blows." These concessions build the strength of a vigorous resistance to adverse circumstances.

72. The correction Pound performed on the French numbering in later editions of this poem—*"l'an trentuniesme de son eage"* (*P*, 185)—reminds us that one is in the thirty-*first* year of one's life, when one is thirty. Pound's alteration is made in his revision to *Personae* (1926), in *Diptych Rome-London* (1958; cited in *GD*, 30, 129), and preserved in subsequent editions by Faber and New Directions.

73. See the influential instance of Davie, *Poet as Sculptor*, 91–101, who regards the sequence mainly as a series of masks, styles, and metrical and stanzaic exercises, and concludes, 100–101: "[I]n *Hugh Selwyn Mauberley* we look in vain for the developing 'plot' that commentators of all persuasions (including the present writer) have thought they found. Such 'plots' can indeed be found—all too many of them. The trouble is that any one of them requires that we give Pound the benefit of every doubt, on the score of elusive shifts of tone, a raised eyebrow here, a half-smile somewhere else, a momentary puckering of the brow." Davie's rejection of "plot" elements in the sequence represents a response to sometimes strenuous attempts to serialize and thematize the movement through the successive poems; see, for example, the attempt by John J. Espey, *Ezra Pound's "Mauberley": A Study in Composition* (Berkeley: University of California Press, 1955), 15–16, who concedes, at the end, that the effort appears "thoroughly arbitrary and dogmatic." If not a linear narrative of point-for-point biographical reference, the poem may be read better as reminiscence and memoir, and, in line with the general recommendation of Kenner, *The Pound Era* (1971; rpt. Berkeley: University of California Press, 1974), 287, as "an elegy to the Vortex"—but in a reading that attends to the complexities that Pound's own development since 1914 enjoined on his perspective. The interpretive element in Pound's retrospect also lends a special significance to the sequencing of the separate poems, e.g., the relation of the war lyrics (IV and V) to the preceding and subsequent narratives, which is discussed later in this chapter.

74. *Cathay: Translations by Ezra Pound* (London: Elkin Matthews, 1915). The setting of several of these poems at the outposts of military empire, e.g., "Song of the Bowmen at Shu" (*P*, 131) and "Lament of the Frontier Guard" (*P*, 136–37), suggests a connection to Pound's historical present. For a consideration of the bearing of the war on "South-folk in Cold Country" (*P*, 143), see Longenbach, *Stone Cottage*, 115–16. See also Kenner, *Pound Era*, 356, who reads *Cathay* as "[a]n effort in arraying items to make a tacit statement"; for Kenner, this is "a book about the War which employs remote Chi-

nese wars as reflectors, and places at the beginning, middle and end three war poems about remote privations, war poems, moreover, of graduated starkness." The imagist aesthetic that the poems of *Cathay* display turns thus to the more direct representation of war in the two lyrics in *Mauberley*.

75. Robert Buchanan, *The Fleshly School of Poetry and Other Phenomena of the Day* (London: Strahan, 1872); the most extended consideration is in his central chapter, "Mr. Dante Gabriel Rossetti," 33–55.

76. "Jenny," in Dante Gabriel Rossetti, *Poems and Translations, 1850–1870* (1913; rpt. London: Oxford University Press, 1936), 62ff.

77. The argument is made for its triumphant *singability*, most of all, by Espey, *Ezra Pound's "Mauberley,"* 98: "[L]eaving the careful quatrains, *Pound now sings* his own farewell in a song based on Waller's *Go, Lovely Rose*, which was set to music by Henry Lawes. The *poem sounds throughout* the suggestion of active passion as earnest against the destruction of Time. The *echoes* of the long line of English poets from Chaucer down are so varied and interwoven as to make a complete unraveling almost impossible, but the *ironic triumph of this lyric in answer to the critical dismissal of Pound in the Ode* is, for the balance of the entire suite, its most important function" (emphases added).

Interchapter 2

1. A comprehensive account of these years and James's influence comes from James R. Mellow, *Charmed Circle: Gertrude Stein & Company* (New York: Praeger, 1974), 31–41, esp. 32–33. Although James's *Pragmatism* would not be published until 1907, Mellow sets out some evidence for the presence of the main attitudes of philosophical pragmatism in the earlier years in Cambridge, 38. The various ideas of American pragmatism, and the diverse expression this developing tradition finds in modernist literature, provide the comprehensive scope of David Kadlec's *Mosaic Modernism: Anarchism, Pragmatism, and Culture* (Baltimore, Md.: Johns Hopkins University Press, 2000).

2. The trip to England and the time in Lockeridge are recounted by Stein, *The Autobiography of Alice B. Toklas* (1933; rpt. New York: Vintage, 1960), 144–55. See also Janet Hobhouse, *Everybody Who Was Anybody: A Biography of Gertrude Stein* (New York: Putnam, 1975), 103–4, and Mellow, *Charmed Circle*, 210–15.

3. Stein, *Autobiography*, 147.

4. An extensive consideration of Russell's developing reaction to the outbreak of war, his sense of disillusionment with the Liberal party and its supposed commitment to the principles of right reason, and his subsequent interactions with the academic liberalism of Cambridge, are provided in the biography (the first of two projected volumes) by Ray Monk, *Bertrand Russell: The Spirit of Solitude* [1872–1921] (London: Cape, 1996), "Against the Multitude," 367–402, esp. 367–70, 383–86. Of particular interest is Monk's investigation into the professional as well as personal relationships between Russell and Irene Cooper Willis, 387–93, which drew her into research work for Russell's antiwar writing and laid the groundwork for her own book, *How We Went into the War: A Study of Liberal Idealism* (Manchester, England: National Labour Press, 1918), "which, in some ways, adheres more closely to Russell's initial intention of analysing and charting the way in which traditional liberalism was subverted and betrayed by the Lib-

eral government that was elected in 1906 among so much hope and idealism," 393. While the conflict between Lytton Strachey and the Liberal government is usually remembered for the sly allusions he made to his homosexuality before the Hampstead Tribunal, during the hearing of his plea for conscientious objector status, his early and ongoing engagement with the political questions and rationales for the war is indicated in an earlier statement, which is quoted by Michael Holroyd, *Lytton Strachey: The New Biography* (New York: Farrar, Straus and Giroux, 1995), 340: "My opinions have been for many years strongly critical of the whole structure of society; and after a study of the diplomatic situation, and of the literature, both controversial and philosophic, arising out of the war, they developed naturally into those I now hold. My convictions as to my duty with regard to the war have not been formed either rashly or lightly; and I shall not act against these convictions whatever the consequences may be."

5. Stein, *Picasso* (1938), in *Gertrude Stein on Picasso*, ed. Edward Burns (New York: Liveright, 1970), 46.

6. Stein, "In One," in *Bee Time Vine and Other Pieces* [1913–1927], vol. 3 of the Yale edition of the *Unpublished Writings of Gertrude Stein*, ed. Carl Van Vechten et al. (New Haven, Conn.: Yale University Press, 1953), 177. Virgil Thomson, in his commentary, 177, situates "In One" with the other writing that Stein undertook during her stay in England.

7. Thomson, in Stein, *Bee Time Vine*, 177, also characterizes it as "the abstraction of an explanation."

8. The judgment is applied by Thomson to a related set of contemporaneous works, in ibid., 179, which he represents as "abstractions again [see n. 7], hermetic works to which I have no key."

9. Stein, "Painted Lace," in *Painted Lace and Other Pieces* [1914–1937], vol. 5 of the Yale edition of the *Unpublished Writings of Gertrude Stein*, ed. Carl Van Vechten et al. (New Haven, Conn.: Yale University Press, 1955), 2. A set of contemporary references in this piece seems clearly to invoke the events of the early days of the war, in a specifically English setting, e.g., 1: "[W]e neither of us have a long journey on the other side of London. . . . Other trains are sometimes added but that does not affect the principal trains that always run. I think so. What will become of us, asked the Czar."

10. "Painted Lace," 1–2.

11. "Accents in Alsace: A Reasonable Tragedy" appeared first in *Geography and Plays* (Boston: Four Seas Company, 1922), and is reprinted in *A Stein Reader*, ed. Ulla E. Dydo (Evanston, Ill.: Northwestern University Press, 1993), 317. The circumstances of its composition in the spring of 1919 are set out by Mellow, *Charmed Circle*, 236.

12. Stein, *Tender Buttons* (1914; rpt. Los Angeles: Sun & Moon Press, 1991), 41; a chronology of composition and publication is provided by Mellow, *Charmed Circle*, 176–78.

Chapter 3

1. Eliot's knowledge of the first several volumes of Frazer's *The Golden Bough* (the third edition appeared in London beginning in 1911) is documented by John B. Vickery, *The Literary Impact of the Golden Bough* (1973; rpt. Princeton, N.J.: Princeton Univer-

sity Press, 1976), 233–34, who also suggests Frazer's bearing on the title and motive theme of *The Sacred Wood*. Vickery proposes, 234, that Eliot positions himself in the role and attitude of the "warrior-priest, who defends [the] honor and sanctity [of the sacred goddess of poetry], and whose function is to prevent inferior poetry and criticism alike from usurping unworthily the role of deity or of priest and attendant." This situation takes as given the mastery or established authority that is at stake in the drama of succession that Eliot stages through the title. This struggle features him, all things considered, more as "usurper" or challenger than "defender."

2. "Sweeney among the Nightingales" appeared first in *Little Review*, September 1918, then as the first poem in *Poems* (Richmond, England: Hogarth, 1919); and in *Collected Poems 1909–1962* (1963; rpt. London: Faber, 1974), 60. Closer work with the various drafts of the poem and the editorial collaboration with Pound will be referenced to the texts cited later.

3. The two parts of the essay were published first in *Athenaeum*, 9 July and 23 July 1920; *The Sacred Wood*, 2d ed. (1928; rpt. London: Methuen, 1953), 1–2. The established character of the opinion that Eliot is addressing and contesting is described as "the ratiocinative, Christianized Aristotle of neoclassicism" by David Goldie, *A Critical Difference: T. S. Eliot and John Middleton Murry in English Literary Criticism, 1919–1928* (Oxford: Clarendon, 1998), 62. Goldie traces this "neoclassical" attitude in its current expression to Murry, for whose *Athenaeum* Eliot wrote many of the essays collected in *The Sacred Wood*, and more distantly to Irving Babbitt, whom Eliot had encountered at Harvard.

4. "The Perfect Critic," *Sacred Wood*, 8–9. One instance in which Eliot indicates some affinity with *political* Liberalism comes in a letter of 28 September 1919 to John Quinn, in *The Letters of T. S. Eliot*, vol. 1, *1898–1922*, ed. Valerie Eliot (London: Faber, 1988), 336: "My own views are Liberal and opposed to the Government in almost everything; but I cannot regard this present expression of Labour discontent [the railway strike of 26 September–5 October] without grave apprehension and distrust." The alliance is obviously provisional, however, and is struck to oppose initiatives undertaken from what may be understood as a more radical flank of Liberalism.

5. "Imperfect Critics" gathers "Swinburne and the Elizabethans" (*Athenaeum*, 19 September 1919) as "Swinburne as Critic," "A Romantic Patrician" (*Athenaeum*, 2 May 1919) as "A Romantic Aristocrat," and "The Local Flavour" (*Athenaeum*, 12 December 1919), and adds "A Note on the American Critic" (on Paul More and Irving Babbitt) and "The French Intelligence"; the quotation is taken from "A Note on the American Critic," *Sacred Wood*, 44.

6. "'Tarr,'" *Egoist*, September 1918, 106.

7. "Contemporanea," *Egoist*, June–July 1918, 84.

8. Edgar Rice Burroughs, *Tarzan of the Apes* (New York: Burt, 1914), the first number of a multiple sequel. Any relevance of this echo for Lewis would require a late date for his naming of the title character. See n. 9.

9. The long process of composition is followed from Lewis's correspondence, internal evidence, and fictional references to biographical events, by Paul O'Keefe, ed., *Tarr: The 1918 Version* (Santa Rosa, Calif.: Black Sparrow, 1990), 361–65. In a preface written in October 1915, Lewis disclaims any connection between the current war and

his presentation of the German character, but generates a lengthy diatribe against German *Kultur*, 13. While the war exerts an arguably negligible bearing on the text of the novel, the current situation is certainly relevant to its critical reception by Eliot and others.

10. Letter of 11 July 1919, from London, *Letters of T. S. Eliot*, vol. 1, *1898–1922*, ed. Valerie Eliot, 318.

11. The milieu of Garsington and its importance for Eliot are conveyed by Peter Ackroyd, *T. S. Eliot: A Life* (New York: Simon and Schuster, 1984), 73, 88. The difficulty that Eliot experienced in his wished-for acceptance at Garsington is recounted by Lyndall Gordon, *Eliot's Early Years* (Oxford: Oxford University Press, 1977), 83.

12. Letter of 23 June 1919, from London, *Letters of T. S. Eliot*, ed. Valerie Eliot, 307.

13. Eliot's interest in the position had evidently been advanced by Graham Wallas, a Fabian and professor of political science at London University. Eliot writes to Wallas to express his disappointment in not getting the post, on 23 March 1917, in *Letters of T. S. Eliot*, ed. Valerie Eliot, 167. On 7 June 1916 Eliot writes to Bertrand Russell about his unsolicited submission to the *New Statesman*, ibid., 142; by 21 August 1916, in correspondence with Conrad Aiken, he summarizes the results of his efforts to make his way in London literary journalism, in a round-up of leading dailies and weeklies that are marked by their affiliations with Liberalism, ibid., 143: "The school takes up most of my days, and in my spare (sic) time I have been writing philosophy for the *Monist* and the *International Journal of Ethics*, reviews for the *New Statesman*, the *Manchester Guardian* and the *Westminster Gazette*. The first two I got in through Bertrand Russell, the others through a man named Sydney Waterlow. I am now trying to get an introduction to the *Nation*."

14. Ibid., 307.

15. Thus Eliot's request for a renewed invitation also asks, ibid.: "I wish Mrs. Woolf could be there too: I have not seen her for a long time." For the reconfiguration of Lady Ottoline as Hermione Roddice and the representation of the Garsington milieu, see D. H. Lawrence, *Women in Love* (1920, 1922; rpt. New York: Viking, 1969), esp. "Breadalby," 74–102.

16. *Sacred Wood*, 25–27.

17. Letter of 31 October 1917, from London, in *Letters of T. S. Eliot*, 205.

18. Ibid., 392.

19. "Preludes" and "Rhapsody of a Windy Night" were first published in *Blast 2* (War Number), July 1915, 48–51. The circumstances are recounted by Materer, *Vortex: Pound, Eliot, and Lewis* (Ithaca, N.Y.: Cornell University Press, 1979), 26–27, who also concludes, 28, that "T. S. Eliot was never a Vorticist in the sense of a modern who accepts the machine age and the 'new multiverse of forces,'" and he points out, 29, that "Eliot joined the Vorticists as the movement was being engulfed by World War I."

20. "Ben Jonson," (London) *Times Literary Supplement*, 13 November 1919; *Sacred Wood*, 105.

21. "Ben Jonson," *Sacred Wood*, 105–6.

22. Ibid., 108–9.

23. Ibid., 116–17.

24. Ibid., 117–18.

25. As emphasized by Eliot, *Letters of T. S. Eliot*, 54. These sentences come at the end of a very long letter, the manuscript of which is still incomplete. It recounts the circumstances of Eliot's departure from Germany (on 3 August) and arrival, via Rotterdam, in London, 51–54.

26. Ibid., 57–58.

27. Letter of 7 or 8 September 1914, ibid., 55. Again, 55: "I find it quite possible to work in this atmosphere."

28. Ibid., 56. Eliot's defense of the German incursion into Belgium echoes the reasoning of 3 and 4 August in the *Manchester Guardian*, among other papers allied with political Liberalism, although he probably picked up the phrases during his time in Germany. In Eliot's notation, this militarization of German civilization into a Prussianized *kultur* of "officers," and a similar regimentation of intellectual life by their "professors," follows the reversal of fellow-feeling currently under way in English Liberal attitudes toward Germany.

29. Letter from Merton College (Oxford), ibid., 93–94.

30. Letter of "21 Mars," from London, ibid., 92.

31. Letter to Norbert Wiener of 6 January 1915, from London, ibid., 80.

32. Letter to his mother of 11 April 1917, from London, ibid., 175: "Then too I have felt more creative lately. . . . I have been doing some writing—mostly in French, curiously enough it has taken me that way—and some poems in French which will come out in the *Little Review* in Chicago." The drought that these exercises have broken is described in his letters of 21 August 1916 to Conrad Aiken, ibid., 144, and 7 June 1916 to Harriet Monroe, ibid., 141, and of Vivien Eliot to Henry Ware Eliot, on 11 October 1916, ibid., 156.

33. Ibid., 145–46. While Eliot may have undertaken the assigned exercise in translating Laforgue's "Hamlet," the paragraph he adds at the end of this letter seems to indicate further work on Laforgue, insofar as the scene of exotic rites represents a reflection not of "Hamlet" but of "Salome," to which his attention would have been drawn already by Pound's work on this Lafourgian source in "Our Tetrarchal Précieuse (A Divagation from Jules Laforgue)," which, as discussed in chapter 2, was completed some time before its appearance in *Little Review*, July 1918; *EPPP*, III:126–31. Cf. "Salome," in Jules Laforgue, *Moralités Légendaires* (Paris: Mercure de France, 1925), 137–75, and Jules Laforgue, *Moral Tales*, trans. William Jay Smith (New York: New Directions, 1985), 87–109.

34. In *Inventions of the March Hare: Poems 1909–1917*, ed. Christopher Ricks (New York: Harcourt Brace, 1996), 86. The translations of Eliot's French are my own, in collaboration with Sophia Sherry. "Inventions of the March Hare" is the title Eliot affixed to the notebook that provides Ricks's source for the earlier verse; the manuscripts of two poems that Eliot left unpublished, "Petit Epître" and "Airs of Palestine, No. 2," are included in the notebook. Much of the poetry that Eliot wrote between 1917 and 1919, in various drafts and with extensive editorial commentary, is also included in this volume (mainly in appendix C), which will be cited parenthetically in the text as *IN*. "Appendix C gives the text—as it first stood in the loose leaves—of the poems in *Poems* (The Hogarth Press, 1919), *Ara Vos Prec* (The Ovid Press, 1920), and *Poems* (Alfred A. Knopf, 1920)," *IN*, xxi. Not all poems in those col-

lections (e.g., "Le Directeur") exist in typescripts, but, when available, these loose leaves provide original or early versions, in relation to which Eliot's (and Pound's) subsequent alterations in manuscript and published form may be identified and assessed. These various versions may also show more comprehensively the range and verve of experimentation that Eliot was undertaking; material that will be reworked or excised in later drafts or in published form is as significant and revealing as the final product.

35. Published originally in *Little Review*, July 1917 (with "Mélange Adultère de Tout," "Lune de Miel," and "The Hippopotamus"), then in *Poems* (1919), *Ara Vos Prec* (1920), and *Poems* (1920) as "Le spectateur"; the title was restored to "Le Directeur" in *Collected Poems 1909–1962*, 48, which provides this text.

36. The illustration, "Passed the Test: A Fragment," is reproduced from *London Censorship 1914–1919* (London: Dept. of Postal Censor, 1919), 32. This book, a collection authored by "Members of the Staff, Past and Present," is marked, 4, "For Private Circulation." This set of jocoserious reminiscences includes poems, personal memoirs, and commentary by the staff, variously named and initialed.

37. Letter of 24 March 1918, from London, in *Letters of T. S. Eliot*, 225.

38. Letter of 21 March 1917, from London, ibid., 165.

39. "Lune de Miel," *IN*, 362; following the *Little Review* publication, the poem appears in the three volumes of 1919–20, which do not vary (except in the addition of accents) from this version.

40. Eliot recalls the moment in his interview with Donald Hall, *Paris Review* (1959), reprinted in Donald Hall, *Their Ancient Glittering Eyes: Remembering Poets and More Poets* (New York: Ticknor & Fields, 1992), 265: "[T]he suggestion of writing quatrains was [Pound's]. He put me on to *Émaux et Camées*. . . . We studied Gautier's poems and then we thought, 'Have I anything to say in which this form will be useful?' And we experimented. The form gave the impetus to the content." The bearing of Gautier's art on Eliot's quatrains may be further observed insofar as the first published, "The Hippopotamus" (*Little Review*, July 1917), echoes in title (if not in wording) Gautier's "L'Hippopotame," which Pound had singled out earlier as exemplary (in a letter to Iris Barry of 27 July 1916, in *Selected Letters of Ezra Pound, 1907–41*, ed. D. D. Paige [1950; rpt. New York: New Directions, 1971], 89). The emphasis Pound places on the expectation of "plain statements" (ibid.) in Gautier's quatrains represents the same capacity for rational straightforwardness that Eliot manipulates in his poems.

41. "Airs of Palestine, No. 2," *IN*, 84–85; the typescript of the poem ("miscellaneous leaves" in the notebook) is marked variously by Pound, with two quatrains bracketed (for excision) and alternative wording suggested for the final two lines. There is a "tightening" aim that would align the final product more identifiably with the Gautier model. The dating that Ricks provides as a chronology of composition, *IN*, xli, places this poem after "The Hippopotamus," roughly in the summer of 1917; for circumstances explaining this placement, as well as the allusion in the title to John Pierpoint's high-minded *Airs of Palestine* (1816, 1840), see *IN*, 283.

42. *IN*, 358; the poem, untitled in typescript, is published as "A Cooking Egg" in *Coterie* (May Day 1919), as in *Ara Vos Prec* (1920) and *Poems* (1920). The last line of the stanza reads as "In a five per cent Exchequer Bond" by the time of the first appearance

in print, and the lowercase formation in the first half of the line is preserved through subsequent printings. The signal capitalization—"Capital"—is preserved.

43. A good account of these circumstances is provided by Tim Redman, *Ezra Pound and Italian Fascism* (New York: Cambridge University Press, 1991), 37–38, 41–42, 52, where he draws the English backgrounds to Pound's later economic theories. Eliot joined the Colonial and Foreign Department at Lloyd's Bank on 19 March 1917, virtually simultaneously with his return to writing verse. See the letter of 21 March to his mother, in *Letters of T. S. Eliot*, 163–64, and the account by Ackroyd, *Life*, 77–78.

44. The first two of these stanzas are deleted in blue crayon in the working (carbon) copy of the poem, an excision recommended (seconded?) by Pound, *IN*, 359. Subsequent printings of the poem include a row of asterisks as the record of that deletion. The nonsense logic that is the conceit of these verses was probably felt to be too strongly concentrated here.

45. In *Coterie* as well as in *Ara Vos Prec* and *Poems* (1920), "Where are the eagles and the trumpets?" is separated into a single line to leave a four-line finale; the rhyme of "trumpets" and "crumpets," however, signals its relation to the closural movement of the poem.

46. These titles are suggested by Pound in version "A-B" (typescript and carbon), *IN*, 366. This version provides my main text.

47. "Try This on Your Piano[:] Whispers of Immortality" is provided for version "D-E" (typescript and carbon), *IN*, 370.

48. By version "G-H" (typescript and carbon), *IN*, 373, "abstracter" has given way (after a deletion in "D-E" [*IN*, 370] and a restoration in "F" [*IN*, 372]) to the more normative "And even the Abstract Entities," which is retained in *Poems* (1920) and in *Collected Poems 1909–1962*, 56. The capitalization represents nonetheless a rhetorical rather than a standard practice. It suggests a mock-ponderous quality reminiscent still of the original motive and wit in "abstracter," which is preserved in any case in the initial publications in *Little Review* and *Poems* (1919).

49. The preponderance of words with visible Latin origins in the following passage is representative of Walter Pater, *Marius the Epicurean: His Sensations and Ideas* (1885; rpt. London: Macmillan, 1910), 1:27: "The religion of Aesculapius, though borrowed from Greece, had been naturalised in Rome in the old republican times, but had reached under the Antonines the height of its popularity throughout the Roman world. That was an age of valetudinarians, in many instances of imaginary ones; but below its various crazes concerning health and disease, largely multiplied a few years after the time of which I am speaking by the miseries of a great pestilence, lay a valuable, because partly practicable, belief that all the maladies of the soul might be reached through the gateways of the body." The complication of Pater's syntax serves at once to replicate the hypotaxis characteristic of Latin texts and to suggest a performative quality, a moderately comic or subironic motive, in this modern version. The rhythm and diction of Swinburne witness a similar incentive and capacity. The heavy repetition of rhymes and homophones clogs in the inner ear, and the hypnotic cadences coalesce to suggest the presence of some antiquated text of unpronounceable phonetics. "Doing antique" entails nonetheless the sort of linguistic ingenuity and verve that injects the performance with considerable élan. See, for example, "The Tale of Balin," in *The Complete Works of Al-*

gernon Charles Swinburne, ed. Sir Edmund Gosse and Thomas James Wise (1925; rpt. New York: Russell and Russell, 1968), 4:196: "As thought from thought takes wing and flies, / As mouth on mouth from sunlit eyes / Tramples and triumphs in its rise, / And wave smites wave to death and dies."

50. Linda Dowling, *Language and Decadence in the Victorian Fin de Siècle* (1986; rpt. Princeton, N.J.: Princeton University Press, 1989), esp. "The Decay of Literature," 46–103, and "The Fatal Book," 104–74.

51. This tradition is followed in its fully complex development by Dowling, *Language and Decadence*, in "Romantic Philology and Victorian Civilization," 3–45, esp. 31, 34, 43.

52. The nationalist dimensions of the *Oxford English Dictionary* (known until 1933 as *A New English Dictionary*) are discussed by Dowling, ibid., 42–43, who also, 58, identifies the origins of this project in "German works of scientific etymology" and "German scientific philology." The nationalist themes in the undertaking are clarified further by John Willinsky, *Empire of Words: The Reign of the OED* (Princeton, N.J.: Princeton University Press, 1994), 54–55.

53. See, for chief instance, Eliot's January 1920 essay, "Swinburne as Poet," *Sacred Wood*, 144–50. Eliot focuses the theme of decadence most urgently in his concern over "morbidity," 149. The "morbidity is not of human feeling," he discerns, "but of language. Language in a healthy state presents the object, is so close to the object that the two are identified." Instead, "[language and the object] are identified in the verse of Swinburne solely because the object has ceased to exist, because the meaning is merely the hallucination of meaning, because language, uprooted, has adapted itself to an independent life of atmospheric nourishment." Nonetheless, 150: "Only a man of genius could dwell so exclusively and consistently among words as Swinburne. His language is not, like the language of bad poetry, dead. It is very much alive, with this singular life of its own." This paradox of vital or nervy morbidity goes to the main conceit of the poetics of decadence and represents a complex to which Eliot remains ambivalent, much like Pound, insofar as the quality of opacity in the dead language presents a departure from a standard of directness, immediacy, or clarity, which Eliot also associates with some earlier (ur-)modernism, 150: "But the language which is most important to us is that which is struggling to digest and express new objects, new groups of objects, new feelings, new aspects, as, for instance, the prose of Mr. James Joyce or the *earlier* Conrad" (emphasis added). The antithetical conjunction that begins this final sentence in the essay suggests that the last statement bears out no principle maintained singly or consistently through the essay. Additionally, Swinburne interests Eliot with his special capacity for logical nonsense. For instance, in citing a poetic chorus, 148, Eliot notes a statement that is "sententious, but it has not even the significance of commonplace. . . . [I]t is effective because it appears to be a tremendous statement, like statements made in our dreams." This quasi-sensible aspect matches the action outlined in Richards's formula of pseudostatement and represents a developmental complexity in the "simpler" poetics of an earlier modernism, to which Eliot, no less than Pound, remains connected.

54. The original typescript (with comments and suggestions for revision by Pound) provides this version, *IN*, 377.

55. Matthew Arnold, *Culture and Anarchy*, ed. J. Dover Wilson (1932; rpt. Cambridge: Cambridge University Press, 1969), 191. The quasi-religious fiction in Eliot's quatrains also shows some connections with Buchanan's usage, as criticized by Arnold.

56. See *IN*, 378. These alterations appear from the first publication in *Little Review*.

57. From the original typescript, *IN*, 355.

58. The conventions of American (New England) representations of the Irish with which Eliot was familiar from his earlier years are rehearsed by Jonathan Morse, "Sweeney, the Sties of the Irish, and *The Waste Land*," in *Critical Essays on T. S. Eliot: The Sweeney Motif*, ed. Kinley E. Roby (Boston: Hall, 1985), 137–40, but are framed as a backdrop to the depiction of Sweeney in *The Waste Land* only. The Irish element in the 1919 poem is mentioned but unfocused thematically by Herbert Knust, "Sweeney among the Birds and Brutes," *Arcadia* (1967), reprinted in *Critical Essays*, ed. Roby, 196–206, where the attention goes mainly to legend, including the story of the Irish king Sweeney, 200; the king's imitation of bird song is recalled, but the mimicry motif is unfocused in this essay. Anti-Semitism centers the attentions of Christopher Ricks, *T. S. Eliot and Prejudice* (Berkeley: University of California Press, 1988).

59. "Gerontion," *IN*, 349 (for textual questions, see n. 79).

60. The text is drawn from the first ("A") of two extant and (slightly) differing carbon typescripts of original typescripts, *IN*, 380. Pound's commentary occurs on both carbon typescripts ("A," "B").

61. The epigraph appears in the initial publication in *Little Review* and subsequently. Additionally, in *Poems* (1919) and *Ara Vos Prec*, there is a second epigraph, from the anonymous Elizabethan play *The Raigne of King Edward the Third*: "Why should I speak of the nightingale? The nightingale sings of adulterate wrong." The relation of this second epigraph to Eliot's knowledge of Vivien's affair with Bertrand Russell is discussed by Ronald Schuchard, *Eliot's Dark Angel: Intersections of Life and Art* (New York: Oxford University Press, 1999), 94. Eliot's relation to Russell, in view particularly of his knowledge of the affair, is recounted well by Schuchard in "The Savage Comedian," 87–101, esp. 91, where Schuchard provides dates for the duration of the affair (1916–19) and for Eliot's awareness of it (December 1917); see also 92ff., where Schuchard interprets the sexual degeneracy of the "Sweeney" poems as the expression of a vindictive poetics. In "Hulme of Original Sin," 52–69, esp. 62, Schuchard also chronicles the evolving articulation of Eliot's antiliberal views. The personal circumstances in which Russell figured may have contributed thus to Eliot's developing view of liberalism, which Russell could be taken to typify. The personal and historical circumstances are a single, complex manifold.

62. This local and timely correspondence goes unobserved among the critics gathered in *Critical Essays*, ed. Roby. In 1974, Marshall McLuhan told me that Eliot once confided to him that a Canadian soldier billeted in England provided one of the models for Sweeney.

63. The misquoted Greek is added in pencil to both carbon typescripts, as noted by Ricks, *IN*, 381.

64. *IN*, 381: "pulls" becomes "draws" in a pencil revision to carbon typescript "A"; "draws" is typed on the original of carbon "B"; "Sits" is revised in pencil to "Stands"

in carbon typescript "A" and becomes "Sprawls" in the *Little Review*, as in subsequent editions.

65. The penultimate line includes "siftings" in *Little Review*, *Poems* (1919), *Ara Vos Prec*, and *Collected Poems 1909–1962*, but "droppings" returned once in *Poems* (1920).

66. "[D]roppings" is marked first by Pound in carbon typescript "A" with quotation marks, then altered by Pound to "siftings," in "B," *IN*, 382.

67. "Ulysses, Order, and Myth," *Dial*, November 1923, 483.

68. The neoclassical element in the construction of literary modernism by the new critics is the most evident demonstration of this legacy and is discussed in the epilogue.

69. In "Hellenist Series (V): Aeschylus," *Egoist*, January-February 1919; *EPPP*, III:258–60.

70. Redman, *Ezra Pound and Italian Fascism*, 41–44, follows the process by which the anti-Semitism of prewar England, which fixed on the image of the Jewish money lender, intensified under the duress of a government borrowing money to finance the war effort. Anthony Julius, *T. S. Eliot, Anti-Semitism, and Literary Form* (1995; rpt. Cambridge: Cambridge University Press, 1997), 13–14, sketches the inverse ratio principle, which measures the decline of civilization in proportion to the prospering of Jewish interests.

71. See, for example, Robert Casillo, *The Genealogy of Demons: Anti-Semitism, Fascism, and the Myths of Ezra Pound* (Evanston, Ill.: Northwestern University Press, 1988), "The Jews, Castration, and Usury," 38–49, and Julius, *T. S. Eliot, Anti-Semitism, and Literary Form*, "A Literary Anti-Semitism," esp. 25–26.

72. For one account of these background circumstances, see Walter Benn Michaels, *Our America: Nativism, Modernism, and Pluralism* (Durham, N.C.: Duke University Press, 1995), esp. "The Rising Tide," 23–29, and "The Vanishing American," 23–40. While Michaels reads the anti-Semitism of Eliot and Pound as an expression initially of an *American* nativism, 101–2, he also notes the expanding frame of international reference in the poets' careers and so marks the other purposes being served by these discourses. Among these subsequent motives, the poets' wish for affiliation with pan-European cultural traditions is the most urgent. Out of the taxonomy of various European and American brands of anti-Semitism that Julius provides in *T. S. Eliot, Anti-Semitism, and Literary Form*, 12–16, a compound of those he describes in his summary, 16, appears clearly applicable to Eliot's cultural background, present situation, and literary motive: "American [patrician] anti-Semitism fed Eliot's desire to identify himself with Europe, and therefore with European prejudices. France showed Eliot that a vigorous anti-Semitism could yet be thoroughly literary, and that it was compatible with cordial, salon relations with Jews. English anti-Semitism made available to Eliot a literary tradition in which the adverse characterisation of Jews was consistent with work of the highest quality."

73. Ibid., 28, 75, and, in the same volume, "Anti-Semitism and the Non-Propositional," 92–110, esp. 93, where Julius draws the character of the anti-Semitic imagination as essentially nonverbal, or subverbal: "Anti-Semitism is not limited to a series of opinions. It derives from corrupt imaginations that neglect truth; it is a 'passion.' It lives in fiction; it is, in Maurice Blanchot's phrase, a 'portrait-accusation.' It comprises a parcel of descriptions of 'Jews' that are adverse, and hostile, but also incoherent and con-

tradictory. The descriptions of 'Jews' in Eliot's Symbolist poetry are pulled out of that parcel."

74. From the original typescript ("A"), titled "Bleistein with a Cigar," *IN*, 353; there is also a carbon typescript ("B") of a later version (see *IN*, 354), which includes the full title, "Burbank with a Baedeker: Bleistein with a Cigar," and has the text, with minor punctuational variants, of the first publication in *Arts and Letters* (Summer 1919).

75. *IN*, 354. "Descending at a small hotel" occurs in all of the published versions, from *Arts and Letters* to *Collected Poems 1909–1962*.

76. The most extensive account of the subject comes from Benjamin Arbel, *Trading Nations: Jews and Venetians in the Early Modern Eastern Mediterranean* (Leiden: Brill, 1995). In Arbel's report, local tolerance for Jews is wholly a function of the rising fortunes of exchange between the Venetian Republic and the Ottoman Empire, with whose resources the Jews had proven themselves indispensable as middlemen.

77. The theme of the cycles of cultural vitality and decline pervades Ruskin, *The Stones of Venice* (1851; rpt., 3 vols., Boston: Estes, 1899), and is fairly sampled in the opening paragraph, 1:15: "Since the first dominion of men was asserted, over the ocean, three thrones, of mark beyond all others, have been set upon its sands; the thrones of Tyre, Venice, and England. Of the First of these great powers only the memory remains; of the Second, the ruin; the Third, which inherits their greatness, if it forget their example, may be led through prouder eminence to less pitied destruction." The moral dimension of this account is strengthened in Ruskin's *Seven Lamps of Architecture* (1849; rpt. Boston: Estes, 1900), where the first and last of the seven essays gathered are "The Lamp of Sacrifice" and "The Lamp of Obedience," which opens, 188: "It has been my endeavour to show in the preceding pages how every form of noble architecture is in some sort the embodiment of the Polity, Life, History and Religious Faith of Nations. Once or twice in doing this, I have named a principle to which I would now assign a definite place among those which direct that embodiment; the last place, not only as that to which its own humility would incline, but rather as belonging to it in the aspect of the crowning grace of all the rest; that principle, I mean, to which Polity owes its stability, Life its happiness, Faith its acceptance, Creation its continuance—Obedience." Venetian architecture provides the largest set of examples for Ruskin's illustrations of these moral principles.

78. Hugh Kenner, *The Invisible Poet: T. S. Eliot* (New York: Obolensky, 1959), 12.

79. The text of "Gerontion" is from an original typescript, "A," *IN*, 351. Points of illustration and comparison will be made with the carbon typescript of a revised version, "B," which includes penciled revisions by Pound (see *IN*, 351).

80. The bearing of the Versailles treaty on the linguistic imagination of "Gerontion" is elaborated by Stan Smith, *The Origins of Modernism: Eliot, Pound, Yeats and the Rhetorics of Renewal* (Hemel Hempstead, England: Harvester Wheatsheaf, 1994), esp. 103, 104, 107–8, where, in the context of postwar uncertainties, the instability of older orders is borne out in the poetic text by a special indeterminacy of verbal meaning and unreliability in literary citation and allusion.

81. Thus, in the introduction (by "E. B. L.") to Newman's *The Dream of Gerontius* (London: Longmans, Green, 1907), 10–11: "On the 29th of October, 1888, Mr. Gladstone wrote to Mr. Lawrence Dillon about the 'Dream': 'It originally came into

the world in grave clothes; swaddled, that is to say, in the folds of the anonymous, but it has now fairly burst them, and will, I hope, take and hold its position in the literature of the world.'" The correspondence first emerged in a circumstance that is redrawn in this introduction, 11, and that reflects the appropriation of the poem by the agents of political history. Here a "Paper on General Gordon's Copy of Newman's Dream of Gerontius, Read before the Manchester Literary Club, 12 November, 1888" records the reception and reading of Newman's poem by General Charles Gordon, on the eve of his fateful entry into the city of Khartoum, summarized thus in the introduction, 11–12: "[F]eeling a presentiment that he was to die at Khartoum, whither he was bound . . . the General duly marked some passages, and on the 18th of February, 1884, the very day he entered the doomed city, gave the copy to Frank Power. Power forwarded it to his sister in Dublin, who sent it on for Cardinal Newman's inspection, and the latter wrote to her: 'Your letter and its contents took away my breath. I was deeply moved to find that a book had been in General Gordon's hands, and that a description of a soul preparing for death.'" This Newman-Gladstone-Gordon conjunction was much publicized, as witnessed by reprints of the cited "Paper" in the *Manchester Quarterly* of January 1889 and *Longman's Magazine* for October 1890.

82. These lines begin as a penciled addition by Eliot to the verso of "B," with a revision of "driven by the horn" to "running on the Horn" by Pound, *IN*, 352, which Eliot incorporated (along with the shift from "driven by the trades" to "driven on the trades").

83. The extent of the practice and its establishment in the public culture of the war are summarized by Nicoletta F. Gullace, "White Feathers and Wounded Men: Female Patriotism and the Memory of the Great War," *Journal of British Studies* 36 (1997): 178–206.

84. Thus in "A" and recto of "B," *IN*, 351, before the addition (revision) cited above, n. 82.

85. "Nature," a first reading, is altered to "History" in "A," *IN*, 350, 351.

86. Added in version "D-E," *IN*, 370, whereafter the phrasing varies in draft and published versions.

87. Newman, *Dream of Gerontius*, 41, has the "soul" of Gerontius ask why, after his sight has been extinguished, his other senses have been preserved: "How comes it then / That I have hearing still, and taste and touch." The echoing correspondence is noted by William Van O'Connor, "*Gerontion* & *The Dream of Gerontius*," *Furioso* (1948): 54, who observes other similarities also, 53–56, esp. 54, to substantiate the case for the bearing of Newman's poem on Eliot's.

88. "Gerousia," a first reading, is altered to "Gerontion" in "A," *IN*, 349, 351, synchronizing thus with the shift from "Nature" to "History" (n. 85).

89. It seems hard to miss the note of deliberate obfuscation in these lines, but a particularly credulous reading of the piece, which measures the success of Eliot's rhetorical fiction of reason-seemingness, comes from Harvey Gross, "*Gerontion* and the Meaning of History," *Publications of the Modern Language Association of America* 73 (1958): 299–304, where, 300, Gross finds a "closely reasoned" answer to the meaninglessness of "history," which he understands as some inferior dimension of existence, to which the

poet's rational capacity is manifestly superior, 301: "[The speaker Gerontion] moves from reverie to intellectual commitment, to a position."

90. The other Anglo-American modernist poet resident in London in these years is H. D. Her verse does not animate to the changes registered and developed by Pound and Eliot. H. D.'s ongoing (and, arguably, increasingly embattled) commitment to articulate individualism may locate one of her main points of difference with her American contemporaries. Her attempt to remain true to the ideals of a prewar imagism may be seen to underlie and unify the plot of her autobiography, an account of her London experience of the war, which was published ultimately as *Bid Me to Live: A Madrigal* (New York: Grove, 1960) but undertaken initially in 1921 as *Asphodel,* ed. Robert Spoo (Durham, N.C.: Duke University Press, 1992). Her attempt to preserve and nurture the private subject of the lyric voice reads indeed as the project and challenge of the one story these two memoirs comprise. The poetic record of this same effort shows throughout the verse contemporaneous with the war. Of the poems gathered in *Collected Poems 1912–1944,* ed. Louis Martz (1983; rpt. New York: New Directions, 1986), "The Tribute" (1916), 59–68, appears as the most sustained engagement. As in much of H. D.'s verse at this time, mythic antiquity affords a setting that casts the representation of the contemporary situation on an oblique angle. Here, the depiction of the demise of "the old gods of the city" and the new rule of "the *one* god, / *one* tall god with a spear shaft, / *one* bright god with a lance" (61; emphases added) summons the reigning deity of total war. The voice of ritual plea that this poem features does not substantially alter the style of lyric invocation and the standard of expressive sincerity that mark her prewar verse. Cf. "Acon" (February 1914), 31–32.

91. This mythos of recuperation in literary and artistic modernism finds one of its most eloquent witnesses in the commentary of the Anglo-Welsh poet and painter David Jones (1895–1974). As a second-generation modernist, who began writing only in the late 1920s, Jones received the work of modernism as an entity largely accomplished, indeed mythologized. See, for example, his "Notes on the 1930s" (1965), reprinted in *The Dying Gaul and Other Writings,* ed. Harman Grisewood (London: Faber, 1978), 45–46. While Jones's (relative) youth did not preclude his service in the Great War (he fought with the Royal Welch Fusiliers at the Battle of the Somme, among other places), he did not assimilate the import of the political culture of the Liberal war in a way that made any direct or pointed impact on the book-length poem he composed out of his military experience, *In Parenthesis* (London: Faber, 1937).

92. T. S. Eliot, *The Waste Land: A Facsimile and Transcript of the Original Drafts Including the Annotations of Ezra Pound,* ed. Valerie Eliot (New York: Harcourt Brace Jovanovitch, 1971), 148. This edition also includes the text of the first edition of the poem (New York: Boni and Liveright, 1922) and will be referenced parenthetically as *WLM.*

93. The most ambitious attempt to assess the effect of Pound's intervention on the *whole* poem comes from Marshall McLuhan, "Pound, Eliot, and the Rhetoric of *The Waste Land,*" *New Literary History* 10 (1979): 557–80. McLuhan contends that Pound's influence was indeed global, and that the editor is fully responsible, not only for the existence, but for the specific character and function of the poem's fifth (final) part. McLuhan understands the four- and five-part versions of the poem in terms of particular, rival intellectual traditions, the import of whose differences he summarizes as the

opposition between a "four-part meditation" and a "five-division pattern of classical oratory," 570. The ultimate effect of Pound's influence and additions, contrary to one's readiest impression of the finished product, is to have "de-sacrilized" the poem. This assertion seems so much at odds with the manifest character of the fifth part that its rationale seems to derive entirely from the logic of McLuhan's schematic thinking. Consider also the eloquent resistance Pound himself would soon witness to schematic imaginative patterns, in the parallel instance of Joyce's *Ulysses* ("Paris Letter: *Ulysses*," *Dial* 6 [June 1922], 623–29). My focus on the poem's characters-in-voice has profited from an unpublished paper on the editorial intervention by Sharon Cournoyer Howell, who gives special attention to Pound's work to establish the dominance of Tiresias.

94. Charles Dickens, *Our Mutual Friend* (New York: New American Library, 1964), 226.

95. The parenthesis is not closed in the manuscript.

96. The chronology and contents of Eliot's various deposits of the manuscript with Pound are established by Ackroyd, *Life*, 165–67.

97. Letter from Paris, dated "24 Saturnus" (24 December?) in Pound, *Selected Letters*, 169. In this letter, Pound allows momentarily for the possible inclusion of these "superfluities," as an insert that will come before the poem. In a subsequent (January?) letter from Paris, however, he withdraws that concession, in response to Eliot's attempt to reprint "Gerontion" as a preface to *The Waste Land*, in Pound, *Selected Letters*, 171: "I do *not* advise printing 'Gerontion' as preface. One don't miss it *at* all as the thing now stands. To be more lucid still, let me say that I advise you NOT to print 'Gerontion' as prelude."

Interchapter 3

1. The four novels—*Some Do Not* (1924), *No More Parades* (1925), *A Man Could Stand Up* (1926), and *The Last Post* (1928)—are collected as *Parade's End* (New York: Knopf, 1992). While Ford composed the first three novels as a sequence, the addition of the fourth is, arguably, an afterthought; the problems are rehearsed in the introduction by Malcolm Bradbury, xxvi–xxvii. Page numbers are to this Knopf edition, which will be further referenced by the title of each novel.

2. Ford, *Some Do Not*, in *Parade's End*, 3, 13, 21, 307.

3. Ford, *A Man Could Stand Up*, in *Parade's End*, 549.

4. The circumstances compelling the change in title are recounted by Ford in the 1927 "Dedicatory Letter to Stella Ford," in *The Good Soldier*, ed. Martin Stannard (New York: Norton, 1995), 5. For the prewar completion of the manuscript, see Arthur Mizener, *The Saddest Story: A Biography of Ford Madox Ford* (New York: World, 1971), 252: "Ford always said that he had finished it by July, 1914, and the evidence suggests that date is substantially correct." That Ford's revisions after 4 August 1914 included a featuring of this date, as the day of recurrent disaster in the fictional chronicle, is suggested by Stannard, ed., *Good Soldier*, 187: "[A]t least one series of corrections was made to the novel *as a whole* after August 4, 1914, to determine its final shape and tone. An aspect of this revision was his attempt to juggle with the dates. True, there is one instance [in a prewar holograph] of coincidence in his choosing the date randomly while dictating, but it is the correction which elaborates it as a structural motif."

5. Ford, *Some Do Not*, in *Parade's End*, 3.

6. Ford, *No More Parades*, in *Parade's End*, 317.

7. Ibid., 320.

8. Ford, *A Man Could Stand Up*, in *Parade's End*, 543.

9. Wyndham Lewis, *Blasting and Bombardiering*, 2d ed. (Berkeley: University of California Press, 1967), 58.

10. Ford, *Some Do Not*, in *Parade's End*, 253.

11. Ibid.

12. Ford, *No More Parades*, in *Parade's End*, 529.

13. See, for example, Ford Madox Hueffer (his postwar change of name will reflect the same sensitivity), *When Blood Is Their Argument: An Analysis of Prussian Culture* (London: Hodder and Stoughton, 1915).

Chapter 4

1. Virginia Woolf, *A Room of One's Own* (1929; rpt. San Diego, Calif.: Harcourt Brace, 1989), 11–12.

2. Thus the "humming noise" Woolf overhears beneath the "rational intercourse" in prewar days is tuned to the music of love poems by men and women, which Woolf rearranges here as an exchange between Tennyson and Christina Rossetti, ibid., 12. The convention obviously confers a secondary or subsidiary position to the female part of the exchange.

3. George Duckworth is recalled by Woolf in a 1939 memoir, "A Sketch of the Past," in *Moments of Being: Unpublished Autobiographical Writings*, ed. Jeanne Schulkind (New York: Harcourt Brace Jovanovitch, 1976), 131. The circumstances of Duckworth's sexual predation are recreated and analyzed at length by Louise DeSalvo, *Virginia Woolf: The Impact of Childhood Sexual Abuse on Her Life and Work* (Boston: Beacon, 1989).

4. Concise but comprehensive portraits of her father's and paternal grandfather's intellectual characters are provided by Hermione Lee, *Virginia Woolf* (London: Chatto & Windus, 1996), 69–71; the contemporary's remark is quoted on 69. The most detailed account of her father's position in British intellectual culture comes from Noel Annan, *Leslie Stephen: The Godless Victorian* (Chicago: University of Chicago Press, 1984), esp. "British Rationalism," 165–91, "The Revelation of the Eighteenth Century," 221–33, and "The Moral Society," 267–99.

5. The compound values of rationalism and masculinism are to be found in Leslie Stephen's conceptual positions no less than in his incidental rhetoric; see Annan, *Leslie Stephen*, "Moral and Immoral Man," 303–7, esp. 306.

6. "A Sketch of the Past," 126.

7. Ibid., 125.

8. Virginia Woolf, *Three Guineas* (1938; rpt. San Diego, Calif.: Harcourt Brace Jovanovitch, 1995). These three essays represent a joint response to the problem adduced in the opening paragraph of the first, 3, "How in your opinion are we to prevent war?"

9. Accounts of Thoby Stephen and the intellectual milieux of Cambridge and early Bloomsbury are provided by Lee, *Virginia Woolf*, 220–31, and Lyndall Gordon, *Virginia Woolf: A Writer's Life* (New York: Norton, 1984), 121ff.

10. This early diary entry is cited by Lee, *Virginia Woolf,* 207.

11. The expedition, consequences, and sense of personal loss are set out in ibid., 227–31; by Gordon, *Virginia Woolf,* 125–26; and by Quentin Bell, *Virginia Woolf: A Biography* (New York: Harcourt Brace Jovanovitch, 1972), 1:107–11.

12. *Jacob's Room* (1922; rpt. San Diego, Calif.: Harcourt Brace Jovanovitch, 1990), 160: "In Greece and the uplands of Albania and Turkey, the wind scours the sand and the dust, and sows itself thick with dry particles. . . . Now the agitation of the air uncovered a racing star. Now it was dark." Subsequent references to *Jacob's Room* are to this edition, cited as *JR*.

13. A good account of the intellectual influence of Moore on Clive Bell and of Woolf's transactions with Bell during the early stages of *The Voyage Out* (then titled *Melymbrosia*) is provided by Lee, *Virginia Woolf,* 253–55. A sample exchange of letters between her and Bell on the early progress of the work (October 1908 and February 1909) is provided by Bell, *Virginia Woolf: A Biography,* 1:207–12. For a text-based account of the long process of the novel's composition, see the extensive record and commentary provided by Louise A. DeSalvo, ed., *"Melymbrosia" by Virginia Woolf: An Early Version of "The Voyage Out"* (New York: New York Public Library, 1982), "Introduction: Recovery of the Text of *Melymbrosia*," xxiii–xliii. The literary text that DeSalvo provides is based upon a draft begun (roughly) in March 1910 and revised from late October to December 1910. One of the important points to be drawn from this version is its attention to a variety of contemporary social issues and political themes, as summarized by DeSalvo, *"Melymbrosia,"* xxxvi–xxxvii.

14. *The Voyage Out* (1915; rpt. San Diego, Calif.: Harcourt Brace Jovanovitch, 1990), 64–65. Subsequent references are to this edition, cited as *VO*. This (American) edition includes the best representation of the corrections and revisions that Woolf incorporated in late 1919 and early 1920 into the text of the first English edition; a good account of that process comes from Louise A. DeSalvo, *Virginia Woolf's First Voyage: A Novel in the Making* (Totowa, N.J.: Rowman and Littlefield, 1980), "Revisions for the First American and Second English Editions 1919–1920," 110–25.

15. E. M. Forster, *A Passage to India* (1924; rpt. New York: Holmes and Meier, 1979), 138ff., and Joseph Conrad, *Heart of Darkness* (1899); 3d ed., ed. Robert Kimbrough (New York: Norton, 1988), 68.

16. Karen L. Levenback, *Virginia Woolf and the Great War* (Syracuse, N.Y.: Syracuse University Press, 1999); Alex Zwerdling, *Virginia Woolf and the Real World* (Berkeley: University of California Press, 1986). Levenback's main critical point about Woolf's exposure to the war involves the novelist's ability to see through the insulating language of war propaganda and euphemized record. Levenback reconstructs this linguistic situation in its typical instances, if not in ways that take specific account of the verbal rationalism of English Liberalism. See "Myths of War, Illusions of Immunity, Realities of Survival," 9–43, esp. 13, 19. Of the varied political topics and historical sites that Zwerdling registers as points of imaginative attention for Woolf, the Great War is featured mainly from the vantage he stakes in a later chapter, "Pacifism without Hope," 271–301, which follows the evolving consciousness of this philosophical position from the early influence of Leslie Stephen through the formative days of the Great War. The resistance to war that Zwerdling establishes in Woolf's intellectual conscience informs a

literary attitude and practice he discusses most consistently under the heading of "satire." While Zwerdling does not recover the substance of political Liberalism as the major occasion for this satire, he goes on to indicate Woolf's growing apprehension—unlike most other members of Bloomsbury—of the failure of rationalism as a practical standard and value.

17. "The Evening Party" may be dated through a letter of Woolf to Vanessa Bell of 26 July 1918, in *Letters of Virginia Woolf*, vol. 2, *1912–1922*, ed. Nigel Nicolson and Joanne Trautmann (New York: Harcourt Brace Jovanovitch, 1976), 262. The manuscript history of the piece (unpublished in Woolf's lifetime) is provided in *The Complete Shorter Fiction of Virginia Woolf*, 2d ed., ed. Susan Dick (San Diego, Calif.: Harcourt Brace Jovanovitch, 1989), 298. References to Woolf's shorter fiction will be made to this edition, as *CSF*, which includes details of initial publication and composition. This gathering also provides valuable information on manuscripts and variant texts in its appendices and notes. The text of "The Evening Party" is taken from *CSF*, 99.

18. As "Fragment 56," in T. M. Robinson, ed., *Heraclitus: Fragments: A Text and Translation with a Commentary* (Toronto: University of Toronto Press, 1987), 39.

19. While the account of Leonard Woolf is far from objective or clinical, see his *Beginning Again: An Autobiography of the Years 1911–1918* (London: Hogarth, 1964), e.g., 163–64: "What tends to break one down . . . is the terrible sanity of the insane. . . . [Virginia's] beliefs were insane because they were in fact contradicted by reality. But given these beliefs as premises for conclusions and actions, all Virginia's actions and conclusions were logical and rational; and her power of arguing conclusively from false premises was terrific."

20. The assumptions are set out by Louis A. Sass, *Madness and Modernism: Insanity in the Light of Modern Art, Literature, and Thought* (1992; rpt. Cambridge, Mass.: Harvard University Press, 1994), "Prologue: The Sleep of Reason," 1–12, esp. 4, 10: "What if madness, in at least some of its forms, were to derive from a heightening rather than a dimming of conscious awareness, and an alienation not from reason but from the emotions, the instinct, the body? This, in essence, is the basic thesis of this book." "A careful comparison with modernism suggests that schizophrenic experience may have less in common with the spirit of Dionysus than with what Nietzsche, in *The Birth of Tragedy*, associates with the god Apollo and the philosopher Socrates: it may be characterized less by fusion, spontaneity, and the liberation of desire than by separation, restraint, and an exaggerated cerebralism and propensity for introspection."

21. Pound exerts no pressure in Sass's account, in which he appears in two inconsequential references (*Madness*, 34, 419 n. 84), while Eliot appears chiefly as a name in comprehensive lists of references or as a subsidiary complement to the figures of Sass's focused interest, 28, 86, 135, 137, 186, 260, 280, 344, 357, 419 n. 78, 421 n. 96, 482–83 n. 45, 522 n. 29, and 532 n. 51. Surprisingly, Woolf gains no clarity of individual definition in the appearances she makes, 28, 30–31, 495 n. 40, 525–26 n. 59, and 544–45 n. 75, where she takes her place in round-up accounts that feature her as a relatively undistinguished instance of general tendencies. The major headings (and subdivisions) in Sass's chapters are drawn from the language of clinical psychology; historical location is not a significant feature in this organization.

22. Leonard Woolf recalls the major movements in his professional biography during the war and its effect on his evolving politics in *Beginning Again*, 176ff., esp 183–97, where he details his relation to Fabian views, his involvement with the Webbs at the *New Statesman*, and his acquaintance with intellectual celebrities such as H. G. Wells. His intersections with the various institutions of London Liberalism are traced by Lee, *Virginia Woolf*, 347–51, who also, 344–47, recounts the actions and attitudes in regard to the war by various representatives of Bloomsbury.

23. *The Diary of Virginia Woolf*, vol. 1, *1915–1919*, ed. Anne Olivier Bell (New York: Harcourt Brace Jovanovitch, 1977), 5.

24. Entry of 4 January 1915, *Diary*, 1:7.

25. Entry of 4 January 1918, *Diary*, 1:99. The echo of *King Henry V* is conjectured editorially, 99 n. 7.

26. Entry of 13 April 1918, *Diary*, 1:138.

27. On the question of conscription or "compulsion" in Ireland, see Keith Jeffery, *Ireland and the Great War* (Cambridge: Cambridge University Press, 2000), 9. In "Obligation," 5–36, Jeffery argues convincingly that a number of reasons for enlisting, ranging from the idealistic to the pragmatic, resulted in no shortage of Irish recruits.

28. As punctuated by Woolf, *CSF*, 89. "The Mark on the Wall" appeared in July 1917, along with Leonard Woolf's "Three Jews," as the first publication of the Hogarth Press. It was reprinted, with minor revisions, in *Monday or Tuesday* (London: Hogarth, 1921), which provides the basis for the text in *CSF*.

29. Entry of 15 November 1918, *Diary*, 1:218–19.

30. Entry of 3 December 1918, *Diary*, 1:223.

31. Woolf describes herself as having "just started another story," in a letter to Vanessa Bell of 26 November 1918, in *Letters of Virginia Woolf*, 2:299. She proceeds to describe the opening scene of the story, 299. "Solid Objects" was first published in the *Athenaeum*, 22 October 1920, which provides the text of *CSF*. The collector motif that provides the theme and plot for the story is situated well in relation to leisure-class consumption in a book that recovers related elements in turn-of-the-century transatlantic culture (as the basis for a wide-ranging analysis of modernism), by Douglas Mao, *Solid Objects: Modernism and the Test of Production* (Princeton, N.J.: Princeton University Press, 1998), 26–31, 39–42.

32. Complete entry of 11 November 1918, *Diary*, 1:216.

33. For the contemporary tradition of *l'écriture feminine*, the major works of reference are Luce Irigaray's *This Sex Which Is Not One*, trans. Catherine Porter, with Carolyn Burke (1985; rpt. Ithaca, N.Y.: Cornell University Press, 1986), esp. "This Sex Which Is Not One," 23–33, "Cosi Fan Tutti," 86–105, and "The Mechanics of Fluids," 106–18; and Hélène Cixous, "First Names of No One" (1974), "La—The (Feminine)" (1976), and "To Live the Orange" (1979), in *The Hélène Cixous Reader*, ed. Susan Sellers, trans. Sellers et al. (London: Routledge, 1994), 25–33, 57–67, 82–92. A slightly later observation and critique of the essentializing element and limiting condition in this notion of gendered writing comes from Julia Kristeva, in her 1980 "Interview with Elaine Hoffman Baruch on Feminism in the United States and France," reprinted in *The Portable Kristeva*, ed. Kelly Oliver (New York: Columbia University Press, 1997), 370–72.

34. *Mrs. Dalloway* (1925; rpt. San Diego, Calif.: Harcourt Brace, 1990), 20ff.; cited subsequently as *MD*. In regard to the church bell tolling the signal number of eleven: the cult of remembrance on 11 November was already solidly established by the early 1920s, as witnessed in the events cited by Hynes, *A War Imagined: The First World War and English Culture* (New York: Atheneum, 1991), 275. Background information on the practice of skywriting and its connection with memories of the recent war is provided by John Young, "Woolf's *Mrs. Dalloway*," *Explicator* 58 (2000): 99–100.

35. *Night and Day* (1920; rpt. San Diego, Calif.: Harcourt Brace, 1990). Arguably, the composition of a novel that followed the conventions of established narrative and (once) secure values served a use in the "recovery" Woolf was undergoing in the years (1917–19) she was drafting it. In readying the typescript to be taken to her publisher, she hints at the self-composing quality of the exercise, in an entry of 27 March 1919, *Diary*, 1:259: "I don't suppose I've ever enjoyed any writing so much as I did the last half of N[ight] & D[ay]. Indeed, no part of it taxed me as The Voyage Out did."

36. The story was published in the *London Mercury*, July 1920, and, slightly revised, in *Monday or Tuesday*, which provides the text for *CSF*, 112. Woolf refers to "An Unwritten Novel" (under this title) in an entry of 26 January 1920, *The Diary of Virginia Woolf*, vol. 2, *1920–1924*, ed. Anne Olivier Bell and Andrew McNeillie (New York: Harcourt Brace Jovanovitch, 1978), 13, where she also indicates the relation between its way of proceeding and "some idea of a new form of a new novel. Suppose one thing should open out of another—as in An Unwritten Novel—only not for 10 pages but 200 or so— docsn't that give the looseness and lightness I want: doesn't that get closer & yet keep form & speed, & enclose everything, everything? My doubt is how far it will enclose the human heart." The growing points of *Jacob's Room* (referred to under this title in an entry of 10 April 1920, *Diary*, 2:28) are clearly intimated as well in the 26 January 1920 entry, 14: "I see immense possibilities in the form I hit upon more or less by chance 2 weeks ago."

37. "Character in Fiction" was first published in *Criterion*, July 1924, and represents a substantial expansion of "Mr. Bennett and Mrs. Brown," which appeared initially in the *New York Evening Post*, 17 November 1923; the earlier version focuses on the limitations of those "Edwardian" authors but does not reference her own writing as working in accord with Eliot and Joyce (and Forster, Lawrence, and Strachey). The texts of the two essays may be found in *The Essays of Virginia Woolf*, vol. 3, *1919–1924*, ed. Andrew McNeillie (San Diego, Calif.: Harcourt Brace Jovanovitch, 1988), 384–89, 420–38; some of the work of revision and enlargement can be followed in appendix III, *Essays*, 3:502–17.

38. In "Character in Fiction," 427.

39. Woolf's recourse to romance conventions in her first two novels and her surpassing of the "marriage requirement" are analyzed well by Rachel Blau DuPlessis, *Writing beyond the Ending: Narrative Strategies of Twentieth-Century Women Writers* (Bloomington: Indiana University Press, 1985), "'Amor Vin—': Modifications of Romance in Woolf," 47–65.

40. William Handley, "War and the Politics of Narration in *Jacob's Room*," in *Virginia Woolf and War: Fiction, Reality, and Myth*, ed. Mark Hussey (Syracuse, N.Y.: Syracuse University Press, 1991), 110–33, esp. 111, 113, where Handley discusses the

relation of the completed character and the appropriated subject, and 121–25, where the narrative form of the novel is compared and contrasted to the organization of an authoritarian state.

41. Ibid., 111.

42. Stephen's declaration is made in the second chapter, "Nestor," in *Ulysses: The Corrected Text*, ed. Hans Walter Gabler et al. (New York: Random House, 1986), 2:377: "History, Stephen said, is a nightmare from which I am trying to awake." This chapter takes "history" as its "art" (in the categories of the "Linati schema").

In a good deal of the criticism on Woolf and the war, she is given an attitude of outraged offense, which, if not untrue at some elementary and unnegotiable level, serves to debar any imaginative attempt on her part to interact with and develop in response to the culture of war. Many of the essays collected by Hussey in *Virginia Woolf and War: Fiction, Reality, and Myth* are extremely valuable in establishing the extent and depth of Woolf's engagement with the atrocities of modern history, thus countering an earlier perception of her distant and even diffident aestheticism. The orientation formed in the editor's introduction, however, sets these essays the task of mapping the lines of literary resistance to the ordaining occasion of war, in effect precluding the possibility that the war is a fostering circumstance for her verbal and imaginative intelligence. In this construction, war and its supporting social formations may need to be analyzed and understood but may never be comported with. In framing the essays, Hussey gestures indicatively to the first, "Virginia Woolf's Keen Sensitivity to War," where the coauthors, Nancy Topping Bazin and Jane Hamovit Lauter, open, 14: "War inspired horror in Virginia Woolf. Her antipathy toward those who cause war is evident in her two essays, *A Room of One's Own* and *Three Guineas*. The impact of war on her fiction expands from a portrayal of individuals as victims to a vision of war that encompasses the possible annihilation of civilization." Shocked recoil follows as the response to such a prospect; active or profitable engagement on the novelist's part with these conditions is obviously not to be readily countenanced. A similar implication may be taken from the influential formulations of Zwerdling, *Virginia Woolf and the Real World*, where, in "Pacifism without Hope," phrases such as "Virginia Woolf's lifelong contempt for war," 271, seem to annul the possibility of any reciprocating engagement with the verbal culture of conflict.

43. See "A Dramatic Scene: The House and Sir Edward Grey's Statement: Logic of Events," *Westminster Gazette*, 4 August 1914, 10; "'conversations'" is used with these marks of skepticism, for instance, in "The German Invasion," (London) *Times*, 3 August 1914, 7.

44. While it is tempting to find in this figure a reflection of the phrases Sir Edward Grey is supposed to have uttered so movingly on 3 August 1914, "The lamps are going out all over Europe. We shall not see them lit again in our time," the uncertainty of Grey's wording, and even the questionableness of the attribution, are rehearsed revealingly by Hynes, *A War Imagined*, 3, 470–71 n. 1. The words do not seem to have entered print before 1925.

45. Kate Flint, "Revising *Jacob's Room*: Virginia Woolf, Women, and Language," *Review of English Studies* 42 (1991): 366–67. Among the critics exploring the principles of *l'écriture féminine*, Bonnie Kime Scott offers the most comprehensive account of

Woolf's career in *Refiguring Modernism*, vol. 2, *Postmodern Feminist Readings of Woolf, West, and Barnes* (Bloomington: Indiana University Press, 1996), "Woolf's Rapture with Language," 3–70; not only the physical body of language but consistent resistance to single vision and rationalistic reduction in linguistic fictions provide the standards and values that Scott thematizes in this reading.

46. "Mrs. Dalloway in Bond Street" was first published in *Dial*, July 1923, which provides the basis for the text in *CSF*, 158. The process by which the work at shorter pieces of fiction evolved into the plan and ambition for the novel is outlined by Dick, *CSF*, 302.

47. A good account of the work situation for women and the attendant sense of equal partnership and citizenship in the war effort is provided by Sandra M. Gilbert and Susan Gubar, *No Man's Land: The Place of the Woman Writer in the Twentieth Century*, vol. 2, *Sexchanges* (New Haven, Conn.: Yale University Press, 1989), "Soldier's Heart: Literary Men, Literary Women, and the Great War," 258–323, esp. 270–79.

48. Margot Asquith, *An Autobiography*, 2 vols. (London: Butterworth, 1920; New York: Doran, 1920).

49. A responsible account of this regimen of the "rest cure" and the symptoms it addressed may be found in Lee, *Virginia Woolf*, 182–83. The same period is recalled by Leonard Woolf, *Beginning Again*, 172ff., where, however, the memoir is overshadowed by the larger circumstance of the war and a set of oddly irrelevant reminiscences about the eccentricities of the domestic staff.

50. Woolf, *A Room of One's Own*, 91. DuPlessis, "Breaking the Sentence: Breaking the Sequence," in her *Writing beyond the Ending*, 31–46; DuPlessis gestures to "the sentence broken," 32–33; she engages the possibilities and complications of "breaking the sequence" at far greater length, 34ff.

51. E.g., "Hades," in *Ulysses: The Corrected Text*, ed. Gabler et al., 6:316–20: "Dead side of the street this. Dull business by day, land agents, temperance hotel, Falconer's railway guide, civil service college, Gill's, catholic club, the industrious blind. Why? Some reasons. Sun or wind. At night too. Chummies and slaveys. Under the patronage of the late Father Mathew. Foundation stone for Parnell. Breakdown. Heart."

52. *To the Lighthouse* (1927; rpt. San Diego, Calif.: Harcourt Brace, 1990), 133; cited subsequently as *TL*.

53. Variations on this pattern include May Sinclair's *The Tree of Heaven* (London: Cassell, 1917), which celebrates the endurance of family and the sanctity of marriage against the background cataclysm of the war; Rose Macauley's *Told by an Idiot* (London: Collins, 1923), where the saga of the Garden family is related in the context of historical events from the last two decades of the nineteenth century through the first two of the twentieth, and where the family achieves a degree of coherence that allows those major eventualities to play as summary allusions against the centers of domestic attention in the expanding clan; and Rebecca West's *The Return of the Soldier* (London: Nisbet, 1918), which rehearses the scheme it subverts in bringing the soldier Chris Baldrick, who is suffering alternative personality disorder (or "fugue") as a function of "shell shock," back to a home he does not know.

54. James M. Haule, "*To the Lighthouse* and the Great War: The Evidence of Virginia Woolf's Revisions of 'Time Passes,'" in *Virginia Woolf and War*, ed. Hussey,

166–75; Haule is summarizing in representative instances the results of an earlier reconnaissance of the manuscripts, "'Le Temps Passe' and the Original Typescript: An Early Version of the 'Time Passes' Section of *To the Lighthouse*," *Twentieth-Century Literature* 29 (1983): 267–311, which, in the later article, he interprets further.

55. Haule, "*To the Lighthouse* and the Great War," 167, 174, 177.

56. For Haule, ibid., 171, the bracketed reference to Andrew Ramsay's death in battle enacts in practice what Woolf states in principle with the bracketed reference to Mr. Carmichael's success with poetry, i.e., the necessity for a purging of "violent commentary" from literature, from this final version in particular.

Epilogue

1. Wyndham Lewis, *Men without Art* (London: Cassell, 1934), "T. S. Eliot: The Pseudo-Believer," 65–100, 69; cited subsequently as *MWA*.

2. Eliot's first response comes in a review of *Science and Poetry* in *Dial*, March 1927, 239–43, where the approval he confers on Richards's formulations about poetry and psychology is offset already by an objection to Richards's imprecise use of the term "belief." While he appreciates in particular Richards's inquiry into the relation "between *truth* and *belief*, between rational and emotional assent," he demurs, 240: "[I]t is a psychological theory of value, but we must also have a moral theory of value." A record and assessment of Eliot's process of disavowal may be found in John Paul Russo, *I. A. Richards: His Life and Work* (Baltimore, Md.: Johns Hopkins University Press, 1989), 349–51, which follows developments from the mid–late 1920s and connects the later literary attitudes to the developing intensity of Eliot's religious views. Russo also provides valuable background on "belief theory" in Anglo-American thought, 346–48, a tradition in which Lewis's objections to Eliot figure interestingly as a difference of Protestant and Catholic attitudes.

3. The statement is made in the preface to Eliot's *For Lancelot Andrewes: Essays on Style and Order* (1928; rpt. Garden City, N.Y.: Doubleday, Doran, 1929), vii. Eliot's "conversion" and reception into the Anglican communion occurred over the course of 1927; see the accounts in Lyndall Gordon, *Eliot's Early Years* (Oxford: Oxford University Press, 1977), 120ff., and Peter Ackroyd, *T. S. Eliot: A Life* (New York: Simon and Schuster, 1984), 159ff.

4. Emphases by F. R. Leavis, *New Bearings in English Poetry: A Study of the Contemporary Situation* (1932; rpt. Harmondsworth, England: Penguin Peregrine, 1963), 19; cited subsequently as *NB*.

5. Richards, "The Poetry of T. S. Eliot" (1926), in his *Principles of Literary Criticism*, 2d ed. (1928; rpt. New York: Harcourt, Brace & World, n. d.), 294. See n. 96 and n. 98 in chapter 1.

6. After situating Pound's earlier verse as a derivative and outcome of the 1890s (*NB*, 113), Leavis pays it the inverted compliment of providing the material that Pound critiques in the self-objectifying autobiography of *Mauberley* (*NB*, 115), to which he assigns a purity of intention for direct expression, all in all, the antidecadent standard of sincerity, 115: "In *Mauberley* we feel a pressure of experience, an impulse from deep within. The verse is extraordinarily subtle, and its subtlety is the subtlety of the sensibility it expresses. No one would think here of distinguishing the way of saying from the

thing said. It is significant that the pressure seems to derive (we are reminded of Mr Yeats) from a recognition of bankruptcy, of a devoted life summed up in futility." The profounder irony in Leavis's reading of *The Waste Land*, we know from the poetic manuscripts, goes to the agreement he expresses with the effect of Pound's heavy interventions on behalf of comprehensive statement, integral consciousness.

7. By the time Leavis gets to a direct consideration of the war, near the end of this lengthy chapter (*NB*, 64), he relegates the verse that these events generated to an unexceptional extension of precedent poetic convention: "Edward Thomas died in the war. The war, besides killing poets, was supposed at the time to have occasioned a great deal of poetry; but the names of very few 'war-poets' are still remembered. . . . Edward Thomas, Owen, and Rosenberg together, even if they had been properly recognized at once, could hardly have constituted a challenge to the ruling poetic fashions."

8. Eliot, "The Idea of a Literary Review," *Criterion*, January 1926, 5.

9. Laura Riding and Robert Graves, *A Survey of Modernist Poetry* (1927; rpt. St. Clair Shores, Mich.: Scholarly Press, 1972), 138–39. The sensibility that "modernist" poetry opposes is set out in "Modernist Poetry and the Plain Reader's Rights," 9–34, and "The Unpopularity of Modernist Poetry with the Plain Reader," 83–109. The poem is Riding's "The Rugged Black of Anger," to be published in her *Love as Love, Death as Death* (London: Seizin, 1928).

10. The poem is attached to the 1929 date by Edward Mendelson, ed., *The English Auden: Poems, Essays, and Dramatic Lyrics 1927–1939* (1977; rpt. London: Faber, 1988), 32, which provides this text. It remains untitled in Auden, *Poems* (1934; rpt. New York: Random House, 1937), 36, where, in numbered series, it appears (with some changes in spelling) as poem XX. Changes in punctuation accompany the titled version in Auden, *Collected Shorter Poems 1927–1957* (London: Faber, 1966), 30–31.

11. Riding and Graves seem nonetheless to wish to deauthorize the category of judgment when they place those inverted commas around "'obscurity,'" *A Survey of Modernist Poetry*, 138. Their defensive aggressiveness about "Decadence," 197, however, seems wholly earnest; that capitalized abstraction retains a menace so evident they must reject it unambiguously.

12. John Crowe Ransom, *The New Criticism* (Norfolk, Conn.: New Directions, 1941), 3; cited subsequently as *NC*.

13. *NC*, 54 ff., e.g., 55: "The liking that occurs with a beautiful poem is exercised (a) within its dense objective detail, and (b) *sub specie virtutis*, or in the light of going on with the sober duty of completing the 'argument.' The definition calls for a poetic 'texture' without trying to have one outside a logical discourse." Also see 219: "A poet must do two things at once; one is to make a logical structure, the other is to make meter. . . . [T]he relation of the meter to the meaning is that of a texture to a structure; this texture is adventitious, and irrelevant to the structure, but highly visible, and to the innocent reader like a curious increment of riches that had not been bargained for."

14. Richards, *Science and Poetry* (New York: Norton, 1926), 9–10.

15. Ibid., 12.

16. Ibid., 44–45.

17. Richards, *Practical Criticism: A Study of Literary Judgment* (1929; rpt. London: Kegan Paul, 1946). As Richards's subtitle indicates, it is not the poetic "object" but

rather the (vagaries of) subjective response that will constitute the interests of his study. For example, 6, he frames the method of offering poetry as "an eminently suitable *bait* for anyone who wishes to trap the current opinions and responses in this middle field for the purpose of examining and comparing them, and with a view to advancing our knowledge of what may be called the natural history of human opinions and feelings."

18. Kenneth Burke, *Permanence and Change: An Anatomy of Purpose*, 2d ed. (Los Altos, Calif.: Hermes, 1954), 24.

19. Ibid., 73.

20. Ibid., 99.

21. Ibid., 255; Burke's emphases.

22. Some indication of the bearing of current historical circumstances on Burke's formulations may be found in a statement like this, ibid., 33, where the Great War is shuffled among other events in a miscellany of disasters that add up most urgently to invoke the economic conditions of America in the 1930s: "Our nomadism, our vast reversals from year to year in economic status, our cataclysmic shifts in the organization of the nation under war, prosperous peace, and depression, our wide diversification of occupational habits, our total blankness of expectancy as to how the world is going or where we may fit into it all five years from now, the complete disappearance of the 'like father like son' attitude except perhaps in our rural districts—all such factors . . ."

23. William K. Wimsatt, Jr., "Eliot's Comedy: *The Cocktail Party*" (1950), reprinted in *Hateful Contraries: Studies in Literature and Criticism* (Lexington: University of Kentucky Press, 1965), 190.

24. Cleanth Brooks, "T. S. Eliot as 'Modernist' Poet," in *Literary Theory and Structure: Essays in Honor of William K. Wimsatt*, ed. Frank Brady, John Palmer, and Martin Price (New Haven, Conn.: Yale University Press, 1973), esp. 365–66, where the discussion of the quatrain poems tends either to praise the preservation of "thought" or to present the poet's attitude toward the absence of "logical structure" as a worthy regret that such estimable intellectual activity cannot be guaranteed in "our [modern] world." The ideal to which Eliot's poetry aspires is drawn by Brooks, 359, through the poet's own stated praise for Andrew Marvell, who "achieved 'a tough reasonableness beneath the slight lyric grace.'"

25. The genealogy and development of this critical concept are set out by Brooks in the memoir and retrospective testament "I. A. Richards and the Concept of Tension," the piece he wrote for *I. A. Richards: Essays in His Honor*, ed. Reuben Brower, Helen Vendler, and John Hollander (New York: Oxford University Press, 1973), 135ff., esp. 150: "Without going into the various criticisms made of Richards' psychological terminology, I can say that to most of us it did not prove very helpful, for the psychological machinery was, at best, irrelevant to our interests. I mention here my own early experience in reading Richards only because it is representative of what occurred in more mature and acute minds. . . . The psychological machinery not only did not help; it actually got in my way. It was worse than a distraction."

26. Ibid.: "On the other hand [as opposed to the "psychological terminology"], when Richards got down to cases—in the *Principles* as well as in the great casebook on the reading of poetry, *Practical Criticism*—I found him immediately rewarding, usually very exciting, and in general a powerful educative force."

27. Wimsatt, "Horses of Wrath: Recent Critical Lessons," in *Hateful Contraries*, 6–7. The essay is an amalgamation of three articles, which were published between 1956 and 1962 and which Wimsatt dates and cites in the acknowledgments, vii.

28. Ibid., 7–8.

29. Gerald L. Graff, "The Later Richards and the New Criticism," *Criticism: A Quarterly for Literature and the Arts* 9 (1967): 241.

30. Ibid.

31. See, for further instance, Graff's "Statement and Poetry," *Southern Review* (Summer 1966): 499–515, and his *Poetic Statement and Critical Dogma* (Evanston, Ill.: Northwestern University Press, 1970), an undertaking he frames by the appeal he repeats in concluding "The Later Richards and the New Criticism," 242: "We might do well to reconsider whether propositional truth may have importance in relation to poetic value after all; we might well reexamine the possibility that poems may indeed offer statements and generalizations which can be taken as such and yet may continue to be poems."

32. John Crowe Ransom, *God without Thunder: An Unorthodox Defence of Orthodoxy* (1930; rpt. Hamden, Conn.: Archon, 1965), 44.

33. The explicit provocation for the essay was a recent gathering of scientists in New York, convened under the heading that Ransom's chapter title confers on it, "The New God." These scientists attempted to align their methods and ethics with a god of progress and logical optimism; see esp. ibid., 6–13.

34. Ibid., 45.

35. Thus the church of "the new God" of scientific logic is presided over by "Mr. Harry Emerson Fosdick, the liberal clergyman," ibid., 7, as the representative of the sensibility that Ransom characterizes thus in the intellectual history he sets out later, 27: "[U]pon that date ["the close of the medieval period"] rose Protestantism, and rose also modern science. The two have been quite contemporaneous, and it is hardly possible to find in this fact nothing but a coincidence. For Protestantism has always figured to itself as a determination to rationalize the antiquated religious doctrines. And as for modern science, that, of course, is the sweeping rationalization of the universe under a minimum of definitive principles known as 'scientific.'"